Seeing the Light: The Case for Nuclear Power in the 21st Century

Nuclear power is not an option for the future, but an absolute necessity. Global threats of climate change and lethal air pollution, killing millions each year, make it clear that nuclear and renewable energy must work together as noncarbon sources of energy. Fortunately, a new era of growth in nuclear power is underway in developing nations, though not yet in the West. *Seeing the Light* is the first book to clarify these realities and discuss their implications for coming decades. Readers will learn how, why, and where the new nuclear era is happening, what new technologies are involved, and what this means for preventing the proliferation of weapons. This book is the best single work yet available for becoming fully informed about this key subject, for students, the general public, and anyone interested in the future of energy production, and thus, the future of humanity on planet Earth.

SCOTT L. MONTGOMERY is a geoscientist, professor, and author who has published twelve books and many articles, essays, and papers both in the sciences and humanities. His most recent title, *The Shape of the New* (2015), with Daniel Chirot, was selected by the *New York Times* as one of the 100 Best Books of 2015. In addition to teaching at the University of Washington (Seattle), he has lectured widely in North America and Europe and is often interviewed for his expertise on energy-related topics. An earlier work, *The Powers That Be: Global Energy for the 21st Century and Beyond* (2010) has been widely used as a text in energy courses and translated into a number of foreign languages.

AMBASSADOR (RETIRED) THOMAS GRAHAM JR. is Executive Chairman of Lightbridge Corporation, which develops new types of nuclear power fuel. He also does extensive part-time teaching at major universities, presently including Stanford University and Oregon State University. He lectures worldwide and appears before Congressional Committees. Since 2009, he has been a member of the International Advisory Board for the United Arab Emirates' peaceful nuclear power program. Internationally known as a leading authority on international arms control and nonproliferation, he served as a senior US diplomat in every major international arms control and nonproliferation negotiation in which the US took part from 1970 to 1997.

Seeing the Light: The Case for Nuclear Power in the 21st Century

SCOTT L. MONTGOMERY AND THOMAS GRAHAM JR.

CAMBRIDGE
UNIVERSITY PRESS

CAMBRIDGE
UNIVERSITY PRESS

University Printing House, Cambridge CB2 8BS, United Kingdom

One Liberty Plaza, 20th Floor, New York, NY 10006, USA

477 Williamstown Road, Port Melbourne, VIC 3207, Australia

4843/24, 2nd Floor, Ansari Road, Daryaganj, Delhi – 110002, India

79 Anson Road, #06–04/06, Singapore 079906

Cambridge University Press is part of the University of Cambridge.

It furthers the University's mission by disseminating knowledge in the pursuit of education, learning, and research at the highest international levels of excellence.

www.cambridge.org
Information on this title: www.cambridge.org/9781108418225
DOI: 10.1017/9781108289511

First published 2017

Printed in the United States of America by Sheridan Books, Inc.

A catalogue record for this publication is available from the British Library.

Library of Congress Cataloging-in-Publication Data
Names: Montgomery, Scott L., author. | Graham, Thomas, 1933– author.
Title: Seeing the light : the case for nuclear power in the 21st century / Scott L. Montgomery and Thomas Graham Jr.
Description: Cambridge, United Kingdom ; New York, NY : Cambridge University Press, 2017. | Includes bibliographical references and index.
Identifiers: LCCN 2017023561| ISBN 9781108418225 (hardback ; alk. paper) | ISBN 1108418228 (hardback ; alk. paper) | ISBN 9781108406673 (pbk.) | ISBN 110840667X (pbk.)
Subjects: LCSH: Nuclear energy. | Power resources – Forecasting.
Classification: LCC TK9145 .M66 2017 | DDC 333.792/4–dc23
LC record available at https://lccn.loc.gov/2017023561

ISBN 978-1-108-41822-5 Hardback
ISBN 978-1-108-40667-3 Paperback

Contents

v

Preface and Acknowledgments

This book is the product of a diplomat and a scientist. Thomas Graham Jr. is a senior US diplomat who, from 1970 to 1997, helped negotiate every international arms control and nonproliferation agreement put forth by the world. Scott L. Montgomery is a geoscientist who spent twenty-five years in the energy industry before becoming a university professor and author. Ambassador Graham has devoted his entire adult life to reducing the threat of nuclear war. It is because of this work that he sees nuclear power as a key means to reduce another global threat – that of climate change. Montgomery belonged to antinuclear organizations before being transmuted into an advocate by years of study and teaching, and by many discussions with nuclear professionals, health physicists, government officials, and, finally, by the implications of climate change.

Employing their backgrounds to hopefully good effect, the authors have sought to cover a wide array of subjects in this book that point up the troubled history, flaws, required re-evaluations, benefits, and necessity of nuclear power for the world. It is their firm belief that such coverage is required to make the reader a truly informed citizen in this domain. The task is significantly large but well within the bounds of possibility. It may even happen that nuclear professionals themselves will find novel and useful material in the pages that follow. We, the authors, would maintain that this is not entirely an accident.

A word about the text. While chapters have been written so that they can be read individually and not necessarily in order, the reader would do well to learn the basic material covered in Chapters 3 and 5 (on nuclear energy and radiation) at an early point. Much later discussion draws on the knowledge and terminology covered there.

Acknowledgments are important to any book, but they are especially necessary to a work where so much direct aid has been given.

Thomas Graham wishes to thank Richard Rhodes, Pulitzer Prize- and National Book Award winning- author; Dr. KunMo Chung, two-time Energy Minister of Korea; and Dr. Karen Hallberg, Principal Researcher of the Argentine National Research Council, for their encouragement to become involved in the fight against climate change and the inspiration to be an author of this book. I also am grateful for the support of other signers of the 2015 Manifesto in support of the December 2015 Paris Conference on Climate Change: Dr. Hans Blix, former Director General of the International Atomic Energy Agency; Jayantha Dhanapala, former United Nation's Under Secretary General for Disarmament; Ambassador Sérgio Duarte, former United Nations High Representative for Disarmament Affairs; Kathleen Kennedy Townsend, former Lieutenant Governor of Maryland; and Jody Williams, 1997 Nobel Peace Laureate for the International Campaign to Ban Land Mines.

Gwyneth Cravens and her book, *Power to Save the World* (2007), were also an important inspiration leading to the writing of the book. Ahlan Al Marzouqi of the Executive Affairs Authority, Abu Dhabi, United Arab Emirates, was of great assistance in telling the story in this book of the admirable and highly successful nuclear power program in the United Arab Emirates. Frances Eddy, as always, was an enormous help in putting chapters together and other related tasks.

Lastly, to Christine, whom I owe so much. With consistent understanding, she accepted many interrupted Saturdays, Sundays, and late nights, and gave me the encouragement necessary to complete my contribution to this book.

Scott L. Montgomery wishes to thank, above all, Annie Fadely for her deft and invaluable assistance that will never be forgotten. Nick Touran, nuclear engineer extraordinaire with TerraPower, offered valuable comments on other parts of the manuscript and companionship on stage. Gratitude must also be given to Mary Manous, Paula and Brian King, and Zaki Hamid of Humanities Washington for their gracious help in arranging public venues where I could discuss my views. A nod is also needed to Bryan Miller of Naked City Brewing & Taphouse, whose rostrum I occupied more than once, and to Chuck Johnson for being my anti-nuclear opponent. Among my University of Washington colleagues, I have had helpful discussions with Dan Chirot, Chris Jones, Chris Kessler, Tom Leschine, Saadia Pekkanen, Kathy Friedman, and Steve Harrall. My students of the past ten years have always been important and have more than once driven me to learn more than I believed was necessary. I'm also indebted to individuals at NIOSH, CDC, NRC, Brookhaven, and Virginia Mason Medical Center (Seattle), who took the time to offer their opinions and perceptions.

Finally, it is to Kyle, Cameron, Marilyn, and Clio that I am most indebted, as will always be the case. Their support, understanding, and patience live within these pages as much as anything of my own.

Abbreviations

AEC	Atomic Energy Commission (US)
AMD	Acid Mine Drainage
BEAR	Biological Effects of Atomic Radiation (report)
BWR	Boiling Water Reactor
CANDU	Canadian Deuterium Uranium Reactor
CF	Capacity Factor
CTBT	Comprehensive Test Ban Treaty
DOE	Department of Energy (US)
EIA	Energy Information Administration
EPA	Environmental Protection Agency (US)
FNR	Fast Neutron Reactor
FOE	Friends of the Earth
GCR	Gas-Cooled Reactor
Gen	Generation (nuclear reactors, e.g. Gen IV)
GHG	Greenhouse Gas
GW	Gigawatt (billion Watts)
HEU	High-Enriched Uranium
HGR	(HTGR) High-Temperature Gas-Cooled Reactor
HWR	Heavy Water Reactor
IAEA	International Atomic Energy Agency
IEA	International Energy Agency
IPCC	Intergovernmental Panel on Climate Change
ISL	In-Situ Leaching
kW	Kilowatt
kWh	Kilowatt-hour
LCOE	Levelized Cost of Electricity
LEU	Low-Enriched Uranium

LFTR	Liquid Fluoride Thorium Reactor
LNG	Liquefied Natural Gas
LNT	Linear No-Threshold
LSS	Life Span Study (Atomic Bomb Survivor Study)
LWR	Light Water Reactor
MOX	Mixed-Oxide Fuel (uranium and plutonium oxides)
MSR	Molten Salt Reactor
MW	Megawatt (million Watts)
MWh	Megawatt-hour
NAS	National Academy of Sciences (US)
NEI	Nuclear Energy Institute
NPT	Nuclear Non-Proliferation Treaty
NRC	Nuclear Regulatory Commission (US)
OECD	Organization for Economic Cooperation and Development
PWR	Pressurized Water Reactor
RBMK	Reaktor Bolshoy Moshchosty Kanalny (High-Power Channel Reactor)
SFR	Sodium-Cooled Fast Reactor
SMR	Small Modular Reactor
TMI	Three Mile Island
UNSCEAR	United Nations Scientific Commission on the Effects of Atomic Radiation
VVER	Vodo Vodyanoi Energetichesky Reaktor (Pressurized Water Power Reactor)
WHO	World Health Organization
WNA	World Nuclear Association

Introduction

On December 7, 2015, seventy-one Nobel Laureate scientists presented a document that spoke in one voice to the United Nations climate summit in Paris. The document they had signed, known as the Mainau Declaration, was a forceful call to action for all the world's nations. The threat faced by humanity from a warming climate, it stated, was greater than any that had ever existed, with only one possible exception.

Indeed, human civilization on planet Earth clearly faces a growing existential crisis. This risk is beyond denial, confirmed many times by scientific work, and is now fully evident in the climatic changes that people are witnessing and, increasingly suffering from in their own experience, from the poles to the equator. Science is conservative in embracing new truths. The requirements for evidence are prodigious and the place of doubt and debate central. Climate change, however, has not only moved well past these stages of validation. It has repeatedly exceeded every forecast for its effects.

So strong is the scientific consensus today, in fact, that fossil fuel industries, not least major oil and coal companies, have accepted it and have pressed the US government under President Donald Trump to retain American membership in the Paris Climate Agreement. Though some prominent officials and commentators do continue to discount the role of human activity in warming of the globe, it is abundantly clear that they do so for ideological reasons, above all the fear of government gaining the power to irrevocably take command over the economy by means of energy choices and control of the environment, writ large. An overwhelming majority of the world, however, including the global scientific community, understands that this is not the real matter at stake. Changes to modern energy, partly or largely through government policies and decisions, will not bring hopeless tyranny. They are far more likely, if intelligently planned, to bring hope that the worst, most oppressive impacts of global warming will not happen. One thing, after all, is certain: carbon emissions must be brought under control and reduced, not a little but a minimum of 40 percent below 2010 levels. It is a colossal undertaking, and it will not be completed soon, in a few short decades. This is because of the immense scale of what needs to occur – the unmaking of 200 years of modern energy.

To achieve what is needed will require every means that nations can employ to produce energy from low- and, especially, noncarbon sources. Fortunately enough, modern society has created sources of this kind, those that can now be expanded and advanced to address the challenge. Simply choosing a few options, because they seem the "greenest" and are backed by wishful computer models, will never be enough. The task is too real, grave, vast, and demanding for diversions that treat it as an opportunity for ideological preferences on the other side of the political spectrum.

Yet climate change, for all its risks, is only part of the existential crisis today. There is another type of threat, once thought to be quelled but that has returned with a vengeance and which looms over large parts of humanity with impacts now known to be spectacularly lethal. Nearly 18,000 people lose their lives every day due to toxic material in the air they breathe. This amounts to 6.5 million deaths annually, which the World Health Organization (WHO) emphasizes is significantly greater than combined fatalities from HIV/AIDS, tuberculosis, and traffic accidents [1]. Energy production defines the main contributor to this global threat to health, above all the burning of fossil fuels, particularly coal. Hundreds of millions of people live in cities today whose air cannot be called fit to breathe. Worst of all are those urban areas blanketed with smog containing very small particulate matter that enters and damages the lungs and circulatory system. In China's eastern cities, up to a million people are now thought to die prematurely every year due to air pollution dense with such matter, whose sources are coal-burning power plants, factories, local businesses, and residences. China is only one example, however. Coal use has grown in many countries around the world, even as it has fallen in most of Europe and North America. That global use may have reached a plateau in recent years and even dropped slightly provides no comfort, as it mainly reflects the change in high-use nations and disguises the continued rise in many smaller nations whose air quality is now worse than at any time in the past. Coal is not the only source of particulate matter (burning of agricultural fields is another potent source in some areas), but it is the most widespread and the most damaging to human health.

It turns out, then, that two of the greatest threats facing humanity largely have the same cause. They therefore can be dealt with, at least in part, using the same means.

A Brief Long Story

The long story of energy has brought us to this point. For many thousands of years human civilization relied on the muscles of large animals, including themselves, for work. They supplemented this with wind and sails, the power of water, the heat of the sun, the burning of wood and, eventually, charcoal. This long era was overturned in a small handful of places between the sixteenth and the nineteenth centuries. The era of coal began most clearly in England as the result of a wood famine, caused by a combination of population growth, growth in local industries (brewing, blacksmithing, glass and brick making, smelting of ores), and a great buildup of merchant and naval shipping. By 1800, the Industrial Revolution had moved from water power to steam, and thus from rivers to coal and the true beginnings of the machine and factory age, which soon spread to other parts of Europe and North America. A point in coal's favor was its widespread occurrence: England, France, Germany, Italy, the Netherlands, Poland, Russia, the US all had significant reserves. Supply was reliable, abundant, cheap, and, for a time, secure. Despite certain drawbacks, especially fouling of the air, exploding boilers, and danger in the mines, coal's risks were deemed acceptable by the ruling powers and were somewhat reduced over time, temporarily.

The coal era lasted a full 150 years, to be replaced by the age of oil. This took time, as enormous amounts of infrastructure had to be disassembled and built. Begun in the 1860s, the oil industry grew rapidly, first as a source of illuminant for lamps and then, in the early 1900s, for land, marine, and air transport, all before 1920. Even so, coal maintained its dominion in core sectors (industry, heating) up until the 1950s and 60s, by which time oil and, to a smaller degree, gas had taken over. The reign of oil was very short, however. From a near-universal source, fueling industry, commerce, power generation, homes, and transportation, it had largely retreated to the last of these sectors by 1980 in the advanced nations. The reason was the oil crises of 1973 and 1978–79. By the 1980s, a greater diversity of sources had been put in place, with coal regaining a good part of the market share it had lost to oil. This was especially true for power generation, which shifted away from oil in these nations toward a combination of coal, natural gas, hydropower, and the first truly noncarbon form of energy generation, nuclear power.

Electricity, in fact, was first generated on a commercial basis in the 1880s. Hydropower developed by conversion of mills into power stations to serve the industrial towns and cities that had grown up in such areas. Very soon, coal-powered generators were added and became preferred, as they were not limited to sites with flowing water and steam power proved able to generate increasing amounts of electricity. With the expansion of the railroads, shipping, large-scale industry, and now power generation, coal use rose to become 80 percent or more of US and European energy consumption by 1900. US consumption alone went from about 35 million tons in 1850 to over 285 million tons at the turn of the century, and by the 1920s, more than 575 million tons [2]. The twentieth century turned out to have an ever-more insatiable use for electricity, spread over nearly every sector of the economy. Coal rode this enormous flood in demand, which only ended for the industrialized, wealthy nations in the next century. By that time, however, a new phase of surging demand was underway in the rest of the world, bringing coal use to unforeseen, even unimagined, heights.

There had been warnings, to be sure. By the 1940s, so-called "killer smogs" were occurring in Western cities with growing frequency. In the US, these happened in Los Angeles, Chicago, New York, and were due to vehicle exhaust mixed with coal emissions. But in Europe, particularly London, it was coal smog that dominated. Seeming without warning, it reached a dramatic peak in the Great Killer Smog of 1952, which took the lives of 4,000 people in two short weeks and nearly 8,000 more in the following few months. Far from the first "pea soup fog" for London, it did translate into the first traumatic demonstration of how lethal air pollution from the burning of coal could be. Still, coal use continued to climb in the advanced nations for another half century. Though power plants built since the 1970s mostly have pollution controls, including those for particulate matter, those that are older do not and were never forced to adopt such controls.

This did not have to be the case. A closer look shows that wealthy nations[1] use of coal for electricity actually declined in the 1960s and 70s, as other sources came to be used, but then returned to a pattern of overall growth that lasted into the 2010s. There are variations within this group of countries, of course: where coal use in the US never decreased until after 2000, and both Japan and Korea's consumption had not declined as of 2017, Europe's consumption did fall significantly, reaching a plateau in the 1990s and then declining again starting in the 2010s.

While there were several reasons for the growth in coal consumption, one deserves mention in particular. The halt to construction of new nuclear power plants in the 1980s, particularly after the Three Mile Island and Chernobyl accidents, decidedly aided coal's return to dominance in electricity generation. If such a halt had not happened, nuclear would have combined with the gradual growth in natural gas consumption to reduce America's level of pollution and carbon emissions substantially. It is likely that many older coal plants without pollution controls would have been retired, reducing emissions and pollution still further.

---

[1] Included here are nations in the Organization for Economic Cooperation and Development (OECD).

So despite its deep disadvantages, coal remained a favored fuel into the twenty-first century, even as the era of oil expanded and a new period of growing source diversity got underway. Yet, there is another way to view the past 200 years of modern energy. It is this: from the 1870s, when coal reached 50 percent or more of energy production, down to the present day, we have never stopped inhabiting the era of fossil fuels. Indeed, if not for hydropower in nations where it can exist and nuclear in most of the wealthy nations and a few others, carbon-based fuels would have fulfilled 100 percent of modern energy needs since the start of the last century. As the world approaches the year 2020, and new sources of renewable power generation along with new nuclear plants come on line, fossil fuels still command more than 80 percent of global energy use. A rough estimate is that systems of carbon energy around the world equal somewhere near \$30 trillion in natural resource value, infrastructure, refining, trade, and labor. To imagine what is needed to reduce all this, to dismantle and replace it or adapt large parts of it, can only be called essential.

A new civilization – modern civilization – unlike anything that had gone before, was created and built on fossil fuels: coal, oil, and natural gas, extremely rich sources of energy. And in the twentieth century these three sources spread throughout the world. Human life has been revolutionized because of this, and will continue to be altered by it, becoming both more prosperous and at the same time more threatened.

It wasn't until the 1970s that some scientists came to understand the Faustian bargain. Means were available to hugely improve the quality of life but if overused could eventually make large parts of the planet much less livable for human beings. This was because the burning of these fuels releases over time vast amounts of carbon, largely in the form of CO_2 gas, into the atmosphere, absorbing and reradiating the Sun's heat, raising the temperature of the lower atmosphere and the oceans. Beginning with the rise of coal use during the Industrial Revolution, the growth of carbon in the atmosphere has raised the world's average, near-surface temperature by 1.3°C (2.3°F) over the past two centuries. This means that the entire atmosphere surrounding the planet has absorbed enough heat so that essentially every cubic meter of it has grown warmer. Because of this, the atmosphere has more energy overall. More extreme weather events, with greater force, causing greater damage and more deaths, now occur. Yet this represents only a small fraction of the total thermal energy that has been added to the Earth's surface and near-surface. Another part has gone to melt sea ice, ice caps, and glaciers around the world, in dramatic fashion. And the largest portion of thermal energy has been absorbed into the upper 700 m (2,310 ft) of the oceans, whose chemistry is being altered and whose volume is actually expanding due to the added heat. Together, these phenomena are causing sea level to rise. It has risen nearly ten inches in the last 135 years, and half of this has happened since the 1970s: the rate of rising is accelerating. As a result, low-lying islands are beginning to disappear, deltas are becoming salinized by encroaching salt water, and coastal areas in many parts of the world are now being flooded far more often by major rainstorms and hurricanes or cyclones. These effects are really only beginning; sea level in many areas will possibly be 3 ft (0.9 m) higher or more by 2100.

Climate change is many threats to many nations – political, social, cultural, economic, and even military. It is a direct challenge to the world's stability, not only because of its impacts but because of the changes that it requires to be made by societies. The core of these changes lies in the realm of energy, which must be moved toward a more noncarbon basis. This means nuclear power and renewables, the only real options that exist today. Neither one of these can achieve what is necessary by itself; to choose one and abandon the other is to amputate an arm from the effort that is needed.

The Paris Climate Agreement of December 2015 brought 190 nations to a consensus that they would work to reduce carbon emissions such that the world's average temperature would not reach 2°C above preindustrial norms, the point interpreted by the scientific community as defining when the most severe impacts will begin in force. These would not just be droughts, storms and higher seas, but effects in the oceans less often described, like more acidic waters reducing the abundance of phytoplankton, a form of life at the base of the marine food chain but that also produces half of the world's oxygen. No small amount of talk at the Paris meetings was devoted to 2015 being the warmest year on record. A year later, 2016 has taken its place. In the decades ahead, it is safe to say that planet Earth will be fine. It is the life that lives upon it that will suffer, indeed that is already enduring.

This book essentially begins with these realities and seeks to inform its readers about the necessity of nuclear power in the new century, the time of climate change and growing air pollution. It takes as a given that readers want and need to know about many aspects regarding nuclear energy – its history, its strengths and flaws, its accidents, the key scientific concepts behind it (in ordinary terms), as well as the potent issues that surround it, like those related to radiation, nonproliferation, cost, waste disposal, safety, and the history and status of public fear.

Nuclear power became available in the immediate wake of the largest, most destructive war ever fought by humanity. For a large number of people, it has been associated with this conflict, with the two monstrous bombs that ended it, ever since. If understandable in some measure, this has ended up as a great misfortune, since nuclear plants could now be everywhere and the climate crisis almost non-existent. Despite having injured or killed the smallest number of people of any major energy source in the past sixty to seventy years, nuclear is thought by more than a few to be the riskiest of all. On the basis of the most extensive, long-term study, between forty-eight and fifty-six deaths (records are less than perfect) and some 4,000 thyroid cancers are associated with Chernobyl after three decades, numbers that are dwarfed by the 12,000 who died in London's killer smog of 1952. This is not to mention the yearly toll of thousands whose lives are lost to extreme weather events today, nor the hundreds of thousands who die from toxic air in Asian cities – deaths that do not require an accident or other extraordinary event. Today, around the world, air pollution from coal and oil kills ever year several times the number of people that died at Hiroshima and Nagasaki. This truth does not in the least alter the horror of the atom bombings and the suffering they caused. It does, however, suggest the dimension of suffering that must be addressed now. It also makes plain that it is time to put away the fear that associates nuclear power with nuclear weapons and face the real threats to society that now exist.

The Mainau Declaration makes this point in terms as clear as we might wish. They are terms with a particular resonance, given the history behind them:

> Nearly 60 years ago, here on Mainau, a similar gathering of Nobel Laureates in science issued a declaration of the dangers inherent in the newly found technology of nuclear weapons ... So far we have avoided nuclear war though the threat remains. We believe that our world today faces another threat of comparable magnitude ... [T]he world must make rapid progress toward lowering current and future greenhouse gas emissions to minimize the substantial risks of climate ... Failure to act will subject future generations of humanity to unconscionable and unacceptable risk.[3]

With these words in mind, it can only be a major step forward that a new age of nuclear power has actually begun. It is to help support and advance this new era, to quicken an understanding of it and why it is much needed, that this book has been written.

References

[1] *Energy and Air Pollution* (International Energy Agency, Paris, 2016), 3.
[2] Energy Sources Have Changed Throughout the History of the United States, US Energy Information Administration (July 3, 2013) (Internet). Available from: www.eia.gov/todayinenergy/detail.php?id=11951
[3] Mainau Declararion on Climate Change (Internet) (December 7, 2015), Available from: www.mainaudeclaration.org/home

1

Why Nuclear and Why Now?

This Time the Future Will Be Different

Nuclear power will be a growth industry for the twenty-first century, and this is a good thing. Two-thirds of humanity now live in countries that utilize this source of electricity. During the next several decades, the figure will likely rise to three-quarters. In 2015, the world had 436 reactors for power generation. Within two years, by early 2017, this number had grown to 449. By 2035, the total number could approach 600, and by mid-century, 1,000 or more. This includes large and moderate-sized reactors (>500 MegaWatts electricity, MW), as well as small modular types (<300 MW), micro-reactors (<10 MW), and even some floating versions. Commercial reactors have operated since the 1950s, mainly in advanced nations. This is already changing: the new nuclear era will be centered in Asia, in developing and emerging states. As a result, billions of tons of carbon emissions and lethal air pollution will not be emitted, and millions of lives will be saved.

And yet, much talk today, about climate change and the energy future ignores or minimizes the nuclear option. A common tendency is to pose fossil fuels against the ascent of renewables, sources of carbon against noncarbon energy, with natural gas as a bridge between them and nuclear power banished from the scene. But in nations like China, India, Russia, South Korea, Saudi Arabia, and Eastern Europe, with key roles in global carbon emissions, nuclear power defines a core part of the effort to replace carbon energy. Just as important will be the expansion of nuclear power into dozens of developing nations for whom coal, not natural gas or renewables, has been the default choice. As this book will show, the future for nuclear power will be larger and more essential than is often assumed in the US and Western Europe.

To many who live in the West or Japan, the idea of a thousand or more reactors in the world may sound absurd or come as a bit of a shock. What about the risks shown by the disaster of Chernobyl and, even more recently, the 2011 accident at Fukushima Daiichi? This incident in Japan, combined with a great earthquake and tsunami, caused massive evacuations and spread the acids of fear and distrust once again in many parts of the world. Nuclear power, it seemed to some, would never again find favor as a major energy option. Humanity was fated to enter a twilight of the nuclear idols.

Not at all. Though of huge impact in Japan, the global significance of Fukushima has been greatly overstated. According to much detailed study, no one is expected to develop cancer or die because of radiation from the accident, as we will show in a later chapter. In the immediate wake of the accident nations did re-evaluate their plans to expand or launch nuclear programs. More than a few considered shutting down or retiring their operating plants. But only a tiny handful ever did so. Moreover, each of these nations – Germany and Italy, for example – remain a "nuclear state" anyway in real terms, as they continue to operate research reactors for materials testing and the production of special isotopes for medicine and industry.

In every other country that discussed a phase out, experts ultimately determined the accident did not warrant such an extreme measure. On the contrary, given that twelve other reactors plus a uranium enrichment plant, all affected by the earthquake, shut down safely was viewed as an impressive success. Adding to this view was that these plants endured the largest earthquake ever recorded in this quake-prone country, undergoing levels of ground acceleration far greater than they were designed to withstand. For nations with less risk of quakes and tsunamis – most of the world, in fact – the conclusion was all the stronger. Such considerations were added to the actual safety record of nuclear power, which, on the basis of repeated research, shows that in fifty years, there have been just three major accidents, only one (Chernobyl) with serious injuries or fatalities. Combined with a small number of plant worker accidents, a total of under seventy deaths have occurred. The great majority of nations with nuclear plants have never experienced anything resembling a major accident. As we will document in more detail later, this record stands in stark contrast to hundreds of fatal accidents every year in the oil and gas industry, many thousands of lives lost in hydropower dam failures during the last half-century, and over 150 fatalities suffered by the global wind power industry since 2005. In brief, the best evidence unequivocally tells us it is simply not credible to call nuclear power a "dangerous" or "risky" technology.

There is another point to consider. Reactors operating worldwide in the 2010s are overwhelmingly based on technology dating from the 1960s and

70s (imagine if this was the case with cars!). They have been superseded by much more advanced reactors now being built and brought into use, reactors that would *not* have suffered the kind of loss-of-cooling accident that happened at Fukushima. Moreover, a future generation of reactor designs with still more innovative features addressing issues of nonproliferation, energy efficiency, cost, waste, and risk is even now undergoing testing in a number of countries.

Nuclear's role in the energy landscape will not only grow, it will become more varied, flexible, complex, and essential. Varied, because of the new array of nations and technologies involved. Flexible, due to new reactor designs and their diverse sizes, ranging from plants larger than today's down to small and even micro-reactors for local power needs. Complex, for these same reasons and for the potent challenges and issues that come with it. And essential, because of how reliable electricity contributes directly to the bettering of human lives – in particular, via improvements to public health, economic development, energy security, and the struggle to deal with climate change. All of these are reasons driving the nuclear future, the next nuclear era, and they will continue to do so for decades. This new era has already begun. It is time to define it, delineate it, and describe why it provides a critical opportunity far too important to waste, deny, or ignore.

A New Era Underway

What concrete evidence do we have that a new era has begun? The answer requires some simple arithmetic. The 436 power reactors existing in 2015 represented a figure that hadn't changed more than a few percent since the 1980s, when Chernobyl (1986) terrified the world and essentially killed any plans for large-scale expansion in nuclear energy. Yet in 2015, as many as seventy new reactors were under construction, a 16 percent rise above the 436 figure. This fact alone reveals something new is happening, a major turnaround from the post-Chernobyl period.

While new reactors were being built, another 165 were planned for completion by 2030–2035. "Planned" does not mean "on the drawing board" or "under consideration." It signifies reactors that have been sited, subjected to government review and approval, and, in many cases, with funding commitments in place [1]. These are reactors, then, that have a good-to-excellent probability of being erected. A total, therefore, of 235 new reactors (70 + 165) will quite likely be built within the first several decades of the new century, bringing the global fleet to a record number. By the beginning of 2017, the total number of operable reactors had already climbed to 449, with sixty under construction, despite the retirement of eight others [2].

This brings up the question of whether many more retirements might happen before long. Couldn't this bring the future global number of reactors down a good deal? Yes, to be sure. But this now looks much less likely than a few years ago. Estimates on retirement numbers vary widely, even wildly, for the next fifteen to twenty years, from dozens to hundreds. Right after Fukushima, claims were made that many nuclear plants around the world would be shut down and not replaced. But just the opposite seems to be happening. Increasing numbers of reactors have been relicensed, allowing them to continue operating for decades. European nations, such as Sweden, Belgium, and Switzerland, that seriously talked or voted on closing their nuclear plants rejected this move as a serious mistake in light of the need to reduce carbon emissions. Despite plans to phase out nuclear in the future in favor of 100 percent renewables, a growing number of energy experts and decision makers are realizing that this vision, based as it is on technologies (e.g. high-efficiency solar power, large-scale energy storage) that do not yet exist, may prove more difficult to achieve than thought and that relicensing of nuclear plants or even replacing them may well be needed.

Such relicensing is not done on a whim or with a simple policy decision. It requires a highly detailed, thorough process of data review, inspection, and more. As we will discuss later on in this book, the original forty-year licensing period for reactors, first established in the US, was never intended to serve as a life span for any nuclear power plant but was instead the amortization period, i.e. the time needed for all loans to be paid off. What this means is that forty or forty-five-year-old nuclear plants are not "past retirement" or necessarily "old".

Some surveys have concluded that nearly 200 reactors will be decommissioned between 2014 and 2040, mainly in Europe, the US, Russia, South Korea, and Japan, thus almost balancing out the increase noted above. Yet, it now appears that most of these will likely be upgraded, if necessary, and relicensed (perhaps for a second time) to remain online till 2040 and beyond. More than a few of those that will be retired may well be replaced with advanced, standardized designs that will cost less and can be built more quickly. None of this is guaranteed, of course. There are economic challenges that nuclear power must face in most Western nations, where it has not (yet) been widely or fully valued for its superior reliability, nonpolluting and noncarbon electricity. Yet recent signs suggest this may be changing. More than thirty-five reactors in the US have been relicensed beyond 2040, while some states like New York and Illinois have decided to do what is needed to keep nuclear plants running so that their carbon emissions can be controlled. Both in the US and Europe, there is a growing awareness that closing nuclear plants has meant increasing emissions, since most such plants are replaced by natural gas, not renewables, and even by coal in some cases.

Meanwhile, another possible scenario, taking such information into account, sees 132 reactors closing by 2035 and 287 new ones coming online[4]. This is a more optimistic view, certainly, but not at all beyond the borders of possibility, for reasons we will mention in a moment. But first, what might such numbers mean for the global reactor fleet? We see that 287 new reactors minus 132 closing equals 155, and when added to the global figure of 450 for late 2016, this gives a total of 605 reactors in 2035. Another scenario, with a minimum growth projection and the above figure for retirees, would be: 60 (reactors under construction in late 2016) + 167 (planned) – 132 (to be retired) equals 95, thus a total world fleet (450 + 95) of 545.

But the picture is not yet complete. There remains an entire category of possible future reactors still to consider. Less certain than "planned" are those that have been "proposed." This means reactors that have been discussed by governments and companies in more than four dozen countries, with specific sites suggested but actual designs not yet decided, approved, or funded. They are, in short, "possible" reactors. Some will surely be built, but there is no way to know how many. Their number, however, is enormous: no less than 345, as of late 2016, rising to 372 in early 2017. Moreover, uncertainty shouldn't detract us from what they show – a depth of interest by nations in all parts of the globe. If only half were actually built, say by 2040, we would be looking at a global fleet of between 700 and 800, depending upon which scenario comes true. If three-quarters were built, we would be looking at 800–900. There is also the small point that, since 2012, the numbers of planned and proposed have risen progressively, year-by-year.

For some, the prospect of such numbers might seem incredible. A *doubling* of global nuclear reactors? In truth, it could be a lot more than this. There is some possibility that we have understated things by no small amount. Hints coming out of China suggest the government, in its desire to reduce coal use, may be considering (or have already decided upon) a goal of *500 or more* nuclear plants by mid-century as a "cornerstone of its national security" [6]. In other words, China alone would more than match the world's total reactor fleet today and thereby push mid-century figures well above 1,000. If true, this should not be a shock. We know, after all, that China does not do things in a small way when it comes to energy. Chinese consumption of coal has been colossal, as is well known, despite being routinely underreported. Also immense have been its dam-building efforts to increase hydropower as well as its world-leading installations of solar and wind power facilities. A program of as many as 500 reactors (including an unknown number of small- and moderate-sized designs), coupled with an enormous scale-up in renewables, would match the immense challenge the country now faces, both in the need for power and for reducing toxic urban air that has become a major public health calamity and source of civil unrest.

China, in fact, is our window into the motives for a new era in nuclear power. This new era will shift the center of the global nuclear industry from West to East, from wealthy to developing nations. A great many in the West have not caught up to this reality, which is rapidly solidifying. Much of the discussion about nuclear in the US and Europe continues to be provincial, lacking a global view. This is especially true of those who argue and wrestle over whether nuclear power is "obsolete" or "a distraction" or is inherently "too expensive." Such discussions, viewed in a global context, show that much of the West still views itself as the center of the nuclear power landscape, that decisions made in the US or Europe will determine the future of this energy source. But this is no longer the case. A new nuclear era is already underway, centered in Asia. While Western nations struggle to decide whether they will be part of this new era, it is moving ahead regardless. The point is that the landscape needs to be seen from a new vantage, with the globe turned so that Asia, the Middle East, and Africa are in full view.

But why do poor and emerging countries want nuclear power, specifically? There are five big reasons: (1) surging demand for electricity, as a fundament to modern life; (2) desire for economic growth; (3) worries over energy security, including reliable sources of power; (4) the need to reverse air and water pollution and lower carbon emissions, which are even now bringing risks to the population in the form of climate change; and (5) politics and prestige, meaning the desire to have a nuclear program because a neighbor or enemy has one, or because it is a sign of a technologically advanced nation.

These reasons do not have equal weight. The first three tend to take priority in most cases, but the fourth, as China's own recent history reveals, is growing in importance on a yearly basis. The final reason is far from trivial; it has certainly had its effects in the past (e.g. in Europe), and more recently has been a factor for Iran, which in turn is a spur for other Middle Eastern nations, particularly Saudi Arabia, to adopt nuclear power. Together, these reasons explain a key reality about the future of nuclear power: even more significant than a doubling (or more) in reactor numbers is the probability that a sizeable number of new countries worldwide will have nuclear power programs in place before 2040. That means around forty-five or more compared to thirty-one in 2016.

This will come with challenges, without doubt. But if done right, it will be excellent progress. Bringing the 1.2 billion people without access to electricity, and two billion more who have it only intermittently, fully into the modern world will mean enormous new possibilities for human benefit. A reliable supply of power is *the* most important factor for making modern life and its advantages possible and one of the most fundamental elements aiding economic growth and advances in social welfare [7–8]. The relationship is not always a simple one, but many paybacks are undeniable: lighting, refrigeration, machinery (medical equipment, water supply and purification, irrigation), computers and digital technology. Large parts of South America, Africa, South Asia, and Southeast Asia lack these things. Altering this situation for the better will advance the lives of a third of humanity.

For governments, meanwhile, it is often the issue of energy security that matters greatly. This is because of the strong connection to national security. Having sufficient amounts of power that are always available that come from dependable and affordable fuel sources provided by reliable suppliers are essential to any nation's stability. This is true not only for electricity, of course. But, again, electrical power is fundamental to every aspect of a modern or modernizing society. Nuclear power's ability to satisfy all of the needs just mentioned makes it highly attractive to nations without large amounts of natural resources.

Many of us in the West might ask where the money is going to come from to build all these new plants? After all, even with every other problem solved, there remains the difficulty of cost. Nuclear plants are expensive to build, and though costs can vary a good deal, they are never low. Nuclear's appeal can be directly affected by the price of other fuels and technologies used to generate power. In the nine years between 2005 and 2014, this appeal rose considerably, as oil and natural gas prices reached historical highs. But in the latter half of 2014, prices collapsed, as world markets had become oversupplied. Natural gas prices in particular fell to levels not consistently seen in decades. The new period of cheap gas has impacted the economics of nuclear power, without doubt. But for how long? Oil and gas prices are historically volatile and unpredictable. Promises that the fracking revolution will keep prices low for many years are not convincing; we have been here before, forgetful that the history of the oil and gas industry is littered with such naive certainties. It is also a reason why a high dependence on natural gas can actually contribute to energy *in*security. Yet, it remains possible that a low-price period lasting ten years, were it to happen, would act to stall the expansion of nuclear power in some parts of the world.

Even so, the hurdle of cost for nuclear is much higher for some nations than for others. As we will discuss in more detail later on, it is higher where first-of-a-kind reactors are typical and construction delays are common, and where the licensing process is especially complex and long. The history of nuclear power in the US, for example, has been typified by competition among a number of companies such that many different reactor designs resulted, each having its own unique components and construction specifications. The very opposite of this was pursued in France, where a very small number of designs were used so that experience and more modular manufacturing of components made things cheaper. Such is the approach now employed in China and South Korea, for example, where reactors are completed in as little as four years (compared to six to ten years, or longer, in the US). There are other factors involved with the economics of nuclear power, but we will save them for a later chapter.

For the moment, there is one more point to make. In 2007, the world crossed a threshold that relates directly to all of this. That year, the number of people living in cities equaled the number living in rural areas. By 2014, urbanites had become 55 percent of humankind. This is a profound change in the nature of the modern world: by mid-century, the figure will be at least 66 percent, a complete reversal from what it was at the end of WWII. This massive trend of urbanization is centered in the developing world, where the most rapidly growing municipalities are not the giant mega-cities of 10 million or more but moderate-sized metropolises between 500,000 and several million, above all in Asia and Africa. There are no big surprises here: Africa and Asia, with more than half of the global population, have the lowest levels of urbanization (40 and 47 percent, respectively) – Europe, Latin America, and North America are all above 73 percent – and the highest levels of rural poverty. To young families, cities provide a host of possibilities beyond what can be expected from a traditional lifestyle at the edge of subsistence. This means better employment, education for their children, improved health care, and a higher standard of living. Cities *can* offer a more rewarding, interesting life, but they can also become centers of urban poverty, crime, and failure. There are many determining factors, but one of the most elemental is electricity to power the homes, businesses, hospitals, human services, and public transport that urban centers need to be successful. More than a third of people living without power are in the slums of cities like Mumbai (India), Karachi (Pakistan), and Lagos (Nigeria).

The future unfolding before us, an ever-more urban future, will be an ever-more electrified one. This is even more true as cities increase their role as the nexus of knowledge-based work, which is materially less-intensive but entirely reliant on electricity. It is due to these simple but relentless truths that developing nations are now facing fundamental choices about how to provide power.

Air Pollution: World's Deadliest Killer?

What they are also realizing, thanks to China's example, is that any successes in urban growth can be undone by the fatal impacts of pollution in the near term and climate change in the long term. Air pollution in China's eastern cities, especially particulate matter, 2.5 micrometers in diameter or less ($PM_{2.5}$), resulting mainly from widespread and massive coal use, is now known to be taking the lives of *at least* 250,000 people annually and probably as many as four times this number [9]. It means that every year more people die in China from air toxicity than all American military deaths in WWII.

We know such massive numbers of coal casualties are legitimate. They come not from eco-extremists or neocon China-haters, but from high-level official bodies like the World Health Organization (WHO) and from reputable researchers at top-level universities. Since the early 2000s, the WHO in particular has been intently restudying the impacts of air pollution, employing new methods and technologies, new evidence on the relationship between particulate matter and health, and new correlations between the rise of air toxicity and the increase of noncommunicable diseases. A key 2014 report revealed that "the risks from air pollution are now far greater than previously thought or understood, particularly for heart disease and strokes" [10]. Data presented for the year 2012 indicated that 1.7 million deaths resulted from air pollution in the western Pacific region, whose highest air toxicity existed in China and Mongolia, both of which depend on coal as their main fuel. The report suggests that as much as 30 percent (507,000) of deaths occurred in these two countries. Given the differences in their populations (3.5 million vs. 1.3 billion) and number of heavily polluted cities, there is little doubt about where the bulk of this mortality took place. A separate investigation of pollution mortality for the same year by a researcher from Tsingua University in Beijing found that when mining, transportation, and water impacts were added in, a death count of 670,000 resulted for China alone. Yet another research study, this one conducted by a group from the Massachusetts Institute of Technology, concluded that 500 million people living in north China where industrialization has been most intense have a life expectancy 5.5 years less than those in south China.

In 2014, a national survey revealed that 90 percent of Chinese cities had pollution levels well above national limits for acceptable air quality. These limits, however, are themselves much higher than those recommended by WHO. For $PM_{2.5}$, WHO's limit is 10 micrograms per cubic meter ($\mu g/m^3$), averaged over a year. China's standard is 35 $\mu g/m^3$. Even so, Chinese cities have been routinely unable to achieve this. Since 2010, many urban areas have exceeded levels of 80–90 $\mu g/m^3$; Beijing's numbers in 2013 and 2014 were above ninety. In the most industrial areas, such as Hebei Province, where coal use in power plants and factories is especially high, levels have gone to 500–900 $\mu g/m^3$ for weeks at a time and have averaged over 150 $\mu g/m^3$. Such levels are off the chart established by WHO for the most hazardous air quality possible.

But China is far from alone in its lethal pollution. By 2015, no fewer than thirteen of the twenty most air polluted cities in the world were in India, where coal use has also skyrocketed [14]. In recent years, India has had the highest death rate from respiratory illness of any country worldwide – nearly twice that of China – and its problems in this domain are already so serious as to require decades for any real improvement. Estimates now suggest that as many as 600,000 deaths per year occur in India and that numbers for many other cities in Asia, though significantly less than this, are growing worse [15].

Indeed, as developing nations have advanced economically, in Asia most of all, their coal consumption has grown as well, so that ambient air quality has degraded in a large number of cities throughout the region – Jakarta, Manila, Hanoi, Kuala Lumpur, Bangkok, Karachi, Dhaka, and Ulaanbaatar [15]. In all of these places, should the pattern continue or improve only slightly, there will be ever-growing aggravations to heart and respiratory disease, circulatory illness, stroke, and premature mortality. Such pollution is now understood to both cause and greatly worsen the conditions of heart disease, lung cancer, chronic obstructive pulmonary disease, and acute lower respiratory infections. In rural areas, where cheap coal is the fuel for heating and cooking in the home, the impact comes down hardest on women and very young children, who spend the most time near stoves and fires.

Year after year, each new study that appears on air pollution in the developing world comes back to a single, chilling truth: such pollution is immensely more deadly than we might ever have imagined. It is killing, injuring, and shortening the lives of more people than malaria, dengue fever, tuberculosis, and HIV/AIDS combined. In truth, we in the West *did* come close to imagining how bad things could be some time ago. The December 1952 "killer smog" in London, resulting from a temperature inversion that trapped the coal smoke from hundreds of thousands of factory, power plant, commercial, and home furnaces in that city, took the lives of 4,000 people in less than two weeks, with another 8,000 or more falling prey to the effects during the next few months. Only three years later, a second such event happened in London, taking over a thousand lives. Fatal smogs, due more to vehicle and industrial exhaust, began to hit Los Angeles in the 1940s, then New York City in 1953, 1962, and 1966, where hundreds of people died. It took more than a few recurrences of such smogs before the first Clean Air Act in the US was passed in 1963. Given the overall situation in coal-hungry states today, it is interesting to read the first part of this Act:

> The Congress finds – 1) that the predominant part of the Nation's population is located in its rapidly expanding metropolitan and other urban areas . . . 2) that the growth in the amount and complexity of air pollution brought about by the urbanization, industrial development, and the increasing use of motor vehicles, has resulted in mounting dangers to the public health and welfare . . . [16]

By the 1970s, clean air laws were passed in North America, Europe, and Japan. Coal plants were now required to employ pollution control systems; new technology was developed to control some of the worst pollutants, like sulfur dioxide (source of acid rain), nitrous oxides (produces ground-level ozone), and particulate matter. Over time, each of these control systems became more efficient and effective; eventually new equipment able to remove most of the mercury that coal gases carry was also developed.

This may sound wonderful, progressive, life-saving, and to a significant degree it was. By the early 1990s, Western and Japanese cities saw far fewer days of deadly air, and very few by the year 2000. The problem was no longer a visible one. It was now possible to expect a future where the air would not be a common enemy to health and well-being. But it turns out that a good part of this is a mirage. In a number of countries, including the US, older coal plants built *before* clean air legislation was passed were allowed to continue operating without pollution controls. Many of these "grandfathered" plants continued operating into the twenty-first century and are still online today (2017), having never put to use the innovations mentioned above. There is no question that this gap in coverage by clean air legislation has had an impact on public health.

No surprise, then, that it is far worse in developing nations, whose main era of industrialization in the 1990s and early 2000s saw air pollution levels rising at alarming rates. Not only in China, but in many other nations coal use rose between five- and eight-fold between 1995 and 2010, in lock step with growing electricity generation and use. A brief list of such nations would include India, Bangladesh, Indonesia, Malaysia, Philippines, Vietnam, Thailand, Burma, Mongolia, Kazakhstan, Chile, and Peru. Despite a global slowing of coal demand after 2014, consumption has continued to rise in South and Southeast Asia at a significant place [17–18]. In none of these countries, moreover, is urbanization near to complete. Great numbers of people will be moving into their cities over the next four or five decades, such that the urban population of the developing world will soar from 2.6 billion to over 5 billion by 2040. And the trend will continue. For by that time, the urban population of

Asia will be under 60 percent, far below the 80–90 percent typical in wealthier nations [19].

In short, the rise in air pollution for these billions of people has possibly only just begun. If, at a minimum, a quarter of a million die each year in China, what might the *global* mortality be like by 2030 or 2040, were coal use to continue its rise? There is no avoiding the conclusion that fatalities would far surpass the combined toll of the most fatal contagions today, such as HIV/AIDS, tuberculosis, pneumonia, malaria, and infectious diarrhea (about 5–6 million total deaths per year). The truth is that toxic air is even *now* a primary contributor to the worst diseases that strike the human community. Future deaths, moreover, would be added to the growing impacts of climate change, a reality whose lethal effects we are already witnessing in 2015.

But wait, the attentive reader says, what about the pollution control systems mentioned above? Can't these be applied to coal-burning plants and industries throughout the developing world? Theoretically, yes. As could "clean coal" technology with capture and storage of CO_2. But realism dictates that we look at the track record for these options, and the record isn't very good.

China and India both have laws demanding the use of pollution control equipment in coal-burning facilities, as do some other emerging and developing nations. But operating such equipment adds cost and therefore lowers profitability for utilities and factories, who are viewed as essential generators of economic growth. In most of these countries, electricity prices are fixed by national and provincial/state governments – kept artificially low to help more people afford power and to spur economic development. The result is two-fold: a refusal by local officials, power plant managers, factory owners, and business CEOs to use the equipment even when installed, and an unwillingness (or inability) by government regulators to enforce related laws and systematically punish offenders. In China's case, we find another hurdle – a deep-seated culture of coal reaching back three-quarters of a century whose mining and transport, sale and distribution, and final consumption weave together many millions of jobs and billions of dollars. China's dependence on coal, though now promised to decrease, is so immense and so deeply integrated into their culture and economy, that a good many decades will be needed to replace even part of it.

As for "clean coal," it has been under development for over two decades now, with little real progress to show. The full complement of technologies under this title, intended to eliminate nearly all air toxins and up to 65 percent or more of carbon emissions, remains too expensive at this writing to be fully commercial. Every such project has run aground on construction delays, politics, and huge cost overruns. While a small retrofit project opened commercially in Canada in 2014, the first full-scale clean-coal power station in the US, located in Mississippi, took nearly six years to complete (two years beyond schedule) at a cost of over $6 billion, more than double the original estimate. For a moderate capacity of 582 megawatts (MW), this qualified as the most expensive electricity in the nation. Such difficulties no doubt reflect the reality that the plant is a first of its kind [20]. Yet this is precisely the point. Decades and dozens of more plants will be needed to mature and fine-tune the technology; how long thereafter to upgrade or replace the more than 5,000 coal power plants now in place worldwide?

It pays to be blunt on this topic – the world does not have decades to wait before a technology that doesn't yet fully exist can begin to make a difference in coal-related air pollution and emissions. Many millions of people will die in the interim. Unfortunately, the same point applies to renewables like wind and, especially, solar power, which remain far from able to run the world's major cities. These technologies will continue to advance and will, almost certainly, help alter our global energy system in profound ways. But there are other sources of electricity able to replace and substitute for coal now and that seem more than likely to alter this system in the next 20–30 years.

The Climate Factor

Here is a striking image: the Earth's atmosphere rolled into a sphere. With a diameter of 1,990 km, the sphere covers New England and part of adjacent Canada. Now gather all the world's cities into one giant square. This turns out to have a side of 1,700 km and to occupy a bit less than 2 percent of the planet's land area. Place the sphere above our great urban square and then imagine the emissions rising from millions of factories, power plants, industries, cars, trucks, etc., and penetrating through the lower walls of the sphere. How long before the atmosphere within starts to change in a fundamental way?

That humanity has had the major part in warming the atmosphere and oceans, and is now seeing the effects of this, stands beyond scientific debate and doubt. The data and knowledge behind this statement have progressed to the point where important skepticism no longer exists, no more than it does for plate tectonics, the existence of DNA, or the fact that ten is larger than five. Scientific consensus is codified in the form of a unique organization, the Intergovernmental Panel on Climate Change (IPCC), whose mission it is to collect, analyze, synthesize, and publish every four or five years, the growing mass of global research on the Earth's changing climate. Scientists, in other words, here report on their fields of work to their colleagues, the press, and to the entire world.

With each successive report, the conclusion of the IPCC about human-caused climate change has grown stronger and clearer. So has the identification of impacts. For example, by 2017, the twelve warmest years on record (since 1880) occurred in the preceding two decades, with 2016 the warmest on record and the year when the extent of sea ice at both poles was the lowest on record. Since the 1950s, the number of record hot days in US cities, across Australia, in the Arctic, and elsewhere has doubled and even tripled. Major, repeated heat waves have struck many nations, killing thousands from Western Europe to India. The planet's cryosphere, its water stored in frozen form, is melting at an ever-growing rate, helping to raise sea levels, increasing coastal erosion, island drowning, and inland surges of major storms. Warming of the atmosphere adds energy to such storms in many areas, so that extreme weather events and related flooding are more common, intense, and lethal.

These are only a few major impacts. According to the IPCC, they will continue and will escalate. About this, too, there is no longer significant dispute though the details remain unclear. Those who reject the consensus, particularly if they is not scientists themselves, do so for ideological reasons, most often the desire to reduce "government control," via environmental policy, over concepts and actions related to the natural world. A common tactic has been to highlight uncertainty, including that involved in computer modeling of the future. Yet the accuracy of one or another model is less important than the unwavering fact that great majority of them support the above overarching conclusions. Moreover, depending where we live, our own experience might be testimony to the changes now underway [21].

Will all this mean the end of civilization? The collapse of societies? A desperate and final escape to begin life anew on a far-off world? Probably not. We do not need an overheated, apocalyptic imagination to convince us that climate change is deadly serious. But if it warps the reality (and distracts attention) to say we are doomed, it does no good to sentimentalize what is happening either. The Earth and its climate are not being "thrown out of balance" or "damaged beyond repair." The planet, its atmosphere and oceans, are not "in peril" or "threatened."

It is the biosphere – life, as we know it – that must be seen as most imperiled by climate change. And this includes human beings, who do not need to "save the planet" but rather themselves and as many of the world's species as possible. This does not mean that humanity faces possible extinction. Our kind inhabits just about every geographic and climatic setting on Earth. But this is scant comfort when hundreds of millions at a minimum are threatened by effects that are even now underway, destroying lives, and growing in severity. Recent heat waves in northern India and Russia, deadly floods in Pakistan and South America, more frequent wildfires and forest fires in the western US, and extreme weather events in many temperate areas of the Northern Hemisphere have together killed many thousands of people. It is no longer legitimate to talk only about possible future impacts.

Real, concrete conclusions emerge from this truth. Humans can accept their powers of control over the Earth's climate and to employ these powers in a way that will best further their own benefit. They are hardly doing so now. To take just one specific example, the effects of abnormally high heat on human health are well-known, and this is especially relevant to developing nations like India. People with cardiovascular ailments, especially the elderly, as well as those who do hard physical labor outdoors, young children and pregnant women who are ill or undernourished, and anyone without adequate access to clean water, are all hugely vulnerable. More than 2,300 people died in India's heat wave of 2015, which affected hundreds of millions and overfilled a great many hospitals in the states of Andhra Pradesh and Telangana. Add to this the prospect of toxic air in many urban centers, and fatal consequences are certain not only in South Asia but in many parts of the globe.

You may view this as a purely secular reality, wrought by the iron laws of physics and chemistry, or as humans interfering with God's Creation, impelled by the sins of pride and greed. The impacts are the same. We are now experiencing the effects of two centuries' buildup of atmospheric greenhouse gases (GHGs), especially carbon dioxide (CO_2). In 2015, the volumetric concentration of CO_2 in the atmosphere surpassed 400 parts per million (ppm) – a level not seen for a million years. As far back as good data goes, about 800,000 years, CO_2 very rarely rose above 290 ppm in the warmest periods and never above 300 ppm. We are at a stage far above this. Human beings have never lived in such an atmosphere. They do now.

Even at lower rates of increase than have been typical (roughly 2–4 ppm/ year), the atmosphere will reach over 500 ppm by mid-century and 700 ppm or more by 2100. If we include other GHGs, converted to CO_2-equivalent, these numbers rise to more than 600 ppm and 850 ppm. Such levels would take us back 56 million years, to the Paleocene–Eocene Thermal Maximum (PETM), when the estimated mean near-surface temperature spiked for 20,000 years at 30°C (86°F), compared to today's 14°C (57°F), and the poles were essentially free of ice. The continents were covered by tropical forests and jungle, and hurricane-type storms occurred as far north as the Arctic Circle, where the seas were at least 23°C (74°F). For much of the year, land temperatures were 35°C (95°F) or above [21].

Is this what we must expect by the end of the century? No one really knows. Best estimates, which remain fairly cautious, tell us that CO_2-equivalent levels of 750 ppm have a 15 percent chance of causing 6°C (11°F) or more of permanent warming. A 15 percent chance may not sound like much. But consider: if the US government had ever thought there existed a 1-in-7 possibility that the Soviets would launch a thermonuclear weapon, the military would have immediately gone to DEFCON 1 (maximum readiness) and remained there permanently. There is much uncertainty about where all the carbon that generated the PETM, and that ocean sediments document, came from. This, in fact, may be one of the biggest differences from today: we know quite well where the main volume of additional carbon is coming from now. And we also know what will slow, stop, and even reverse it.

Primary is the burning of carbon-based fuels. Carbon dioxide accounted for over two-thirds of all human-generated GHG emissions in 2015, with coal representing at least 50 percent of this, and rising. Other contributors include oil at 34 percent, methane (CH_4) 10 percent, and nitrogen oxide 1 percent. Coal defines the dominant source, not only for its release of CO_2 but because it also generates methane (coal naturally contains large amounts of it), nitrous oxides, and black carbon ("soot"), another powerful agent of warming consisting of tiny particles that absorb and reradiate energy from the Sun [21]. This last, in fact, is largely the same $PM_{2.5}$ from coal responsible for so many air pollution deaths every year.

Since the early decades of the Industrial Revolution, the greatest impact on local and global climate has come from the burning of coal. This has not changed. For a single decade, the 1970s, forms of motorization (cars, trucks, planes, etc., both civilian and military) and vehicle ownership grew especially fast in wealthy nations giving petroleum the king's chair in carbon emissions. But after the second oil crisis in 1979, oil consumption dropped, and then grew again more slowly. But in the late 1990s, world coal use took off, led by a developing Asia. By 2005 carbon added to the atmosphere from this source again outstripped oil by an ever-growing amount.

In fact, global coal use fairly doubled in the two decades after 1995, a rate of increase not seen since the nineteenth century. We have already made clear which country did the most to make this happen. The case today, however, is such that even if China holds true to its promise of reduced coal dependence, this can be more than made up by growth in use by other Asian states. All forecasts agree that the world's consumption of coal will continue to rise, more slowly than before due to stricter environmental rules, but rise nonetheless [17].

The Nuclear Alternative

Enter the nuclear alternative. Consider that a new nuclear plant, built with twenty-first century technology, like the 1.4 GigaWatt (GW) designs built by South Korea in the United Arab Emirates, will provide the electricity of three or four coal plants while occupying roughly the same amount of land as one of them and producing no air pollutants, no particulate matter, and no greenhouse gases. Together, the 449 operable reactors plus the sixty under construction at the end of 2016, totaling about 545 GW, represent more than 2,000 coal plants (accounting for the fact that nuclear plants are run at 25 percent to 30 percent higher capacities than coal plants). Given what we have said above, these are vital statistics, to say the least. And they are getting more vital and meaningful by the year.

This is because, while the coal "boom" of the 2000s may have ended, there are still a great many new plants scheduled for the coming decade. In early 2017, despite the decline in coal use in most Western nations, over 560 new coal power plants were under construction worldwide, 90 percent of which were in Asia. Most of these were in China, India, Indonesia, Vietnam, and Philippines, with hundreds more plants already announced and permitted [22]. The increase also includes Japan (eleven coal plants under construction, thirty-four more announced, permitted), where shut down of the country's nuclear power plants after the Fukushima accident has led to a major increase in fossil fuel consumption for power. Outside Japan, the people of the Asian region, and the world as a whole, are fortunate that for each of the new plants approved at least two others have been shelved or canceled. Yet this hardly merits a round of beer hall revelry. The prospect of more than 500 new coal plants coming online by 2030 or before, many of them without the latest pollution control equipment, should instead give us pause. There are clear humanitarian reasons to hope that the greater number will not be built. But for that to happen, something will need to take their place.

Such is one reason to feel thankful that the majority of new nuclear power reactors are being, and will continue to be, constructed in some of these same nations, and in developing nations more generally. This, too, as already noted, defines a change from the past and an important element of the new nuclear era. Until now, nuclear power has been a Western technology, rooted in the wealth and scientific soil of the West and the ex-Soviet Union. Yet such is a Cold War view.

Over half of the 200+ new reactors now planned and underway for the next decades are in non-Western countries, a number of them without existing nuclear programs. Since the 2000s, at least forty-five nations have shown strong interest in launching such programs for the first time. Using the WNA again as a source, we see that these countries include

- *Europe*: Albania, Serbia, Croatia, Portugal, Latvia, Estonia, Ireland, Poland
- *Middle East and North Africa*: Turkey, Saudi Arabia, Qatar, Kuwait, Jordan, Egypt, Tunisia, Algeria, Morocco
- *sub-Saharan Africa*: Ghana, Senegal, Nigeria, Kenya, Uganda, Namibia
- *South America*: Chile, Ecuador, Venezuela, Bolivia, Peru
- *Central and South Asia*: Azerbaijan, Georgia, Mongolia, Bangladesh, Sri Lanka
- *SE Asia*: Vietnam, Thailand, Malaysia, Indonesia, Philippines, Singapore [23]

To say this is a highly varied group of states would be a colossal understatement. Indeed, the variety and geographical spread give testimony to the powerful appeal nuclear now has worldwide. When we say these countries have "shown interest," we mean they have sought information, advice, and guidance from the International Atomic Energy Agency (IAEA), the world's chief organization for nuclear cooperation, safety standardization, and inspections, established in 1957 as part of the United Nations. All the noted countries are among the 190 that are parties to the Nuclear Non-Proliferation Treaty (NPT). Signatories to the NPT that have also joined the IAEA (164 countries as of 2016) are required to seek help and approval from the organization in order to begin a civilian nuclear program. That all of the above nations have done so is an excellent first sign. It tells us they will not be going it alone. They will instead gain the advantage of the most advanced, up-to-date knowledge, technology, and guidance. This is not to say that every country on our list above is guaranteed to launch a nuclear power program soon, or that there won't be others, perhaps many of them. Just as cheap natural gas and coal or another nuclear accident might turn the interest of some governments in another direction, so might the need for noncarbon sources or the success of new nuclear nations like the United Arab Emirates make nuclear power even more attractive.

Yet some nations in the list will undoubtedly bring other challenges. Countries with unstable governments, civil unrest, or major conflict with other states, are not ideal places for building the technical competence and security requirements needed for a nuclear program. This is no less true for nations with rampant corruption or brutal insurgencies. In such cases, the IAEA is likely to advise caution, perhaps postponement, combined with a higher level of monitoring and inspection if the country decides to go forward. Such, at least, would be a minimum.

It may be, too, that the US will seek what are called 123 Agreements with as many of these nations as possible. By such agreements, the US promises to provide nuclear know-how, technology, reactor fuel, and reactor components (built to the highest standard), in exchange for enhanced obligations on nonproliferation. These obligations could overlap those advised by the IAEA, namely more frequent, strict, and thorough inspections of nuclear sites. But they would go further: as in the 2009 Agreement with the UAE, they would ask the country to forgo any interest in enrichment and reprocessing technology, the two technologies by which nuclear fuel can be produced. In fact, in 2015, the US already had twenty-four of these 123 Agreements in place, covering the EU as well as fourteen developing nations including Argentina, Brazil, Colombia, Egypt, Indonesia, Kazakhstan, Thailand, and Turkey. There are thus precedents in place to deal with at least some of the challenges from a more globalized nuclear industry.

This may be made easier by the technology involved. Unlike the coal plants China and India built in the 2000s, many of which had older, less efficient designs, the reactors to be erected in developing nations will use the same advanced technology as in wealthy countries. This is because, with only a few exceptions, the reactors will be designed and built by companies from South Korea, China, Japan, Canada, and Russia. The global nuclear industry has already become a domain of market competition among the world's most sophisticated firms. Those nations that follow the lead of the UAE – and there will be more than a few – will demand the highest level technology for the best price. This means competition to offer superior power output, better safety systems, higher fuel efficiency, decreased waste, and reduced potential for proliferation. As this book will show, new designs are now coming available to answer all these demands.

The only question is whether the US will move forward on these in a significant way. In other words, will America maintain its global leadership role in nuclear matters or continue to watch its nuclear industry languish and weaken, so that this role weakens as well. And further, how might such a reduced standing affect the ability of the US to forge 123 and other non-proliferation agreements in the future? As the new era of nuclear expansion arrives, the US and other Western nations are faced with an epochal decision: will they be part of this evolving, noncarbon realm of technology or will they be left behind.

A First Conclusion

At this point in the history of energy, we know that the source upon which the modern world erected itself has become one of the great threats to human well-being. Whether or not we accept the idea that we are living in the Anthropocene Epoch, defined by when a major human impact on global Earth systems began, there is no denying that such an impact exists, that it is bringing many risks for many forms of life, and that the single largest contributor to it over the past two centuries has been coal.

In 2014, the province of Ontario, Canada, became the first major territory of North America to end all coal use. Soon after, the nations of Belgium, Switzerland, and Norway, all large economies in Europe, became coal free. Then, in April of 2017, none other than Britain went an entire day without a single coal plant operating, a potent symbolic moment for the island that had launched the modern era in energy and transformed itself into "the workshop of the world" on the basis of that single fuel. The reason that any of this has been possible is nuclear power, the one exception being Norway which uniquely gets over 95 percent of its electricity from hydropower (though it has research reactors performing collaborative work with more than a dozen countries and firms, including Norway's own Thor Energy, which is seeking to develop a new, thorium-based reactor fuel for the global nuclear power industry). Where Ontario and Belgium derive about half their power from nuclear, Switzerland is at 34 percent, Britain at 20 percent. Britain has plans to eliminate coal use by 2025 using a combination of renewables and new nuclear plants.

But if the West has increasingly turned from the fuel that powered and polluted its industrial age, this hasn't been the case elsewhere. Declining coal use in the US and Europe has been overshadowed by rising consumption elsewhere. Developing nations with sizeable resources of coal – China, India, Indonesia, Poland, Kazakhstan, South Africa, Mongolia, Pakistan, Turkey, among some others – have typically held fast to the principle that "when you are home, the walls will help you" (Russian proverb), i.e. the most secure resources are those within domestic borders. Yet the problems faced by China have sharpened many eyes about what this can mean. The observation has been made that this one fuel lifted hundreds of millions of Chinese out of poverty in a single generation, and that none of these people would trade their advancement for a slower pace of development using "cleaner" energy. Yet this compels us to ask a question: is it *really* necessary that tens of millions die or fall seriously ill for these hundreds of millions to find progress? Is this the best calculus we can hope for regarding economic development?

The answer, of course, must be "no." This is not a trade-off that should be acceptable or accepted. Nor, as we will see, is there any possibility of miraculously turning development into a dream powered wholly by renewable solar and wind power. These remain unready to power a major city, let alone an entire economy. Another bad trade-off is thinking we can mortgage the energy future of poorer nations to technologies that do not yet exist. This brings us back to natural gas. It is greatly superior to both coal and oil in nearly every way except carbon emissions – it generates fully 55 percent as much CO_2 as coal and

73 percent those of oil. This is good enough to make it a bridge fuel to a more low-carbon future, but not a main pillar of that future. The other challenge with natural gas is that a majority of developing nations must import it, often at elevated prices, and sometimes with political costs and concerns.

Thus, we arrive at a truth about our world today: the drive for economic development, energy security, reliable power, and lower pollution and carbon emissions has impelled nations toward nuclear power. While we will discuss the example of the United Arab Emirates in Chapter 11, there are certainly others. Nations in Asia, from Turkey to Thailand have come to view nuclear as essential to ending power shortages and avoiding the "coal problem." If we need an example of what nuclear might help achieve in the climate area, we might look to France. After the first oil crisis, the French famously decided to switch from oil and coal in power generation to nuclear; rapid build-up of reactors led to an equally rapid decline in emissions of at least 2 percent per year, such that France became the lowest emitter of any OECD country and the world's largest exporter of electricity [24]. For a negative model, where such trends appear in reverse, there is Japan. Shutting down all forty-eight of its reactors, thereby losing a third of its electricity, the country turned to more coal, natural gas, and oil for power, raising carbon emissions by nearly 20 percent in just three years and increasing oil imports from the Persian Gulf.

We have stressed that the new nuclear era does not come without questions and concerns, big ones in fact, as well as advances and advantages. In the pages that follow, we will address many of these, particularly the most pressing among them. But it is essential to understand, at the outset, that this era is "new" in a number of ways. It represents a profound change both in the number of reactors it will see built and where most of these will be – not in wealthy nations of the West but in less-wealthy and even poor countries of the developing world. This reflects the historical stage these countries have entered, the stage of rapid industrialization and economic modernism, when they are lifting themselves out of centuries of poverty and deprivation. The most fundamental need to make this happen is the spread of reliable electricity; nearly everything begins with this. Technology defines yet another key component of the new era: today's advanced reactor designs are a giant step beyond those of the 1970s and 80s that now dominate the landscape, and arrive with new fuel possibilities, greatly improved safety systems, higher efficiency, and larger output. Lastly, there is the nuclear industry itself, which has been actively pursuing a new phase of global cooperation and also competition, one involving a surge in innovative ideas that affect every aspect of peaceful nuclear energy, from cooling systems to financing, and that will extend the very utility of nuclear plants into novel domains.

As the authors of this book, we feel certain that the new era provides reason for both hope and caution. During the next several decades, humanity will be faced with providing more energy services to many more people in less damaging ways. There is no debate here. Without more electricity reliably brought to those who now lack it, any real gains in global health, access to food and water, poverty reduction, and social stability will stagnate, or worse. Yet energy must not, in the obligatory name of development, become a source of detriment and degradation, nor a guarantor of a different, warmer world. The world has options to prevent this from happening. It cannot afford to give up any of them, especially one that can supply power on a massive scale in any climate, weather, or season, at all hours of every day, for decade after decade, with no release of pollution or carbon emissions.

As the following chapters will also emphasize, this option had a fearful beginning in wartime and a troubled infancy wrapped in secrecy, arrogance, and Cold War anxieties. Such an origin, for some, has framed "nuclear" as an embodiment of threats dangerous, dark, and even demonic. But it is time, we contend, to put away these views from the childhood of nuclear power. The history of the last half-century – when viewed with a steady and unstigmatized eye – shows it to have matured into one of the world's safest, most beneficial, and rapidly advancing energy technologies. This book, while taking nuclear fear as a serious and required subject (Chapter 7), will add its voice to those who know the risks of monstrous proportion are naked emperors.

The world cannot afford essentialist thinking about nuclear power, not when carbon pollution kills every year more than the number of people who died at Hiroshima and Nagasaki. Ironic as it may be, the antinuclear ideology today comprises a threat of its own, a way of thinking just as incompatible with solving the pollution and climate crises as the denial that they exist. A better future for humanity depends deeply, inexorably, on expanding the reach of modern energy while reducing its carbon footprint. Lowering the use of coal, and oil too, will not be easy, quick, or cheap. But it is worth believing that human ingenuity will find ways to make it happen. And one of these ways, a major one for many nations, is the nuclear option, designed and managed to the highest standards.

References

[1] World Nuclear Association (WNA), World Nuclear Power Reactors & Uranium Requirements. Available from: www.world-nuclear.org/info/Facts-and-Figures/World-Nuclear-Power-Reactors-and-Uranium-Requirements/
[2] IAEA (International Atomic Energy Agency), Power Reactor Information System. Available from: https://www.iaea.org/pris/

[3] International Energy Agency, World Energy Outlook (2014).

[4] World Nuclear Power Reactors & Uranium Requirements, *WNA*.

[5] C. Buckley, China Burns Much More Coal Than Reported, Complicating Climate Talks, *The New York Times* (November 3, 2015). Available from: www.nytimes.com /2015/11/04/world/asia/china-burns-much-more-coal-than-reported-complicating -climate-talks.html?_r=0

[6] B. Dooley, Forget Fukushima: China Powering Ahead with Plans for New Reactors, *Japan Times* (April 15, 2015). Available from: www.japantimes.co.jp /news/2015/04/15/asia-pacific/forget-fukushima-china-powering-ahead-plans- new-reactors/#.WCueFKIrLkI

[7] R. Ferguson, W. Wilkinson, and R. Hill, Electricity Use and Economic Development, *Energy Policy*, 28 (2000), 923–934.

[8] P. K. Adom, Electricity Consumption-Economic Growth Nexus: The Ghanaian Case, *International Journal of Energy Economics and Policy*, 1: 1 (2011), 18–31.

[9] J. Lelieveld, J. S. Evans, M. Fnais et al., The Contribution of Outdoor Air Pollution Sources to Premature Mortality on a Global Scale, *Nature*, 525 (September 15, 2015), 367–371.

[10] 7 Million Premature Deaths Annually Linked to Air Pollution, *World Health Organization Media Centre* (March 25, 2014). Available from: www.who.int /mediacentre/news/releases/2014/air-pollution/en/

[11] L. Jing, 670,000 Smog-Related Deaths a Year: The Cost of China's Reliance on Coal, *South China Morning Post* (November 5, 2014). Available from: www.scmp .com/news/china/article/1632163/670000-deaths-year-cost-chinas-reliance-coal? page=all

[12] Y. Chen, A. Ebenstein, M. Greenstone, and H. Li, Evidence on the Impact of Sustained Exposure to Air Pollution on Life Expectancy from China's Huai River Policy, *Proceedings of the National Academy of Sciences*, 110: 32 (2013), 12936–12941.

[13] China Says 90% of Cities Failed to Meet Air Standards in 2014, *Reuters* (February 1, 2015). Available from: http://www.reuters.com/article/2015/02/02/us-china- pollution-idUSKBN0L606R20150202

[14] J. Burke, India's Doctors Blame Air Pollution for Sharp Rise in Respiratory Diseases, *The Guardian* (September 23, 2015). Available from: www.theguardian .com/world/2015/sep/23/india-doctors-air-pollution-rise-respiratory-diseases-delhi.

[15] World Health Organization, Ambient Air Pollution: A Global Assessment of Exposure and Burden of Disease (2016). Available from: http://apps.who.int/iris/ bitstream/10665/250141/1/9789241511353-eng.pdf?ua=1

[16] Title 42, The Public Health and Welfare, Chapter 85, Air Pollution Prevention and Control, Section 7401, Congressional findings and declaration of purpose (a)(1), (2). Available from: www.gpo.gov/fdsys/pkg/USCODE-2013-title42/html/ USCODE-2013-title42-chap85-subchapI-partA-sec7401.htm

[17] International Energy Outlook 2016, US Energy Information Administration, Chapter 4: Coal (May 2016). Available from: www.eia.gov/forecasts/ieo/coal.cfm

[18] T. Moss, In Asia, King Coal Hard to Dethrone, *Wall Street Journal* (December 9, 2015). Available from: www.wsj.com/articles/in-asia-king-coal-hard-to- dethrone-1449692644

[19] United Nations Population Division, World Urbanization Prospects: 2014 Revision, Highlights, (2014). Available from: https://esa.un.org/unpd/wup/ Publications/Files/WUP2014-Highlights.pdf

[20] K. E. Swartz and S. Rahim, Kemper "Clean Coal" Project Shows the Costly Perils of Being "First of Its Kind," *E&E News* (August 24, 2015). Available from: www .eenews.net/stories/1060023782

[21] R. K. Pachauri et al., Climate Change 2014: Synthesis Report, Summary for Policymakers, Intergovernmental Panel on Climate Change (2014). Available from: www.ipcc.ch/pdf/assessment-report/ar5/syr/SYR_AR5_FINAL_full_wcover.pdf

[22] Endcoal, Global Coal Plant Tracker. Available from: http://endcoal.org/global-coal-plant-tracker/

[23] World Nuclear Association, Emerging Nuclear Energy Countries (October, 2016). Available from: www.world-nuclear.org/info/Country-Profiles/Others/Emerging-Nuclear-Energy-Countries/

[24] K. Bullis, To Meet Emissions Targets, We've All Got to Be like France, *Technology Review* (August 23, 2013). Available from: www.technologyreview .com/s/518711/to-meet-emissions-targets-weve-all-got-to-be-like-france/

2

How It Began: Weapons and Their Legacy

In the Beginning: A Letter

To fully understand the nuclear landscape of today and tomorrow, we need to see it as part of an evolution that began in the 1930s and 40s. There are aspects of that time that are still very much with us and will continue to be with us for at least another generation or two. Indeed, a look at the past is essential for other reasons, too. It tells us a great deal about how governments, researchers, institutions, and the public have been vital actors in the evolution of nuclear reality since the beginning.

It is a key fact, perhaps above all others, that nuclear power emerged from nuclear weapons which were born in a reactor. Or more precisely, the peaceful uses of nuclear energy grew directly out of efforts to build a weapon of mass destruction, whose possibility was first proven in a pile of graphite blocks containing scattered blebs of uranium oxide. There is a kind of extreme irony in this: a technology to produce electricity, the fundament of modern life, grew out of technology able to destroy life, indeed *all* life. In any case, the association between weapons and power plants has never really waned; this, too, is part of nuclear history. We therefore need to consider aspects about the development of nuclear weapons, as well as treaties meant to control them, before looking at nuclear power.

Nuclear energy is like fire. In fact, it was always there, waiting to be discovered. Someone was going to do it. In his epochal work, "The Making of the Atomic Bomb," Richard Rhodes on the first page quotes Robert Oppenheimer, the scientific chief of the Manhattan Project, as follows: "It is a profound and necessary truth that the deep things in science are not found because they are useful; they are found because it is possible to find them" [1].

32

The pioneer of nuclear physics, the discoverer of the atomic nucleus, Ernest Rutherford, believed that while large amounts of energy could be derived from atoms it was an inefficient way of doing so and that anyone who looked for a source of power in a related process was talking "moonshine." Nonetheless, in a 1914 novel, *The World Set Free*, H. G. Wells predicted atomic bombs and atomic war, followed by a reformed (and much reduced) mankind who builds utopia based on "atomic power."

Indeed, the atom's time had come. If the 1800s were the era of great advances in chemistry, geology, and evolution, the first half of the twentieth century belonged to physics. Leó Szilárd, an important player in all of this, as he was crossing the street in London one day in 1933 while pondering a recent reading of Wells' book, suddenly realized that – Rutherford to the contrary – if an element could be found that absorbs a neutron, splits, and then emits two neutrons, it could sustain a chain reaction. With such an element, thought Szilárd, then "it might be possible to . . . liberate energy on an industrial scale and construct atomic bombs" [2].

In the 1930s – at least in scientific circles – the possibility of realizing Szilárd's vision grew rapidly. Experiments in Germany by Otto Hahn and Lise Meitner demonstrated that slow neutrons bombarding uranium could create barium. This was the first evidence that atoms could be split, releasing a large amount of energy in the process. Like Meitner, many of the physicists in Europe who contributed to related experiments were Jews or opponents of oppression who fled Hitler's growing power for the safety of other nations. In the US, this included, in addition to Szilárd, the likes of Albert Einstein, Edward Teller, and Enrico Fermi, as well as other physicists of the first rank. Yet, as World War II neared, concerns grew that those who remained behind in Germany, such as Werner Heisenberg, might be put to work building a bomb that Hitler could then use to destroy cities and threaten the entire world. In 1939, Szilárd persuaded Albert Einstein to write a letter outlining this danger to President Roosevelt.

Who contributed a lot to projects

The letter itself went through many drafts and the plan for how to get it in Roosevelt's hands went through many labyrinthine twists and turns as well. Finally, however an economist named Alexander Sachs, known well by Roosevelt, to whom Szilárd and his colleagues in this effort (Eugene Wigner and Edward Teller) had been introduced, agreed to be the carrier. Dated August 2, 1939, Einstein's letter explained in fairly direct terms that a nuclear chain reaction had become achievable "in the immediate future," that this would produce "vast amounts of power and large quantities of new radium-like elements . . . and it is conceivable – though much less certain – that extremely powerful bombs of a new type may thus be constructed." Einstein

Alexander Sachs – economist who knew Roosevelt

noted that such a bomb could be delivered by sea to destroy an entire port and the surrounding area. It was essential that the Administration keep in touch with physicists working on related experiments in US universities and possibly help them advance their work with additional funding. The letter ended with an understated, somewhat convoluted, yet unmistakable warning:

> I understand that Germany has actually stopped the sale of uranium from the Czechoslovakian mines, which she has taken over. That she should have taken such early action might perhaps be understood on the ground that the son of the German Under Secretary of State, Von Weizsacker [sic], is attached to the Kaiser-Wilhelm Institute in Berlin where some of the American work on uranium is now being repeated [3].

The threat revealed by these lines would have been clear to most any European: a high-ranking Nazi official has been informed by his son (employed at an advanced research center) that uranium is urgently needed and should be immediately commandeered as state property for work that could prove of enormous benefit to the Reich. To an American, however, even an informed president like Roosevelt, some of this might have been less obvious and striking. What should *not* have been obscure to any educated American, however, was Einstein's strategic use of "radium-like elements." Radium's lethal effects were well-known from the national scandal and trial surrounding the United States Radium Corporation, which, in the 1920s, had allowed its manual workers (all female) to suffer growing sickness and death from radiation poisoning while protecting executives from exposure, then lying about the cause of illness. The case of the "Radium Girls," who sued the company, exposing its venality and the dangers of radium (when ingested), brought a storm of media publicity and change to US occupational hazard law.

Sachs could have drawn on this background but decided not to. Finally securing an appointment with FDR on October 11, he elected not to read from Einstein's letter but to present the ideas therein using a document in his own words which he quoted to Roosevelt (he left the letter and a memorandum from Szilárd in a folder for the President to read later). Sachs emphasized that scientists foresaw nuclear energy could have major use in three areas: peaceful energy, medical applications, and weapons of almost unlimited destructive force.

At the end of his presentation, Sachs turned to a 1936 lecture by British physicist and Nobel Laureate Francis Aston entitled "Forty Years of Atomic Theory" and read from its final paragraph. Aston drew a parallel between "the more elderly and apelike of our prehistoric ancestors," who had undoubtedly objected to the newly discovered technology of fire, and those who failed to understand the powers held within the atom. "Personally," wrote Aston,

"I think there is no doubt that sub-atomic energy is available all around us, and that one day man will release and control its almost infinite power. We cannot prevent him from doing so and can only hope that he will not use it exclusively in blowing up his next door neighbour." Roosevelt got the point immediately. "Alex," said the President, "what you are after is to see that the Nazis don't blow us up." "Precisely," Sachs said [4].

This relatively brief discussion led to a distinct and, to put it mildly, historic sequence of events. First came the establishment of the US atomic weapon program known as the Manhattan Project in 1942. Within a mere three years, this led to the Trinity Test on July 16, 1945, in which the first atom bomb was detonated; less than a month later, there came the use of the bomb against the Japanese cities of Hiroshima and Nagasaki on August 6 and 9, 1945, and thereafter the acquisition of a vast arsenal of such weapons by the United States. As Einstein foresaw, history had been split by the splitting of uranium. The Nuclear Era had begun.

In truth, there was great ambivalence about the use of the atomic bomb from the earliest days. Only a few weeks after President Roosevelt's death on April 12, Secretary of War Henry L. Stimson assembled, with the approval of now-President Truman, a group that he decided to call the Interim Committee to advise the President on the use of the atomic bomb. Stimson was the chairman and its members included such men as James Byrnes, the new Secretary of State; President of the Carnegie Institution, Vannevar Bush; President of Harvard James Conant; and MIT President Karl Compton. Many fateful discussions were held by this Group. There were also interactions with others, including Director of Los Alamos Robert Oppenheimer and Major General Leslie Groves, the Commanding General of the Manhattan Project.

Byrnes was a strong proponent of using the weapon. He informed Truman the United States was developing a new explosive of immense force capable of wiping out entire cities and that this might allow the United States to dictate its own terms at the end of the war. Byrnes also believed that use of the bomb would make Russia more manageable after the war and apparently had been advised by General Groves (incorrectly, as it later turned out) that there was little chance Russia would acquire the bomb for a number of years, as the country lacked uranium resources.[1]

---

[1] Estimates of uranium resources at this time, even for the United States, were based on limited information and vastly underrated what existed. During the next several decades, large deposits were discovered in the United States, Canada, Australia, South Africa, and what is today Kazakhstan, part of the Soviet Union until 1990.

Stimson had a very different perspective. Though in the end he supported using the bomb against Japan, he did so with great reluctance and was adamant that it not be employed on the city of Kyoto, the cultural, artistic, and spiritual center of the country, whose destruction would mean the loss of temples and artistic treasures of great importance to humanity and might well generate eternal bitterness in the Japanese toward the US [5].

Truman, strongly influenced by Byrnes, decided to drop the bomb because he believed it would end the war promptly. He made clear to the Joint Chiefs that he would judge among all options "with the purpose of economizing to the extent possible the loss of American lives." Though General Marshall was of the same view as Truman, believing the atomic bomb was necessary to end the war – especially after the vicious fighting on Okinawa – General Eisenhower was strongly opposed. He had dinner with Stimson in Germany in July shortly after the Trinity test and when asked his opinion told Stimson he was against it on two counts, "First, the Japanese were ready to surrender ... Second, I hated to see our country be the first to use such a weapon" [6]. Eisenhower also spoke to Truman, but the President concurred with Marshall's judgment.

As for the scientists, a good many of those involved in the Manhattan Project opposed actual deployment of the weapon they were engaged in building. Szilárd was certainly among these. A better idea, many felt, was to provide a warning, in the form of a demonstration of the weapon's power – a moral "necessity," it was said, since an attack with the bomb on any population center would kill and injure a huge number of civilians, including women, children, the elderly, and the infirm. This was rejected for a variety of reasons (e.g. what if the demonstration device didn't work?).

In this regard, it is interest to quote something that Szilárd said in a 1960 interview with *US News and World Report*:

> Suppose Germany had developed two bombs before we had any ... And suppose Germany had dropped one bomb, say, on Rochester and the other on Buffalo, and then having run out of bombs she would have lost the war. Can anyone doubt that we would then have defined the dropping of atomic bombs on cities as a war crime, and that we would have sentenced the Germans who were guilty of this crime to death at Nuremberg and hanged them? [7]

Such considerations, often pondered and deliberated since 1945, might lead us to twist the fabric of history in another revealing way. What if the profound series of advances in nuclear science during the 1930s had taken place during an era of peace? Governments, not driven by the crisis of global war, would have had no reason to take control of such advances and turn them toward bombs as the first and most "necessary" application. As Einstein's letter suggests, we might well have begun the Nuclear Era with a vast new source of peacetime energy – the first such new source since the discovery of oil a century earlier. Granted, the threat of developing weapons would always remain; there would be no final guarantees. Still, we should count it a most unfortunate legacy: the world continues to live with many thousands of nuclear weapons yet only a few hundred reactors that provide electricity, the basis for modern life.

Weapons and Tests: Race to World's End

Nuclear weapons came to be regarded with special foreboding and the possibility of their widespread proliferation a cause for deep anxiety. From the beginning, there were different views about the bomb and the threat it represented. Officials also realized that the public had to be informed at some level. Following the successful Trinity test in July of 1945, General Groves commissioned the chairman of the Department of Physics at Princeton University, Dr. Henry D. Smyth, to write an unclassified "report to the nation" on the Atomic Bomb Project. This document defined what might be public and what must remain secret about the Project. But it did something else as well. Paragraph 13.7 of the General Summary took up "The Questions Before the People" and seems worth quoting:

> We find ourselves with an explosive which is far from completely perfected. Yet the future possibilities of such explosives are appalling, and their effects on future wars and international affairs are of fundamental importance. Here is a new tool of mankind, a tool of unimaginable destructive power. Its development raises many questions that must be answered in the near future. [8]

One of these questions, indeed the most pressing of all, was how to deal with the possible proliferation of atomic weapons after the war's end. The prospect frightened everyone, even those most adamant about using the bomb against Japan. Information gathered by the Interim Committee suggested a "competitor" would need perhaps six years to catch up with the United States. There was no confusion about what that meant. Still, some did not believe the Soviet Union had the capability of building a nuclear weapon in that time frame.

The "Smyth Report," as it came to be known, was not particularly helpful in this regard. In many ways, it concealed a great deal more than it "declassified." Though it promised "a general account of the scientific research and technical development" that created the bomb, it offered little beyond the published scientific literature. But it left out nearly the entire engineering dimension – an astounding act of deletion when we consider what was required to turn chemical and mathematical formulae into a weapon that killed over 100,000 people in a few seconds and an equal, or even greater number, through its effects. Looked at in this way, the report seems more an effort to create a certain kind of public memory, one that confused the bomb with physics, thus with heroes and geniuses like Einstein. Some of this appears in the report's language. It was this document – which sold through eight editions and spent months on the *New York Times* bestseller list – that substituted the word "atomic" for the more correct "nuclear." Smyth himself admitted later on: "in 1945 the world 'nuclear' was either totally unfamiliar to the public or primarily had a biological flavor, whereas 'atomic' had a definite association with chemistry and physics. Since ... the report was aimed at a wider audience than nuclear physicists, we decided that atomic was less likely to frighten off readers ... " [9] The Smyth Report proved no small success. "Atomic" came to rule common speech and government institutional labels, like the Atomic Energy Commission (AEC), for the next twenty years.

Meanwhile, historically speaking, the Soviet bomb that everyone feared was a foregone conclusion. This was not solely due to scientific expertise. Thanks to their spy ring at Los Alamos and elsewhere, the Soviets were receiving a steady stream of information about the US Atomic Bomb Project. The Cold War loomed, in other words, even before the final days of WW II.

When President Truman mentioned to Stalin at the Potsdam Summit Conference in July 1945 that the US had a new weapon of unusual destructive force, Stalin did not show much interest, having already been informed about the Trinity test. But after Hiroshima and Nagasaki, the situation dramatically changed. Stalin put the chief of the KGB, Lavrenty Beria, in charge with orders to acquire the bomb or else. The US government soon became aware that the Soviets were seizing all German plants related to the use of atomic energy, as well as the only operating uranium mine in Europe. Yet many American political leaders did not believe that the Soviet Union was capable of producing an atomic bomb anytime soon.

In 1946, the United States put forward the Baruch Plan at the United Nations. Named for the well-known philanthropist and statesman, Bernard Baruch, then US representative to the UN's Atomic Energy Commission, the plan would have placed all nuclear research under international ownership and control – of course, with the US retaining the knowledge it had already acquired. The Baruch Plan was the one real attempt to stop proliferation before it began. Partners in the Manhattan Project – Canada, the United Kingdom, and the United States – further proposed the establishment of a United Nations Atomic Energy Commission for the purpose of "entirely eliminating the use of atomic energy for destructive purposes." The Soviets rejected the Baruch Plan out of hand. Halting proliferation of the bomb was not going to happen for many years. In fact, if the Soviet Union had little interest in such a goal, the US itself was less than devoted to it. Too much international cooperation and world government were required at a time when the American government aimed to keep its monopoly on the most destructive weapon ever created.

Indeed, the same year it proposed the Baruch Plan (1946), Washington held a secret conference at Los Alamos. Its purpose was to review work on a thermonuclear bomb, called the Super, and to recommend the next steps. At the time, the US nuclear stockpile consisted of only nine plutonium bombs, of which seven could be made operational; by the beginning of 1948, this number had increased by ten more. Then, on September 23, 1949, President Truman announced that the Soviets had conducted their first atomic test, known as RDS-1, or "First Lightning" (US personnel referred to it simply as "Joe-1"). Washington's response was to considerably expand the US atomic arsenal. And on January 31, 1950, after intensive internal debate involving scientists, bureaucrats, and politicians, work moved ahead on the hydrogen bomb. Surprisingly, no one during the debate considered that this might lead to an arms race. The focus remained entirely on American superiority [10].

The Americans detonated the first thermonuclear test, code-named "Ivy Mike," on November 1, 1952, at Eniwetok, an atoll of the Marshall Island group in the eastern Pacific. The explosion, at ten megatons, created a cloud one-hundred miles wide and twenty-five miles high, extinguishing all life on neighboring islands. Ivy mike was a test of the so-called Teller-Ulam design (after its creators, Edward Teller and Stanislaw Ulam), by which a nuclear fission reaction generates the needed conditions for a fusion detonation. The test device used liquid deuterium, which required elaborate cryogenic equipment to remain at about minus 250°C, and was very large, at 82 tons, so could not be used for an actual weapon. A year-and-a-half later, on March 1, 1954, a second device, "Castle Bravo," was tested, this time on Bikini atoll. This device was dry and much smaller (nicknamed "Shrimp"), but produced unexpected and, in many ways, disastrous results.

Intended as a 5-megaton explosion, the actual yield was two-and-a-half times larger, 14.8 megatons – a thousand times that of the Hiroshima bomb. Resulting from a theoretical error, Castle Bravo's huge blast spread fallout much farther downwind than expected, necessitating evacuations on other islands, causing severe radiation burns and hair loss, and affecting the crew of a Japanese fishing vessel, the *Lucky Dragon*, with acute radiation sickness. The US never again conducted a test of such magnitude. News of the *Lucky Dragon* incident reached the public later that year, in no small part because of a diplomatic crisis that resulted. Together with the heavily publicized arrival in May 1955 of the "Hiroshima maidens" - twenty-five young women who had been school girls when the first atom bomb was dropped and who suffered severe burns and disfigurement. They were coming to the US for advanced surgical treatment to alleviate their conditions. Together with news of the *Lucky Dragon*, the Hiroshima maidens greatly raised awareness and fear of radioactive fallout from nuclear weapons' testing. Einstein's warning of "new radium-like elements" would not lose its meaning and relevance.

Almost entirely lost in the attention granted Japanese sufferers were hundreds of Marshall Islanders and twenty-eight US servicemen who had been exposed to high levels of fallout. Where Eniwetok, site of the Ivy Mike test, lay more than 200 miles west of the main island group, Bikini was part of the group, only eighty miles from the inhabited Rongelap atoll. A few hours before the test, winds had been deemed unfavorable due to their likelihood of spreading fallout westward over Rongelap and a number of other islands where people lived. This is precisely what happened. A radioactive plume stretching more than 300 miles after only four days dropped major amounts of high-dose fallout (full body exposures ranging from 110 mSv to more than 1.9 Sieverts; see Chapter 5) on a series of atolls, with Rongelap especially affected. Evacuations by sea performed by the US military didn't begin until the second morning after detonation, nearly a day after the American servicemen had been airlifted off Rongerik atoll, a source of much later criticism. Nearly 700 people were exposed to significant levels of radiation. Most of those on Rongelap, and dozens of people on other islands, developed thyroid disorders, including malignant nodules. Full extent of the health impacts has remained a highly debated topic to the present.

Three years after Ivy Mike, the Soviets tested their own first hydrogen device on November 22, 1955, at the Semipalatinsk site in what is now eastern Kazakhstan. That particular day, a temperature inversion had developed over the area. This had an effect that no one foresaw: the inversion reflected part of the shock wave back to ground level, bringing damage to a number of villages that had been thought a safe distance away and killing several people, including a little girl. Like the American Bravo test which this event, in a sense, had echoed, the realities and possible results of setting loose uncontrolled thermonuclear chain reactions lay beyond the full understanding of even the most brilliant scientists.

Andrei Sakharov, key physicist behind the Soviet program, would later reveal in his memoirs that this incident began his shift toward becoming a human rights activist and a supporter only of controlled nuclear energy. He recalls giving a toast at the celebration held in honor of the successful RDS-37 test: "May all of our devices explode as successfully as today's, but always over test sites and never over cities" [11]. His words brought chill and silence. After a few moments, a high-ranking military officer stood up, raised his glass, and told a lewd joke about male potency in old age. The crudity made Sakharov go pale. But the point was lost on no one. Six years later, the Soviets detonated the largest nuclear explosion of all time – 58.6 megatons – on October 23, 1961, in the atmosphere 4,000 meters (13,000 ft) above Nova Zemlya in the Kara Sea. Known as the Tsar Bomba ("Czar of all bombs"), its explosion was so powerful that total destruction would have occurred over a circular inhabited area 50–55 km (31–34 miles) in diameter.

By this time, moreover, the strategic ballistic missile had come into play as well, raising all stakes considerably. Now either side, the Soviets or the Americans, could deliver enormous numbers of nuclear weapons on each other in less than thirty minutes, with impressive accuracy and no possibility of defense. For the first time in human history, it was possible to annihilate an entire nation of people a great distance away, without sending a single soldier. Hitler's dream for the V-rocket program, the *Vergeltungswaffe* or "weapon of retribution," had been doubly realized. From this point forward, the goal of "nuclear superiority" became a chimera.

Indeed, the Cold War arms race was already a decade old. Nuclear tests had grown steadily in number from eighteen in 1951 to fifty-five in 1957, soaring to 116 in 1958 on the eve of a temporary test ban. Nearly all of these early tests, through 1962, were exploded in the atmosphere – more than 420 in all – before the US, Soviet Union, and UK, due to fallout concerns, agreed to underground detonations only. France and China, however, did not sign the partial test-ban treaty and carried out about eighty more explosions above ground, bringing the total atmospheric test figure to about 500. The last such test was by China in 1980. Overall, declassified documents and public information suggest that, for the entire nuclear era, spanning 1945–2015, the number of tests per country approximate the following: US – 1,032; USSR/Russia – 715; France – 210; UK – 45; China – 45; India – 3; Pakistan – 2; North Korea – 3; world total – 2,055; of which US – 50 percent; Soviets – 35 percent [12].

These detonations took place in many different settings, a fact with implications. They were detonated 200 meters underground, 600 meters under the ocean, at the Earth's surface, on barges at sea, from balloons a dozen or more kilometers (km) in the sky, in rockets up to 320 km in space. Geographically, they occurred on warm tropical islands in the Pacific, wind-torn plains of the Russian arctic; the Sahara Desert of southern Algeria; the steppes and Ural Mountains of Kazakhstan; the great dried salt lake of Lop Nur, western China; the open Pacific Ocean; and, of course, the high desert of southern Nevada.

Three points come from all of this. First, fallout from atmospheric explosions was spread over every part of the Earth's surface. Second, in several cases – notably sites in Kazakhstan and Nevada, where the greatest number of tests occurred, and in the Pacific – many thousands of people in downwind areas were affected by fallout, and it's now understood that a fair number of the people most affected grew sick and even died as a result, though others did not. Third, these facts, plus the huge diversity of settings where tests took place, have provided a great deal of scientific information on the effects of such explosions, both in the short- and longer-term, on the environment and on people. What we learn from this can be surprising: for example, parts of the Nevada and Semipalatinsk Test Sites will be dangerously radioactive for centuries, while the Montebello Islands offshore western Australia, where Britain set off three nuclear tests in the 1950s, is now a wildlife conservation area. Another fact: early worries about genetic defects in children born to parents affected by radiation exposure turned out to be unnecessary; such effects have not been observed in decades of study.

One of the worst long-term effects from the era of testing was the aura of secrecy that came to surround all things "atomic" and "nuclear." The hypersecurity enveloping the Manhattan Project never really diminished during the Cold War. Throughout the 1950s, the US AEC told the American public that fallout from testing presented little risk, that all serious hazards were confined to the test site [13]. This kind of purposeful misstatement was itself an outgrowth of the wartime mentality that sought, among other things, to hide the true level of horror in a nuclear attack and danger in radioactive impacts. In the first days after the bombings of Hiroshima and Nagasaki, Japanese medical and scientific teams were sent to study the effects of what had happened. Their research formed the earliest work of its kind – in fact, the *only* work collecting data in the first weeks after the bombings. Despite the invaluable importance of this information, American Occupation forces confiscated it and suppressed publication. Meanwhile, all film footage shot of the two cities after the bombings, as well as the overwhelming majority of photographs, were confiscated. Much of this visual material was not released for decades, until the 1980s. This included footage that had been shot by the American military itself. Such are but a few examples of the censorship practiced to keep the US public from understanding what was really implied and involved in the arms buildup happening in their midst.

> IMP Quote

The Arms Race: A Compressed History

The nuclear arms race that came in the wake of Hiroshima and Nagasaki was a global affair. Discussions concentrate on the US and Soviet Union, given that no other country ever approached the same order of magnitude of these two arsenals. But many other nations were involved early on, and a brief look at this history offers some striking truths about the reasons why nations have wanted, and may want in the future, the power and symbolism of nuclear weapons.

The Cold War officially began in 1946, proclaimed in Churchill's famous "Iron Curtain" speech. And the Soviet coup in Czechoslovakia in 1948 established this conflict as nothing less than a long-term struggle to the death for mastery of the world by the two superpowers. The Soviets would do everything possible to acquire nuclear weapons, and America was going to do everything possible to stay ahead in nuclear weaponry. The first imperative ensured the second. Both imperatives made a nuclear arms race seem inexorable, as if destiny had intervened and related decisions were beyond all control. With such logic essentially shared by the two superpowers, from the very beginning any attempt to create a broad international agreement supporting nonproliferation would be (to put it nicely) an uphill effort. It would only be possible when a new logic intervened, when the world community concluded it simply *had* to be done.

The scale of the arms race came to defy any sense of rational proportion. During the forty-six-year span of the Cold War, the United States built more than 70,000 nuclear weapons and the Soviet Union 55,000. Not all of these weapons existed at the same time; early versions were replaced by more advanced bombs later on. Still, the figures for any single year make our jaw drop. As early as the mid-1960s, the US reached a peak of 32,500 nuclear weapons in its stockpile, while the Soviets had a maximum of over 40,000 in the 1980s [14]. In 1972, strategic weapons deliverable by US missiles reached 5,800, carrying 4,100 megatons, and 2,100 carrying 4,000 megatons for the Soviets. By any measure, these are incomprehensible numbers. In practical terms – the terms of actual military capability – they far exceeded the ability of either nation to destroy every population center in the other many times over, and to kill off most or all of the rest of humanity (and earthly life) in the bargain, through decades of intense fallout.

3 Branches of US mil. wanted their own arsenal

In the US, all three major branches of the military – army, navy, air force – demanded their own brand of nuclear weapon, adapted to bombers, submarines, missiles, and more. Weapons were produced by an enormous defense-factory system, with twelve major government sites, working seven days a week from the late 1940s to the late 1960s, fed by nonnuclear components produced by hundreds of companies and corporations. Even by 1960, the US had over 20,000 nuclear weapons. Thus President Eisenhower's famous farewell speech a year later, warning against "the acquisition of unwarranted influence, whether sought or unsought, by the military-industrial complex," warned of a reality that already existed. By 1996, the US had spent an immense amount of money on its arsenal, around $5.5 trillion (over $8.5 trillion in 2014 dollars), not including the expense of dismantling weapons and cleaning up toxic radioactive sites related to warhead manufacture [15]. Costs are irrelevant, say some commentators; the US won the Cold War, and this justifies whatever was done. We might, however, question such wisdom. What could have been done with 30,000 weapons that couldn't have been achieved with 3,000? At what point, that is, did "nuclear superiority" become a costly anachronism?

IMP Q's to ask...

But proliferation was not slated to stop with the superpowers. After the first Soviet test in 1949, a number of other states began to consider nuclear weapons. First in line were the United Kingdom, France, Sweden, and Switzerland. Later this list expanded to Australia, Brazil, Israel, China, India, and South Africa. Interestingly, Canada, which had been a member of the Manhattan Project, opted not to pursue nuclear arms. Considerations for a global nonproliferation policy had little to do with this decision. Already it was evident that nuclear weapons in the Cold War were going to be the indicia of a state's great power status. Canada had no ambition to be a great power. Its interest was in being a Western state with real influence in the developing world. Protected by America's nuclear deterrent, it could devote the money saved by *not* building weapons on more positive enterprises at home and abroad.

Other countries who pursued nuclear weapons

Canadians didn't participate

The United Kingdom independently began to develop nuclear weapons as soon as the war was over. The new Prime Minister Clement Attlee set up a cabinet subcommittee (known informally as the Atomic Bomb Committee) to examine the feasibility of an atomic weapon for Britain as early as August 1945. America's refusal to continue wartime nuclear cooperation did not affect the British decision – rather, it helped strengthen Britain's resolve to move ahead. Nor did the concept of controlling the spread of nuclear weapons play any role in Britain's considerations. The Committee, that is, concluded that atomic energy was likely to be an important industrial activity and that acquiring the bomb would increase Britain's prestige and influence and

British experience

was therefore a vital national interest. The nuclear program began in 1946 under the control of the Atomic Energy Research Establishment, with the first test (plutonium-implosion device) carried out successfully in October 1952 in the Montebello Islands, roughly 20 km off Australia's west coast. The British program had major significance. Though it would never be able to compete with the American or Soviet weapons efforts, it helped solidify the Cold War concept – still with us today – that, with respect to major states at least, the possession of nuclear weapons distinguishes great powers from all other nations.

The French experience was different, but the result was the same: proliferation of nuclear weapons to another state for reasons essentially of national prestige. Initially, French leaders believed that if France did not pursue nuclear weapons Germany could be kept from them as well. It did not matter that the Americans, Soviets, and British all had, or would soon have, weapons. The memory of the war was too fresh; France could do without the bomb as the price for keeping Germany nonnuclear [16]. But in 1954 the situation changed. Defeat of the French military in Vietnam at Dien Bien Phu, and the signs of German conventional rearmament, convinced Premier Pierre-Mendès-France it was time to reconsider. France needed to keep well ahead of Germany and to re-establish its standing as a major European power with scientific capability. Secret ministerial meetings were held in the fall of 1954, and on December 26, Mendès-France presented officials with a draft decision paper the first sentence of which read: "The making of atomic bombs is decided." A separate paper prepared for the meeting argued that, while "not necessary" for military purposes (since the "USA builds the bomb at an industrial rhythm"), a French bomb did "present a double interest: political [and] technical" [17]. Despite some uncertainties in funding and political support, the project moved forward, so that when de Gaulle returned to power in May 1958, it was soon possible to schedule a nuclear test. This took place on February 13, 1960, in the Algerian Sahara.

Sweden's own program began shortly after the 1945 atomic bombing of Japan. In the initial years after WW II, the country's objective was to become a neutral power that could nonetheless defend itself militarily against any invading nation. Soviet invasion of neighboring Finland in 1939–1940 and seizing of territory was a factor here. But during the 1960s, no firm or final decision had yet been made, and by the end of the decade the Swedish government, because of military budget constraints, had to choose between a nuclear weapon and a new fighter aircraft. The decision went for the plane. Sweden dropped all plans to acquire nuclear weapons when it signed the Nuclear Non-Proliferation Treaty (NPT) in 1968 [18].

Swiss

sgned
NPT

Israel

Swiss interest in the acquisition of nuclear weapons also began with the end of the war in 1945. The idea was to consider the construction of a bomb as a means of dissuading any form of attack on the country. The Federal Council of Ministers established a study Commission for Nuclear Energy in 1946, but it does not appear that any sense of urgency prevailed, and there were concerns about the expense of such a project. With the bloody suppression of the Hungarian Revolution in 1956, however, attitudes changed: the situation in Eastern Europe was anything but reassuring, and a small neutral state that had resisted Hitler had to find a path to postwar security. A period of domestic political conflict over the nuclear issue then ensued, with a national referendum on prohibiting weapons development put before the public on April 1, 1962. The Swiss people voted by a more than two to one margin to reject prohibition. Intensive planning work then began. Only a few months later, the Cuban Missile Crisis enhanced the sense of real threat; if an all-out attack by the Warsaw Pact on Western Europe took place, Switzerland would be an early target. A second national referendum opposing a prohibition on nuclear arms passed by a sizeable majority. However, as no clear threat of an attack emerged, and as financial considerations began to be weighed more seriously, enthusiasm waned. Switzerland decided to sign the NPT on November 27, 1969 [19].

Israel's rationale for the bomb was not status but survival. The first prime minister, David Ben-Gurion, believed that, after the Holocaust, the young state could ultimately rely only on itself [20]. Ben-Gurion also felt Israel's long-term security would be based on science and technology, a domain where the country commanded significant intellectual resources. Until the mid-1950s, only small progress was made. But when Ben-Gurion returned to government in 1955, as Minister of Defense, a first step was taken with purchase of a small research reactor from the United States, as part of President Eisenhower's new Atoms for Peace program.[2] Then, in 1956, a new opportunity arrived. President Gamal Nasser of Egypt initiated the Suez Crisis, announcing his nationalization of the Suez Canal from Britain and France. Despite US opposition, the British and French decided on a military response and asked Israel to join, with France promising a research reactor in return. Postwar relations were strong between France and Israel; the former became a major arms supplier to Israel early on, and the Israelis later provided intelligence to the French on

---

[2] Atoms for Peace Program, named after an important speech by that title Eisenhower gave to the United Nations General Assembly in 1953, was an effort by the US to provide civilian nuclear technology, materials, and expertise to many countries, mainly its allies, in order to promote "the peaceful uses of nuclear energy." Historians are agreed that both the speech and the resulting program also had distinct propaganda aims, including the goal of calming public fears about US nuclear intentions.

independence movements in North Africa. Even though the British and French military response against Egypt failed, Israel had done its part by seizing the Sinai and therefore the Israelis insisted on being sold by France an upgraded research reactor, one capable of producing large amounts of plutonium. The reactor was sited at Dimona in the Negev Desert, which became the center of Israel's weapon program. In 1957, French supplier Saint Gobain Nucléaire agreed to build an underground reprocessing plant for plutonium separation, giving Israel the ability to make its own bomb fuel. Finally, France was also the source of information secretly given to Israel on the design and manufacture of nuclear weapons.

Completed in the early 1960s, the reactor had an ample supply (20 tons) of heavy water purchased from Norway. By this time, the US Intelligence Community had become convinced of Israel's intent to build a weapon. The CIA learned of the heavy water sale and the presence of Israeli observers at the French nuclear tests in the Sahara. With the reprocessing plant finished in 1965, and the first plutonium separated that same year, it was judged that by the time of the Six-Day War in 1967, Israel had two or three nuclear devices in its possession. The country has never claimed a test of a nuclear device, though the close relationship with France suggests that one of its early tests proved the existence of two nuclear powers, not one. As early as 1960, President Kennedy was convinced of the serious risk that nuclear weapons would spread over the world and that Israel represented the greatest short-term danger in this regard. He pressed the Israeli government hard to permit American inspectors at Dimona. This was agreed to in 1961, with occasional further inspection until 1969. But the Israelis concealed the true purpose of the facility, leading American inspectors to believe it was only a small research reactor. The State Department and CIA remained skeptical, however. Israel continued to refuse to sign the NPT and has never admitted to possessing a nuclear weapon. Instead it has practiced what observers call "nuclear ambiguity" or, in more vernacular terms, a "bombs in the basement" policy [21].

The last nation to discuss at this point is China. This nation tested its first nuclear device in 1964 at Lop Nur, Xinjiang Autonomous Region, thereby rounding out the permanent five of the UN Security Council as nuclear weapon states. China signed a secret agreement with the Soviet Union in 1951, agreeing to trade uranium ore for nuclear know-how. Soviet assistance ended in the late 50s, as relations cooled between the two countries, but enough knowledge and technology had already been provided so that the Chinese made rapid progress thereafter. On January 15, 1955, Mao Tse-Tung and senior Politburo members held a secret meeting at a Beijing facility, with only one item on the agenda: initiating a nuclear weapons program for China. Two important scientists were present who lectured Mao and his colleagues on nuclear physics and uranium geology. At the end of the briefing and subsequent discussion, there were toasts by Mao and Zhou Enlai with Zhou calling on the scientists "to exert themselves to develop China's nuclear program." While there were several reasons urging Mao to take this step, a key influence was the recent war in Korea, at the end of which China had been threatened with nuclear weapons by the United States if an armistice could not be concluded. Other motivators were the ongoing crisis in the Taiwan Strait, the US Taiwan defense treaty signed in December 1954, and a desire for international prestige and influence. A second crisis in the Taiwan Strait in 1958 only reinforced Mao's view that China must have nuclear weapons [22].

Here is a good place to stop and consider what these brief tales of nuclear acquisition tell us. One overarching point seems clear: the nuclear era began in the midst of the most destructive war in human history, and much fear and secrecy and sense of existential threat of that event bled over into the new Cold War era and came to be concentrated in the ambitions behind building nuclear weapons. Indeed, the bomb (whether "atomic" or "nuclear") both embodied the unparalleled and unprecedented destruction of the war and transformed the struggles it failed to solve. The reasons why individual nations wanted such a weapon were individual in some sense, reflective of their positions in the new era. But there were also patterns. For the US, instead of turning from aggressive buildup, as the world's first true superpower and "protector of the free world" it believed it must achieve supremacy in the nuclear arena. The Soviets under Stalin felt they could not let that happen; in their view, the power of the Soviet empire would be crushed, and the "war against capitalism" lost. What's more, the Americans had shown their willingness to actually use the bomb. Both nations therefore saw the arms race as fate, stemming from the nature of the world as it had come to be.

Britain and France, meanwhile, which had been Great Powers for so much of the modern period, had seen their status greatly disempowered by the war. For them, at stake was their own importance, their place in the struggle for history – political, cultural, scientific. It was an idea not merely of pride but of national consciousness and self-image, carried by a generation of politicians and military officials that had matured in the era of colonial empires. The bomb was a means to retain their place in the history of the modern world. It was something more, in that it "promised" independence, security, and perhaps influence as well. Neither France nor England could conceive of their own futures without an essential aspect of what de Gaulle called "grandeur."

As for Sweden and Switzerland, the motive was simpler, above all a matter of defense against Soviet aggression, which had been repeatedly proven in the

Baltics and Eastern Europe. Israel and China may at first seem entirely different from one another in the nuclear context. Yet they both felt themselves to be isolated, threatened, and vulnerable. Moreover, both secretly derived much help from an ally, but also had the scientific and technological capability to carry the program to completion. For these two nations, then, the reasons for having nuclear weapons include a mixture of defense and deterrence, as well as standing as scientific powers. That Israel hasn't officially admitted it has such weapons is of little import.

Such realities are sobering to contemplate. That each weapon these nations worked to acquire would, if used or accidently detonated, unleash death, devastation, and disease on a horrendous scale, not for a short time but for many decades and perhaps even longer, tended to be forgotten in the heat of postwar "strategy" and "deterrence." Weapons that perhaps should have inspired terror and unmitigated rejection became, instead, the tools for political, military, and ideological standing. Though not altogether reassuring, it is at least a hopeful historical sign that, in the midst of such Cold War distrust and obsession, efforts to take better command of the future did take place.

Of Arms and the Ban: Early Treaties

True enough, other countries flirted with or attempted to acquire nuclear weapons. As discussed below, some succeeded: India, Pakistan, South Africa, and North Korea all built arsenals. What were their reasons? India sought prestige, certainly, but also defense against China (with whom it fought a brief and humiliating border war in 1962). Pakistan, mortal enemy to India, followed suit, with much help from China. South Africa's nuclear motives stemmed from its ostracism by the global community for Apartheid and sense of being under threat; yet, when Apartheid ended in the early 1990s, it transformed itself from pariah to positive model by giving up all its weapons. North Korea represents an extreme case, developing weapons as a response to the perception of existential threat, from the US mainly, but also South Korea (with whom it is still officially at war), and Japan. And Iran, in its own likely quest for a weapon, may well be moved by the same motives, reacting to what it sees as the nuclear-armed menace from the US, Israel, and perhaps most importantly Sunni Pakistan. Thus, in pretty much every instance, fear was the motivating factor.

Yet well before any of this happened, calls began for a stop to testing and proliferation. This brought little positive response right away, but by the early 1960s when new nuclear states and news of others on the way appeared, the time had come and the inclination had grown in the international community to try and negotiate some control over what was happening. In the US, the Kennedy Administration received expert predictions that perhaps two dozen states would emerge with nuclear arsenals by the end of the 1970s. From the beginning, JFK displayed an intense interest in nonproliferation. He was particularly worried about China, as US intelligence was convinced Mao Zedong was intent on acquiring nuclear weapons. On the eve of his inauguration in January 1961, he asked outgoing Secretary of State Christian Herter which countries were most likely to become new weapons states. Herter replied, "Israel and India" [23]. He was both right and wrong, of course, since Israel surely had a weapon within several years, while China exploded its first test in 1964, a full decade ahead of India. To the end of his brief presidency, Kennedy worked hard to restrain the Israeli program, perhaps concluding that if the United States could not check its ally, how would it say no to anyone else, even Germany?

Kennedy's concerns might seem a bit ironic. By 1961, after all, the US had amassed a staggering 22,229 nuclear weapons, with the Soviet Union at 2,450, and the United Kingdom, 50 [24]. Though these numbers were kept under tight security, Kennedy was undoubtedly aware that the US had a huge lead on the Soviets and, perhaps, a far larger stockpile than it could ever make use of. In a press conference of March 1963, he stated outright: "... personally I am haunted by the feeling that by 1970 ... there may be 10 nuclear powers instead of 4, and by 1975, 15 or 20 ... I regard that as the greatest possible danger and hazard" [25]. It seems fair to assume his worries were both about further increases in the number of weapons, as well as the number of states pursuing them. Such worries were far from his alone. Many officials in other nations agreed that if the diversion of nuclear materials from peaceful use to weapons programs could not be halted by a system of international safeguards, and if as a result proliferation continued to expand, the chances of nuclear war would rise greatly, whether as a result of accident, unauthorized use, or escalation of conventional conflicts. Starting in 1959, the United Nations General Assembly took up the issues of nuclear testing and proliferation with more than mild concern and adopted several resolutions that led to an historic treaty.

Over the next decade, a profound and much-needed change came about in the global nuclear picture. This change did not end the arms race between the Soviet Union and the United States. Nor did it greatly reduce Cold War tensions, as the Cuban Missile Crisis so plainly showed. Yet, in the end, urged by a guiding mixture of concern and hope (among other passions), it yielded a global agreement that the world found reason to obey for decades thereafter, with very few exceptions. To be sure, the making of the Nuclear Non-Proliferation Treaty (NPT) was anything but a simple, straightforward

[handwritten: 18 Nation Committee in Disarmment]

affair. Indeed, a tense, complex, and uncertain world guaranteed the process would be no different, and it wasn't. But it moved forward, in stages, some of which deserve mention.

A watershed came in 1961. That year, the General Assembly established an Eighteen Nation Committee on Disarmament (ENCD), including nations from both Eastern and Western blocs and also eight nonaligned countries representing Asia, the Middle East, South America, North America, and Europe.[3] We should see this for what it was – a remarkable coming together of interests in a time of global conflict. In further action, the General Assembly unanimously passed what is known as the "Irish Resolution." This called on all states to forge an international agreement prohibiting the transfer or acquisition of nuclear weapons. It was put forward by the assertive and magnetic Frank Aiken, Ireland's Minister of External Affairs, who had developed a unique reputation as a voice for decolonization, neutrality, and international order and peace (the Irish had the friendship of both Israel and Arab nations and Aiken's delegation famously sat in the General Assembly between the Israelis and Iraqis). More specifically, the Irish Resolution called for an agreement whereby "the nuclear states would undertake to refrain from relinquishing control of nuclear weapons and from transmitting the information necessary for their manufacture to states not possessing such weapons, and ... states not possessing nuclear weapons would undertake not to manufacture or otherwise acquire control of such weapons" [26].

Such was the first major step toward the NPT, which has proved to be one of the most successful and (given the nature of the weapons involved) important international arms treaties in history. A further advance came in 1965 when a new United Nations resolution outlined the actual components of such an agreement, including the goals of halting the arms race and beginning actual disarmament. As written, these components defined much of what a nonproliferation treaty needed to have:

(a) The treaty should be void of loopholes that might allow nuclear or nonnuclear powers to proliferate, directly or indirectly, nuclear weapons in any form.
(b) The treaty should embody an acceptable balance of mutual responsibilities and obligations of the nuclear and nonnuclear powers.
(c) The treaty should be a step towards the achievement of general and complete disarmament and, more particularly, nuclear disarmament.

---

[3] Countries included: Western Bloc – US, UK, France, Canada, Italy; Eastern Bloc – Soviet Union, Poland, Czechoslovakia, Bulgaria, Romania; and Nonaligned – Brazil, India, Mexico, Sweden, Ethiopia, Burma, and United Arab Republic.

[handwritten right margin: countries included]

[handwritten bottom: UN resolution / agreement for disarmament]

(d) There should be acceptable and workable provisions to ensure the effectiveness of the treaty.

(e) Nothing in the treaty should adversely affect the right of any group of states to conclude regional treaties in order to ensure the total absence of nuclear weapons in their territories [27].

In addition to these points, there was a pivotal statement issued by the eight nonaligned members of the ENDC. Representatives of these nations had gone on record with a memorandum stating that "... measures to prohibit the spread of nuclear weapons should...be coupled with or followed by *tangible* steps to halt the nuclear arms race and to limit, reduce, and eliminate the stocks of nuclear weapons and the means of their delivery." Egyptian Ambassador Mohamed I. Shaker in his definitive work, *The Nuclear Non-Proliferation Treaty, Origin and Implementation, 1959–1979*, opines that this "joint memorandum can be considered as the immediate origin of principle (b)" [28].

Again, given the atmosphere of the time, it was no mean achievement for nations to find agreement on such goals. One big reason they did so was the balance of obligations struck between nonnuclear and nuclear states. Five states – the US, UK, France, China, and the Soviet Union – had both nuclear technology and nuclear weapons and thus stood stratospherically above all nonnuclear nations in uses of nuclear energy and military power. The goal was thus to find an equitable solution to this hugely inequitable reality. A bargain, based on the principles mentioned above, was found: nonnuclear countries agreed never to seek or acquire nuclear weapons, and in return the nuclear states pledged to allow unfettered access to peaceful nuclear technology and to pursue negotiations toward nuclear disarmament with the aim of eventually eliminating all stockpiles. In blunt terms, nonweapon states would give up any chance of getting weapons, while nuclear states would work to eventually give them up, while also acting as knowledge and know-how providers to the rest of the world. Such terms were articulated in Article IV and Article VI of the NPT. It is interesting to note that Article VI, relating to the five nuclear states, is quite short: these nations, it says, must "pursue negotiations in good faith on effective measures relating to cessation of the nuclear arms race at an early date and to nuclear disarmament, and on a treaty on general and complete disarmament under strict and effective international control." Part 1 of Article IV, meanwhile, established the "inalienable right" of all NPT parties to the peaceful use of nuclear energy and related research. Part 2 of the same article lays out essential trade-offs, as follows:

> All the Parties to the Treaty undertake to facilitate, and have the right to participate in, the fullest possible exchange of equipment, materials and scientific and

1 problem is its hard for inspectors to test reactors

technological information for the peaceful uses of nuclear energy. Parties to the Treaty in a position to do so shall also co-operate in contributing alone or together with other States or international organizations to the further development of the applications of nuclear energy for peaceful purposes, especially in the territories of non-nuclear-weapon States Party to the Treaty, with due consideration for the needs of the developing areas of the world [29].

The bargain was never one-sided and had advantages for all parties. But future decades would reveal problems too. Lack of specificity in Article VI (e.g. deadlines) allowed nuclear states to "pursue negotiations in good faith" and to create significant disarmament agreements without ever really halting the arms race. Nonnuclear states, meanwhile, were allowed the technologies related to electricity production, and this included not only power plant reactors but uranium enrichment and plutonium reprocessing – technologies able to make fuel for reactors *and* for bombs (as we will discuss in Chapter 3). Though safeguards would be included, with inspections among them, it turned out that inspectors could be fooled. A larger problem, however, came from states that refused to sign the NPT – India, Pakistan, Israel, all of whom secretly developed weapons – and, in one case so far, states that decide to withdraw from the treaty, as North Korea did in 2003.

2nd problem – some countries refused to sign

Yet it would be entirely wrong to call the NPT a failure in any sense. Though nuclear power has expanded to thirty-one nations, only a fraction of these have ever developed weapons. Indeed, it is fair to say that not a single peaceful nuclear power program has been used to generate weapons.[4] Instead of the two dozen weapons states predicted during the Kennedy Administration for 1970, the world has only nine in 2015, more than three decades later. Four other states that once *had* such weapons – South Africa, Ukraine, Belarus, and Kazakhstan – gave them up. India's first detonation in 1974, utilizing plutonium from a research reactor, proved that nuclear technology provided for peaceful uses had been turned to the making of weapons. This made it evident that unrestricted, blanket transfer of such technology could not be allowed. To decide which dual-use technologies and materials needed to have export controls, an organization called the Nuclear Suppliers Group was formed in 1974, and, after several years of discussion, produced a series of guidelines

---

[4] In the case of India, a small 40 megawatt (MW) research reactor, supplied by Canada, was the source of plutonium used for the country's first "peaceful nuclear explosion" (code-named "Smiling Buddha"). The reactor was not used for power generation but had been supplied for peaceful purposes of research. India broke the terms of the original contract, which stipulated the unit could not be used for any weapons purpose. To this day, India has not signed the NPT.

("trigger list") that have been periodically updated to keep pace with technological advances. More will be said about this in Chapter 12.

There have been other dangers along the road to the present, such as the case of Iran and the black market in weapon technology set up by Pakistan's "father of the Islamic bomb," Abdul Qadeer Khan; we will discuss these too (see Chapter 12). But the record is clear: the Nuclear Non-Proliferation Treaty has made the world far safer than it might have been.

The Kennedy Speech

The NPT was bolstered in part by a separate agreement, the Limited Test Ban Treaty. Signed in 1963 by the Soviet Union, United States, and United Kingdom after eight long years of struggling negotiations, the treaty banned once and for all "any nuclear explosion" in the atmosphere, under water, and in space. Pressure for such a ban had come from the American public in the wake of the *Lucky Dragon* incident, and also from portions of the Soviet populace, especially those in the vicinity of the Semipalatinsk test site. Despite official attempts to downplay any sense of danger, people in many nations had become frightened about fallout and the rising number and size of nuclear detonations. As it happened, the Soviets were the first to propose such a ban, in 1955. But the three Western nations involved, England, France, and the US, wanted such a ban linked to disarmament measures. Eventually they dropped this condition but demanded there be ways to verify compliance with a ban. They had distrust of the Soviets continuing tests in secret and thus gaining "an edge." Soviet premiers, first Bulganin and then Khrushchev, repeatedly called on President Eisenhower to end all tests, which Eisenhower rejected, responding about the need for a monitoring system, with on-site inspections. This last was always going to be a problem, for the US too, given the code of secrecy about nuclear matters. More dead ends and deadlocks followed. But then, in 1959 and 1960, a fragile moratorium on testing occurred. For two full years, neither the Soviets nor the Americans nor the British, set off any explosions (the French, however, conducted three atmospheric tests).

The moratorium did not last; it was shattered by the shooting down of an American U-2 spy plane in 1960, which had been taking pictures of the Mayak weapons complex in southeastern Russia. Relations deteriorated between the two nuclear superpowers, and testing resumed with the 58.6 megaton Tsar Bomba detonation. Then, in October 1962, the Soviets began to install nuclear-armed missiles in Cuba, 90 miles from the US coastline. The resulting US blockade and stand-off frightened the entire world; a war between the nuclear superpowers seemed imminent. As we know, this did not happen; a deal was struck whereby the Soviets would remove their missiles if the US promised not to invade Cuba *and*, as JFK secretly agreed, took its own missiles out of Turkey. The Cuban Missile Crisis gave a jolt to public anxiety over the threat of nuclear war, and all three leaders, Kennedy, Khrushchev, and Harold MacMillan, were energized to seek again an agreement. This once again proved challenging, but a series of letters between Kennedy and Khrushchev helped set a new tone. Then came a historic speech by JFK at American University on June 10, 1963, which was hailed by Khrushchev himself as a new start.

The Soviet leader proposed a treaty that would prohibit detonations causing fallout and possible danger to people, i.e. in the atmosphere, under water, and in space, but would allow underground testing to continue. Above ground and under water explosions, all parties knew, could be easily verified by existing technology; there would be a need for monitoring stations, but these could be far away, and there would be no need for on-site inspections. Britain and the US were soon persuaded. Moreover, signing a test ban treaty with the Soviets was viewed as a way to possibly curb China's nuclear program. At the very least, it would isolate the Chinese and bring pressure to bear on them by the international community, while also placing them on the opposite side from the Soviet Union. France, however, refused to sign the Limited Test Ban Treaty, continuing to demand a link to disarmament; the Chinese, too, chose not to sign and to continue atmospheric tests until 1980 (the French stopped such testing after 1974).

A few words might be said about JFK's speech at American University. Written by Ted Sorensen, Kennedy's speech writer, it was delivered at a time when oratory by a powerful leader still had the potential to alter history for the better. Kennedy's remarks on the issue of peace and how to build it: this would "not [be] a Pax Americana enforced on the world by American weapons of war. Not the peace of the grave or the security of the slave" [30]. Total war was now without sense. Though spending billions on weapons for the purpose of preventing their use was essential to peace, Kennedy said, there must be ways to mitigate this and redirect ideas elsewhere. This meant that, if the Soviet Union adopted "a more enlightened attitude," Americans must examine their own views toward Russia.

This was one of several points Khrushchev found particularly moving. "As Americans, we find communism profoundly repugnant," Kennedy said,

But we can still hail the Russian people for their many achievements—in science and space, in economic and industrial growth, in culture and in acts of courage. Still more, "No nation in the history of battle ever suffered more than the Soviet Union suffered in the course of the Second World War. At least 20 million lost their lives. Countless millions of homes and farms were burned or sacked. A third of the nation's territory . . . was turned into a wasteland – a loss equivalent to the devastation of this country east of Chicago [30].

Such recognition of Russia's great suffering and sacrifice had never appeared in an American presidential speech before. That Kennedy described such suffering in terms that, in 1961, evoked the aftermath of a nuclear attack – thereby suggesting, in a sense, that Russia was in a better position to understand what such an attack meant than the US – was not lost on the Soviet leader. Neither was a striking passage that followed:

> Today, should total war ever break out again . . . our two countries will be the primary target. It is an ironic but accurate fact that the two strongest powers are the two in the most danger of devastation. All we have built, all we have worked for, would be destroyed in the first 24 hours. And even in the Cold War, which brings burdens and dangers to so many countries . . . our two countries bear the heaviest burdens. For we are both devoting massive sums of money to weapons that could be better devoted to combat ignorance, poverty, and disease. We are both caught up in a vicious and dangerous cycle with suspicion on one side breeding suspicion on the other, and new weapons begetting counter-weapons [30].

If this were not enough to bend Khrushchev to the reality that the US truly wanted some kind of agreement, Kennedy followed up such words with a promise: "To make clear our good faith . . . I now declare that the United States does not propose to conduct nuclear tests in the atmosphere so long as other states do not do so . . . Such a declaration is no substitute for a formal binding treaty, but I hope it will help us achieve one."

It did. Khrushchev was led to say that this was "the greatest speech by any American president since Roosevelt." After having faced down the Soviet Union in Cuba only a few months before, Kennedy had the vision to offer terms of recognition and equal standing in the face of the relevant threat. Both nations had the same enemy, he said. Or, using the most quoted part of the speech: "For, in the final analysis, our most basic common link is that we all inhabit this small planet. We all breathe the same air. We all cherish our children's future. And we are all mortal" [30].

The Widening Gyre: Postwar Legacy

However miraculous it may seem when all things are considered, our world survived the Cold War arms race without the exploding of a single nuclear weapon in a single heavily populated area, anywhere. Nor has there been such an incident since 1991, when the Soviet Union came apart and nuclear weapons were suddenly in the hands of three new states (Belarus, Ukraine, Kazakhstan) without any experience managing and securing nuclear weapon stockpiles. All of these weapons have now been accounted for and secured in other nations.

For over seventy years now, Hiroshima and Nagasaki have remained the horrific events that have never been repeated, whether accidentally or intentionally. Though rarely (if ever) spoken of in such terms, this amounts to a tremendous, even spectacular close call. Were there actual near misses, even *very* near misses? Yes, there were. On a November night in 1979, National Security Advisor Zbigniew Brezinski was awakened and told the Soviets had launched hundreds of nuclear missiles at the US and that the country would be largely destroyed within less than 15 minutes; the only option seemed the launching of a counterstrike of equal scale. Fortunately, a triple check of all systems showed a computer error at the North American Aerospace Defense (NORAD). Three years later, Soviet early warning systems detected several incoming US missiles that should have triggered a counter launch. But the officer on duty at the relevant command center, Stanislav Petrov, decided not to relay the information to his superiors, instead judging the attack a false alarm, which indeed it was. Then, in 1995, a combined US-Norwegian research team fired a rocket toward the Artic island of Svalbard, intending to collect data on the aurora borealis. This was misread by Russian nuclear forces as a submarine-fired missile, putting Russian submarines on high alert and causing the "nuclear briefcase" to be brought before then-President Boris Yeltsin. It did not take long for radar operators to realize the rocket was headed north and out to sea, not east and south toward Russia. In fact, the US and Norwegian scientists had alerted thirty nations, *including* Russia, of their intended launch, but somehow this information never found its way to radar command.

Close calls there have certainly been, in other words. On both sides the personnel involved have held back from the final choice of retaliation. Is this comforting, then? Can we depend on it happening again in the future, if needed? Not in the least. Now, we are not so much faced with a prospect of global war, but instead regional nuclear conflicts. How long, that is, might Pakistan refrain from a counterstrike launch, if it thought a missile from India was on the way? What if the two nations involved were Israel and Iran? How might North Korea respond to a misidentified missile attack from a US submarine?

Yet the greatest amount of fear and anxiety are reserved for power plant reactors, not weapons. If the chances of world nuclear war are less now than at any time during the Cold War, humanity in the late 2010s still lives with many thousands of nuclear weapons – according to nongovernment sources such as the Federation of American Scientists and Arms Control Association, roughly 4,018 of them in the US (1,411 deployed), and roughly 7,000 in Russia (1,765 deployed), with as many as 1,100 split among the other seven nuclear states [31]. There is no diminishing the threat these arms will continue to pose, nor the extremely challenging and ever-pressing matter of total disarmament in a world where the knowledge of how to build a weapon, if certain materials are in hand, is readily available. And despite the thankful absence of another Hiroshima and Nagasaki, there did take place over 2,000 intentional detonations in the Earth's precious atmosphere, at a time when the dangers of radioactive fallout were well known.

Without the Limited Test Ban Treaty in 1963, which took a full eight years to create, how much longer might these atmospheric tests have continued? We simply don't know; nor can we be assured that either the US or Soviet Union would have soon moved to only underground detonations and set a precedent for the other weapons states. In fact, both nations continued to perform near-surface tests of nonweapon nuclear detonations for more than a decade after the treaty, these being explosions that were applied to civil engineering projects like creating artificial lakes, reservoirs, canals, and other large-scale excavations, as well as putting out gas-well fires. A number of these nonmilitary tests (of which there were about 150 in total, 85 percent in the Soviet Union) ended up spreading fallout over large areas, though in nondangerous amounts. Even after signing the 1963 limited ban, the two nuclear superpowers refused to fully accept the nature of the legacy their testing had already produced.

We thus return, yet again, to Einstein's 1939 letter to FDR, calling attention to "large quantities of new radium-like elements." What seems so striking today is not merely the level of military paranoia that led both the US and USSR. to conduct tests endangering the health and lives of their own people, but the underlying assumption that people would bear it without major complaint, that they could be dissuaded, distracted, fooled about the repercussions and that this was somehow justified by national security.

* * *

It may seem strange that we have begun this book, which seeks to promote nuclear power for the global future, on such a dark note. Why focus on weapons, after all, and the arms race? Why start with war and conflict? Because this is the setting from which nuclear power emerged. The first reactors of any kind were built as part of the Manhattan Project, though their purpose was to generate plutonium, not electricity. Nonetheless, they established the fundamentals of what a reactor was, how it worked, what it could do. Civilian reactors in the US, meanwhile (as we will discuss in Chapter 3), were based directly on the design of those developed for nuclear submarines of the US Navy. But in broader terms, too, reactors to supply power to the public emerged out of the circumstances and ideas related to weapons and the weapons industry. Eisenhower's Atoms for Peace speech was intended to stimulate new uses for a technology that had remained entirely in the hands of the government, mostly the military. This was also true in the other five original nuclear states. This had lasting importance for public attitudes, above all those of the generations that came of age in the postwar era.

To be sure, there was a whole other dimension presented to the ordinary citizen. Nuclear energy bore two faces: one of gargantuan threat, the other of measureless progress. Since early in the twentieth century, there had been promises of atomic energy bringing a future of wonders and marvels, from flying cars to longer life. Many of these myths were erased by Hiroshima and Nagasaki and then the arms race. Yet the idea of "atomic power" as a source of wondrous progress returned after the war, this time often in the form of propaganda. The most avid promoters of the "Atomic Age" as heralding a new and glorious future were, unsurprisingly, the government and the military, and this was true in the US, France, Britain, and to some degree, China and Soviet Union as well. Atomic (or nuclear) medicine would soon help cure disease, bring food and water to impoverished millions, and replace all other energy sources for the rest of time. A good deal of this atomic optimism was either funded or directly encouraged by government sources, such as the AEC in the US and the Foreign Office in Britain.

But in terms of its overall impact, this discourse was largely, if not entirely, a failure. In many ways, it could not have been otherwise. Promises of progress could not thin the ubiquitous backdrop resulting from the threat and fear of nuclear war. As we've mentioned, too, conflicting reports about the effects of radiation did much to damage the credibility of government as a reliable source for vital information. In the US, the AEC came in for significant criticism and distrust. To be fair, its mission was impossible from the beginning: to watch over the nation's nuclear arsenal, carry out classified research, advance private nuclear enterprise, and act as an outlet to the news media and the public, defined responsibilities often in direct conflict with one another. In late 1952, the Commission waited more than two weeks to issue a statement about Ivy Mike, the world's first thermonuclear explosion, and when its official announcement finally came, it said merely that "experiments" had been conducted and "satisfactory" results obtained. Reports, however, had already

arrived by letter from witnesses testifying to the gigantic scale of the blast; the
AEC threatened to investigate such "leaks" and to pursue disciplinary action
[32]. Such was the type of "press release" that earned the Commission a less
than gleaming image. It suggests, as well, the authoritarian stance that the AEC
often took and its arrogant attempts to control the press. By the end of the
1950s, the positive face of nuclear energy had largely become a silhouette.
Further reverses came from the Cuban Missile Crisis a few years later, which,
despite the victory achieved by the Kennedy Administration, played out as
a truly traumatic event for the American people.

It is thus the viewpoint of this book that the feelings and visions, under-
standings and anxieties, sensibilities and suspicions about things "nuclear" that
have dominated the last half-century, above all in the West, emerged from this
post-WWII legacy. We have spoken of this legacy several times already, in less
than glowing terms. From the late 1940s into the 1950s, nuclear technology
gained an aura of secrecy and fear. If this began during the war, it never really
weakened thereafter. The arms race itself ran on the fuel of fear to a great
degree, as did the pursuit of nuclear weapons by states like China, Pakistan,
Israel, and North Korea. The overwhelming reason for such pursuit was always
the sense of existential threat, what the military came to call "deterrence."
It helps to be frank about this: the many tens of thousands of nuclear weapons
were never wholly about preventing attack or achieving superiority. Such
numbers are orders of magnitude beyond what the military itself said would
ever be needed. As early as 1945, for example, the Pentagon estimated
that only about 310 warheads would be enough to destroy the Soviet Union.
And in 1948, Los Alamos scientists predicted that a maximum of a hundred
large-yield hydrogen bombs would be sufficient to bring "world-wide
destruction . . . from radioactive poison" [33]. While the public never knew
how many weapons actually existed in either the US or the Soviet Union, they
understood that true, global annihilation was a real possibility during their
lifetime.

Nuclear energy during the first decades after WWII acquired a complex
mixture of meanings and imagery. For a great many people, not least in the
US but also in the UK and Israel, the realm of the "nuclear" could not but be
tinged with secrecy, fear, distrust, and even, in some cases, a sense of betrayal
by a democratic government that was supposed to be accountable to its people.
This was all very unfortunate for what came after. It was impossible that
civilian nuclear power, when it arrived, would somehow be free of this troubled
legacy.

* * *

It seems worthwhile, given what has been said here, to end this chapter with a thought experiment. Szilárd, as we remember, in a sense began the nuclear era with his own experiment of this kind. Ours, however, is a bit different in kind. It goes like this: what if the profound advances in nuclear physics during the 1930s had taken place during a period of relative peace, a period free of the conflicts leading up to world war? Would weapons have been the technology that emerged from this work? Most likely not; in fact, almost *certainly* not. This is not the direction that scientists would have naturally turned, especially in a capitalist society. We would therefore have had nuclear power long before nuclear weapons, and the sensibility attached to "nuclear" ("atomic" would not have been used) would have been very different. To be sure, weapons would have made their appearance at some later point; yet how might the world have responded?

The point, then, is that the troubled legacy of the "nuclear" was not foreordained. It was never inevitable, as if commanded by a higher or lower power. Nor was it innate to the science and technology of controlled nuclear energy. The crises of war, both hot and cold, lasting for many decades with the sense of existential threat, brought it into being and maintained its presence. How might the landscape have evolved if even a fraction of the immense effort and cost and intelligence expended on weapons gone toward peaceful uses of nuclear science? There is a chance, in fact, for this to be more than a mere thought experiment for a large part of the world.

References

[1] R. Rhodes, *The Making of the Atomic Bomb* (New York: Simon & Schuster, 1986), p. 11.
[2] S. R. Weart and Gertrud Weiss Szilard (eds), Leo Szilard: His Version of the Facts: Selected Recollections and Correspondence, (Cambridge, MA: MIT Press), 1978, reprinted in *New Scientist*, May 31, 1979, p. 738. Ibid., p. 36.
[3] Einstein's Letter to President Roosevelt – 1939 (Internet), *Atomic Archive, Historical Documents*. Available from: www.atomicarchive.com/Docs/Begin/Einstein.shtml
[4] Rhodes, p. 314.
[5] Ibid., pp. 640, 641.
[6] Ibid., p. 688.
[7] President Truman Did Not Understand, an Interview with Leo Szilárd, *US News & World Report* (August 15, 1960), 68–71, 70.

[8] H. D. Smyth, *Atomic Energy for Military Purposes, The Official Report of the Atomic Bomb under the Auspices of the United States Government, 1940–1945* (Princeton: Princeton University Press, 1945), p. 226.

[9] H. D. Smyth, The Smyth Report, *The Princeton University Library Chronicle*, 37:3 (Spring 1976), 173–190, 185.

[10] Cold War: A Brief History—The Soviet Bomb, atomicarchive.com (Internet). Available from: http://www.atomicarchive.com/History/coldwar/page03.shtml

[11] A. Sakharov, *Memoirs*, trans. R. Lourie (New York: Knopf, 1990), pp. 190–194.

[12] Comprehensive Test Ban Treaty Organization, Preparatory Commission, Nuclear Testing (Internet). Available from: www.ctbto.org/nuclear-testing/history-of-nuclear-testing/world-overview/

[13] P. Ortmeyer and A. Makhijani, Worse Than We Knew, *Bulletin of the Atomic Scientists* (November/December 1997), 46–50.

[14] R. S. Norris and W. M. Arkin, NRDC Nuclear Notebook: Global Nuclear Stockpiles, 1945–2000, *Bulletin of the Atomic Scientists* (March–April 2000), 79.

[15] S. I. Schwartz (ed.), *Atomic Audit: The Costs and Consequences of US Nuclear Weapons Since 1940* (Washington, D.C.: Brookings Institute, 1998). Available from: www.brookings.edu/about/projects/archive/nucweapons/weapons

[16] J. E. C. Hymans, *The Psychology of Nuclear Proliferation* (London: Cambridge University Press, 2006), pp. 89–91.

[17] Ibid., pp. 105.

[18] P. Cole, *Sweden Without the Bomb* (Washington, D.C.: RAND Corporation, 1994).

[19] J. Stussi, Historical Outline on the Question of Swiss Nuclear Armament (Internet), *The Nuclear Weapon Archive*. Available from: http://nuclearweaponarc hive.org/Library/Swissdoc.html

[20] A. Cohen, *Israel and the Bomb* (New York: Columbia University Press, 1958), pp. 12, 13.

[21] J. T. Richelson, *Spying on the Bomb* (New York: W. W. Norton, 2006), pp. 236–242, 254–262.

[22] Ibid., pp. 137–138.

[23] Ibid., p. 254.

[24] Norris and Arkin, op. cit.

[25] R. Dallek, *An Unfinished Life, John F. Kennedy* (Boston: Little, Brown and Company, 2003), p. 615.

[26] M. I. Shaker, *The Nuclear Non-Proliferation Treaty, Origin and Implementation, 1959–1979* (London: Oceana Publications, 1980), p. 933.

[27] Ibid., p. 37.

[28] Ibid., p. 55.

[29] United Nations Office for Disarmament Affairs, Treaty on the Non-Proliferation of Nuclear Weapons (NPT) (Internet). Available from: https://www.un.org/disarma ment/wmd/nuclear/npt/

[30] John F. Kennedy Presidential Library and Museum, Commencement Address at American University, (June 10, 1963) (Internet). Available from: https://www .jfklibrary.org/Asset-Viewer/BWC7I4C9QUmLG9J6I8oy8w.aspx

[31] K. Davenport and K. Reif, Nuclear Weapons: Who has what at a glance, Fact Sheets and Briefs (Internet) Arms Control Association. Available from: https://www.armscontrol.org

[32] J. Walz, Experiments for Hydrogen Bomb Held Successfully at Eniwetok; Leaks About Blast Under Inquiry (Internet), *The New York Times* (November 16, 1952). Available from: www.nytimes.com/learning/general/onthisday/big/1101.html #article

[33] P. Bienaimé, In 1945, the Pentagon Estimated That 204 Atomic Bombs Could Destroy the Soviet Union (Internet), *Business Insider* (October 3, 2014). Available from: www.businessinsider.com/the-pentagon-estimated-204-atomic-bombs-could-destroy-the-soviets-2014-10

3

What is Nuclear Energy? Some Helpful Background

Beginnings: Rutherford's Atom

For nearly a century, the atom was eternal. The theory had been set down by the English school teacher, John Dalton, in 1808, and it dominated without peer for many decades. Though it came to be modified by later discoveries, scientists continued to believe that atoms could neither be created nor altered, let alone destroyed. The universe, in short, was in a steady, perpetual state.

But in 1897, it began to collapse. This was when the young physicist Ernest Rutherford (1871–1937) got hold of the atom, and the end soon came for Dalton's neat and tidy hypothesis. "Another beautiful theory destroyed by an ugly fact," is how Thomas Huxley once described such a loss. Yet the new facts were anything but unsightly. They were startling, even violent in a manner of speaking, but also energetic, elegant, and most of all, world-changing.

Rutherford remade the atom into a stunningly dynamic entity. He did not do this alone; far from it. He began as a follower of French scientists, especially Henri Becquerel and Marie Curie, who identified a new phenomenon that Curie named "radioactivity." It was astonishing to find there were forms of matter able to burn images into a photographic plate while it was stored away in a dark drawer. Becquerel first saw this in 1896 and understood what it meant: there were atoms that could somehow produce their own energy. Physicists knew that some kinds of matter could absorb and then give back energy from a source like the Sun. But atoms generating energy hadn't been imagined.

The finding quickly spread through the scientific community and ignited the young Rutherford, barely a year from having completed his doctorate. People have speculated that his unmatched brilliance in conceiving simple but revealing experiments – exactly what was needed at the time – might have come from growing up one of twelve children on a farm in New Zealand, where he repaired machinery, built devices, and worked on clocks.

Be that as it may, in 1898, when only twenty-seven, he applied for and was accepted to the Macdonald Chair in Physics at McGill University, Montreal. Immediately, he set about studying the "uranium rays" that Becquerel had discovered two years earlier. No mean experimenter himself, Becquerel had wanted to find out just how penetrative such rays might be. By putting different materials, like glass and metal, between the uranium and the plates, he observed how the images changed, weakened in some cases, concluding there was more than one kind of "ray." This was the idea that Rutherford seized upon.

Following Becquerel's lead, he experimented with a number of materials. He saw that an extremely thin sheet of aluminum could stop one type of ray but not another. The first type he called "alpha," beginning letter of the Greek alphabet, and the second, more penetrating type, "beta," the next letter. A third type, discovered by the French physicist Paul Villard several years later, was far more penetrative than these two, and Rutherford dubbed it "gamma." Next, he found that alpha and beta "emanations" (as he called them) could be bent by magnetic fields, indicating they were probably not rays at all but instead charged *particles*. Beta particles were not hard to identify as electrons, as these were already partly understood in their basic behavior. Alpha particles, which were bent in the opposite direction, were positively charged. Gamma emanations, however, weren't bent at all, even by the strongest magnets; they were deemed "true rays."

Rutherford was only just getting started, however. He wanted to see exactly how penetrative these types of radiation really were. Using thorium as a source (a better producer of alpha and beta particles than uranium) and aluminum foil of precisely measured thicknesses, he found that alpha, beta, and gamma rays could be largely stopped at 0.0005, 0.05, and 8 centimeters thick, respectively. This suggested that alpha rays, or particles, could even be blocked by a person's skin, while beta rays would be able to penetrate our epidermis to some degree but would be halted by heavy clothing or a glass window. Gamma rays, however, had the energy to go through nearly any object except a metal wall several or more inches thick.

In the midst of these experiments, Rutherford had stumbled on a disturbing conclusion. So contrary was it to ideas about the atom that it seemed to call upon magic. Many scientists rejected it outright. Rutherford surmised correctly, however, that by emitting an alpha particle, thorium must be losing some of its mass and energy and therefore transforming itself into another element. It was the "parent" changing into a "daughter element." This was in 1902, and he was now working with the chemist Frederick Soddy at McGill. Using chemical tests, Soddy confirmed a new element was indeed produced. He later recalled having said: "Rutherford, this is transmutation; the thorium is disintegrating and transmuting itself." To which Rutherford answered: "don't call it 'transmutation' ... they'll have our heads off as alchemists!" [1] He wasn't entirely joking.

They agreed to the term "spontaneous transformation" and so kept their heads. Indeed, they moved rapidly forward, playing a central part in the most intoxicating era that modern physics had yet seen, each year revealing new phenomena on the basic nature of matter. Excitement gained intensity from competition among research teams. Rutherford at one point confessed to his mother: "I have to publish my present work as rapidly as possible in order to keep in the race" [2]. Together with Soddy, however, he more than kept pace. One of their key findings: the first "daughter element" of thorium was radium, which of course was radioactive too and decayed into another element, actinium, also radioactive, and so the process continued. At one stage along this "decay series" of thorium, Rutherford and Soddy observed a daughter element that was a radioactive gas (later identified as radon) that quickly lost its "emanations." That is, its radioactivity rapidly declined until it reached very low levels. Both men realized it must have decayed quickly and that such decline must be true of *all* radioactive elements, since they are continually losing mass and energy. But some, like uranium and thorium, do this more slowly, requiring many thousands of years to weaken significantly. Others needed perhaps only minutes or hours. This supported Rutherford's idea of a "half-life period." He now defined it as the time needed for *half the atoms in a sample to decay into non-radioactive "daughters."*

There was an essential corollary to this. The degree of atomic change created by radioactivity meant that very large amounts of energy must be involved. Even French researchers, who rebuffed "the British idea" of radioactivity as a process of one element decaying into another, agreed with this conclusion. Marie Curie, and her husband, Pierre, both felt that the energy released on an atomic level was immense. Rutherford and Soddy began speaking of "atomic energy," a term quickly adopted by physicists and chemists working on related phenomena. The idea circulated that it might even be the energy in stars. Soddy, in particular, would later speculate in books and lectures about the powers this would one day bring into the hands of humanity.

In 1904, Soddy moved to the University of Glasgow, and Rutherford's next assistant, Otto Hahn, was at McGill for only a year (1905–06) before transferring back to Germany (Berlin). Rutherford himself accepted in 1908 a chance to move to Manchester University. In less than a year, his new lab began to generate important discoveries, keeping him "in the race." Proving, at last, that alpha rays were actually helium nuclei (two protons plus two neutrons) stripped of their electrons was one of these. The finding completed an essential part of the radioactivity puzzle, since beta rays were known to be high-speed electrons and gamma rays were true high-energy rays.

So the three major components of radioactivity, or what was already called "radiation," were now finally known. It would be a few decades before gamma radiation was more fully understood. It still needed Einstein's hypothesis that light and other kinds of rays were actually made up of discrete little bundles or packets of energy that could act both as waves and particles. Such packets were accepted under the name of "photons" in the late 1920s. A decade before this, however, Rutherford had unleashed his most startling discovery of all about the atom.

The experiments that led to this, conducted by Rutherford's Manchester team, are legendary and have been widely known to scientists ever since. They were a direct result of the realization that alpha particles sometimes did not behave as they were supposed to, given the updated model of the atom. This was called the "plum pudding" model, a bit too English and obscure for the rest of the world, so it was also called the "blueberry muffin." It portrayed the atom as a group of electrons embedded in a (poorly understood) spherical mass of positive charge. As atoms were understood to have no total electrical charge, this mass had to balance out the electrons' negative charge. As a whole, the atom was spread out, diffuse, without any real solidity. But when electrons were removed, as they were in the creation of alpha particles, the remaining positive mass was thought to somehow condense and act as a solid. A solid alpha particle should therefore go right through a sheet of atoms, like a cannon ball through fog (or pastry).

But when Rutherford's two assistants, Hans Geiger (of Geiger Counter fame) and Ernest Marsden, set up experiments that fired alpha particles at thin sheets of metal, including gold foil, they encountered an incredible result: though most alpha particles went through as they were supposed to do, a small number were scattered at many angles, and a few were actually deflected *right back* at the source, as if they had bounced off something extremely hard. Rutherford could not contain his amazement: "It was quite the most incredible event that has ever happened to me in my life . . . as incredible as if you fired a 15-inch shell at a piece of tissue paper and it came back and hit you" [3].

This was in 1909, and by 1911 Rutherford had published a wholly new model of the atom. The new, twentieth-century atom had a tiny but hard center of concentrated mass and positive charge surrounded by "satellite" electrons. Thus was born the atomic "nucleus" (a term borrowed from biology) and a new era in physics.

By 1920, Rutherford had moved to Cambridge. He was now Cavendish Professor of Experimental Physics, the most eminent post for anyone in that field in Britain. At Cambridge, he wasted no time in extending his work. Between 1919 and 1920, his lab had established that the positively charged part of the nucleus was made up of particles each of which Rutherford had named the "proton." As the charge of these was balanced out perfectly by the surrounding electrons, the other particles making up the mass of the nucleus had to be electrically neutral. One of Rutherford's former students, James Chadwick, is credited with proving the existence of this particle, the "neutron." Chadwick's paper on this in the journal *Nature* was a mere 700 words but it packed a punch. The neutron, it suggested, when emitted by a nuclear reaction of some kind, would have a high velocity and, due to this speed and its electric neutrality, would be able to penetrate any kind of matter. These two aspects would prove of great importance.

The atom's solid core implied a colossal amount of binding energy able to keep the nucleus together, given that the protons would want to fly away from each other. So great must the energy be, felt Rutherford, that, in his later years, he turned away from the idea that it could ever be harnessed for use. He viewed such hopes as "moonshine." Soddy, however, was more prescient on this score.

Soddy was right about other matters, too. He was the discoverer of isotopes – different forms of an element that have the same number of protons (atomic number), but different number of neutrons. Uranium, for example, was eventually found to have as many as eight isotopes – U-232 through U-239 – all of them possessing ninety-two protons but a number of neutrons ranging from 140 up to 147. The reality of isotopes proved essential for a fuller understanding of nuclear energy, since isotopes of a single element may have widely differing half-lives, types of radiation, and may act in very different ways when bombarded by subatomic particles.

After receiving the Nobel Prize for chemistry in 1921, Frederick Soddy left science. He turned instead to economics, applying the laws of thermodynamics to the working of a nation's economy. Most economists at the time considered Soddy out of his area of expertise and rather out of his mind (the word "crank" was applied to him). Yet some of his ideas strike us today as entirely sound, even prescient:

> That this still is the age of the energy of coal is unfortunately only too true, and the whole earth is rendered the filthier thereby ... [B]ut these last years have wrought a wonderful revolution in our knowledge of energy ... It is possible to look forward to a time, which may await the world, when this grimy age of fuel will seem as truly a beginning of the mastery of energy as the rude stone age of Paleolithic man now appears as the beginning of the mastery of matter [4].

How Much Energy?

Ernest Rutherford died on October 19, 1937. The cause was a strangulated hernia whose care he had ignored too long. The man who had won the race to alter humanity's understanding of matter was brought low at sixty-six by neglect of a small injury. But even as the world of physics mourned him, one of Rutherford's assistants at McGill, Otto Hahn, helped bring about the next great leap toward an understanding of nuclear energy.

During the 1930s, major effort went into studying the effects of bombarding various elements with neutrons. The ability of neutrons to create changes in the nuclei of elements, producing new isotopes and even transmutation of one element into another, had been discovered and confirmed. This opened a whole new field of work, pursued in a number of labs, such as those of Enrico Fermi in Italy, Frederick and Irene Joliot-Curie in France, Ernest Lawrence in the US, as well as Rutherford. Fermi, in particular, using neutrons of different velocities, went through nearly all elements in the periodic table, creating many new isotopes. Nearly all labs used "fast" neutrons, those naturally produced by some materials, for their experiments. Fermi was among the first to work with "slow" or "thermal" neutrons – those that had been passed through a material reducing their energy to where it was equal, or in thermal equilibrium, with surrounding atoms. He found, in fact, that thermal neutrons were especially good at producing reactions with heavy elements, like uranium. It would be discovered in fact, that they could create a bizarre reaction whose explanation would come with immense implications.

Hahn, together with colleague Lise Meitner and apprentice Fritz Strassmann, worked at the Kaiser Wilhelm Institute in Berlin in the late 1930s. They were particularly interested in creating new elements beyond uranium, last in the periodic table at the time. But before they could get very far, Nazism intervened. Meitner, an Austrian Jew by birth, had remained in Germany far too long, caught up as she was in the exciting research with Hahn. Since Hitler's ascent to power four years earlier, nearly all Jewish scientists had been dismissed, and many left Germany, sensing a dire future. By 1938, the situation had become perilous with Hitler's annexation of Austria. Meitner escaped to Sweden with the help of scientist-friends. But she kept in touch with her two colleagues and remained, as it turned out, a vital participant.

This was because of certain "strange" results, as Hahn put it. Bombarding uranium with thermal neutrons did not create a heavier element or isotope, as normally happened. It yielded a *lighter* one. Hahn, a chemist, analyzed it to be either radium (atomic number 88) or, more likely but incomprehensibly, barium (number 56). This made no sense at all and was initially excluded. The reason was simple: shooting neutrons at nuclei had always produced either an isotope of that same element or else a close neighbor in the periodic table. Barium, however, was nowhere near uranium.

Thus, after much further experimentation and repeated testing had confirmed that the product was indeed barium, Hahn and Strassmann faced a real enigma. Repeating the experiment several times, they found other lighter elements, like strontium (38) and yttrium (39). What could it mean? It was Lise Meitner, together with her nephew, Otto Frisch, who had come to visit her in Sweden, who came up with the answer. Instead of knocking away a small portion of the target nucleus or being adding to it, the thermal neutron had been absorbed, causing the nucleus to become unstable. Meitner envisioned the uranium nucleus deforming like a drop being stretched so that it thinned in the middle until, finally, it ruptured into two smaller nuclei. Meitner and Frisch used the word "fission" – following a growing tradition of adopting terms from biology. Meitner and Frisch wrote up their interpretation in English, in a brief, two-page paper for the journal *Nature*. It appeared in the March 1939 issue and contained these words:

> It seems therefore possible that the uranium nucleus has only small stability of form, and may, after neutron capture, divide itself into two nuclei ... These two nuclei will repel each other [as they are both positively charged] and should gain a total kinetic energy of *c.* 200 Mev [5].

Physicists who read this at the time would have paused for breath. This was a colossal amount of energy. How colossal? One fission event yielded more than 200 million times the energy of the neutron that caused it. In different terms, 1 gram of uranium (a sphere the size of a large pencil dot) undergoing complete fission could produce the equivalent of 3 *million* grams (3.3 tons) of coal.

It was this short little paper by Meitner and Frisch that alarmed the émigré physicists in America. Scientists who understood nuclear matters, including those in Germany and Japan, would immediately understand what it meant. This is what led to the urgent request that Einstein write his famous warning letter to FDR. The real worry was not only that uranium fissioned, but that every time it did, it *also* released two to three neutrons, which could then cause other nuclei to fission, unleashing a chain reaction. If such a chain reaction continued in a sizeable mass of uranium, the explosive power would be beyond imagining. That the Nazis in particular might be working on such a weapon was therefore a threat that rose above all others.

In 1944, despite the war, the Swedish Nobel Committee awarded Otto Hahn the Nobel Prize in chemistry "for his discovery of the fission of heavy nuclei." Neither Strassmann, Frisch, nor above all, Lise Meitner were included. It was an error never corrected, even though Hahn, in his Nobel reception speech, attributed the discovery to Meitner and Frisch and their short paper in *Nature* (he notes that they also coined the term "nuclear fission"). Meitner received many other scientific awards thereafter, both in Europe and the US. Indeed, she was treated as a celebrity of the highest order by the American press in 1946, when she paid the US a visit, and was even handed a script from Hollywood about her life, which she declined to endorse. "It is based on the stupid newspaper story that I left Germany with the bomb in my purse ... " [6]

If these brief historical notes from the birthing room of nuclear physics have been comprehensible, then the reader already has an excellent background for this book. Let us summarize, in simple terms, a few of the major points:

– Radioactivity is the decay of a parent nucleus into a new, daughter nucleus by emission of radiation (particles and energy).
  • It is often the transmutation of one element into another.
  • Radioactive decay produces alpha, beta, and gamma rays
  • Half-life is the time needed for half the nuclei in a sample to decay into other nuclei.
  • When we use the term "element," we are really talking about an *isotope*, a variety of the element
– Nuclear fission involves a nucleus capturing a free neutron, becoming unstable, and dividing into two lighter nuclei, which are radioactive.
  • When the nucleus is fissile, as it is with certain isotopes of uranium and plutonium, the process releases huge amounts of energy and two to three neutrons.
  • These neutrons can cause fission in other nuclei, creating a chain reaction.
  • Fission can be greatly enhanced in some isotopes by neutrons that are slow (thermal).
  • Fission produces fast neutrons, but these can be slowed down, or "moderated," by certain materials such as graphite and water.
– Nuclear scientists prefer their atoms to be solid matter, not pudding or muffins.
– Lise Meitner still deserves a Nobel Prize.
  • In 1982, a new element (no. 109), was named for her, Meitnerium
  • She never had a bomb in her purse.

How to: The Bomb

This is a fair bit of nuclear physics, simply rendered. But as you might imagine, it leaves a few gaps. The most important of these, for our purposes, relate to the particular isotopes of uranium and plutonium that undergo fission most readily, and that release enough neutrons in the process to create a chain reaction. It is easiest just to list them:

– Three isotopes can produce a chain reaction: U-235, Pu-239, and U-233
  • Only U-235 exists in nature in any significant amount
  • U-235 and Pu-239 are the fuel for bombs and reactors
  • Pu-239 is created in reactors by neutron capture in U-238
  • U-233 is created in reactors by neutron capture in thorium-232

Among these isotopes, U-235 has been the prime reactor fuel worldwide, mainly because it occurs in nature together with U-238 and can be cheaply mined. U-235 has a relatively long half-life, 704 million years, so that some of it remains from the creation of the Earth, 4.54 billion years ago, when such heavy elements were incorporated into our planet from the primordial material of the solar system. The half-life for U-233 is only 160,000 years, and for Pu-239 just 21,100 years. They have long ago decayed into the stable end product, lead (Pb).

Otto Hahn and Lise Meitner revealed to the world of physics that a nuclear explosion would be a runaway chain reaction. By contrast, a reactor creates a *controlled* reaction. In fact, controlling fission is not at all difficult. A fundamental factor is the fuel.

This starts with natural uranium. It is made up of 99.3 percent U-238 and 0.7 percent U-235. The first of these, U-238, has a half-life of 4.5 billion years, roughly the same as the age of the Earth, so about half its original amount still exists. Though it doesn't fission well, U-238 is called "fertile," because it can absorb a neutron to become U-239, which then decays fairly quickly into Pu-239, the fissile isotope of plutonium.[1]

For a weapon, the fuel must have enough of the fissionable isotope so a runaway reaction can happen extremely quickly. This means it is enriched in either U-235 or Pu-239, typically to over 90 percent. With U-235, this kind of fuel is called *highly enriched uranium*, or HEU. Manufacturing it for the first atomic bomb defined the greatest challenge faced by scientists and engineers of the US Manhattan Project during WW II. This is because U-235 and U-238 have identical chemical behavior and so have to be separated mechanically, based on the tiny difference in their mass. To do this today, the uranium is combined with fluorine to produce a gas (uranium hexafluoride, UF_6), which is then injected into a system of centrifuges that spin very rapidly (thousands of times per second), forcing a partial separation of the two isotopes, with the

---

[1] The actual reaction involves U-239 decaying into neptunium-239 (Np-239) in 23.5 minutes, which then decays into Pu-239 in 2.4 days.

heavier U-238 further to the outside. The gas has to be put through the centrifuges many times to achieve 90 percent or higher enrichment in U-235.

With Pu-239, creating enriched fuel can be done in a reactor, where U-238 will absorb neutrons. Timing is important. As fuel is exposed to fission-derived neutrons, more and more of the U-238 is turned into Pu-239. But the plutonium itself will absorb neutrons, and if it doesn't fission will create other isotopes, Pu-240 and Pu-241. This dilutes the total amount of Pu-239 and also introduces problems related to the decay of these other isotopes. It turns out that removing fuel from the reactor after around three to four months will minimize these other isotopes and maximize the amount of Pu-239. Weapons-grade plutonium is therefore made in special reactors not suitable for power production, since the fuel is switched out quite frequently.

Having the right fuel isn't sufficient by itself to create a chain reaction, however. There has to be enough of it. If there isn't, too many neutrons are able to escape into the surrounding environment, so fission stops. The critical limit where enough fuel exists to support a sustained chain reaction is called the *critical mass*. It depends on the enrichment level. If we are talking about 95 percent U-235, the critical mass is 52 kg (114 lbs). For Pu-239 at this enrichment, the critical mass is only 10 kg (22 lbs). The difference here tells us that Pu-239 produces more neutrons per fission than does U-235 and creates a more vigorous chain reaction.

What about lower enrichment levels? The less pure the fuel is, the more mass is needed. Theoretically, an explosion is possible even at 20 percent U-235, but the critical mass for this is hundreds of kilograms, making such a weapon wholly impractical. Little Boy, the bomb dropped on Hiroshima by the US in 1945, destroying everything over an area over 3.5 km (2.2 mi) in diameter and killing over 80,000 people, had 64 kg (141 lbs) of uranium enriched to an average of 80 percent. This was just under the critical mass for such an enrichment level[2] and wouldn't have produced a large explosion, except for one thing. Manhattan Project scientists added a thin shield of neutron-reflecting material (tungsten carbide). This sent a good many escaping neutrons back into the fuel, significantly raising the number of fissions. Because of this, the 64 kg turned out to be about *twice* the critical mass. In other words, only half of the fuel was really needed.

Obviously, the smaller the required (critical) mass, the more efficient the use of fuel. We just learned one way to reduce the critical mass for a given enrichment level: add a neutron reflector. Another way is to increase the density of the fuel, so that the atoms are much closer together and fewer neutrons will escape.

---

[2] At 80 percent enrichment, the total amount of U-235 was: 0.8 × 64 kg = 51.2 kg, just under critical mass for a sphere.

Both of these methods were employed in the Fat Man bomb dropped with horrendous effect on Nagasaki. In this case, the fuel was Pu-239 that had been chemically separated from remaining U-238. This was fashioned into two small hemispheres, encased in a "tamper" layer that acted as a neutron reflector and was itself surrounded by specially shaped explosive charges. When detonated, these charges created a spherical shock wave that collapsed the tamper and compressed the plutonium into a super-dense sphere. Inside the two plutonium hemispheres was a neutron source that initiated the fission. This *implosion* type of design, with neutron reflector, was able to reduce the needed mass of plutonium down to 6.2 kg (14 lbs), a tenth of the mass of Little Boy.

Because of its success in decreasing the amount of fuel, the implosion design became standard for the great majority of nuclear weapons (nonhydrogen bombs). By the late 1940s, when the Soviet Union first tested its own nuclear device, the US had given up the gun-type Little Boy weapon in favor of implosion designs that used a mixture of U-235 and Pu-239 as fuel. Plutonium, in general, has remained the more preferred fuel for weapons in other nations, especially those without thermonuclear capability, because Pu-239 is easier and cheaper to make, can be fit to many different weapon sizes, and produces a higher yield, i.e. more kilotons of TNT per unit mass.

No discussion of this kind should be allowed to end so clinically. The bombs dropped on Japan and the monstrous suffering and devastation they caused are known to nearly every human being on the planet. Images of the horror, real and imagined, have been seared into the imagination of a great many millions of people. But not widely known, and all too often ignored, is that the Little Boy bomb that produced this ruin was mostly a failure. Less than 2 percent of its fuel actually exploded. Put differently, *more than 98 percent* of the weapon did not contribute to the devastation. In the case of Fat Man, as much as 15–20 percent of the fuel was effective; at least 80 percent was not.

The meaning of this is simple. No matter what visions of nuclear Armageddon we may have in our mind, no matter how informed our ideas may be by what happened in Japan, they do not match what the reality could have been.

How to: Reactors

These basic facts reveal the main ideas for how to control fission. The key is two-fold: reduce the level of enrichment *and* control the supply of neutrons.

Neither of these goals has been difficult to achieve. In fact, the very first fission chain reaction was a controlled one – produced under the direction of Enrico Fermi at Chicago Pile 1 reactor (CP-1) on December 2, 1942. Bombs came second.

Reactor fuel should be low enough in U-235 so that a nuclear explosion is impossible. For the past fifty years, civilian power plant reactors have used fuel enriched to levels between 2.5 and 5 percent, what is called *low enriched uranium*, or LEU. The rest of the fuel, as we noted above, consists of U-238. Again, by absorbing a neutron this becomes the Pu-239 produced in a reactor. Once created, however, some of this isotope will itself undergo fission in the same reactor. It's estimated that as much as half of the plutonium created this way is burned in the reactor, producing over one-third of the heat generated. The reactor is thus capable of "breeding" part of its own fuel (a capability we will discuss in more detail later on). But, as already mentioned, some of the Pu-239, instead of undergoing fission, captures a neutron to become Pu-240, and the process repeats to yield Pu-241 and 242 isotopes.

Spent fuel from the most common civilian power reactor contains about 93 percent U-238, roughly 5 percent radioactive fission products (the smaller nuclei left over from the split atoms), 1 percent U-235, and about 1.2 percent plutonium by weight, which turns out to be a kind of isotopic casserole consisting of about half Pu-239, 25 percent Pu-240, 15 percent Pu-241, and 5 percent Pu-242. The fuel is considered "spent" because of the buildup of fission products, which increasingly "poison" the fission by absorbing neutrons that might otherwise contribute to the chain reaction. As a result, the fuel's ability to generate predictable heat decreases. Overall, most of the original energy potential in the fuel is still there, in the U-238, with its capability to be converted into Pu-239. The original plan devised in the US, aimed at replacing coal and oil use with nuclear energy, involved such conversion on a routine basis in special "breeder" reactors. This plan, partly due to its dependence on large-scale plutonium production, ran into serious domestic opposition in the 1970s and was abandoned.

Returning to our main topic, we need to answer: how can fission be made self-sustaining if enrichment levels are so low? The answer lies with the neutrons. Slowing them down, as we've seen, greatly increases their ability to be absorbed by a U-235 nucleus and to result in fission. Since the neutrons released by fission are themselves fast, the fuel needs to be divided up into many portions all surrounded by a moderator. Thus, fast neutrons escaping from one portion of fuel will be slowed by the moderator before entering another fuel portion and generating fission there. By separating the fuel and moderator, neutrons can be slowed without the risk of being unproductively captured by U-238 during their journey.

But what to use for the moderator? Experiments of the 1930s, especially those by Fermi himself, had shown that neutrons were most effectively slowed by collisions with very light nuclei – we might think of a billiard ball striking head on another ball, which absorbs most of the first ball's energy causing it to slow. Both hydrogen and carbon (no. 6) proved the best choices for a moderator. Four other elements are between them in the Periodic Table, helium, lithium, beryllium, and boron, but they all had difficulties: helium, a gas, wasn't dense enough (neutrons go right through it); boron and lithium are neutron absorbers; beryllium is both toxic and expensive. Carbon had none of these problems. One of its purest forms is graphite, which, as nearly pure carbon, is very stable and can be manufactured.

The other choice for moderator was hydrogen, which meant water. Here, there were actually two possibilities: its common form, ^{1}H (one proton in the nucleus) or its "heavy" form, ^{2}H (proton + neutron), known as Deuterium (D). Because hydrogen is too reactive to exist on Earth and quite expensive to generate, a special fluid was chosen as moderator that is particularly rich in hydrogen atoms: water. This meant either H_2O or D_2O. Nature, however, has a habit of offering options and hurdles at the same time. Both hydrogen and deuterium absorb a relatively small but important number of neutrons, with hydrogen absorbing more. Thus, if regular, "light" water is chosen as the moderator, nuclear fuel definitely needs to be enriched for there to be enough neutrons available for fission. Choosing heavy water (D_2O) instead means that natural uranium can be used as fuel, with no enrichment. But there is a trade-off: heavy water occurs as only a tiny fraction (less than 1 part in 5,000) of regular water and artificially separating it out is an expensive process. Nonetheless, Canadian scientists and engineers designed a successful reactor based on use of heavy water, called CANDU (Canada Deuterium Uranium).

Fermi and his team at the University of Chicago chose graphite as the moderator for the world's first human-built reactor. In late 1942, they assembled the prosaically named but historically epochal "Chicago Pile 1." On December 2, the reactor "went critical," i.e. its fission became self-sustaining – the term "critical" being related to the idea of critical (sufficient) mass, not any sort of crisis – on December 2, a date many have viewed as the launch of the Atomic Age. Though a true breakthrough in the history of modern physics, the forty-nine scientists who were present at the event celebrated with a few sips of Chianti and a paralysis of silence. They were all too aware, as war raged in Europe and Asia, what it meant. But they also had hope for what it might also mean.

Roughly a decade later, the first nuclear reactors would be put into common use. What isn't widely known: these early reactors were not used for generating electricity, but instead for powering submarines, the first of which, the USS *Nautilus*, was launched on January 21, 1954.

How a Modern Nuclear Reactor Works

If erected today, CP-1 would be considered a dismal failure for its power output. It would barely be able to light a single 100-Watt bulb. Compare this to a newly completed reactor in 2016, such the ones at Sanmen in Zhejiang Province (China), each capable of delivering 1,200 MW, enough to power a city the size of San Francisco.

The comparison is unfair, of course. CP-1 was never meant to produce electricity. Not until 1951 was the very first power-generating reactor built in the US. This happened at the Argonne reactor test facility in southern Idaho. Capable of 2 MW, it was hooked up to the local grid and supplied electricity to the town of Arco, population 1,200, for about an hour. A year earlier, in Obninsk, the Soviets had connected their own first power reactor, at an output of 5 MW. England, in 1956, topped everyone with Calder Hall 1, which produced 50 MW. Though differing in design, these early examples, like their relatives today, employed the same fundamental principles. Each was a heat engine, boiling water to make steam, which spins a turbine generator to produce electricity.

Worldwide today, 85 percent of all nuclear power plants are built using *light water reactor* (LWR) designs. Fission generates the heat in the reactor core, which is immersed in water. The water serves both as a *coolant*, removing heat from the core so it doesn't get too hot, and as a *moderator*, slowing down neutrons released by fission so they will be more easily absorbed and keep the chain reaction going. The resulting steam is transmitted through pipes to the turbine, which is like that of a jet engine. It has many blades set at a slight angle on a central shaft, so the flow of incoming steam causes it to spin. The steam then goes to a condenser, where it enters a set of pipes surrounded by cooler water, which turns it back into a liquid so it can be recycled. The turbine shaft, meantime, is fairly long and extends into a separate compartment where the generator sits. This is a powerful electromagnet attached to the shaft and spins inside a large cylinder of coiled wire. Spin of the electromagnet causes induction in the wire, producing electricity. The process is about 33–35 percent efficient. The efficiency, in fact, is limited by temperature; other types of reactors able to operate at very high temperatures have higher efficiencies (reasons why LWR uses lower temperatures are noted below). In these cases, if some of the generated heat is used for other purposes, an industrial process or desalinating water, efficiencies can rise to 60 percent or more. This approach is known as "combined heat and power."

The basic set up of a nuclear plant is the same as for any steam-driven power plant, whether it burns coal, natural gas, oil, or biomass. There is one major difference: all choices *except* nuclear involve burning a carbon fuel and so, along with heat, they produce carbon dioxide and other waste gases, as well as particulate matter. With nuclear, fission creates new radioactive material as waste, but no airborne pollution or carbon emissions. Furthermore, all nuclear waste is captured and stored. Airborne waste from carbon fuels can be mostly removed by pollution controls, but these are not used on thousands of power plants worldwide, especially in developing countries, due to the added expense. Even in the most advanced power plants today, only part of this waste is apprehended, with toxic metals like mercury uncaptured. No commercial plants anywhere remove carbon dioxide, the main greenhouse gas driving climate change. And the truly vast amount of ash and liquid waste from coal plants is often left exposed to the air behind dams or in landfills, abandoned mines, and other near-surface settings.

Fuel and the Fuel Cycle

Nuclear fuel is most abundantly made for LWRs, which comprise 85 percent of the global reactor fleet currently. While this will likely change in the future, the dominance of LWRs will probably continue for a couple of decades at least. But in talking about fuel, it helps to look at its entire history and what options exist for how it is used.

It begins with mining and refining of uranium ore, which yields a bright yellow or orange powder known as *yellowcake*. As we've noted, the composition of this material is 99.3 percent U-238 and only 0.7 percent of the fissionable isotope U-235. Enrichment to 3–5 percent U-235 cannot be done with chemistry, because the two isotopes are chemically identical. Several different kinds of industrial processes have been developed to separate them by other means, the most widely used employing gas centrifuges.

The process starts by turning yellow cake into a gas, uranium hexafluoride (UF_6). This is injected into centrifuges about 13–18 ft (4–6 m) tall, often rotating 90,000 times per minute. Spinning forces a portion of the heavier U-238 toward the outside, with the lighter U-235 left behind, closer to the center. Each centrifuge does only a tiny part of the job. In an enrichment plant, there are thousands arranged in parallel banks or "cascades," so that when the slightly enriched portion of gas leaves one centrifuge is sent to another in the next bank, and so on. The time needed to enrich a particular amount of UF_6 to a specific U-235 level depends on factors like how much starting material there is, how many centrifuges there are, of what size and technology, and so on. In round figures, a given (not small) quantity of UF_6 can be enriched to 3.5 percent in several months with current centrifuge technology, and to 90 percent (weapons grade) in less than a year. But again, this can vary greatly depending on technology.

An important division is made between low enriched uranium (LEU) and highly enriched uranium (HEU). Based on proliferation considerations, it defines 20 percent as the lower limit of HEU. The reason is not that a bomb can be made at this level of enrichment (it would need a ton or so of uranium!), but because it represents the greater amount of effort needed to produce weapons grade material, 90 percent or above. This is why the IAEA and the Non-Proliferation Treaty seek to prevent any nonweapon nation from enriching to 20 percent and above and why, in the particular case of Iran, the finalized nuclear deal involved removing all 20 percent uranium and down-blending it to less than 5 percent. We might recall, too, that enrichment was by far the greatest challenge of the Manhattan Project: to produce the 62 kg (137 lbs) of 83 percent U-235 that went into the Little Boy bomb took four tons of uranium ore, a gigantic building that needed, by one estimate, nearly 10 percent of US total electricity, and 12,000 people to work the centrifuge system [7].

For commercial reactor fuel, the LEU is converted to uranium dioxide (UO_2), forming a black powder that is mixed with a bit of ceramic binder and pressed into cylindrical pellets about 1 cm in diameter and 1 cm long. *Fuel pellets* are made small for a reason: UO_2 is limited in its ability to conduct heat, the ultimate goal, and this ability can be maximized by making the volume relatively small and the surface area large (conversely, a large chunk of fuel would retain most of its heat internally). In a way, this little piece of terrestrial material, not much bigger than a vitamin pill, represents the endpoint of the Rutherford atom: with as much energy content as nearly a ton of coal, it argues for a release of society from that nineteenth-century carbon source.

Before they can be used, fuel pellets are heated to about 1,700°C, so that they solidify by partial melting (sintering). They are then packed into a thin, hollow tube called a *fuel rod* (also: fuel pin), 3–5 m (10–16 ft) tall. Fuel rods are made from a special alloy of the element zirconium, chosen because of its toughness and ability to both withstand and conduct heat. This fuel *cladding*, as it's called, is an essential barrier between the fuel and the water coolant in the core. Thus, it also separates fuel from whatever the water touches, like the components of the pressure vessel, piping, valves, and more. The cladding also places certain limits on LWR performance: because it begins to corrode above 350°C, these reactors cannot operate at the high temperatures needed for efficiencies of 40 percent or more.

About 160–265 fuel rods are bundled into a single *fuel assembly*, a kind of frame holding the fuel rods close together in a square or hexagonal pattern. A fuel assembly, weighing about half a ton, is the basic component of the reactor core, which has between 120 and 195 assemblies (60–87 tons). In addition, a fuel assembly will also have empty slots where *control rods* can be inserted, either by gravity from above or mechanical force from below. Control rods absorb neutrons: when lowered into the core, they slow the rate of fission; when raised, they increase it. Elements useful for this purpose include isotopes of boron, silver, cadmium, indium, and hafnium. Taken as a whole, the production of heat and electricity in a reactor is a carefully modulated process. Enrichment level, arrangement of fuel rods, and use of control rods can all be part of this. But on a more immediate level, some other factors related to temperature (thermal feedback, actually) are used to govern reactor stability. For example, allowing the core temperature to rise will make the fuel expand, which causes the chain reaction to slow down. This works with water, too, which loses some of its moderating capability when it thermally expands. It also happens that the neutron-capturing ability of U-238 increases with temperature, also slowing the reaction. Thus, reactor stability is maintained in a number of ways.

One point to consider: beginning with the fuel pellet itself, a nuclear reactor can be defined as a system of containments. Fuel pellets are sealed and sintered and held within zirconium alloy, which, in its fuel assembly is surrounded by water, which slows and absorbs neutrons. All of this, the reactor core, exists within a thick steel container, known as the *reactor pressure vessel* (RPV), specially designed to resist corrosion and thermal expansion and coated on the inside with a material able to reduce the effects of neutron and other particle bombardment. These effects, including a phenomenon known as embrittlement, counter each other in part but will accumulate over decades and eventually limit the lifespan of an RPV. In a great majority of cases, this lifespan is now understood to be fifty to sixty years or even more, the original forty-year span for licensing having been decided for financial reasons (total loan payment). However, examples of corrosion and small-scale cracking have made it clear that RPV monitoring and inspections need to be done on a regular basis. The reactor vessel exists within a thick, 1.2-m (4-ft) containment shell made of reinforced concrete, a good neutron-absorber. Surrounding this containment, finally, is the reactor building itself. There are also ditches, berms, and channels around the margins of a plant to catch and contain any fluids that might leak from the power-generating system.

The concept of a *nuclear fuel cycle* is an essential one for understanding what happens to any batch of fuel and what can be done to maximize the amount of energy derived from it. The front end of the fuel cycle includes everything we have been talking about – the mining, conversion to UF_6, enrichment, fuel fabrication, and loading into a reactor. The back end of the fuel cycle includes storing spent fuel, then either keeping it in storage or sending it to a facility for *reprocessing*, where plutonium and remaining U-235 are separated out and used to make new fuel, thus *closing* the fuel cycle. This needs a bit more discussion.

Fuel can last from eighteen to thirty-six months, depending on reactor type and operation. Every two years or so, therefore, the reactor is shut down and refueled. Spent fuel assemblies are removed by an overhead crane and placed in a nearby spent fuel pool, where they remain under meters of water for three to five years, sometimes longer. Initially, spent fuel is highly radioactive and hot due to fission products with short half-lives. After several years, most of these have decayed away, so the spent fuel is no longer hot and is less dangerous. It is now put into interim storage. If not recycled, it will be stored in a manner that can last decades, for example in a cask of concrete with internal shielding. It can then be permanently stored in an underground repository, if one exists, or left onsite in a special protected area. This is called a *once-through* or *open* fuel cycle. It leaves around 95 percent of the energy content in the original fuel unused.

To recover more of this energy, the fuel can be recycled. There are two possible stages of this recycling, and these make up the back end of the fuel cycle. The first stage involves reprocessing. As mentioned, spent fuel goes to a facility where the 1.0–1.5 percent of generated plutonium is separated (reprocessed) and used to make new fuel. Reprocessed U-235 can be used to make new LEU. Reprocessed plutonium, on the other hand, is not pure Pu-239 but includes several other Pu isotopes. It is blended with depleted uranium to create a fuel known as MOX ("mixed oxide" fuel). Such fuel makes up about 5 percent of the global total used in any specific year. A second possible stage of recycling, rarely pursued at present, involves the remaining uranium, mainly U-238, that made up at least 95 percent of the original fuel. It is now down to about 93 percent, counting the 5 percent of fission products and the 2 percent of reprocessed uranium and plutonium. Nearly all of that 93 percent can be chemically processed and used as a "blanket" in what is called a *fast reactor*. This does not have a moderator and thus employs fast neutrons to breed plutonium in this blanket, thus creating new fuel and getting far more out of the original spent fuel. Fast reactors, however, have only been rarely used to date, though they will likely become much more common in coming decades. Recycling spent fuel, meantime, is said to *close the fuel cycle*.

Reprocessing, meanwhile, has been a subject of debate and controversy since it was first conceived. Advantages include reducing the total amount of nuclear waste and increasing the energy recovered from the original fuel by up to 90 percent. These are true benefits, without doubt. Disadvantages center on the separation and storage of plutonium (not yet converted into MOX), which is felt to pose risks both as a highly toxic material and a lure to proliferation by nations or terrorists. As discussed elsewhere in this book, plutonium is not more toxic than a number of chemicals with wide use in many countries (forms of cyanide in gold mining, for example). Proliferation concerns are more serious and legitimate. Yet total volumes, in actual size, are quite small and should not be difficult to keep secure – the 270 tons of plutonium from civilian reprocessing over fifty years by various nations would fit in a single-car garage.

Nonetheless, reprocessing is today performed by only six of the thirty nations with nuclear power. In the 1950s, scientists believed that it would be necessary before long, because there was very little natural uranium to be found on Earth. They were wrong about that, quite wrong in fact. The truth was that very little exploration had been done for uranium, and when it got underway in a serious manner, much more began to be discovered in a number of nations, including Canada, the US, South Africa, Australia, and Russia. In fact, so much uranium was discovered that reprocessing became economically unnecessary. Still, six countries have proceeded ahead with it.

These include France, UK, Russia, India, Japan, and China. The US stopped the practice after India used reprocessed plutonium from a research reactor to build a weapon, conducting a test ("Smiling Buddha") in May of 1974. The reactor had been constructed by Canada, using heavy water supplied by the US. Because the US had helped build research reactors in many nations by that time, and because the NPT allowed any member nation to reprocess spent fuel, President Jimmy Carter decided in 1977 to halt civilian reprocessing and set an example that would help prevent further weapons proliferation. This move did not persuade any of the nations listed above from going ahead with the technology. For other countries, it may have had some clout, but at least as important was the cheap price of uranium. This alone provided little incentive to build expensive reprocessing facilities and generate more costly secondary fuel. US policy, meanwhile, was continued until 1999, when the US Department of Energy contracted the building of a MOX fabrication plant at the government's Savannah River nuclear reservation. Intended as a means to meet conditions of a treaty with Russia to reduce surplus plutonium (military origin) in the US, the project encountered delays and cost overruns, such that its future at this writing appears uncertain.

The radioactivity in spent fuel produces what is called *decay heat*. Such heat is mainly generated by short-lived fission products. It is always present, in other words, and will take over any time a reactor shuts down and fission stops. If the cooling system stops working for some reason, decay heat will either boil away the water or, if water is under pressure, heat it up so that the pressure increases, possibly to dangerous levels. If the coolant water boils away, fuel is exposed and heats up very rapidly. In about twenty to thirty minutes, it can reach 1,200°C, where the zirconium cladding begins to burst, releasing fuel particles. If there is steam, oxidation of the cladding is happening as well, releasing hydrogen gas. Within another hour or so, temperatures will approach 1,900°C, where the cladding melts and dissolves part of the fuel into a growing lava known as corium. Because hydrogen is a source of explosions (Fukushima) and melted fuel has some potential to burn through the reactor containment structure, new reactor designs have systems to deal with both possibilities. These include simple technologies to vent or chemically store any hydrogen gas and to capture and isolate corium melt.

Besides such advances, there are also ongoing efforts to create new fuel technologies able to improve reactor performance and reduce costs. Some of this work focuses on fuel that would have a significantly higher melting temperature than conventional ceramic-uranium pellets. This would extend the length of time in a loss-of-coolant accident before the fuel begins to melt, thereby providing more opportunity to reestablish cooling and prevent a meltdown. Another approach has involved a different type of fuel rod made not of uranium oxide pellets packed into a tube but of solid metal alloy, blending uranium and zirconium and shaped into a four-lobe rod whose cross section resembles a + sign and that is twisted into a licorice-like spiral. The increased surface area of the fuel in contact with water allows for a better transfer of heat and thus an increase in power production. Moreover, with a sufficient amount of zirconium in the alloy, the metal fuel will not swell, as conventional fuel pellets do because of the buildup in fission products, which include gases. Such swelling decreases the efficiency of heat transfer and reduces how long the fuel can remain in the reactor. A different way to address the issue is to make fuel pellets porous, and this defines another area of research and innovation.

Everything discussed to this point relates to only one type of fuel and fuel cycle, involving U-235. There are other fuel cycles as well, involving fissionable isotopes of plutonium, thorium, and some other heavy elements. One of these that has attracted a great deal of attention in the nuclear industry and energy circles is related to thorium fuel. Thorium-232 is not a fuel itself but is fertile and can be "primed" with neutrons to become U-233, which is fissionable. This can be done in a reactor with graphite as moderator, and it can be done in a liquid form, as thorium-fluoride molten salt. Thorium has certain advantages over uranium, and they are not trivial. It is three to four times more abundant in nature (even produced as a waste product in the mining of rare earth metals) and requires no enrichment, though it does need a small amount of enriched fissile material to start up. A thorium molten salt reactor would require a small fraction of the fissile material and would produce far less waste, which would also be radioactive for a much shorter time. Because it does not breed a large surplus of U-233 and produces only small amounts of plutonium, mostly Pu-238, a molten salt design arguably reduces proliferation concerns. In addition, such a reactor could be refueled while operating and achieve higher efficiencies (45–50 percent) than current reactors (~33 percent).

While there are still other advantages that have convinced many observers, there are also drawbacks. Undoubtedly the greatest of these is the lack of experience with such reactors and thus the need for pilot, demonstration, and experimental full-scale versions. An early prototype operated from 1965–1969 at the Oak Ridge National Laboratory (US) under the capable direction of Alvin Weinberg proved the concept of such a reactor (called the Molten Salt Experimental Reactor), it was shut down after completing its mission. Planned follow-up work, however, was canceled by the Nixon Administration, due in part to political considerations favoring the liquid metal fast breeder program. After forty-five years, such work has finally begun under new management. This includes some effort at Oak Ridge itself in partnership with state-owned nuclear companies in China.

Waste and Waste Disposal

The term "nuclear waste" applies to any material no longer used that is radioactive. This includes medical, industrial, military, and power-plant-related material. Globally speaking, different countries have used their own definitions for types of waste. Yet a majority of schemes recognize three main categories.

– *Low-level waste* (LLW) includes lightly contaminated materials like clothing, lab supplies, filters, and other solid matter. Radioactivity in LLW decreases rapidly within months. It is about 90 percent of all nuclear waste by volume.

– *Intermediate-level waste* (ILW) is solid and liquid material radioactive
  enough to need shielding. It includes components from inside the reactor
  vessel, chemical sludges, fuel cladding. Such waste is treated and packed
  into steel drums, then sent to a repository. The US does not use "ILW" as
  a category.
– *High-level waste* (HLW) includes spent nuclear fuel, waste from
  reprocessing, some military waste, and small volumes from medical isotope
  production (in research reactors). HLW is highly radioactive and heat-
  producing and requires special shielding. It comprises 3 percent of the total
  volume of nuclear waste but has 95 percent of the radioactivity. The great
  majority of HLW is spent fuel.

Most attention tends to focus on HLW, and not without reason. As noted,
spent fuel from civilian power reactors makes up the great majority of this. To
review, spent fuel from a LWR consists of about 95 percent U-238, ~1 percent
U-235, 1–1.5 percent plutonium isotopes, 3–5 percent fission products, plus
about 0.1–0.15 percent minor actinides. This last group, the minor actinides,
include heavy metallic elements of atomic number 89 (actinium) to 103
(lawrencium), except for major actinides uranium and plutonium. Minor
actinides generally have long half-lives and so pose the longest-term hazards.
Most radioactive of all, however, are fission products, which resulted from the
breaking apart of U-235 nuclei. Most are short-lived, with half-lives under
30 years, and some under a week (recall: the shorter an isotope's half-life, the
more radioactive it is).

HLW is extremely hazardous material when fresh. Less than a minute's
exposure to unshielded spent fuel right from the reactor, at a distance of several
meters, would be fatal. While its radioactivity declines rapidly, it remains
harmful for millennia. Even more radioactive is the liquid waste left over
from reprocessing. It does not *stay* dangerously radioactive for more than
about three centuries, and is thus far better than spent fuel in those terms. But
it is still very nasty stuff in the meantime. Such is why we have innovative ways
to immobilize it in the form of a glass-like solid or artificial rock.

At the same time, the volume of HLW is petite. In weight, roughly 280,000
tons have been amassed over sixty years. Compared to any other type of
industrial waste, this is tiny. That 280,000 tons is quite dense, averaging about
10–11 g/cm^3 (density of lead is 11.3). We can imagine the total HLW volume as
covering a single soccer field to a depth of about 18 m (60 ft). This compares to
millions of tons of far less dense but highly toxic chemical wastes produced
worldwide each year.

No really serious technical problems exist for disposing of HLW. Scientists and engineers have long decided the best method is to store it underground in a geologic repository, preferably below the water table and any aquifers. This doesn't mean "deep" underground, as often said. Most proposals are for storage sites less than 2,000 m (6,600 ft); oil and gas wells are often several times this, while some mines are below 3,000 m (9,900 ft). Host rock for a repository should also be naturally sealing, made of impermeable rock, like salt, certain shales, or granite. By these terms, the Yucca Mountain site in Nevada, until recently the chosen site for a US repository, doesn't do very well. It lies above the water table, in fractured volcanic material, and in an overall oxidizing environment.

Geologic disposal, however, makes perfect sense. This is particularly true, given that 9 billion gallons (34 billion liters) of industrial waste, much of it toxic and some of it lethally so, is stored thousands of meters/feet underground in specific formations *each year*. There are certainly other specifications needed for an HLW repository: isolation from inhabited areas and low geologic activity are the big ones (the second of which is also not met very well by Yucca). But to put the matter succinctly, permanent disposal of nuclear waste is not a scientific-engineering problem. It might be called a political problem instead. But the greater truth holds that it remains a problem of public fear and distrust of authorities. This is commonly known as the challenge of "social acceptability." It is a nice euphemism. Fear and distrust, however, remain a very real and ironic barrier to permanent waste disposal, especially in democratic nations where transparency, accountability, and respect for the views of affected groups are required for any repository project. Even when these requirements have been met, efforts have been often thwarted to locate a final resting place for HLW. Ultimately, there is no victory in such rejection: the waste stays above ground, far more vulnerable than if stored at depth.

There are exceptions, however, notable ones. Two advanced nations with high environmental standards and public awareness have moved forward with nuclear repositories. Finland in 2004 began work on a facility at Olkiluoto, a small island and nuclear power plant site on the country's southwest coast. Olkiluoto is already home to a shallow repository (60–100 m/180–330 ft depth), for LLW and ILW. The new repository, to open in 2020, will be a series of horizontal tunnels in the same granitic rock about 430 m (1,420 ft) below ground. An above-ground plant will encapsulate spent fuel rods in copper canisters filled with argon gas (copper resists corrosion; argon is chemically inert). Holes will be bored into the floor of each tunnel and the canisters lowered into them, with plugs of bentonite clay below and above to seal against water. When all canisters are in place, the tunnel will be filled with clay blocks and its entrance closed with a cement plug. The cost will be about

€3.5 billion ($5.3 billion, 2016 dollars). As for social acceptability, people in the area have had a nuclear power plant at Olkiluoto for decades and are in favor of the project. They believe the waste will be safer a thousand feet underground, carefully contained, than if sitting in plain sight.

Sweden, meanwhile, has plans for a similar facility at Forsmark, on its eastern coast. As in the Finnish example, Forsmark has one of the country's nuclear plants as well as a repository for LLW and ILW. The same basic design is planned for a depth of about 500 m (1,520 ft). In this case, the granitic rock is fractured but has been stable, in terms of major movement or heating, for millions of years, with fracture waters posing no risk for the bentonite or copper canisters. At this writing, the license application isn't complete, though it has passed review by an international team of experts. The matter of social acceptability is not a problem; a critical point is that local people believe the authorities involved are trustworthy [8]. Both Olkiluoto and Forsmark repositories are designed for 100,000 years, in order to endure one or more future glacial ages.

Could Sweden and Finland serve as precedents for other nations? Definitely yes. They have demonstrated that "social acceptability" will be greatly aided by involving affected residents from an early stage. Regulators must appear independent and accountable; public trust is fundamental. And such trust has proven to depend on people being informed, on having their concerns and questions answered truthfully, and on being treated with respect. This last, in fact, has been proven with respect to another underground repository, the Waste Isolation Pilot Plant (WIPP) located in southeastern New Mexico. Opened in 1999, WIPP handles transuranic waste from the manufacture of nuclear weapons, not spent fuel from civilian power reactors. Yet, the important point here is that the local community remains strongly in favor of the facility, despite several minor accidents, due in part to the large amount of information provided and the involvement of local officials in certain areas of decision-making. In combination with the Scandinavian examples, WIPP highlights past errors by efforts that have emphasized technical and scientific matters at the expense of local issues. Selecting sites where nuclear facilities already exist and have been accepted by the community seems another useful criterion.

Another example of success, with a caveat, is offered by South Korea. This nation has had a particularly difficult time locating any kind of repository, in part due to an authoritarian approach. The government in 2005 changed course, inviting interest from towns that *wanted* such a facility (and had the geology to make one feasible). A referendum was held, with the town showing the highest level of public support being chosen. This was Gyeongju, in the southeastern part of the country, close to the Wolseong Nuclear Station. Having opened in

2015, the repository is for LLW and ILW, at a depth of 100–130 m (330–430 ft), possibly a first step toward a deeper HLW site. The Korean government ended up sweetening the deal with a subsidy of about $230 million and the promise of locating a major corporate headquarters locally.

National efforts like these are limited, since not every country has the right geological conditions said to be needed for a repository. A different approach, put forward by the IAEA, is to have one or more international sites operated on a commercial basis. One location recently proposed is in the state of South Australia. This seems an excellent choice, given the long-term geologic stability of the continent and the options in granitic and other well-suited host rock. There are ethical grounds as well: having long resisted nuclear power, Australia is nonetheless a top exporter of uranium (a seeming "hypocrisy" widely recognized in the country). In 2016, the South Australian Royal Commission into the Nuclear Fuel Cycle released a study in favor of building a repository, on conditions that the state own the facility, to ensure any generated wealth would be equitably dispersed, and that there be local consent. Whether or not a site will result, a valuable new precedent has been set for discussing waste disposal.

These efforts sound excellent. Rationally conceived, based on solid science, they are motivated by a commitment to protecting the public and the environment. Indeed, all the thought, study, and work needed to ensure such waste will be isolated from contact with living things for 100,000 years testifies to this commitment. And yet, from another viewpoint, such endeavors can only seem incredible. Is nuclear waste so much more deadly than every other hazardous material that it requires exponentially greater effort and expense? Almost certainly, more scientific study, political struggle, and money have been expended on behalf of nuclear waste than all other forms of toxic disposal combined. No such repositories exist for the many millions of gallons of lethal chemical wastes injected below ground, nor for the mercury, lead, selenium, and arsenic in coal ash that is left in tailings ponds, landfills, and abandoned mines, and whose toxicity *never* declines. Indeed, a nuclear waste repository could be rightly called an embodiment of fear, wrapped in anxiety, buried in dread.

In the US, the story has been one long tale of expensive failure. Yucca Mountain was chosen as the single repository site in the 1980s, when Nevada had little political influence in the US Congress. All other candidate states had found ways to bow out of the process. Thirty years later, Nevada's senator Harry Reid had become majority leader of the Senate and demanded of President Obama, who needed powerful allies in an exceptionally hostile Congress, that Yucca be put on a shelf. It was – after a total of $15 billion had been spent on studying it over the decades. Given this, we might wonder, was the site ever suitable in the first place? A new and different chapter in this long, sad story might be written, however, in the form of studies exploring the possibility of storing waste in liquid form, using deep disposal wells.

Here we enter interesting territory. What radiation standards were established? These might well be applied to any sites chosen in the future. The numbers are these: an upper limit of 0.15 mSv per year (~1.5 chest x-rays) above natural background for the first 10,000 years, rising to 1.0 mSv/yr until 1 million years has passed. Natural background is about 3.5 mSv/yr at Yucca, so the ceiling for the first 10,000 years is 3.65 mSv and 4.5 mSv for the next 990,000 years. This compares with 6 mSv/yr average for the US public from both natural and medical exposure. Meanwhile, natural background in the city of Denver (Colorado) averages 5 mSv. How is it, then, that we have dose standards for a million years to "protect" a desert area where nobody lives, yet "allow" people to inhabit a major city where levels are above those same standards? Or, to use another comparison, what are the standards used at WIPP, the operating repository for transuranic waste from nuclear weapons in southeast New Mexico? Workers here, in fact, are held to a maximum limit of 50 mSv per year – *50 times* the limit at Yucca Mountain.

Reactor Designs – Yesterday, Today, and Tomorrow

It happens that the primary goals of generating heat with fission and controlling it with a cooling system can be achieved by many different reactor designs – hundreds, in fact. This is due to the large number of possibilities for fuel, moderator, and coolant. By far the most common designs in use today and since the early stage of commercial nuclear power are known as "light water reactors" (LWR). The term "light" distinguishes them from "heavy water" models (HWR), which the Canadians have developed as CANDU (Canada Natural Uranium Deuterium). LWRs (and HWRs) employ water as moderator and coolant. This might seem clever and efficient, but it has some limitations and drawbacks, too. Every design has its pros and cons, just as every energy source does.

Reactor designs are divided into generations – Gen I, II, III, III+, IV – based on chronology and technology. Gen 1 were prototypes built in the 1950s and early 60s, before commercialization. Gen II were the first fully commercial designs, mainly LWRs and CANDU, with a few others like the British gas-cooled, graphite-moderated design (Magnox), and the Soviet RBMK, a problematic LWR involved in the Chernobyl accident. Gen II last from the 1960s to the early 1990s and today represent about 80 percent of all operating reactors. Many Gen II designs were used for just a few reactors. This made first-of-a-kind builds common, adding significantly to costs. Beginning in the mid-late 1990s, Gen III brought more advanced LWR designs, with better thermal efficiency, passive safety systems (no human action needed), and standardization. There are not many of these yet operating (2016), due to few reactor orders in Europe and the US China, however, is building a number of them.

The division between Gen III and III+ designs is somewhat arbitrary. Gen III+ take the improvements of Gen III a few steps further. Though LWR designs, they represent a series of major advances over Gen II. Not only do they use fuel more efficiently, reduce waste, and deliver more power, they are simpler, modular, and have more complete passive safety systems that rely on natural convection of heat or use gravity for supplying emergency coolant. Companies in number of countries, particularly France, Japan, South Korea, Russia, Canada, China, and the US, have produced Gen III/III+ designs, often in collaboration (sharing of "best ideas"). One of the more popular designs is by Westinghouse (owned by Toshiba): the AP1000 (AP = "Advanced Passive"), with 1.1 GW capacity. This is an LWR with all of the above advantages, plus a small footprint that requires far fewer components and only one-fifth the amount of steel and cement as Gen II designs. With some upgrades and adaptations, the AP1000 is the basis for twelve reactors under construction: four in China, four in the United Arab Emirates (see Chapter 11), and four in the US. Both China and South Korea have created their own, scaled-up versions of the design in the CAP1400 and APR1400, both with 1.4 GW capacity.

Gen IV designs represent an entirely different future for nuclear power stations. Unlike previous generations, a number of these designs have emerged not from company boardrooms but instead from an independent body called the Generation IV International Forum, founded in 2000. In this case, a hundred experts from various nations evaluated a total of 130 reactor concepts before selecting six primary designs. Criteria included sustainability, cost, safety, proliferation resistance, and security from attack. A key objective is to eliminate any concern about long-term fuel supply. Three of the designs are fast reactors with helium, lead, and sodium as coolants. Others are molten salt, very high temperature gas, and supercritical water reactors. Some of these designs, such as sodium-cooled and molten salt reactors, were demonstrated in the 1950s and 60s in the US but were never commercialized. Most Gen IV concepts are forecast to have a closed fuel cycle and to use some of their heat for non-power purposes, such as producing hydrogen gas. Closed fuel cycles would involve such processes as reprocessing, breeding, and fuel fabrication to be done onsite, thus with no need to transport any fuel material.

Added to these designs are those created by smaller innovative companies that have similar criteria but may focus on one or another advantage in particular, such as sustainability (long-term operation without refueling) or nonproliferation. At the present time, several Gen IV designs are in the testing and prototype phase, particularly in China and Russia, with India, Europe, and South Korea also planning such work.

One final technology that deserves mention, as it has received considerable attention in the past decade, is the small modular reactor, or SMR. As the same suggests, these are much reduced in size, with compact designs for producing 25–300 MW and for being manufactured in factories and rapidly assembled on site. Most designs have reactors largely or entirely underground and able to operate without refueling for five years or longer. Individual sites can install single or multiple reactor units. Due to their small size, sites can be located in areas where a large-scale power station is not feasible. Among the many specific applications are dedicated power for industries, urban districts, rural areas away from a grid, mining and other isolated operations, oil refineries, military bases and installations, and ports. SMRs are also appropriate for adding power to small and fragile grids that exist in many developing nations. Finally, these reactors might find use as backup or baseload support for renewables, creating 100 percent noncarbon systems.

There are several key ideas behind the interest in SMRs. They can greatly lower the negative effect of large capital costs for building a nuclear plant. They also provide improved flexibility and simplified designs with reduced operation and maintenance, plus reduced proliferation risks. Also in the minds of company CEOs is the goal of raising public acceptance: whether "small is beautiful," it is likely to be viewed as less threatening or risky. Between these ideas that apply mainly to advanced nations, and the possibility that tremendous opportunity exists in developing nations too, the time may indeed be right for the SMR. At this writing, very few SMRs are yet operating but dozens of companies have moved forward assertively. By 2020, a number should be under construction in North America and Europe, with others in China, Russia, India, and South Korea already operating. Though most designs are for LWR, there are others for fast reactors and high-temperature gas-cooled types.

The following describe a number of reactor designs now in use and in various stages of demonstration for the future.

Pressurized Water Reactor (PWR): This is the most common reactor operating today, comprising about 65 percent of the global fleet. It has a core typically enriched to 3–5 percent U-235 and two recycling water systems, or coolant loops. The first of these loops cycles through the core and is kept under pressure so water reaches a temperature of about 315°C and doesn't boil. Instead, water in this primary loop passes through a heat exchanger – essentially, a series of pipes in a chamber of cooler water – to produce steam that then goes to the turbine-generator. CANDU versions of this basic design are known as pressurized heavy water reactors, or PHWR.

Boiling Water Reactor (BWR): The second most common design in use, BWRs are about 18 percent of the global fleet. In design, they are similar to PWRs except that they have only one coolant loop. Water in this loop is at a lower pressure and allowed to boil, creating the steam to drive the turbine-generator. It is then sent to the condenser and cooled back to a liquid that is recycled to the reactor core. To remove radioactive material it may have picked up, the water passes through a series of dense filters. BWR usually refers to Gen II designs, while the *advanced boiling water reactor*, ABWR, is Gen III (four exist).

Gas-Cooled Reactor (GCR): Pioneered by the British, this design uses graphite as a moderator and carbon dioxide as coolant. As of 2016, there were around fourteen such reactors in operation. With gas as a coolant, higher temperatures can be used (up to about 650°C in existing models but higher in future designs). The CO_2 circulates from the core to a steam generator (again, pipes filled with water), with steam going to a condenser and then recycled. Advanced designs, particularly the *high temperature gas-cooled reactor* (HTGR), operate at temperatures up to around 900°C, use CO_2 or helium gas as coolant, and may have two steam generators placed inside the reactor vessel. Elevated temperatures allow HTGRs to achieve thermal efficiencies as high as 45–50 percent. This also requires special materials compared to other reactors.

Fast Neutron Reactors (FNR): This is a category of reactors that do not include a moderator and use a dense core to generate a large supply of neutrons. About twenty such reactors have been built since the 1950s, with the longest operating example in Russia (at Beloyarsk, since 1980). Nearly all have been experimental. They have proven challenging and expensive to build and also controversial in some countries because of their ability to "breed" plutonium (proliferation worries). Yet FNRs also have potent advantages. When a "blanket" of fresh U-238 or spent LEU fuel (~95 percent U-238) is added, the fast neutrons convert U-238 into Pu-239. Such fast breeder reactors (FBR) can create more fuel than they consume, offering the potential for many centuries of power production. They can also burn as fuel the heavier, longer-lived minor actinides in LEU waste, thus reducing the time such waste is highly radioactive from hundreds of thousands to only hundreds of years. For these reasons, FBRs were originally part of an overall plan to move to plutonium as main fuel in nuclear power. Be that as it may, the benefits of FNRs argue strongly for advanced designs that avoid past difficulties, and indeed several such designs are currently in development with the goals of nonproliferation, higher efficiency, burning of actinides, and generation of heat for multiple purposes.

Sodium-Cooled Fast Reactors (SFR): This design, a type of FNR, uses liquid sodium metal as coolant. Sodium has distinct advantages, as it absorbs very few neutrons and is an excellent conductor of heat. It is also noncorrosive and has a low melting point (98°C) but a high boiling point (887°C), so it remains a liquid over a wide temperatures range and won't boil away, exposing the core. It also doesn't need to be pressurized, a significant cost and safety benefit. SFRs can burn a diversity of fuels: LEU, actinides, MOX, plutonium. SFR breeder reactors, a type of *liquid metal fast breeder*, generate their own fuel. Sodium, however, is highly reactive with air or water and requires special design features to prevent leaks. One SFR breeder, the Monju reactor in Japan, had leakage problems and has been viewed as evidence the technology is dangerous and unreliable. Countering this is the less well known but more significant EBR-II (Experimental Breeder Reactor-II), a prototype that operated safely and reliably for thirty years (1965–1994) in southern Idaho. EBR-II was even put through a worst-case experiment involving a loss of coolant flow at full power, yet the system shut itself down within minutes, proving the ultimate safety of the design. This capability, which also exists in the MSR, has attracted a great deal of attention in the nuclear community for its long-term promise. Yet, in its day, striking one of the more profound ironies of nuclear history, the EBR-II event took place in early 1986 and was on the verge of being widely reported when Chernobyl occurred.

Molten Salt Reactors (MSR): Between 1965 and 1969, Alvin Weinberg, then director of the US Oak Ridge National Laboratory, successfully demonstrated a reactor using uranium fuel dissolved in liquid fluoride salt coolant. Fission occurs within the coolant, whose temperature increases to a prescribed level (e.g. ~700°C) without being pressurized (an important point). It goes to a heat exchanger, where it is cooled by a secondary loop of molten salt, free of radioactive matter, while the primary loop undergoes chemical processing to remove neutron-absorbing matter. Heat in the secondary loop can then be used to generate steam and run a turbine and do other work as well. This basic set up means an MSR cannot melt down (as it is already "melted") or build up pressure, and any leak of fuel-coolant solidifies, preventing radioactive mate-rial from spreading. If built as a fast reactor, an MSR can burn the actinides (including plutonium) that fission produces. A special type of MSR is *the liquid fluoride thorium reactor* (LFTR), noted previously. This involves breeding Th-232 into U-233, with both isotopes dissolved in the liquid fluoride salt.

This salt is chemically stable and does not interact violently with air or water the way sodium does.

A Brief Word at the End

We have come a long way from Ernest Rutherford and the dynamic atom he helped introduce to the world. Rutherford in middle age did not believe nuclear energy would be practical. Had he lived another decade, into the late 1940s, he might well have played some role in the Manhattan Project and, in the company of Fermi et al., would have found much reason to change his mind.

Sadly, Rutherford died before the truth of fission and the chain reaction it makes possible had been proven. In a way, these discoveries were the culmination of what he had started. Finding that the nucleus of an atom is solid and hard and will return an alpha particle "as if you fired a 15-inch shell at a piece of tissue paper and it came back and hit you," Rutherford began a great circle that closed when Lise Meitner and Otto Frisch realized the same nucleus could be split, releasing an unimaginable amount of energy.

It was one great circle to open another. Nuclear energy for productive human use was born directly from the greatest era in the history of physics, and something of this brilliance is repeated in the ingenuity expressed by nuclear technology today. It is clear that this ingenuity will not cease anytime soon. There is much to anticipate.

References

[1] M. Howorth, *Pioneer Researcher on the Atom: The Life Story of Frederick Soddy* (London: New World, 1958), p. 83.

[2] A. S. Eve, *Life and Letters of the Rt. Honorable Lord Rutherford* (Cambridge, UK: Cambridge University Press, 1939), pp. 80–81.

[3] E. N. da C. Andrade, *Rutherford and the Nature of the Atom* (Garden City, NY: Anchor, 1964), p. 111.

[4] F. Soddy, *Matter and Energy* (New York: Henry Holt, 1912), pp. 15–16.

[5] L. Meitner and O. R. Frisch, Products of the Fission of the Uranium Nucleus, *Nature*, 143 (March 18, 1939), 471–471, 472.

[6] R. L. Sime, *Lise Meitner: A Life in Physics* (Oakland: University of California Press, 1990), p. 332.

[7] R. Rhodes, *The Making of the Atomic Bomb* (New York: Simon and Schuster, 1987), p. 647.

[8] A. Hedlin and O. Olsson, Crystalline Rock as a Repository for Swedish Spent Nuclear Fuel, *Elements*, 1:4 (August 2016), 247–252.

4

Nuclear Energy for Society: The Beginnings

The First Reactors

Despite a small chance of success, the world's first nuclear reactor proved able to operate cheaply and safely for a good many years, with almost no environmental impact and not a single breakdown or equipment failure. If this seems impressive, consider that it existed 1.7 billion years ago in the Oklo area of southeastern Gabon, West Africa. At four closely linked sites, self-sustaining fission, in pulsed mode, continued here for roughly 150,000 years. We know this from detailed study of the Oklo uranium mine, which leaves little doubt about what happened. A natural accumulation of U-235 occurred in porous sands filled with water, which acted as moderator and coolant. When fission established a chain reaction, the water heated up until it boiled away, at which point the reaction stopped, only to begin again when enough water accumulated in the sandstone. At some point, the U-235 decreased to where a chain reaction was no longer possible. But after so many centuries, what about the waste? None of it migrated more than a dozen centimeters or so from the "core" [1].

Fast forward about two billion years, and planet Earth has 449 artificial reactors to generate power, the great majority of which also use water as both moderator and coolant. The light water reactor (LWR), both in its boiling and pressurized versions (BWR and PWR), accounts for nearly 80 percent of all civilian nuclear plants, plus hundreds more research and naval propulsion reactors. While it may be replaced in the future as the favored design, it has dominated built reactors for nearly sixty years.

Given that a very large number of designs are possible for generating electricity, how did this one approach become so prevailing? The answer comes back to the early history of nuclear power in the US, where the LWR

95

was invented and developed as a general standard. Several other nations, particularly the UK, France, and Canada, nurtured their own designs, since the US, under the banner of military secrecy, refused to share its own technical information even with allies who had worked on the Manhattan Project. Yet these countries were by far the exception. By the early 1970s, other nations with nuclear programs had adopted the LWR as an option already commercialized by the world's most advanced scientific and technological, not to say industrial, superpower.

None of this means that the LWR was the inevitable or best choice. Many nuclear scientists and engineers felt then, and feel today, that it wasn't. Analysts point out it was more costly, therefore less economical in a time of low fossil fuel prices, than other designs [2–3]. Why it became "the chosen one" had less to do with technical factors than with institutional and social realities, particularly those related to the Eisenhower Administration and the newly formed Atomic Energy Commission. But in order to understand this, a fair amount of background context is needed.

We might begin with the first artificial reactor. As discussed in Chapter 2, this was built in a squash court under the stands of Stagg Field at the University of Chicago. It was under the direction and close watch of Enrico Fermi, as part of the Manhattan Project, in late 1942, a period in the war when the Germans and Japanese were still very much on the offensive, and succeeding. Fermi was one of the great physicists of the twentieth century, who had received the Nobel Prize in 1938 for his work on the absorption and diffusion of slow neutrons. He was a calming presence, rarely ruffled, one who inspired confidence in others. He was also known for a dry sense of humor. Asked after the war about Robert Oppenheimer and his directorship over the Manhattan Project scientists, Fermi commented, "He was simply unable to let things be foggy. Since they always are, this kept him pretty active."

The reactor Fermi built, known by the thrilling title of "Chicago Pile-1," or CP-1, was extremely simple compared to today's designs. It had a wooden frame supporting layers of graphite blocks (graphite being the moderator). There were alternating layers, with one being pure graphite and the next graphite embedded with slugs of uranium fuel. Vertical holes were drilled through the pile for control rods made of wood wrapped with cadmium foil (cadmium being a strong neutron absorber). These rods were largely worked by hand. A team on one side had the job of flooding the pile with cadmium salt solution if the control rods didn't stop the reaction. As it was an experiment, some amount of improvisation was needed. Fermi's original idea was that the pile had to be in the shape of a sphere, to maximize neutron capture. But he then calculated, based on the actual neutron flux, that far fewer layers were needed for a chain reaction. The final shape resembled a door knob: 6.1 m (20 ft) high and 7.6 m (25 ft) wide. The entire mass was enveloped in a thin balloon, which would have been filled with carbon dioxide if neutron radiation from the pile had reached a significant level. It never did [4].

At 3:25 p.m. on December 2, 1942, the pile went critical. Twenty-eight minutes later, at 3:53 p.m., Fermi signaled for the main control rod to be released into the pile. The chain reaction stopped, and the "Atomic Age" began. As Fermi later wrote:

> At this moment we knew that the self-sustaining reaction was underway. The event was not spectacular, no fuses burned, no lights flashed. But to us it meant that release of atomic energy on a large scale would be only a matter of time ... We hope that [with the end of the war] perhaps the building of power plants, production of radioactive elements for science and medicine would become the paramount objectives [5].

Something of this hope can be found, tempered though it may be, in the words of an epochal government act four years later, which turned over all further research in nuclear energy to a new body, the US Atomic Energy Commission (AEC). "It is reasonable to anticipate," Section 1 of the Atomic Energy Act of 1946 notes, "that tapping this new source of energy will cause profound changes in our present way of life." The bill had gone through several versions, with scientists speaking loudly against attempts to put the AEC under military control. A more civilian-centered bill ensued, only to be rendered more cautious, with military connections, as revelations emerged in early 1946 of nuclear information stolen and leaked to the Soviets. In its final iteration, the Act stated:

> [S]ubject at all times to the paramount objective of assuring the common defense and security, the development and utilization of atomic energy shall ... be directed toward improving the public welfare, increasing the standard of living, strengthening free competition in private enterprise, and promoting world peace [6].

The order in which these goals appear is not without historical meaning.

The Earliest Years

From its beginning, the war had forced people to think in such terms. Fascism and Japanese militarism had threatened huge parts of the world. This time, war had not been about alliances or sovereignty, but about national survival. Now that much of Europe and Japan lay smoldering in ash, their societies in need of rebuilding, it was inevitable that intelligent, hopeful individuals, scientists, and engineers (responsible for the weapon to end all weapons) perhaps most of all, would want to view the peaceful possibilities of nuclear energy as world-changing, even as they naively called for a new world government to banish the weapons made from it.

Such hopes were not lost on other nations. Britain, for example, began operating its own design, using graphite as moderator and air as coolant, as early as August of 1947, then followed with a second version in 1948. Canada opened its Chalk River, Ontario, research facility with an experimental heavy-water reactor in 1947. Another heavy-water design emerged in 1951 from a joint effort between Norway and the Netherlands. Since the US also had a monopoly on uranium enrichment, these other nations explored different pathways to reactor technology. Eisenhower's Atoms for Peace program, begun in 1954, changed everything, opening up US technology to others. Canada, however, continued to develop its own alternative approach, using heavy water and natural (nonenriched) uranium.

When was the first *designed* use of nuclear energy for power generation? This happened in Obninsk, a city southwest of Moscow, where a small power reactor (5 MW) called the APS-1 was built. Connected to the grid in June of 1954, the Obninsk reactor marked a big step in the creation of this Soviet "scientific city," as it was called, a site where there came to exist a collection of major research institutes focused on nuclear science and engineering. Such was part of the Soviet Union's own embrace of a hopeful future in this domain. It could not, however, compete with the gigantic weapons complex at Mayak, 1,700 km to the southeast, where facilities covering 90 km² were devoted to the production, refining, and weaponization of plutonium (and where several of the worst nuclear accidents and environmental contamination in history occurred). The Obninsk reactor, meanwhile, was "a dangerous mix of technologies," as it had "a coolant that could explode ('water turned to steam' and a moderator (graphite) that could catch fire"[7]. For such reasons, it would never have been built outside the Soviet Union. This was also true of its immediate successor, the RBMK (Reaktor Bolshoi Moshchnosty Kanalny, or high power channel reactor), whose similar problematic features would one day contribute to the disaster at Chernobyl.

The first commercial nuclear power plant went critical (established a fission chain reaction) and was connected to the national grid in England. This was in the second half of 1956. Located in Cumbria, along the northwest English coast, the Calder Hall 1 was treated as a great national achievement and cause for celebration. At 40–50 MW, it generated about eight times the power of the Obninsk reactor, using a graphite-moderate and gas-coolant design. The site, in a rural part of the country, soon was expanded to include a number of other reactors, a reprocessing facility, and more, as part of the Windscale-Sellafield complex. True to the mixed motives of the time, Calder Hall was actually built as a dual-use system like Obninsk, for production of plutonium and electricity. It fed power into the grid but at a low level compared to most of England's coal plants, which then accounted for over 95 percent of all power generation.

Finally, in 1957, the world's first civilian nuclear station opened in the US along the Ohio River in Beaver County, northwest Pennsylvania. The Shippingport reactor, an early part of President Eisenhower's Atoms for Peace program, was ironically located in the same region where the petroleum industry had begun a century earlier, in the 1860s. Built for around $79 million, Shippingport's pressurized water reactor (PWR) achieved criticality on December 2, 1957, exactly fifteen years to the day after CP-1, and began producing power to the grid a few weeks later. Though civilian in its use, the reactor core was actually taken from a cancelled aircraft carrier. It had highly enriched uranium (HEU), 93 percent U-235, instead of the 3–5 percent that became normal for a PWR. The reactor was built by Westinghouse for a cancelled project, in direct cooperation with the Division of Naval Reactors of the AEC. But undoubtedly the most impressive military connection at Shippingport regarded the man chosen to oversee its creation – Admiral Hyman Rickover, "father of the nuclear navy."

At the same time, Shippingport had some exotic, nonmilitary touches. Though built to produce power, it was also experimental, a breeder reactor intended to test the "seed and blanket" design, in which a central "seed" fuel was surrounded by a "blanket" of natural uranium. When the "seed" went critical, it supplied enough neutrons to cause plutonium (Pu-239) production and fission in the "blanket," such that each portion contributed roughly half of the total heat output. At maximum, the unit generated 68 MW at a cost ten times that of a contemporary coal plant. Shippingport continued operating for twenty-five years, until 1982, and did so with two other cores. The second core employed the same basic design – HEU surrounded by natural uranium blanket – but roughly five times larger. The third core, however, was altogether different, using a fuel made of thorium-232 and U-233 (as a neutron source), surrounded by a thorium blanket. When removed after five years, the blanket showed that breeding had indeed taken place. It confirmed that a light water reactor could be turned into a breeder with the right core design [8]. Because of the experimental nature of the reactor, some observers prefer to name a different plant, the Yankee Rowe, the first truly commercial nuclear power station.

All of these early attempts had a larger context. To call it "mixed" is certainly accurate, but perhaps understated. Politically, in the West at least, there was the hope of bringing to fruition a major benefit from nuclear energy to offset the focus on weapons and the inevitable anxiety this brought. Many wonders and spectacles had been promised the public from atomic energy, above all new forms of transport and electricity that would be universal and universally cheap. Aside from a gleaming (and affordable) future of techno-marvels, however, this addressed an anxiety about energy supply itself.

American oil had powered the greater part of the recent war on the allied side, and nerves were stretched about how long national and global supplies might last.[1] In Europe, the same anxiety was directed at coal, whose extraction continued to exhaust the more accessible deposits. As for transport, a good many shiny promises were made about atomic cars, trains, plains, and boats, all of which had been first proposed, in fictional terms, by H. G. Wells in *The World Set Free* (1914). The only result, however, was a special reactor to power submarines and aircraft carriers (though the military did spend some $1.5 billion on a program to build nuclear planes). The reactor design, a PWR that would come to serve an outsized role, was determined by US Admiral Hyman Rickover in 1951. Its first craft was the submarine *Nautilus*, costing $55 million, more than any of the plants mentioned above. It was sleek but not cheap, and its dark, formidable shape called to many minds a huge bomb, not a technologic miracle.

In Europe, meanwhile, an enormous surge in the demand for electricity began in the 1950s. This was due to reconstruction and renewed industrial activity, but also growing consumer demand for electronic appliances, TVs, refrigerators, and so on. For Britain, air pollution in the form of killer smogs due to coal burning, such as the one that cost 12,000 lives in December 1952, provided another reason for developing a new form of power generation.

But there was also a military dimension to all of this, too. Much information related to nuclear energy was kept secret in every nation that had a weapons program in progress or in the planning stages. Particularly true in the case of the Soviet Union, it was a lesser but no less real phenomenon in the US, Britain, and soon France, China, and India. It was a pattern that, together with hostility between the US and USSR, helped ensure failure for the proposal by Western diplomats and scientists that a new international political order, a World Government, be established and given control over nuclear technology, especially weapons [9].

By late 1948, it had become evident that this would not happen. A year later, the Soviets tested their first weapon. Every year thereafter for the next decade,

---

[1] A case in point was a widely read series of articles by Secretary of the Interior Harold Ickes about America's petroleum reserves, published between 1943 and 1947, with titles such as "Oil from Coal, A Must for America," "We're Running Out of Oil," and "The War and Our Vanished Resources."

the number of weapons tests in the atmosphere by the two superpowers grew. By the mid-late 1950s, fallout had become an issue of public concern in many nations, especially the US, where it began to affect people's views of nuclear power. The newly created Atomic Energy Commission, in charge of bringing nuclear power to public life, was also put in charge of the nation's weapons production program. Its officials found themselves in the position of having to try and calm public worries, often bending the truth to do so. By the time the first civilian nuclear plants were coming online, the AEC was widely viewed as something approaching a propaganda organization for the arms race. President Eisenhower's plan to separate peaceful uses of the atom from those commanded by the armed forces did not succeed.

Promises of Atomic Wonder

Nonetheless, nuclear energy had its ardent public supporters during its early years. Promises made on behalf of "the peaceful atom" were often grand and even grandiose. Not only did they tap a standing belief about "the wonders of science." They called directly upon a deeply felt desire that the postwar era would be a turning point, a period of stability and advancement full of special effects powered by science. Far from a fatal collapse into Armageddon, the Atomic Age would be a fresh start for the free world. Some measure of this can be found in speeches by those directly involved in making the Atomic Age come true. AEC's first chairman David Lilienthal, for example, told reporters in 1949 that "atomic energy" would bring nothing less than a new "beginning of human history in which faith in knowledge can vitalize man's whole life."

Related imagery in books, films, articles, and popular culture has been well documented by a number of authors [10]. Much of what they reveal can be found in writings by the popular science writer David O. Woodbury, whose book *Atoms for Peace* (1955) was among the most widely read on atomic energy and could still be found on the recommended reading list of the AEC in the mid-1970s. Woodbury wrote a brief summary of his book for the August 9, 1955, edition of *Look* magazine, whose cover carried a story, "Inside Hell," by a survivor of Hiroshima. Woodbury began his peace with a transition to his message: "Our generation lives between Hell and Utopia. For the very force that can destroy the human race can create wonders without end . . . It is small wonder that men's minds today shuttle between fears of doom and dreams of unprecedented bounty" [11].

Woodbury did not dwell on this paradox. By the mid-1950s, it had advanced to the borders of cliché. But this was because of the utopic side of the equation;

"doom" was beginning to gain a new face in the form of fallout, a source of fear that would soon engulf much of the US public. And for science, too, there was a vein of deep worry over the effects of radiation and nuclear reactors placed in public settings. If it was the age of innocence in some respects, it was also the era when disillusionment and nuclear fear had their broader and darker beginnings.

Woodbury wished to turn toward the sun and to clarify the "unprecedented bounty." The wonders would be impressive: radioisotopes to cure cancer and other diseases; "radiogenetics" to grow hardier crops that will end famine; "atomic gadgets" for industry, from materials testing to oil refining; desalination to supply water for all nations; and new forms of propulsion for a new era of transport. Readers were informed that government scientists could already "create hundreds of new substances called 'radioisotopes.' All the familiar chemical elements ... [can] be 'soaked' in an atomic pile similar to that which made the A-bomb's plutonium, and would come out exploding with tiny particles." The result was "a whole new kit of tools for medical research, thousands of times cheaper than radium and infinitely more versatile."

The author reserves his greatest enthusiasm for "electric power made by the atom." America's AEC is doing its part to push forward advances in this area, since it remains too expensive. But in just a few years' time,

> You will hear of small atomic plants going into action in obscure areas of the world, where economy is less important than ending a power famine: India, for instance, where there is virtually no power ...; Spain, with insufficient coal; North Africa, with limited waterpower ...; even frozen Greenland. Already, the US Army is well started on a portable atomic-power plant that can be knocked down and taken anywhere by plane.
>
> There is little doubt that, within a few years, atomic power will have become a major diplomatic weapon throughout the world. Even now, the US and Russia are in a race to pioneer the atom in the backward countries. Power, and other atomic products, can be the deciding argument in Indochina, India, perhaps in Africa as well ...
>
> Energy is the key to civilization. The world demand for power increases about 25 per cent every ten years. By A.D. 2000, if this keeps up, the supplies of petroleum and cheap coal will have sharply diminished. But atomic energy will be as commonplace as gasoline [13].

Woodbury, akin to most of his contemporaries, was no mere fantasist. He is distinctly aware of the larger global picture. He finds purpose in highlighting that the US and Soviet Union were heading into a double race, one for weapons of mass destruction, the other for influence through nuclear power. This, too, was a goal of the Atoms for Peace program. The non-Soviet world would be urged to adopt US nuclear technology, a goal that, if achieved, would create both a major new industry for American companies and global industrial and possibly political alliances with America.

Promises of technologic marvels are present too, of course. But this is not the most striking thing the future will bring, especially from the viewpoint of public awareness. Rather, the most outstanding feature of Woodbury's writing and that of most other journalists at the time is what was missing. Almost nowhere is the layperson taught, in accurate fashion, the essentials of nuclear energy itself. Woodbury himself, as quoted above, speaks of elements "soaked in an atomic pile" so that they emerge "exploding with tiny particles." Such a confused stew of metaphors was typical and not exactly helpful. Driving this home was a perceptive and much-cited 1955 article in the *Bulletin of Atomic Scientists* written by San Francisco journalist Gene Marine. It pointed out that the problem of poor understanding and even poorer attempts to remedy it could be found everywhere in the American press, which had essentially abandoned its democratic purpose to inform, critique, and educate. Marine writes sharply of the anti-intellectualism inherent in the constant use of "mysterious" and like words applied to everything "atomic." He implies, in fact, that it served well as a stand-in for the claim of secrecy that some members of the military and the AEC would much prefer. The press, he says, by accepting the need for secrecy, has become self-intimidated. Its people are "obsessed, first with the fear that they might say something wrong and thus commit inadvertent treason, and second ... that atomic phenomena are so obscure and difficult that nobody but an Oppenheimer or a Szilard could understand anything about them anyway" [14].

This author could have, and perhaps should have, gone further with his theme and turned a page of bitter irony. Only the year before, Robert Oppenheimer had been stripped by the AEC of his security clearance and thus any ability to act as a government advisor, due to trumped up accusations of being a communist and even a Soviet spy. The actual reasons for this attack were several. Above all had been Oppenheimer's opposition to developing the H-bomb, his criticism of the logic behind an arm's race, and his recommendation to Eisenhower for "a policy of candor" towards the American public regarding the scale of the US and Soviet arsenals and their rate of growth [15]. Later that same year, 1953, Oppenheimer gave a series of lectures to the British public on the basics of nuclear science and the necessity for "the unrestricted access to knowledge." Published in the US as *Science and the Common Understanding*, the author made clear his position that "improving [humanity's] lot ... alleviating hunger and poverty and exploitation, must be brought into harmony with the over-riding need to limit and largely to eliminate resort to organized violence between nation and nation" [16].

Oppenheimer's removal, engineered by AEC Chairman Lewis Strauss with help from FBI Director J. Edgar Hoover, greatly enraged and alienated the scientific community. Einstein even suggested "AEC" stood for Atomic Extermination Conspiracy. As Oppenheimer's reputation was international, the scandal reflected badly on the US image in foreign scientific eyes as well. It turned out the FBI had even illegally wiretapped conversations between Oppenheimer and his lawyers. When the facts came to light, the AEC actions appeared ugly and unjustified to a fair portion of the public. Strauss, in particular, seemed to have pursued the matter for personal reasons, as an effort of character assassination. Indeed, the American scientific community never looked at the AEC the same way again. Something had gone wrong in the halls of authority when it came to atomic energy. One of America's most popular scientist-heroes had been attacked and disowned by the very officials who owed their position to the project he so successfully directed. Could the words of such officials, say about nuclear tests, fallout, safety, and more, be trusted?

First Generation Electricity: A Mixed Tale

The AEC was established by the McMahon Atomic Energy Act of 1946, which was supposed to transfer stewardship of atomic energy from military to civilian control. To a degree, it was the child of an earlier proposal put before the United Nations only months before, regarding an international body that would be responsible for advancing nonmilitary uses of nuclear science and sharing such knowledge and technology with the world. This had been brought forward by the US but was rejected by the Soviets. It then became the basis for the AEC, with some not-so-minor differences. Its five commissioners would be appointed by the president, yet it would also be answerable to three committees, a Joint Congressional Committee on Atomic Energy, a General Advisory Committee of high-level scientists, and a Military Liaison Committee.

This probably seemed like a good idea at the time, having the commission be accountable to the executive, legislative, and military branches of government, as well as the scientific community. But it was actually a recipe for trouble, even (in some ways) disaster. Each domain, after all, had its own agendas and demands, and these were often in direct conflict. If scientists wished to make knowledge and data about fission available to researchers, the military demanded it be kept secret, while Congress sat in the middle, knowing that some information would be needed by companies if civilian nuclear power were ever to exist. There were still bigger problems. The Act made the AEC command central for every kind of use to which nuclear energy might be put. It had regulatory power over all public forms of nuclear technology and control of the vast national lab system set up as research centers for the Manhattan Project. Finally, the AEC also was responsible for building and advancing the US nuclear arsenal.

It was, by any account, an impossible task. Taking only the public side of the equation, the AEC had to sell atomic energy for war and for peace, as a weapon of strategic annihilation and a guarantor of progress and amity. To try and achieve this, it aimed its many messages at both children and adults. It both wrote and commissioned pamphlets, brochures, posters, technical reports, and radio programs. It sponsored lectures, science fairs, television interviews, and school visits. It produced a continuous series of films about basic nuclear science, the importance of "atomic" (not bomb) tests, and "safe atomic cities," to be shown in schools throughout the country (e.g. *The Magic of the Atom*, 1954). Its commissioners testified regularly, even routinely, before Congress. It nourished forms of press coverage, creating releases and other informational supplies for reporters, including strategic leaks. Certainly, it had a darker side, as the Oppenheimer scandal revealed. Under Lewis Strauss in particular, it lied to the public and worked to quash any criticism and to discredit scientists or engineers who disputed AEC statements [18–19].

But of all the conflicting tasks it was given, the Commission struggled hardest and longest with building a civilian nuclear power industry. As early as 1951, when the Soviets detonated their first nuclear device, it was evident that hopes for an era of global cooperation on a remarkable new source of energy would not be met. "Secrecy that we thought was an unwelcome necessity of the war," Fermi wrote in 1955, "still appears to be an unwelcome necessity" [20]. This being penned in the later stages of McCarthy Era paranoia, which had begun in 1950 and would extend into 1956. Yet, by this time, the "Atomic Age" had also broadened into the realm of power production. The ways and means in which this was done proved extraordinarily important for the future.

This was because the US made decisions that came to determine the type of reactors that would dominate civilian nuclear power worldwide. Such decisions were not necessarily the most informed, well-advised, or even rational, but they were beyond all doubt the most influential. Looking at the quoted statement from the Atomic Energy Act again, we can see that the AEC was created to further political, military, social, and also economic aims all at the same time. Early on, this meant it was involved in both weapons and reactor development, in promoting the latter for civilian power, as well as in public relations to support all these efforts. Then, once commercial reactors became a reality, it was also tasked with subsidizing early power plants *and* acting as the federal regulatory body over them. No leaps of imagination are needed to understand how some of these goals might conflict and thus how the AEC was quite likely to find itself falling into difficulty. If it had to obey certain demands for secrecy, pressed from the military side, it also was required to promote, partly fund, and regulate the nuclear domain from the commercial side. In the middle of this tug-of-war, moreover, the AEC carried out the world's most advanced program to design and test actual reactor technologies.

Titled the Power Reactor Development Program (PRDP), this R&D effort began in late 1952 and continued to 1960, with further demonstration projects to 1969. During this period, Congress provided the AEC with research monies to fund a series of prototype reactors that tested different design concepts. Such concepts included light water, fast breeder, graphite-moderated, gas-cooled, liquid-metal, molten salt, and certain combinations of these (e.g. liquid-metal fast breeder). All of these test reactors yielded valuable information about physical parameters related to fission rates, neutron production, heat production, steam generation, behavior of materials, and a great deal more. There were only two small problems with this essential knowledge. First, it was being urged forward not for reasons of research per se but to provide a basis for rapid commercialization – the "free competition in private enterprise" aim. Second, despite the importance of such knowledge for any privatizing effort, large portions of it were kept secret by the military for reasons of national security [21].

Giving the AEC both civilian and military tasks and not separating them in any clear way led to this situation. It was, in fact, an expression that the Eisenhower Administration wanted to move forward quickly, indeed too quickly, pushing nuclear power out the door of its birthing room in government hands and into the marketplace where it would be rapidly turned into a mature technology. Released from federal control, that is, handed to private enterprise, the free market could work its magic. Companies would engage in competitive innovation, lowering costs, improving quality, and advancing the technology so that it could compete directly with fossil fuel power generation, especially coal and oil,[2] the cheapest then available. Such had long been, and has remained, an idea dear to the heart of conservative thought and economics. In the case of nuclear power, however, there has always been the question of whether such a large-scale, expensive technology fits with the free market concept. Certainly the Eisenhower Administration thought it did. And the AEC, despite internal conflicts, strove to make it happen under the directorship of Lewis Strauss

---

[2] Between roughly 1935 and 1973, the first oil crisis, liquid petroleum provided fuel that was burned for electricity. Following the oil crisis, prices for all petroleum products shot up more than 300 percent, making fuel oil for power generation non-competitive and wasteful, particularly compared with fuel for vehicles. Some parts of the world, such as the Middle East, still burn fuel oil in power plants. In general, however, advanced nations reduced the practice to very low levels decades ago.

(1953–1958). A close friend of Eisenhower's, Strauss remained fiercely loyal to the vision of nuclear power becoming commercial and competitive with fossil energy within a decade.

The Administration's desires, in fact, were several. To provide America with both a vast new source of energy and leadership in an entirely new industry that would soon become global in extent. This would reveal, once again and in a new age, the preeminence of American industry and its commitment to the free market, as opposed to the state-controlled economy of communism. To stay in the forefront of nuclear technology and fulfill the role of world leader in science and technology, the US had to prove dominance in the use of atomic energy, and prove it soon, before other nations could catch up. Both the British and the Soviets had the knowledge to do exactly that. America needed to demonstrate full command over the atom, therefore, in convincing fashion. Finally, Eisenhower wished to show the world that his Atoms for Peace speech (1953) was in earnest, that the US would pledge itself to peace, even as it kept itself strong. "[T]he United States pledges before you, and therefore before the world," he had announced in that speech to the U.N. General Assembly, "its determination to help solve the fearful atomic dilemma – to devote its entire heart and mind to finding the way by which the miraculous inventiveness of man shall not be dedicated to his death, but consecrated to his life." Such high promises could not be made to seem mere words.

Much of the earliest work, before the Atomic Energy Act of 1954, amending the original 1946 law, was carried out by the government. This meant small, experimental reactors at the Argonne National Lab in southern Idaho and the Oak Ridge National Lab in Tennessee. Some real successes emerged from this research work. An example was the Experimental Breeder Reactor-1, or EBR-1, built in 1951 at Argonne. The design involved using a small amount of fissionable U-235 to produce neutrons that would be absorbed by a much larger mass of fertile U-238, a significant part of which would be transmuted into fissionable Pu-239. The concept was proven correct. It solidified in many minds the potential for a planned future where a small number of breeders could provide fuel for a large fleet of power plants. These would operate cheaply and reliably, with no dependence on foreign nations (for fuel). The possibilities for exporting such a plan, for repowering human society, seemed inebriating. EBR-1 came with an added prize. It also had the honor of becoming the world's first reactor to generate usable electricity: in December of 1951, it illuminated four 200 W light bulbs, then all the lights in its building.

That EBR-1 was funded by the government not only made sense from the point of view of the potential benefit for American society but also because of cost – even small, experimental reactors turned out to be much more expensive than anticipated. This did not matter so much at first, when the "R" part of R&D was the focus. But it did not last. Indeed, it was very short-lived. The demand for a shift to the "D" side was made entirely evident in the wording of the 1954 Act:

> Many technological problems remain to be solved before widespread atomic power, at competitive prices, is a reality. It is clear to us [Congress] that continued Government research and development, using Government funds, will be indispensable to a speedy and resolute attack on these problems. It is equally clear to us, however, that the goal of atomic power at competitive prices will be reached more quickly if private enterprise, using private funds, is now encouraged to play a far larger role . . . In particular, we do not believe that any development program carried out solely under government auspices, no matter how efficient it may be, can substitute for the cost-cutting and other incentives of free and competitive enterprise [22].

In short, the rush was on. With barely five years of research into this new realm of large-scale technology, the Eisenhower Administration and Congress were united in the demand that nuclear power begin its move into the marketplace. To be fair, their hopes were partly fueled by the spectacular success of the naval PWR used in the first nuclear submarine, *Nautilus*, a program completed in a mere four years, from start to launch. Indeed, Rickover had rejected all advice and gone straight to building a full-scale prototype in southern Idaho, this being the very first PWR ever erected. The achievement, remarkable by any measure, had more than a little to do with Rickover's own meticulous oversight and care for every last detail and insatiable appetite for perfection. Some irony, there-fore, is to be heard in his famous words about management philosophy: "Good ideas are not adopted automatically. They must be driven into practice with courageous impatience." The tale of the *Nautilus*, however, should probably have been a warning more than a precedent. Rickover was one of a kind, and believing his success could be approximated again and might stand as a standard was ill-advised at best.

It was also true that some industrial leaders came forward quite early with the idea of participating in reactor design and construction. Their hope was to get in early on a new industrial technology they could build themselves and then either operate or sell at a profit to the utilities. These leaders came from major American companies – Dow Chemical, Commonwealth Edison, Bechtel Corporation, General Electric (GE), and Westinghouse. That all of this might be a bit premature, given where things stood research-wise, was emphasized in 1955 when EBR-1 suffered a partial meltdown during a test to determine the cause of certain unexplained reactor responses. "Technological problems," in other words, might well take more time and cost more to solve than a "speedy" transition to commercialization might want. Another hint that nuclear power wasn't yet ready for prime time came from another part of private industry itself. Utilities, it turned out, were not quite so ecstatic about pouring hundreds of millions of dollars into a new power technology that hadn't yet been proven reliable or cost-effective – a technology, moreover, with no commercial track record at all [23–24].

The PRDP went ahead. Between 1955 and 1964, three rounds of government-industry projects were pursued. For each round, the AEC invited design applications with cost estimates, from potential industry partners. By this time, more technical data was declassified and made available to companies. Their own scientists, therefore, were now able to decide what kind of reactors might be worth pursuing. Yet, without understanding it, they were putting themselves in a much riskier position than assumed. The problem wasn't money or engineering or safety. It was larger; it was conceptual. Incredibly enough, PRDP reactors were to be built not at government facilities, as research prototypes, but near towns and cities throughout the country, as demonstration projects. The haste to make nuclear power commercial led to essentially pure test reactors being located where proven, working power plants were needed. It was a strategy driven less by boldness than urgency. And it turned out to have worse than mixed results. In a majority of cases, because of the commercial context, any design that did not perform well was likely to be shut down and abandoned. As most nuclear scientists and engineers agree today, a goodly number of high-potential designs were simply and brutally terminated before they could be properly evaluated. Forcing the transfer of a technology as complex and costly as nuclear power to the "free market," a technology still very much in the *experimental* stage, was fated to flounder in some part and to squander opportunities.

In its first, 1955 round of invited proposals, the AEC chose two to fund. Yankee Rowe was a PWR built in western Massachusetts to generate 185 MW. Considered an unmitigated success, it can be described largely as a scaled-up version of the Rickover's PWR submarine reactor. While it was not the first commercial nuclear power plant in the US, it was the first of its kind – the kind that would come to dominate the global industry. Yankee Rowe came in on time and 20 percent under budget. It began generating power to the grid in 1961, and for the next thirty-two years, the rest of its operating life, it continued to produce electricity with few problems and at low cost. As such, it stood as a counterexample to the other design selected by the AEC. The Fermi-1, built on the shores of Lake Erie, 35 miles (56 km) south of Detroit, was a sodium-cooled fast breeder reactor that began testing at low power in 1963 and then started supplying power in 1965. A year later, a plate at the bottom of the reactor pressure vessel got loose and blocked nozzles for coolant flow to some of the fuel assemblies, two of which heated up and partially melted. Shut down for nearly four years in order to discover the cause, perform repairs, reload fuel, restart and test the reactor, Fermi-1 was ready to go back online in 1970 but then suffered a small sodium leak and explosion. After further repairs, the reactor was deemed overly expensive and unworkable and was shut down in 1972.

Between 1957 and 1965, the AEC held two more rounds of proposal submission, plus helped support a number of other efforts by various consortia involving various companies and utilities. Altogether, the US government was involved in more than two dozen prototype projects, often paying part or most of the upfront costs of preparation and construction. From a high altitude, these projects look as if they emerged from hands of ambitious and explorative, even daring, leaders. The diversity of designs is more than impressive. In the second and third rounds, they included organic (hydrocarbon fluid replacing water as coolant and moderator), boiling water, boiling water with recycled steam, and pressurized heavy water reactors, as well as a sodium-cooled, graphite moderated design and a full-scale PWR, the Connecticut Yankee (490 MW). Though most of these designs had problems and were terminated, others emerged more solid and dependable. In particular, the PWR appeared to prove itself repeatedly as a reliable option.

Yet, upon closer view, we find the AEC more like a struggling animal, given too many commands all at once. It had hoped to find several designs that might be brought to market quickly and profitably. But few could be given the necessary iterations of research and testing, failure and innovation, that a complex technology normally requires before it can enter an existing market. AEC administrators had a mandate to rush the process. Often enough, "the most that was 'demonstrated' was that some particular species of reactor was not quite ready for demonstration" [25]. We might call it the Rickover syndrome – skip the lab work, forget a small-scale pilot version, defeat all trial-and-error effort, go straight to product demonstration. Rickover, however, was building a war machine on a wartime schedule, not a commercial facility for the marketplace. The *Nautilus* did not need to make money. Nor did it depend on bringing aboard the financial support of "free and competitive enterprise." Indeed, the *Nautilus* program had a single objective, and after its director made the final decision about what design to employ, every effort could be devoted to testing and improving and testing again each element, material, and component. The thoroughness was breathtaking. When the *Nautilus* performed flawlessly on its very first run, some found it incredible. Others, however, understood it as the most likely culmination of an incredible process.

Triumph of the LWR

In fact, Rickover's nuclear submarine work could not be called an unmitigated success. With input from Alvin Weinberg, he had actually chosen three differ-ent designs that might be built small enough for a submarine. Besides the PWR, these were a gas-cooled and sodium-cooled design. As Westinghouse worked on the PWR for the *Nautilus*, Rickover had GE build a sodium-cooled reactor for the *Seawolf*. As with the PWR, a land-based prototype was first built, then two final reactors for use, one to be installed and the other a spare. Because of the strong results at EBR-1, Rickover had hope for the *Seawolf*. As noted in Chapter 3, liquid sodium has much better thermal conductivity than water, so it can deliver a lot more heat, thus steam and power. But the *Seawolf* had problems. During its test voyage in 1955, cracks and a sodium leak developed in two pipes, forcing the ship to dock for repairs and then run on reduced power. Rickover decided the reactor was too expensive, complex, and difficult to repair. In the end, he may also have had doubts about taking liquid sodium, which explodes on contact with water, out to sea. The *Seawolf* had its core replaced with a PWR like that in the *Nautilus*. The gas-cooled design remained on paper.

Rickover knew that the PWR was neither the best nor the cheapest alter-native. But the goal was to determine which design could yield reliable results and be developed quickly. Needed in the new Cold War era was "a decisive weapon" that might render the US navy superior for many years [26–27]. Physical principles were loud and clear: the PWR would not deliver the most power. But it would produce enough to make a sub far faster than the best diesel-electric models and give the ability to remain submerged for far longer. It could also be built quickly, giving the US a lasting lead. The PWR achieved all of this. No surprise, then, that when placed in charge of a civilian power reactor at Shippingport, despite the wholly different goal of generating elec-tricity, Rickover chose the PWR.

This brings us back to our main topic. Beyond the reach of naval propulsion, besides the efforts of the PRDP, the government built many experimental reactors at its two national nuclear research labs, Argonne (Idaho) and Oak Ridge (Tennessee), in the 1950s and early 60s. These labs were also under the purview of the AEC, which allowed them to remain more purely research-oriented, though always with a certain view to applications too. Many of the reactors built as Argonne and Oak Ridge were small and intended for training, materials testing, and other experimental inquiry. But others could be called prototypes to test various design ideas that might have commercial potential. In all, the two labs fabricated twenty-seven reactors, and if we include

Argonne's second lab in Chicago, the number rises to forty-one. Light water, heavy water, graphite-moderated, fast breeder, gas-cooled, homogeneous (HEU dissolved in water as fuel), molten salt, and, later at Argonne, a unique system known as the integral fast reactor. More than half of these design concepts were successfully proven. All had advantages and disadvantages, as did Rickover's PWR. Some, such as the boiling water, gas-cooled, liquid metal breeder, molten salt, and integral reactors, had real commercial possibilities. Only one, however, has ever been used for an actual power plant.

Even well before 1970, the LWR had emerged as the sole likely survivor of all the varied reactor designs tested in the US for actual power generation. Why was this the case? We have seen hints of the reasons already. On the one hand, there was the push and rush to commercialize nuclear power by the AEC, largely at the behest of the Eisenhower Administration. At issue, in part, was the fundamental idea of conservative economics that the marketplace of competitive free enterprise was always a more nutritive home for any technology than the wasteful clutches of government. But other factors had influence too. A felt need to remain the world's scientific and technological leader was one of these. Another was Eisenhower's own desire to demonstrate to the world that the US was indeed developing peaceful uses of nuclear energy, uses which it might well share with most of humanity. Doubtless, too, there was an interest in proving to the American public that nuclear energy could be a benefit to daily life, not just a weapon of mass death. From the government side, therefore, pressure was high to transform nuclear power into a profitable new industry.

On the other side, however, were the utilities, they who needed to invest in power plants for the industry to grow. They found themselves hesitant to embrace a brand new, complex, and costly technology before its commercial promise had been confirmed. They were not really R&D companies and were not interested in committing large sums of money to projects that had no short-term payoff and might need years of adjustments, fixes, and other changes before the result became fully reliable. As companies in business to provide a service (electricity) and turn a profit, they were cautious about taking big financial risks and wary of serving as guinea pigs. They wanted indications that a nuclear reactor could generate power at costs competitive with those of existing fossil fuel plants.

As we have seen, starting in 1954, the AEC was willing to move the process forward by subsidizing all or part of the reactors built as part of its commercialization program, the PRDP. Part of the amended Atomic Energy Act of that year also allowed the sharing of technical information from prior reactor testing that the military had previously kept confidential. In 1957, a further amendment to the Act was passed as the Price-Anderson Act. This required the budding nuclear industry to have liability insurance for compensating the public in case of an accident, and it put a limit on such liability (the act has been renewed several times; the limit in 2016 was $13.6 billion). These actions by the AEC helped generate participation by a number of utilities. But whatever enthusiasm they may have had was tempered by the problems encountered in a number of the reactors built and then abandoned during the three rounds of the PRDP.

By the early 1960s, it was obvious that very few designs had actually been demonstrated; most could still be called "experimental." In fact, only one reactor type – the PWR – had been repeatedly built with consistent success. Rickover's choice for the US navy and for Shippingport solidified the PWR's credentials. Yankee Rowe confirmed them. The PWR soon had company. One set of reactors at Argonne, called Borax (Boiling Water Reactor Experiment), showed that a simpler design with coolant water producing steam, was stable and did not overly contaminate the turbine with radioactivity. Borax III was hooked up to the local grid on July 17, 1955, and powered the town of Arco, population 1,800. A year later, GE broke ground for the Dresden-1 in northern Illinois, the first privately financed nuclear plant in the US. The BWR began operating in 1960 and was followed by others at various sites around the country over the next eight years. Most were small, less than 100 MW, and some suffered from steam leaks and other problems. But others, like the Big Rock Point plant in northern Michigan, worked well. Information from these aided the building of the first truly large-scale power plants, such as the Oyster Creek plant in eastern New Jersey, with 636 MW capacity. Commissioned in 1969, it remains the nation's oldest nuclear power plant, relicensed to 2029.

The triumph of the LWR was therefore due to a combination of factors more related to ideas and institutions than engineering and technology. By "ideas and institutions" is meant the influence of Hyman Rickover, which itself was determined by the forced urgency for commercializing nuclear power and the need for workable reactors able to convince utilities the new technology was viable. Until the late 1960s, it barely made money. Coal and oil were cheap, and reactors were much more expensive to build than first estimated. The economics of nuclear power did not appear so promising. But in the late 1960s coal prices began to rise, and in 1973 the first oil crisis hit. When, as a result, the price of petroleum jumped 400 percent, nuclear economics looked a good deal better. A clear lesson from this was made emphatic when a second oil crisis struck in 1978–79. The lesson was evident, though it tended to be overlooked: fossil fuel prices, oil and gas especially, are volatile, unpredictable, and tied directly to political events.

None of this was true for nuclear. Uranium was consistently cheap, since resources had burgeoned due to new exploration. But upfront costs were another matter. Competitive "free enterprise" had led to a host of different, competing LWR designs, which were thus built on a first-of-kind basis. Unexpected problems and changes were therefore common, increasing construction time. Together with evolving regulations, extensive licensing requirements, and anti-nuclear protests that challenged the process at every step, nuclear power faced its own set of economic difficulties. This, unfortunately, allowed coal use to rise rapidly from the 1970s to the 1990s, when nuclear was the main competitor in terms of US power generation. Since 1970, in fact, the struggles faced by nuclear contributed directly to coal's long-term rise.

As for the LWR, by 1970 it was solidly on its way to becoming a global standard. It had already been chosen by France, Germany, Japan, and several other nations. Soon the UK would begin to shift from its home-grown gas-cooled design to LWR. Starting in the 1990s, after Chernobyl and the fall of communism, Russia too, using its VVER technology, moved toward more Western-style PWRs. In France, the oil crisis of 1973 led to the so-called "Messmer Plan," under Prime Minister Pierre Messmer. Choosing a PWR design, the country launched a massive development to replace imported oil for power. In contrast to the US, the plan was guided but not financed by government and employed a standardized design that rapidly reduced costs as construction experience grew. Within a single decade, between 1975 and 1985, the French had built more than forty-five reactors and nuclear-generated power had risen from about 10 percent to over 65 percent of the country's total. By 1990, there were fifty-six reactors producing more than 75 percent of French electricity [28]. France's nuclear achievement elevated still further the status of the LWR. Indeed, the only real competitor to it has remained the Canadian CANDU heavy water design, a success in its home country and several others, like India.

In 1982, Admiral Hyman Rickover delivered a farewell testimony to the US Congress, which included some statements about the future of nuclear power. Rickover said he did not think that nuclear would be worth pursuing if it produced radiation and threatened future generations. His words came in a period of heightened nuclear anxiety. Less than two years earlier, the Three Mile Island accident had occurred, and with the election of Ronald Reagan as president, an aggressive military buildup began along with provoking and partly threatening comments aimed at the Soviet Union. Only a few weeks after Rickover spoke, Jonathan Schell's widely read book, *The Fate of the Earth*, appeared to draw dramatic landscapes of a world wasted by nuclear war. Rickover, however, was speaking about his own creation, the PWR, and of LWRs in general. His own creation, the nuclear navy, seemed to frighten him; he said he would sink all of it if he could. Yet when asked by Senator William Proxmire if he thought civilian reactors could be operated safely: he responded,

"Absolutely, sir." Much else about this part of his speech seems ambiguous. Because the world would very soon run out of oil and coal, he said, it would need nuclear power. Yet radiation from this energy source could set things back two billion years, when the Earth was so radioactive that life could not exist. Rickover was wrong about these topics – wrong at a fundamental level. Few, if any geoscientists thought oil or coal was nearing an era of scarcity, and the last thirty-five years have more than borne out their abundance (indeed, this is precisely the problem regarding carbon emissions). Moreover, radiometric dating had shown that life began at least 3.5 billion years ago, a number that has since been pushed back further still. So the admiral, like many at the time, seems to have overjudged some of the threats facing humanity, nuclear power among them.

Though most reactors built today are LWRs, their limits are well and widely understood. The future promises a marked change. Of the six Gen IV designs chosen for testing and development, only one uses light water (at temperatures above 500 °C, so with key differences from Gen II/III). All other designs use either gas, liquid metal, or molten salt, and will operate at temperatures up to 800–900 °C, greatly improving efficiencies. They can be built smaller and still generate large amounts of power and, based on knowledge acquired over six decades, will have marked improvements regarding earthquake, accident, and proliferation resistance. A few designs are now in the testing phase, especially in China, and during the next fifteen to twenty years they will undergo further testing and prototype development. There is no rush to make them commercial.

Conclusion: Chances Missed

It is well known among engineers and historians of science that the best versions of a technology are not always the ones that succeed. The future of nuclear power, employing Gen IV designs, will almost certainly prove this true in the case of the LWR.

In the 1950s, a plan emerged for the future of US electricity. Uranium appeared scarce; its energy had to be maximized. With LWRs as the favored technology, used fuel could be recycled via breeders, the result burned as new fuel. Calculations showed this would provide power for many centuries, possibly even millennia if somewhat more uranium could be found. Like many plans that seem able to solve diverse problems (energy security, fossil fuel pollution, etc.) at a single bound, this vision of a nuclear future crashed on the craggy shores of history. But in its conception, it depended on forsaking alternatives that were valid and deserving.

Two designs in particular would likely have drawn Rickover's approval. They require mention, not only because of their value, but because they are likely to return in Gen IV forms. First is the EBR-II, a sodium-cooled fast breeder reactor that operated at Argonne's Idaho site from 1964 to 1994. This was a prototype that demonstrated the idea of a "complete power plant," one with a closed fuel cycle that burned original fuel, reprocessed the spent fuel (in a separate onsite facility), then burned the result. It had other successes as well: it validated a pool-type design, with liquid sodium filling a space containing the reactor core, heat exchanger, and other systems; it operated at 80 percent of capacity for a decade, showing it could compete with LWRs; it proved an advanced form of reprocessing (pyroprocessing) and passive safety. This last, noted in Chapter 3, deserves special mention. At full power, with emergency systems disabled, all electricity was cut, shutting off pumps that circulated coolant. But the large pool of liquid sodium, with its high thermal conductivity, absorbed decay heat from the fuel (fission had stopped) and worked by natural circulation until the reactor shut itself down. This was hugely important proof of passive safety. Despite such promise, though, the EBR-II was terminated by President Bill Clinton in 1994, a sign of how the US had turned away from nuclear in the post-Chernobyl era [29].

The second abandoned success was the Molten Salt Reactor Experiment (MSRE) built and operated at Oak Ridge from 1966 to 1969 under the director-ship of Alvin Weinberg. This design has fuel dissolved in the coolant and reprocessing taking place chemically while the reactor continues to operate. Graphite is the moderator, and liquid fluoride salt serves both as coolant and carrier of the fuel in the form of dissolved uranium or plutonium (or both), and actinides. Fission heats the fluid salt to temperatures about 700 °C with no pressurization, allowing for a higher heat transfer and thus power production than LWRs. Weinberg was attracted to the MSR idea because of its greater safety – it cannot melt down or explode, as fluoride salt does not react like sodium – its higher temperatures and efficiency, and its ability to be refueled while at full power. By demonstrating the MSRE for several years, Weinberg and his team also showed that this kind of reactor should be significantly cheaper than LWR designs, as it requires no fuel fabrication, thinner containment, and less cement and steel, while its fuel can last four to seven years. The MSRE was the first reactor to operate with U-233, another important success. Though the U-233 was bred from thorium in other reactors, the experiment essentially showed it could be generated from thorium in the liquid salt. The MSRE was cancelled in 1969 by President Nixon, and Weinberg was fired soon after. While the project had reached its time and funding limit, it was not continued despite its clear success. Many have speculated that the molten salt concept didn't fit with the LWR-liquid metal breeder plan, which had the ability to generate plutonium for fuel and weapons both. The weapons connection does not seem likely, given that separate facilities for military plutonium production, such as Hanford in Washington State, already existed. Another explanation was offered by Weinberg himself, who noted that the use of liquid fuel was too different from conventional ideas of a reactor, too much the province of chemists rather than physicists.

If past history is important, it is raised to a higher level by the status of advanced nuclear power today. In the US, this includes over forty nuclear start-up companies, led not by ex-CEO's of large nuclear firms or emeritus professors but by young, highly trained scientists, engineers, and businesspeople [30]. Such companies can be called visionary, in that they take the issues of climate change, air pollution, and demand for power in the developing world as potent motivation for helping create a better future. Each new start-up firm has solidified around a single reactor design, and, as we might guess, the designs that dominate are those inspired by Weinberg and by EBR-II. It is a testament to the true achievements won by government investment in nuclear technology that so many start-ups of this kind have now emerged. How many of these may succeed can't be decided at this early point. It is evident, however, that vision and commitment are strongly present in the US nuclear landscape.

What we can say for certain is that both of the reactor designs we have called missed opportunities have returned in Gen IV reactor designs. This is only as it should be. Both, after all, were experiments that turned into demonstrations. The international task force, Generation IV International Forum, has determined they belong among the concepts chosen for the new nuclear era of the twenty-first century, a determination now being brought to the fore by a new industry of nuclear start-ups in the West, as well as programs in China and collaborations involving EU nations, such as Horizon 2020, as well as others that bring together companies and universities from Russian, Chinese, South Korean, and US entities. Designs beyond the LWR will get a second chance, and so will the world.

References

[1] A. P. Meshik, The Workings of an Ancient Nuclear Reactor (Internet), *Scientific American* (January 26, 2009). Available from: https://www.scientificamerican.com/article/ancient-nuclear-reactor/

[2] M. M. Waldrop, Nuclear Energy: Radical Reactors (Internet), *Nature*, 492:7427 (December 5 2012), 26–29. Available from: www.nature.com/news/nuclear-energy-radical-reactors-1.11957

[3] R. Perry et al., *Development and Commercialization of the Light Water Reactor, 1946–1976* (Rand Corporation, 1977).

[4] R. Rhodes, *The Making of the Atomic Bomb* (New York: Simon and Schuster, 1986), Ch. 13.

[5] C. C. Kelly (ed.), *The Manhattan Project* (New York: Black Dog & Leventhal, 2009), pp. 67–68.

[6] Atomic Energy Act of 1946, Public Law 585, 79th Congress, Section 1(a).

[7] J. McAffey, *Atomic Awakening: A New Look at the History and Future of Nuclear Power* (New York: Pegasus, 2009), pp. 206.

[8] Ibid., pp. 228–230.

[9] A. Einstein, *The Einstein Reader* (New York: Citadel, 1984), pp. 125–162.

[10] M. A. Amundson and S. C. Zeman, (eds.), *Atomic Culture* (Boulder, CO: University Press of Colorado, 2004).

[11] David Woodbury, Here Is the Utopian Peacetime Promise of the Atom, Look (August 9, 1955), 26.

[12] Ibid., p. 29.

[13] Ibid., pp. 29–30.

[14] G. Marine, Atoms in the Press, *Bulletin of the Atomic Scientists*, 11:7 (1955), 250–252, 264.

[15] K. Bird and M. J. Sherwin, *American Prometheus: The Triumph and Tragedy of J. Robert Oppenheimer* (New York: Vintage, 2005).

[16] J. R. Oppenheimer, *Science and the Common Understanding* (New York: Simon and Schuster, 1954), p. 97.

[17] A. Buck, The Atomic Energy Commission (Internet), *Office of History and Heritage Resources*, US Department of History (July 1983). Available from: http://energy.gov/sites/prod/files/AEC%20History.pdf

[18] S. Weart, *The Rise of Nuclear Fear*, revised edn. (Cambridge: Harvard University Press, 2012).

[19] P. Boyer, *By the Bomb's Early Light* (Durham: University of North Carolina Press, 1994).

[20] Atomic Heritage Foundation, Fermi on Chicago Pile-1 (Internet). Available from: www.atomicheritage.org/key-documents/fermi-chicago-pile-1

[21] R. Perry et al., p. 4–5.

[22] Ibid., pp. 10–15.

[23] W. Allen, *Nuclear Reactors for Generating Electricity: US Development from 1946 to 1963* (Rand Corporation, 1977), pp. 20–24.

[24] R. Perry et al., pp. 14.

[25] W. Allen, pp. 20–24.

[26] F. Duncan, *Rockover and the Nuclear Navy: The Discipline of Technology* (Washington, D.C.: Naval Institute Press, 1990).

[27] T. Rockwell, *The Rickover Effect: How One Man Made a Difference* (Bloomington: iUniverse, 2002).

[28] World Nuclear Association, Nuclear Power in France (Internet). Available from: www.world-nuclear.org/information-library/country-profiles/countries-a-f/france.aspx

[29] C. Westfall, Vision and Reality: The EBR-II Story, *Nuclear News* (February 2004), 25–32.

[30] S. Brinton, The Advanced Nuclear Industry, *Third Way* (June 15, 2015) (Internet). Available: http://www.thirdway.org/report/the-advanced-nuclear-industry

5

Radiation: A Guide for the Perplexed

What It Is

Radiation is no less a part of nature than the Sun or the atom. It is a movement of energy that takes place in all matter, everywhere in the universe. Better said, traveling electromagnetic waves and subatomic particles fill all space in the cosmos, every square centimeter, every second. This includes the Earth and everything on it, from rocks to humans. It is in all that we eat, drink, and breath, and is as much a part of us as blood and bone. The question, then, is not how to escape or minimize it, but how to understand it.

Health physicists, radiobiologists, and others who study its effects on the body speak of two fundamental kinds. *Non-ionizing* radiation, such as radio waves, visible light, and microwaves, has relatively low amounts of energy, too low to remove an electron from an atom (ionization). *Ionizing radiation*, however, is able to do this and therefore to create changes in matter. X-rays and gamma rays plus particles like protons and high-energy electrons, comprise this category, our focus.

Radioactive elements are one source of ionizing radiation. Such an element has an unstable nucleus that must eject some part of its energy or mass. It does this in the form of radiation, which can take one or more of three main forms:

– *Alpha* particles. These are helium nuclei (2 protons + 2 neutrons) and are emitted especially by heavy elements like uranium and thorium. Because of their size, alpha particles collide with air molecules. They cannot travel in air more than about an inch (2 cm). They are stopped by a sheet of paper or human skin and are not harmful if external. They are more dangerous if emitted within the body.

- *Beta* particles are high-energy electrons, blocked by a thin sheet of metal foil or thick clothing. If energetic enough, they can penetrate slightly below the skin and, with significant exposure, may produce burns. Like alpha particles, they cannot go through the walls and windows of a building or car.
- *Gamma rays* are packets of electromagnetic energy called photons but act like waves, with especially high energy. They can pass through most objects, including the human body, but lead or thick concrete will stop them. Because of their penetrative capability, gamma rays can affect the body more than either alpha or beta particles when Text come from outside.

Neutrons can also be ionizing. When they have high energies, they are directly so. At lower energies, they can be captured by nuclei which then become unstable and thus radioactive. Of zero charge, neutrons are highly penetrating like gamma rays. They are not normally harmful because low in abundance (free neutrons are themselves unstable, decaying to a proton and electron). But when produced in great numbers by fission and fusion reactions, they are highly damaging to living matter. Neutrons are produced naturally by heavy nuclei like uranium and thorium that undergo fission in a scattered and dispersed way.

As implied by their different abilities to penetrate matter, alpha, beta, gamma, and neutron radiation do *not* have the same effects on living tissue. Nature is complicated this way; biological impact can differ considerably depending on radiation type, energy level, and also whether it is outside or inside an organism. Both alpha and beta radiation can have much more serious effects if their sources are ingested, whether swallowed or inhaled. But more on this topic below.

One other kind of radiation that can be ionizing is x-rays. These are not produced from the decay of nuclei, like alpha, beta, and gamma radiation, but from the interaction between high-energy electrons and the nuclei of metal elements.[1] Made up of photons like other kinds of rays, x-rays are weaker than gamma rays but at their highest energy levels overlap with gamma radiation.

A key fact about radiation is that it spreads out and thus weakens rapidly with distance from its source. This change follows what is called the *inverse square law*, which also applies to gravity, sound, and some other physical realities. It means that the amount of radiation reaching an object (or person) is inversely

---

[1] More specifically, as fast electrons approach near an atom, their path is bent by the protons in the nucleus and they are slowed down slightly. This loss of energy is given off by the electron in the form of an x-ray.

proportional to the square of the distance – every time a given distance from the source doubles, the radiation level falls by a factor of four.

Where It Comes From

We are subject to radiation at every moment of our lives. This includes ionizing radiation, which comes to us from every direction. Let us count the ways:

- from *space*, in the form of cosmic rays, a hugely diverse array of particles including the nuclei of most elements, whose intensity increases with altitude;
- the *ground*, due to the decay of radioactive elements, mainly potassium (K-40), uranium (U-238), and thorium (Th-232);
- the *air*, mainly as radon (R-222), a decay product of uranium and thorium;
- from *plants*, which contain radioactive potassium and carbon (C-14);
- from *fresh water* in rain, ponds, creeks, rivers, and lakes, and in *sea water*. In both cases, K-40 is a main contributor. Levels in fresh water will depend directly on the local environment and regional watershed and so can vary greatly. The oceans have a more limited range but many radioactive isotopes, including uranium.
- from *food and drinking water*, due to K-40 and C-14, plus smaller amounts of uranium;
- from *buildings, sidewalks, highways*, whose bricks and concrete contain grains or pebbles of granitic rock, richer than other rocks in uranium and thorium;
- from *human use of radiation*, in medicine, industry, occupations. Medical diagnosis, dentistry, and airport scans use higher energy x-rays, which are less energetic than gamma rays.
- from *each other*, since we eat, drink, and breathe radioactive substances, mainly K-40 and C-14, which are continually replenished within us. Also, this will depend on where we live; some areas have more uranium or thorium in the soil, therefore in dust that can cling to clothing, skin, hair, and so forth.

All of this combines to make up the background radiation of a specific area. The first five sources are considered "natural background," while the latter four qualify as "artificial" or "manmade background." Obviously, there is overlap here, since human activity can directly affect the natural environment and vice versa. What is the largest of these sources that people are exposed to? Before the mid-1990s, it was radon gas pretty much everywhere, and this is still true in many nations. For advanced nations, however, the largest source now comes from medical diagnosis and radiotherapy. This worries some people, who feel such exposure contributes to rising cancer rates. Yet the data do not support this. Cancer incidence has not surged in nations that employ these technologies, which have saved many millions of lives and contributed greatly to *decreased* rates of death due to cancer. This is strongly evident in the US, for example, where medical imaging and forms of radiation therapy are especially well used [1].

What does the above list of radiation sources tell us, generally speaking? That natural radiation is a kind of medium uniting all living and non-living things. Also, that during our lifetime, even in a single month, our exposure levels can go up and down a great deal. Every time we take a plane trip, for example, drive or hike in the mountains, move to a city at a greater elevation, radiation levels increase because of the higher intensity of cosmic rays. If we visit a friend or relative who lives above 5,000–6,000 ft (1520–1820 m) where the bedrock is granite, levels go up by an order of magnitude. There are areas on Earth – including those that are densely inhabited – where levels of exposure are even 100 times the global average. And yet we find people still live there and do not drop dead in the streets by the thousands. Nor are cancer rates any higher than elsewhere in the same country. They may even be lower.

How It's Measured

Like gravity or magnetism, radiation can't be seen, heard, tasted, or smelled. It becomes visible through measurement. Numbers and their meaning help take the mystery out of radiation and give us the power to talk about it as an ordinary phenomenon.

As it happens, we need more than one set of numbers to do this. Radiation begins at source, then flows outward, interacting with the air, before encountering something more solid, where it deposits some or all of its remaining energy. There are thus three stages in the life of radiation where we make measurements to understand its progress. And if we want to know (as we often do) what specific effect it may have on living matter, we make a final type of measurement that is especially useful.

The US Nuclear Regulatory Commission has a simple scheme that helps sort all this out, using the letters R.E.A.D. [2]. This system is shown below for completeness and reference, but in this book we will be mostly concerned with only the first and last stages (R and D). Also for completeness, two sets of units are given in each case, an unfortunate necessity related to the tendency of some countries (e.g. the US) to hang on to an older system. This book will make use of the newer International System of Units (SI), begun in the 1960s, and now adopted by most of the world.[2] These units are given second.

- **R**adiation emitted by the source material, often called "activity." The original unit of measure is the curie (Ci), the activity of one gram of radium. The SI unit now used is the becquerel (Bq). One Bq = one atomic nucleus disintegration per second, thus a very small unit (1 curie = 3.7×10^{10} Bq). A typical measure is becquerels per volume for liquids, written as Bq/liters, or becquerels per mass for solid matter, Bq/kg. Ground contamination is measured in Bq/m^2. For foodstuffs, the unit is Bq/kg (or Bq/l for water and milk). And in air, as Bq/m^3.
- **E**xposure, meaning the amount moving through the air. More precisely, it means how many ions of air are created per kg of air affected by the radiation. Units in this case are the roentgen (R) and coulomb/kilogram (C/kg)
- **A**bsorbed dose refers to the amount of energy that radiation deposits in (transfers to) objects, living or non, which it encounters. Units here are the rad and the gray (Gy). One Gy = 1.0 joule deposited per kg of tissue.
- **D**ose-equivalent, or "effective dose," which provides a measure of the biological effect resulting from the absorbed dose. These measurements are given in rem (**r**oentgen **e**quivalent in **m**an) or Sieverts (Sv). In comparison, 1 Sv = 100 rems. But since rems and Sv represent very large dose-equivalents, in most cases dealing with human beings 1/1000th of a rem or Sv are used, i.e. mrem or mSv. Most often these units are given in relation to time, e.g. average worldwide dose from natural background radiation is 2.4 mSv per year, or 0.27 µSv per hour.

Becquerels and Sieverts (usually as mSv) are the units now most often used around the world to talk about radiation levels (many in the US, however, continue to hang on to the older system). This is true whether we're talking about natural background levels or nuclear power accidents. The becquerel is straightforward and clear in meaning. The Sievert, or

---

[2] Frequently abbreviated "SI" (for *Système international d'unités*), this system represents the work of international scientists to construct a coherent, standardized set of essential units for global use, to replace a growing chaos of diverse measures that tended to change between fields and even nations. Over time, SI units have come to dominate more and more, as international journals, organizations, scientific projects, and programs demand their use. However, earlier units still make their appearance, especially in material intended for a local audience. Such is very much the case with radiation.

mSv, is a kind of close approximation. This needs to be said for accuracy. A big reason the measuring of biological effect isn't so direct and simple is that each type of radiation affects the body somewhat differently. For example, at the same absorbed dose level, alpha particles have twenty times more impact on human tissue than do either beta or gamma rays. This doesn't matter when exposure is external, since alpha particles can't even penetrate the skin. It matters more when alpha radiation has a source inside the body. Another interesting complexity is that radiation affects different organs and tissues differently. Such variation means that the Sievert is a kind of average. Yet its use for this is based on decades of data gathering, application to actual incidents (including Chernobyl), and adjustment, confirming its value and utility [3].

But what do becquerels and mSv mean in the real world? The Bq, after all, is a tiny measure.[3] Because of this, we usually need to speak in terms of kBq (thousand becquerels), MBq (million), GBq, or TBq. Here are some examples [4]:

185 lb or 84 kg man (100 Bq/kg):	8273 Bq
Coffee Beans	1000 Bq/kg
Granite	1000 Bq/kg
Coal ash	2000 Bq/kg
Low grade Uranium ore (0.3 percent):	500 kBq/kg
Radioisotope, medical diagnosis:	70–200 MBq
Chernobyl total radiation released:	~5200 PBq (10^{15} Bq)
Fukushima total radiation released:	~ 800 PBq 10^{15} Bq)

Here is an interesting comparison. The global upper limit on radioactivity in food, as designated by the Food and Agricultural Organization (FAO) of the United Nations, is 1000 Bq/kg. This limit is today considered quite conservative (note coffee beans in the list above). It applies specifically to radionuclides most abundant in nuclear accidents.[4] The US has decided on a 1,200 Bq/kg limit for food and 1,200 Bq/l for water, and milk. The EU limit is 1,250 for foods and 1,000 for water and milk. Prior to the Fukushima accident, Japan had limits similar to the EU. *After* the accident, however, responding to widespread fears, the government cut all limits by half. When this failed to inspire calm, limits were dropped to 100 Bq/kg for food, 200 Bq/l for milk, and 10 Bq/l for water. The result was chaos; in markets, formerly safe foods were suddenly

---

[3] In contrast, the curie is a very large unit, with 1 Ci = 3.27×10^{10} disintegrations, or Bq. This means that 1 Bq = 2.7×10^{-11} Ci.

[4] These nuclides are: Iodine-131; Cesium-134; Cesium-137; and Strontium-90.

banned. A spillover of concern led to prohibition of most Japanese food products in South Korea and China. People who left Japan for the US or Europe, however, could be assured that they ate and drink safely at radio-activity levels many times higher.

For discussions about the impacts of radiation on people, however, the most important measure is "effective dose," measured in mSv or, as recorded by dosimeters, microSieverts/hour (μSv/hr). The following is a list similar to the one above for some marker levels. Unless otherwise specified, each number refers to a total dose absorbed either at one time or over a short period (e.g. < 1 week).

10,000 (10 SV)	= Acute radiation poisoning; death < 1 month
6,000	= Level received by Chernobyl workers who died
3,000	= Average 50 percent survival rate
1,000 (1 Sv)	= Temporary radiation sickness, nausea, not fatal; 5 percent chance of cancer incidence later in life
500	= Max. short-term limit for rescue workers in life- saving work
250	= US federal max. yearly limit for astronauts
100 (11.4 μSv/h)	= Statistical link to cancer begins (1 percent risk)
20–50	= Upper yearly limit for nuclear industry workers
10 (1.14 μSv/h)	= Full-body CT scan
6	= Average yearly total background in US
2.4	= Global average from natural sources only
0.3	= one-way flight to Tokyo
0.1	= Chest x-ray

A few of these numbers are helpful to keep in mind for gauging dose levels you may hear about, as well as those we'll be discussing in this book. Start with 1,000 mSv (1 Sievert): when someone receives a whole-body dose of this amount at one time, cells die and the person will usually suffer from temporary acute radiation sickness. This dose, in other words, is high enough to kill living tissue. Note, however, that it isn't fatal, and the lifetime risk it is estimated to have for causing cancer is low, 5 percent. It is important to stress that we're talking about very short-term exposure, e.g. all at once or within a few weeks, *not* over the span of a lifetime (a good many of the world's people approach or exceed 1,000 mSv during their lives).

A second number to remember is 100 mSv. This is the lowest dose where any discernible link to cancer occurs, absorbed over a year or less. In this case, the link is purely *statistical*, which means it is a kind of grand average, not a certainty but a possibility. It works only for a large population (tens of thousands). There is so much variation between people in terms of their background exposure, living conditions, individual genetics, diet, exercise, smoking, drinking, and so on, that only by including a huge number can all this be somewhat averaged out and a separate signature for radiation begin to be identified for the general public. We can't say, in other words, that any individual exposed to 100 mSv will develop cancer at some point in their lives. We can't say it about a few dozen or even a few hundred individuals either. The variations are too large and too unpredictable to make any correlation meaningful [5].

Radiation exposure must also be weighed against the backdrop of normal cancer incidence. Rates here, as we all know, are high – 20–30 percent – for the general population in most advanced and emerging nations. We know of hundreds of substances and influences that increase the risk of cancer. Besides tobacco, there is, benzene, asbestos, food toxins, chemical dyes, chronic inflammation, obesity, and air pollution, to name only a few. Viewed in these real-world terms, radiation may well have to stand near the back of the line unless doses are quite high.

Some people become nervous when they learn that radiation levels go way up during a long-distance flight. This is certainly true, due to cosmic radiation, but not very significant. Commercial pilots and flight attendants are in the air as much as 900 hours each year. They are right behind uranium miners as receiving the highest doses of any occupation. Their dose depends a good deal on where they fly. If they (or us) go over the pole, they will receive about 7 μSv/h while there, dropping to 2.5 μSv/h as they approach the equator. The first figure equals 61.4 mSv/yr, well shy of the 100 mSv/yr number discussed above. But then, to achieve that figure, they would need to circle the Arctic Ocean for 12 months (8,064 hours); 900 hours would never be enough. In fact, airline crews rarely receive yearly dose levels above 3 mSv/yr. Anyone who might still be uneasy can find comfort in a seventeen-year study of 10,000 pilots, which found no discernible cancer risk from cosmic radiation [6].

What about background dose levels? The world average for natural background radiation is 2.4 mSv/yr. But levels actually vary greatly both within and between nations. Any grouping of countries will show this nicely. For example, parts of England are below 2 mSv per year, while Norway, Sweden, and Finland, with large amounts of granitic rock, are over 6 mSv/yr and in places above 10 mSv/yr. Similar variation is seen in the US: average figures for some states, like Florida, are as low as 1.3–1.4 mSv/yr, while Colorado and South Dakota are in the range of 7.1–9.6 mSv/yr. For Washington, meanwhile, we find doses under 1.4 in Puget Sound but more than ten times this (17 mSv/yr) in the northeastern part of the state [7]. Dose levels can and do vary greatly between geographic areas. A six-month visit in Denver by someone from Miami would give them nearly four times the yearly dose they would otherwise receive.

When artificial sources, such as medical procedures, buildings, etc. are added in, levels increase by 3–4 mSv/yr in most advanced nations, where such procedures are common. If we return to Florida, we can see that this means *most* of the yearly dose in that state is now due to medical (including dental) diagnosis and therapy. This is more than a little significant. Prior to the 1990s, widespread and routine use of nuclear medicine was quite restrained, being concentrated in x-rays and radiation therapy for cancer. Concerns continuing from the 1950s existed about levels of exposure, especially regarding x-rays. But the accumulation of data over three decades indicated that such concerns were higher than necessary. Expansion of new diagnostic equipment (e.g. CT-scan) and therapies thereafter have essentially doubled the yearly background dose level for most people in the developed world. In short, we are now exposed to twice the yearly ionizing radiation as in former decades. In the US, we have gone from about 3.1 to 6.2 mSv/yr, while in Europe, the rise has been from roughly 2.2 to 4.1 mSv.

Should we be worried? But as we just saw, these are very low levels, below a single CT scan. As we will see, there are areas on Earth where *natural* background levels are many times higher. Study of the effects of these dose levels on people living in such places are revealing, and we will visit them to find out what such study has found.

Why Effects Can Be Different

We usually think about the link between radiation and cancer, and this is not wrong. Radiation is able to cause almost any kind of common cancer. But again, it is not monolithic. Its effects on the human body depend on a number of factors. Type of radiation is one of these. A rule of thumb says that gamma rays have the greatest effect when exposure comes from outside the body, while all three kinds are capable of important impacts when inside. This makes sense when we remember the penetrative capabilities of each (alpha least, beta small, gamma large).

At the same time, different parts of the body respond differently to radiation. Some tissues are more sensitive than others. The most radiosensitive are where cells multiply quickly as part of normal processes. This is why children are more vulnerable to radiation harm than adults. Especially radiosensitive in both children and adults are bone marrow, reproductive organs, intestines, and the lymph system (thymus, spleen, lymph nodes). Next are the skin and portions of the body with cell linings, like the mouth, esophagus, rectum, vagina, ureter, and bladder. Less radiosensitive are our respiratory organs, kidneys, liver, mature (nongrowing) bones and cartilage. Most resistant to radiation damage are the muscles, spinal cord, brain, and red blood cells.

Another factor has to do with the specific isotope or isotopes involved. This means how radioactive they are, how abundant, and also how *mobile*, how easily can they spread through the environment Certain radioisotopes, because of their chemical properties, form compounds that dissolve readily in water and so can be transported anywhere that water goes, including into soils, lakes, streams, plants, animals, food, and humans. Isotopes that do not dissolve in water are far less mobile and will tend to remain in place, unless washed away, when deposited on solid ground. Some isotopes form compounds with minerals in the soil and can be fixed there for long periods of time.

Chemistry also determines where an isotope goes once it enters the body. Some are concentrated in specific organs. This happens because these isotopes are able to take the place of elements that are normally present. The thyroid gland, for example, draws the stable isotope of element iodine (I-126) out of the blood stream to help make hormones essential to growth for children and that continue to regulate our metabolism as adults. One of the most common products of uranium and plutonium fission is I-131, a radioisotope with a half-life of only eight days (recall: the shorter the half-life, the more rapidly an isotope decays). The isotope I-131 is in the chemical family of the halogens and has similar properties to chlorine or fluorine, meaning that it readily changes into a gas. When released, it will quickly disperse and then settle over a wide area. If this area is crop- or pastureland or has a source of water for people, the isotope will be integrated into food, milk, drinking water, and more. Taken into the body, I-131 is concentrated in the thyroid, replacing some portion of I-126. Once there, it emits very high energy beta particles; while these only penetrate a few millimeters, they are energetic enough to do significant damage to thyroid cells if the isotope is concentrated enough.

Data from Hiroshima and Nagasaki, from studies of fallout victims, and from the Chernobyl accident, show that if ingested in sufficient amounts, I-131 can result in thyroid problems, including cancer. While thyroid cancer, a fairly rare disease, is among the most successfully treated of all cancers, with very few fatalities if detected early, it remains a distinct danger from fallout sourced by uranium/plutonium fission. To minimize such danger, iodine pills are handed out, which saturate the thyroid with the stable isotope and so keep out I-131. If this is done and no further spread of the radioisotope occurs, the danger from I-131 will fall fairly rapidly. One of the largest and most comprehensive studies of exposure to I-131 where iodine pills were not available comes from Chernobyl. The following paragraph from a 2006 summary by the World Health Organization (WHO) of Chernobyl's effects is particularly informative:

> A large increase in the incidence of thyroid cancer has occurred among people who were young children and adolescents at the time of the accident and lived in the most contaminated areas of Belarus, the Russian Federation, and Ukraine . . . Radioactive iodine was deposited in pastures eaten by cows who then concentrated it in their milk which was subsequently drunk by children. This was further exacerbated by a general iodine deficiency in the local diet causing more of the radioactive iodine to be accumulated in the thyroid. Since radioactive iodine is short lived, if people had stopped giving locally supplied contaminated milk to children for a few months following the accident, it is likely that most of the increase in radiation-induced thyroid cancer would not have resulted [8].

Lack of iodine pills *plus* deficiency of this element in local foods combined with I-131 fallout to cause some 4,000–6,000 cases of thyroid cancer over the next twenty years, resulting in a total of fifteen deaths. For Fukushima, on the other hand, iodine pills were available and no dietary deficiency existed (seafood, including seaweed, which Japanese eat in abundance, are very high in I-126). At the time of this writing (2017), no cases of thyroid cancer have been confirmed to result from the nuclear accident of March 2011.

Since we will have much more to say about these nuclear accidents in Chapter 6, there are three other radioisotopes, all common fission products, we should introduce. The most important of these is Cesium-137, a radio-isotope of stable Cs-133 that emits beta and gamma radiation, with a half-life of thirty years. As one of the alkali metals, Cesium is highly reactive, forming compounds that are called salts (Sodium and Potassium are also alkali metals), which dissolve quickly and completely in water. Thus, when released in quantity, C-137 also ends up in plants, animals, drinking water, and foods. When ingested, Cs-137 spreads throughout the body, where it can stay for up to four to five months before being entirely excreted. Because of this *and* its high mobility and relatively long half-life, it is a major concern in any large-scale nuclear incident. Another fact adds to this. Because Cesium can substitute for potassium, it can also become fixed in nonedible plants and in clay minerals. This renders it immobile and therefore a continuing presence in the landscape. A second radioisotope, Cs-134, has identical chemical properties to its Cs-137 sibling and similar emissions, but a much shorter half-life of 2.1 years. There are no "Cesium pills" to take for protection.

One final radioisotope of concern is Strontium-90, an artificial isotope of stable Sr-88. As a beta emitter (it also emits weak gamma radiation), it is not usually a threat unless ingested (it is not dangerous if inhaled). Its quality of potential harm comes from a half-life of twenty-nine years and a strong chemical similarity to calcium, which gives it high mobility and a concentration in dairy products, especially milk. It thus ends up in bones, teeth, and also in the kidneys. It can reside in the body for several decades or more. At sufficient concentrations in bone and bone marrow, Sr-90 can cause bone cancer or even leukemia. By far the largest source of Sr-90 in the world (~99 percent) is atmospheric nuclear testing. The second large source is the Chernobyl accident. No increase in Sr-90 above natural background has been found associated with the Fukushima event.

When Is It Harmful?

This is perhaps the question most people would like answered, clearly and definitively. Do such answers exist? Yes – but, like all answers in science, in terms of probability. Or, to coin a phrase: there is no such thing as risk without uncertainty.

Take radon, for example, a common source of exposure for most of us. It is a decay product of U-238 and the largest contributor to natural background radiation, something we breathe every day. Mainly Rn-222, with a half-life of 3.8 days, it is a gas that emits alpha particles. In areas where soils have more uranium than is common, Rn-222 can build up inside homes over time, especially basements that lack air circulation. Long-term exposure for underground uranium miners has been proven a risk for lung cancer, yet estimates of risk for the public are complicated by lack of scientific understanding about exactly *how* lung cancer is initiated and by people's exposure to tobacco smoke, asbestos, particulate matter, or other lung-damaging substances. Large-scale studies able to correct for some of this have given contrary results. Most interpret a rise in risk with higher radon levels, but others argue for the exact opposite (healthful) effect [9]. At base, the controversy is not about data but a powerful interpretive idea.

We see this idea come alive in the numbers used, for example, by the US Environmental Protection Agency (EPA) to define recommended limits for radon in homes. Since 2005, the limit has been 4 picoCi/liter, or, in SI units, 148 Bq/m^3. This is stricter than in many other nations, where the limit varies from 400 Bq/m^3 to 1,000 Bq/m^3 [10]. EPA estimates that at 148 Bq/m^3 "about 7 people" will contract lung cancer out of 1,000 who never smoked. For smokers, the risk leaps nine-fold, to 62 people. At 400 Bq/m^3, the numbers are "about 18 people" for nonsmokers and 150 (15 percent) for smokers. When we plot these figures on a graph (Bq/m^3 vs. modeled risk level), we see a linear relationship: for every 100 Bq/m^3, the modeled risk will go up 0.47 percent for nonsmokers and 4.7 percent for smokers. This plot, however, doesn't end at the 148 Bq/m^3 limit but is extrapolated to smaller levels. At 48 Bq/m^3, the risk has fallen to "about 2" nonsmokers (out of 1,000).

But here we encounter a problem. Reducing radon this low, the EPA says, "is difficult" in most homes [11]. This is an official way of saying it can't be done; the great majority of us can't reduce our radon activity this low. We have opened basement windows, put fans in, taken out the bar, whatever. We are at a real-world physical limit. *And yet*, the linear relationship doesn't stop here. The mentioned graph, as routinely drawn, continues all the way to zero. This essentially means there is still some level of risk even when we are faced with a single atom of Rn-222. Thus, the answer to the question of this section is simple: ionizing radiation is always harmful, at *any* level. Or, rephrasing the query as "When are we safe?" The answer is just as final: never.

However excessive this may seem, it has been a fixed idea in radiation studies since the 1950s and remains in place as the foundation of official protection philosophy. Experts in related fields know it is excessive, of course. But there is so much uncertainty involved in risk estimates – uncertainty due to differences in people's genetics and life styles, and in the effects of radiation itself at doses below about 500 mSv and especially below 100 mSv – that the linear relationship will help guide experts in setting dose limits that will be able to protect everyone.

To understand this better, a bit of history helps. A good deal is known about the body's response to levels around 1,000 mSv and above from studies of atom bomb survivors. The most famous and long-lived effort has been the Life Span Study (LSS) of bomb survivors and their children, including some 121,000 people.[5] Coordinated by Japanese and US scientists, the effort continues today and will likely pursue its work decades hence, until the number of its subjects declines considerably. While it represents unparalleled work, able because of the nature of exposure to

---

[5] Conducted first by the Atomic Bomb Casualty Commission, which later became the Radiation Effects Research Foundation, this extensive study has followed 94,000 people (reduced to 86,500 over time) directly exposed to bomb radiation and 27,000 individuals who were not exposed. Its reports can be downloaded from its website: http://www.rerf.jp/index_e.html http://www.rerf.jp/library/archives_e/lsstitle.html

examine effects on both genders in all age groups, LSS is limited in one major way: destruction of prebomb medical records and data censorship under American military occupation during the first five years after the war. Nonetheless, the long-term value of the study cannot be gainsaid.

LSS found early on that at distances of 1–1.2 km from the explosion hypocenter, corresponding (in today's terms) to about 3,000–4,000 mSv, survival rates were 50 percent, increasing fairly rapidly with distance. At about 1.5 km, dose rates fell to 1,000 mSv, where symptoms of radiation sickness were common but not fatal, and at 1.75 km to about 400–500 mSv, where such symptoms ceased but where there was a decrease in lymphocytes (white blood cells). These types of data produced a linear plot of biological impact with decreasing dose. Below about 500 mSv, the data for atom bomb survivors becomes increasingly scattered, allowing for a number of interpretations [12].

Some of the broad findings by LSS tend to surprise and even shock people when they hear them. This is because findings utterly contradict commonly held views about bomb survivors. For example, the idea that most survivors affected by bomb radiation became sick and later died is untrue. More than fifty years after the bombing, over 90 percent of affected children who were under ten at the time remain alive, while over 40 percent of people who were then adults were still living (the figure was estimated at more than 70 percent in 1950). It also turns out that only about 8–10 percent of all cancers observed in survivors could be attributable to radiation [13]. Another widely held belief is that birth defects were frequent in children born to irradiated parents. This is also false. A total of 31,150 children born to affected parents were compared with 41,066 from other Japanese cities, with the result that *no increases in birth defects* among the first group were seen, even over decades. This doesn't mean a complete absence of defects due to radiation. It does mean they were not frequent enough to stand out in any detectable way [14].

The suggestion from LSS findings seems evident. We may need to scale back our ideas about how threatening alpha, beta, and gamma radiation truly may be. At *moderate* and *high* doses, biological impacts from radiation, including cancer risk, increase as the dose rises, in a linear way. But at *lower doses*, especially below 100 mSv, no final relationship has been established, and there is growing controversy about this, some of it quite heated. This remains the case despite studies that appear every few years claiming to have ended the debate [15]. But LSS has its limits too. It can tell us a great deal about the effects of one-time doses, but not as much about long-term, low-level exposures. The latter defines the radiation experience for the great majority of humanity, including most of those affected by nuclear accidents. Thus more needs to be said here.

Hermann Muller and the LNT Hypothesis

The no-safe level idea about radiation began, in large part, during the late 1940s with Hermann Muller. Muller was a top-level geneticist responsible for discovering in the 1920s the power of x-rays to cause mutations in fruit flies, work for which he was awarded the 1946 Nobel Prize in medicine. In his Nobel speech, Muller stated that 99 percent of mutations were harmful, noting that their frequency "is directly and simply proportional to the dose of irradiation applied ... whether x- or gamma- or even beta-rays." He had little trouble, scientifically or emotionally, extending his work on insects to human beings. He felt the data left "no escape from the conclusion that there is no threshold dose" below which damaging mutations ceased [16]. Ionization of even a small group of atoms in a single cell could be harmful. In an address to the National Academy of Sciences in 1955, he stated: "it is no longer a matter of doubt" that any exposure, no matter how tiny, carries its corresponding risk [17]. Because of this, moreover, any long-term study of bomb survivors was a waste of time. It could not reveal the real mutations that had been produced in individuals. This was because of a still more insidious reality:

> Each detrimental mutation, even though small in effect and lost to view in the jumble of a heterogeneous population, tends to continue from generation to generation and to hamper successive descendants, until at last it happens to tip the scales against one of its possessors, and that line of descent then dies out in consequence ... And the individual sufferers will be unable to trace their troubles to the source. At long last, the damaged heredity must become eliminated from the race by the painful process of extinction of lines [18].

If there be any doubt about Muller's meaning, he further noted in a *Time* magazine interview that it would be "fortunate" if all irradiated bomb survivors were made sterile [19].

We may not be shocked to find that Muller was a life-long believer in eugenics. It was a core belief of his, one he repeated until his death in 1967, that there is a first-order need for the genetic improvement of humanity. Programs aimed at reversing harmful mutations, through "a rationally directed guidance of reproduction" should be seen as a required effort of civilization and thus "must continue to constitute our ultimate biological hope" [20]. Therefore, anything created by humanity that worked in the opposite direction, to increase our "genetic load," especially on a global scale, defined a threat of the deepest kind (Muller was not loath to employ moral terms like "good" and "evil"). Such, without any doubt, was radiation.

This was close to an extremist view, even at the time. Yet in the aftermath of Hiroshima and Nagasaki and in the midst of nuclear weapon testing, with growing worries over fallout, Muller's ideas gained force. As an eminent geneticist who spoke often in public (a rare thing), his influence extended well beyond the journal literature. That he was an excellent, path-breaking scientist is beyond doubt. That he accurately judged the impacts of radiation on humans, not fruit flies, is questionable at best. There was little or no knowledge at the time of how cells and, especially, DNA were able to self-heal. Today we know most mutations have neutral impacts. Despite advances in the 1960s, Muller never modified his views.

In a highly influential National Academy report published in 1956, Muller's no-safe-dose hypothesis became official policy. This report, *Biological Effects of Atomic Radiation* (which we will discuss in Chapter 7), was partly written by Muller himself and established what became known as the *linear no-threshold* (LNT) model. As suggested by our discussion of radon above, LNT remains the basis for methods that estimate the risk from radiation. LNT, in fact, has been re-evaluated and officially re-established over the past six decades as an international standard. This is largely due to the lack of a recognized alternative and to the reigning idea, noted above, that only very conservative dose limits can guarantee a high level of protection. In fact, LNT advises *against* any such limits (no safe dose). But governments have decided, correctly or not, that such limits are easier to administer, monitor, and use for communicating levels of risk. A key problem, however, is that very low dose limits tend to exaggerate risk. When applied in nuclear accidents, as revealed by Chernobyl and Fukushima, they act to help spread fear and to support official responses that are hasty and add greatly to the level of suffering.

Yet, while LNT has many loyalists in the radiobiological community, it has come under increasing fire. This is largely due to new data that refuses to support it [21–22]. Included here, for example, is updated information on A-bomb survivors who received low doses, as well as studies of patients who have undergone radiation therapy. A growing number of professionals point out that the LNT model for low doses (e.g. <100 mSv) has become ever-more shaky and inadequate and deserves to be challenged [23]. They emphasize that studies claiming to prove LNT at low doses come up with numbers so vanishingly small (e.g. 0.0001 percent) that they call into question the very idea of "risk" itself [24]. Doubtless one of the more important studies whose results counter the LNT hypothesis involved mice subjected for five weeks to dose levels of 890 mSv/y, roughly 400 times natural background [25]. Though receiving a total dose of about 105 mSv, the subjects showed no signs of significant DNA damage. If this seems questionable due to the use of animal subjects, we might consider that the origin of the LNT concept was based on Hermann Muller's experiments with fruit flies in the 1920s.

A possible competing hypothesis, known as *hormesis*, has attracted storms of interest and debate. It claims that low doses of radiation are actually beneficial, as they stimulate DNA repair and other immune system responses [26]. Hormesis refers to the healthful effect that tiny doses of a toxin or other "stressor" can generate. The phenomenon, long established in Asian medicine, has gained acceptance in the West via laboratory studies, for example on use of snake venom to treat arthritis [27]. But with radiation, hormesis remains a battleground. Accepted by official organizations in France, Japan, China, and Korea, it has been repeatedly rejected in the US, much of Europe, and by the United Nations Scientific Committee on the Effects of Atomic Radiation (UNSCEAR) [28]. A common objection points to the lack of a clear mechanism for hormesis. Yet there is no complete understanding of how radiation produces cancer either. For now, the debate seems worthy but unresolved.

How low *are* official dose limits based on LNT? Let us look at those for the US, published by the Nuclear Regulatory Commission [29]. These are limits that apply to government facilities and refer to the maximum that is allowed for annual exposures above normal background. For any member of the general public: 1 mSv. For adult workers in facilities where radioactive materials are present: 50 mSv. For pregnant adults and minors (sixteen to eighteen years old) who work in such facilities: 5 mSv. In Europe, dose limits are still lower for workers, 20 mSv, and for pregnant workers, 1 mSv. These limits agree with what is recommended by the International Commission on Radiological Protection (ICRP), an independent organization whose mission is to minimize harmful effects of ionizing radiation worldwide. Comparing these figures with our list of doses given earlier in the chapter, we see that most are half or less than the radiation from one CT scan. If extended to cover our personal decisions in daily life, we would not be allowed to take more than three transoceanic plane trips, or, for that matter, to move our family to a location above an altitude of 7,000 ft (2,120 m).

It helps to go back to a point that offers some perspective. When talking about radiation risk, after all, we are really talking about a risk *above* the expected incidence of cancer. For the US population, the average lifetime chance for having cancer (fatal or not) is 41 percent; in other words, 1 in 2.4. The odds are worse in the UK, at around 50 percent [30]. Cancer, in fact, is one of the most intensively studied sets of diseases, and global statistics are abundant. For wealthy nations, the cumulative probability of developing cancer by age 75 is 30 percent for men (1 in 3.3) and 15 percent for women (1 in 6.7). In "less developed" countries, the rates fall to 17 percent for men (1 in 5.9) and 12.7 percent for women (1 in 7.9) [31]. What do these numbers tell us? First, that if cancer is our main worry, low doses of radiation are trivial compared to other influences. Second, that one of the most dangerous decisions a man in Cambodia or Kenya can make isn't to work in a nuclear plant or waste facility in his home country. He can simply move to a wealthy country and adopt its lifestyle.

A Plane Trip to Kerala

It is time for a journey. We are ready, that is, to visit some parts of the globe to sample its radiological diversity. We begin with a plane ride from New York to southwestern India. The state of Kerala, part of the famous Malabar Coast, is blessed with gleaming beaches, palm trees bending in the trade winds, and rainforest green of the Western Ghats ranges.

Kerala's beaches are unique. They have among the highest levels of natural radiation on Earth. Their sand is rich with the mineral monazite, source of rare earth metals and thorium. The monazite sands of Kerala were created over millions of years by rivers that drained inland areas where veins bearing the mineral once existed. Transported to the sea, eroded material was distributed along the coast by longshore currents. Kerala's beaches contain the largest concentration of thorium in the world.

Researchers have not been shy about studying them. They have found much variety in their readings. At the low end are doses of 1–10 mSv per year, at the mid-level 40–50 mSv/yr, and at the upper end, 60–75 mSv/yr, with over 100,000 people living in areas where the yearly dose is 10–40 mSv [32]. Roughly a quarter of this comes from internal exposure to radon. Within five years, most of these people will have received 50–200 mSv, more than radiation workers are allowed, and if they are born and grow up in these areas, they will have a lifetime dose of will over 1,000 mSv, much of it while they were children. This might make us want to get back on the plane, until we learn that rates of serious illness have fallen dramatically in recent years (a source of pride). There is, too, the small fact that cancer rates are a bit lower than those in the general population [33–34].

After a few months of reassured relaxation at our Kerala resort, it is time to move on. We board an Iranian Airlines flight to Tehran. From here we drive north about 200 km, through the magnificent Elburz Mountains, the great volcano of Mt. Damavand, over 5,600 meters (18,400 ft) high, always in view. Passing through the ranges, we turn west along the coast of the Caspian Sea and eventually come to Ramsar, a popular resort town known as the "gem of northern Iran." Ramsar, in fact, has prospered in modern times from its offerings of coastal recreation, urban culture, and, in the searing Iranian summer, cool and misty mountain walks. Its population has grown to about 60,000 but can swell to nearly ten times this number at the height of the season. One of Ramsar's core attractions, open all year, are a series of hot springs. Visited for their presumed healthful benefits, these waters have a singular character. Migrating upward through fractured granite rich in uranium and its decay products, they are highly enriched in radium. Where they emerge from the ground are thick deposits of travertine, a form of precipitated limestone, which is itself enhanced in radioactive elements. Easy to quarry and shape, the travertine can be found in the walls of many homes nearby the springs.

The town has been famous among radiation experts for decades. Effective dose levels here are the highest known on Earth, varying from a low range of 10–50 mSv to a high-range of 130–260 mSv per year, with up to a third of this from internal exposure [35–36]. Highest doses are near the hot springs, of which around 150 exist, with the nine largest developed into spas. Geothermal activity has been high for many thousands of years, so elevated amounts of radium and radon have been present in the air, soil, ground and surface water, and, more recently, crops (such as rice) that are locally grown. People who live here are immersed their whole lives in natural radiation that can be five times or more the international limit for radiation workers. And cancer rates? No higher than normal for the Iranian public, whose rates are lower than in the West [37–39]. If our sense of irony is thereby put in motion, we might recall that during the Fukushima nuclear accident, some wealthier residents escaped the area by going to Japan's famous radium hot springs, Misasa Onsen.

Spending months enjoying the cool mountain air in the daytime and hot spring water at night, we are again ready to continue our journey. Let us, however, be brief this time. Our next stop, Guarapari, Brazil, is yet another lovely monazite beach area (with "black sands" especially rich in the mineral), a tourist destination with annual dose rates locally up to 30 mSv and above 100 mSv in a few places [40]. After splashing in the southern Atlantic for a month or two, we take off once more, this time for Yangjiang, a semi-tropical area in southern China with monazite-bearing clay soils used to make bricks for houses. Being invited to stay in cottages made of this material, we too are able to sample background radiation levels of 5–10 mSv/yr, most of it internal and much higher than in surrounding areas [41].

There is one final stop on our global itinerary. For this we must leave the Earth's temperate zones and visit the far north. Here, in the Barents and Kara seas, off the northeastern Arctic coast of Russia and along the east-facing inlets of Novaya Zemlya, we will not stay long. It is not a pleasant place to visit for the reasons we are doing so. Novaya Zemlya was one of the Soviet's primary nuclear testing sites and is where the largest such test of any kind – the Tsar Bomba in 1961, at 50 Megatons – was detonated. But that's not why we're here. In the 1960s and 1980s, the Soviet Union dumped 17,000 containers of radioactive waste into the Barents Sea, fourteen submarine nuclear reactors, five still containing spent fuel, in the bays of Novaya Zemlya, and nineteen ships with radioactive waste in the Kara Sea. If this were not enough, it also scuttled a nuclear submarine, both its reactors loaded with fuel [42]. On our trip to the area, we learn that this has been known since the early 1990s. A number of international research missions have been to the area, conducted sampling, monitoring, analytical work, held conferences, shared data, and produced reports. Some researchers, perhaps, expected to find an environmental disaster, with much threat to nearby humans (the city of Murmansk, towns of northernmost Norway, indigenous people like the Sami and Nenets) via contaminated seafood.

Nothing of the kind has been found, however. Rather than spreading through the water column and into food webs, thus affecting the Arctic ecological system, leaked radionuclides have remained in the immediate vicinity of their sources [43]. Continuous monitoring, moreover, shows that this hasn't changed since the early 1990s when the first studies were done [44]. None of this means all is fine and we can just go back to reading Pushkin. Such nuclear material needs to be recovered and disposed of properly, like so much other waste that has been dumped into the seas. But not because it qualifies as a catastrophic threat to the Arctic and its people. Such a threat very definitely exists and is in progress: climate change. But it is linked to a different set of energy sources.

Having now completed our year-long journey, we return to New York and take stock of our exposures. Three months in Kerala provided 15 mSv (60 mSv/yr × 0.25 yr), as we spent much time walking the beaches and building sand castles. Enchanted by Ramsar, we remained six months, taking our ease, chipping off samples of travertine, enjoying the warm mineral waters each evening, and sampling the locally grown (organic) dishes, gaining an impressive 65 mSv (130 mSv/yr × 0.5 yr). In Brazil, where we stayed two months, the beaches drew us once more, especially the black sand (we saved a bag of it!), but in Yangjiang we arrived at the start of the monsoon and spent the entire month confined indoors to our clay-brick cottage. These places, then, provided another 15 mSv, bringing the sum to 95 mSv (no exposure from the Russian Arctic). Adding 3 mSv for our total flying time (eighty hours, with bags of travertine and black sand), plus a doctor's visit and CT scan (spine, 10 mSv) for back pain due to so many long flights in economy class, and we arrive at a final figure for the year of 108 mSv.

Should we be worried? Our exposure, after all, is more than ten times what people in the Chernobyl and Fukushima evacuation zones received. Regarding Iran, the US Centers for Disease Control advises travelers to be fully up to date on vaccinations and to be watchful for food and water contamination: malaria, typhus, polio, yellow fever, and Hepatitis A are diseases of concern. Not a word is said about radiation.

Our radiological journey, then, has been revealing. We may even wish to return for a second visit to one of our sites in the future, like the Malabar Coast, with its truly ancient history. If so, we might well arrive when India has begun mining its thorium-bearing sands, fulfilling its long-term plan to build reactors that can't meltdown and generate no plutonium so are largely without proliferation risks.

How Dangerous, Really?

Part of the research for this book involved speaking to a variety of scientists in the field of radiobiology. Some of these people were involved in radiation protection, some were academic researchers, others were hospital radiologists and government health physicists. Few were eager to discuss in any but a general way the current system of dose limits and the LNT hypothesis. About the latter, most acknowledged the existing debate over its accuracy at low doses but, in the words of one well-known researcher, would rather keep their "head down" about it. As one government scientist put it, "the topic is often too politically and emotionally radioactive" for rational discussion.

In the end, it is difficult to avoid concluding that our system for estimating the biological risks of radiation creates more risk than it solves. This system, that is, remains overly indebted to the fearful view of Hermann Muller. It is thus never very far from the eugenics-inspired idea that radiation represents a power that degrades the human prospect. It is a singular idea. There are, after all, concentration thresholds for many other substances, be it a neurotoxin, poison, or bacterial/viral abundance. Only radiation is treated as if it will do us harm if even one atom is involved. Only in this realm does it seem risk is infinite and inexorable.

There are serious implications to such a view. The LNT concept is not merely a hypothesis. It is a philosophy. It puts forth a metaphysics and an ethics of living in a world where one of the most elemental processes in nature becomes a ubiquitous carrier of the most dreaded disease known. Of course, there exists another dimension here. Humans have themselves contaminated the Earth with radiation, especially with weapons of annihilation. The limitless peril of exposure therefore becomes a mirror of this, too, *and* a punishment for it.

A growing number of professionals now agree that the fear industry surrounding radiation has been much more perilous to public health than radiation itself [45]. It has clearly fed antiscience views among the general public. Radiation fear, for example, has turned many people away from the use of nuclear medicine in diagnosis and therapy, thereby lowering effective care. It has fed worries about cancer produced by power lines, cell phones, computer screens, and the like. It has led to widespread and scientifically unfounded suspicion of irradiated foods, in the belief that these become radioactive or damaged. As a result, the technology is barely used in many advanced nations, especially in Europe, but also rejected by many health-conscious individuals in North America and East Asia. Because of this, meat, seafood, and dairy products, in particular, have for fifty years been subject to higher-than-necessary rates of contamination by pathogens, leading to outbreaks, for example, of *E coli*.

Among the worst consequences of radiophobia are the many lives lost and damaged by the accidents at Chernobyl and Fukushima. As we will see later, it has been firmly established that the most serious public health impacts from these events came from panic evacuations by each government but still more from the mental health problems suffered by many tens of thousands. Taking the case of Chernobyl, thousands of young women in Europe decided to abort perfectly healthy fetuses in order to avoid birth defects they believed would happen due to Chernobyl fallout [46–48]. Workers in the Soviet Union who helped clean up the accident showed significantly high rates of suicide in years afterward [49]. There were roughly 600,000 "liquidators" (as they were called), and it is these workers along with many of the evacuated residents that suffered from depression, anxiety attacks, post-traumatic stress disorder, and other symptoms up to four times higher than the general population [50].

At some point, one feels, society must come to its senses about radiation. Ultimately, because of its factual ubiquity in nature, the no-threshold philosophy tells us we were not really meant to survive long-term in this universe: our "little spaceship Earth," in the famous words of R. Buckminster Fuller, is actually a chamber of slow execution. Life on Earth began roughly 4 billion years ago, when the atmosphere was thin and radiation levels were far higher than today. A host of radioactive isotopes existed then in the shallow planetary crust that have long since decayed away. Over the span of geologic time, levels have fallen, continuously and greatly. All living things have adapted to this dynamic. There is no evidence that human beings define an exception.

References

[1] American Cancer Society, Cancer Facts and Statistics (Internet). Available from: https://www.cancer.org/research/cancer-facts-statistics.html

[2] US NRC (Nuclear Regulatory Commission), Measuring Radiation (January 4, 2016). Available from: www.nrc.gov/about-nrc/radiation/health-effects/measur ing-radiation.html

[3] T. Henriksen and D. H. Maillie, *Radiation and Health* (Boca Raton, FL: CRC Press, 2002).

[4] Ibid., Chs. 4 and 8.

[5] T. Jorgensen, *Strange Glow: The Story of Radiation* (Princeton: Princeton University Press, 2016).

[6] E. Pukkala al., Incidence of cancer among Nordic airline pilots over five decades: occupational cohort study (Internet), *British Medical Journal*, 325 (September 14, 2002), 1–5. Available from: www.bmj.com/content/bmj/325/7364/567.full.pdf

[7] J. Mauro and N. M. Briggs, Assessment of Variations in Radiation Exposure in the United States (Internet), US Environmental Protection Agency, Contract EP-D-05–002. 2005. Available from: www.orau.org/ptp/PTP%20Library/library/ Subject/Environmental/radiationbackground.pdf

[8] World Health Organization, Health Effects of the Chernobyl Accident: An Overview (Internet). Available from: www.who.int/ionizing_radiation/cherno byl/backgrounder/en/

[9] J. M. Samet, Radiation and Cancer Risk: A Continuing Challenge for Epidemiologists. *Environmental Health*, 10 (Supplement 1, 2011), S4, 1–9.

[10] H. Zeeb, International Radon Project: Survey on Radon Guidelines, Programmes and Activities (Internet). World Health Organization, WHO/ HSE/RAD/07.01. Available from: www.who.int/ionizing_radiation/env/radon/ IRP_Survey_on_Radon.pdf

[11] US Environmental Protection Agency, Health Risk of Radon (Internet). Available from: www.epa.gov/radon/health-risk-radon

[12] M. Doss, B. L. Egleston, and S. Litwin, Comments on 'Studies of the Mortality of Atomic Bomb Survivors, Report 14, 1950–2003: An Overview of Cancer and Noncancer Diseases. *Radiation Research*, 178:3 (September 2012), 244–245.

[13] B. Schaal, What We've Learned from the Atomic Bomb Survivors (Internet). Insights from the Chair, National Academy of Sciences (February 26, 2013). Available from: http://nas-sites.org/insights/192013/02/26/what-weve-learned-from-the-atomic-bomb-survivors/

[14] Radiation Effects Research Foundation, Birth Defects Among the Children of Atomic Bomb Survivors (1948–1954) (Internet). Available from: www.rerf.jp/ radefx/genetics_e/birthdef.html

[15] S. T. Corneliussen, Experts Publish Dueling Messages on Low Radiation Doses (Internet). *Physics Today* (July 6, 2015). Available from: http://scitation.aip.org/ content/aip/magazine/physicstoday/news/10.1063/PT.5.8124

[16] H. J. Muller, Nobel Lecture – Nobel Prize in Physiology or Medicine, 1946 (Internet). Nobelprize.org, Official Web Site of the Nobel Prize. Available from: www.nobelprize.org/nobel_prizes/medicine/laureates/1946/muller-lecture.html

[17] H. J. Muller, Genetic Damage Produced by Radiation, *Bulletin of the Atomic Scientists*, 11:9 (November 1955), 210–212, 230; 210.

[18] Muller, Genetic Damage, p. 211.

[19] The Gloomy Nobleman, *Time*, 48:20 (11 November, 1946), 96, 98; 96.

[20] H. J. Muller, Our Load of Mutations, *American Journal of Human Genetics*, 2:2 (June 1950), 111–176; 171, 169.

[21] M. Tubiana, The Linear No-Threshold Relationship is Inconsistent with Radiation Biologic and Experimental Data, *Radiology*, 251:1 (2009), 13–22.

[22] D. R. Wigg, Radiation: Facts, Fallacies and Phobias, *Australasian Radiology*, 51 (2007), 21–25.

[23] B. L. Cohen, Test of the Linear-No Threshold Theory; Rationale for Procedures. *Nonlinearity in Biology, Toxicology, and Medicine*, 3 (2005), 261–282.

[24] A. Abbott, Researchers Pin Down Risks of Low-Dose Radiation (Internet), *Nature*, 523:7558 (June 30, 2015). Available from: www.nature.com/news/researchers-pin-down-risks-of-low-dose-radiation-1.17876

[25] W. Olipitz et al., Integrated Molecular Analysis Indicates Undetectable Change in DNA Damage in Mice After Continuous Irradiation at ~400-fold Natural Background Radiation, *Environmental Health Perspectives*, 120:8 (August 2012), 1130–1136.

[26] A. M. Vaiserman, Radiation Hormesis: Historical Perspective and Implications for Low-Dose Cancer Risk Assessment, *Dose Response*, 8 (2010), 172–191.

[27] A. Gomes et al., Antiarthritic Activity of Indian Monpcellate Cobra (Naja Kaouthia) Venom on Adjuvant Induced Arthritis, *Toxicon*, 55 (2010), 670–673.

[28] T. D. Luckey, Radiation Hormesis: The Good, the Bad, and the Ugly, *Dose Response*, 4:3 (2006), 169–190.

[29] US Nuclear Regulatory Commission, NRC Regulations (10 CFR) (Internet), Part 20 – Standards for Protection Against Radiation, Subpart C – Occupational Dose Limits, Subpart D – Radiation Dose Limits for Individual Members of the Public. Available from: www.nrc.gov/reading-rm/doc-collections/cfr/part020/

[30] Cancer Research UK. Cancer Risk Statistics (Internet). Available from: www.cancerresearchuk.org/content/cancer-risk-statistics#heading-Zero

[31] A. Jemal, F. Bray, M. M. Center et al., Global Cancer Statistics. *CA: A Cancer Journal for Clinicians*, 61 (2011), 69–90; Table 1, 73.

[32] J. H. Hendry et. al., Human Exposure to High Natural Background Radiation: What Can it Teach Us About Radiation?, *Journal of Radiological Protection*, 29 (June 2009), A29–A42.

[33] C. R. Soman, V. R. Kutty, S. Safraj et al., All-Cause Mortality and Cardiovascular Mortality in Kerala State of India: Results from a 5-Year Follow-up of 161,942 Rural Community Dwelling Adults, *Asia-Pacific Journal of Public Health*, 20:10 (2010), 1–8.

[34] R. R. Nair et. al., Background Radiation and Cancer Incidence in Kerala, India – Karanagappally Cohort Study, *Health Physics*, 96:1 (2009), 55–66.

[35] M. Sohrabi, Recent Radiological Studies of High Level Natural Radiation Areas of Ramsar, *Proceedings of International Conference 'High Levels of Natural Radiation'*, (Ramsar: November 3–7, 1990), 39–48.

[36] J. H. Hendry et. al., Human Exposure to High Natural Background Radiation: What Can It Teach Us About Radiation? *Journal of Radiological Protection*, 29 (June 2009), A29–A42.

[37] M. Ghiassi-Nejad, F. Zakeri, R. Gh. Assaei, and A. Kariminia, Long-Term Immune and Cytogenetic Effects of High Level Natural Radiation on Ramsar Inhabitants in Iran, *Journal of Environmental Radioactivity*, 74 (2004), 107–116.

[38] S. M. J. Mortazavi and P. A. Karam, Apparent Lack of Radiation Susceptibility Among Residents of the High Background Radiation Area in Ramsar, Iran: Can We Relax Our Standards?, *Natural Radiation Environment VII*, 7 (2005), 1141–1147.

[39] S. M. J. Mortazavi and H. Mozdarani, Non-Linear Phenomena in Biological Findings of the Residents of High Background Radiation Areas of Ramsar, *International Journal of Radiation Research*, 11:1 (January 2013), 3–9.

[40] R. Veiga et al., Measurement of Natural Radioactivity in Brazilian Beach Sands, *Radiation Measurements*, 41 (2006), 189–196.

[41] Z. Tao et al., Cancer and Non-cancer Mortality Among Inhabitants in the High Background Radiation Area of Yangjiang, China (1979–1998), *Health Physics*, 102:2 (February 2012), 173–181.

[42] C. Digges, Russia Announces Enormous Finds of Radioactive Waste and Nuclear Reactors in Arctic Seas (Internet), *Bellona*. Available from: http://bellona.org/news/nuclear-issues/radioactive-waste-and-spent-nuclear-fuel/2012-08-russia-announces-enormous-finds-of-radioactive-waste-and-nuclear-reactors-in-arctic-seas

[43] B. Salbu et al., Radioactive Contamination from Dumped Nuclear Waste in the Kara Sea – Results from the Joint Russian-Norwegian Expeditions in 1992–1994, *Science of the Total Environment*, 202: 1–3 (August 1997), 185–198.

[44] G. G. Matishov, D. G. Matishov, I. S. Usyagina, and N. E. Kasatkina, Multiannual Variations in Radioactive Pollution of the Barent-Kara Region (1960–2013), *Doklady Earth Sciences*, 458, Part 2 (2014), 1249–1255.

[45] G. Walinder, *Has Radiation Protection Become a Health Hazard?* (Swedish Nuclear Training and Safety Center, 2000).

[46] L. B. Knudsen, Legally Induced Abortions in Denmark after Chernobyl, *Biomedical Pharmacother*, 45:6 (1991), 229–231.

[47] T. Rytömaa, Ten Years After Chernobyl, *Annals of Medicine*, 28:2 (1996), 83–88.

[48] M. Specter, A Wasted Land – A Special Report; 10 Years Later, through Fear, Chernobyl Still Kills in Belarus (Internet), *The New York Times*, (31 March, 1996). Available from: www.nytimes.com/1996/03/31/world/wasted-land-special-report-10-years-later-through-fear-chernobyl-still-kills.html?pagewanted=all

[49] K. Rahu, M. Rahu, M. Tekkel, and E. Bromet, Suicide Risk among Chernobyl Cleanup Workers in Estonia Still Increased: An Updated Cohort Study, *Annals of Epidemiology*, 16:12 (2006), 917–919.

[50] E. J. Bromet and J. M. Havenaar, Psychological and Perceived Health Effects of the Chernobyl Disaster: A 20-Year Review, *Health Physics*, 93:5 (2007), 516–521.

6

Chernobyl and Fukushima: Meaning and Legacy

Burned into Memory

It was never a picturesque part of the world's most tyrannical state. There are forests, rolling hills, marshes and other wetlands, and grasslands, vast grasslands, many of which had once been pasture for cattle. In the abandoned areas where people have been missing for decades and may never return, the land has fallen back to the trees, grasses, and above all the animals, the wild deer and horses, the Eurasian lynx and elk, Grey Wolves and Brown Bears, wild boar and bison, red foxes, badgers, White-tailed Eagles and the majestic European crane. Where humans fear to tread, a wild kingdom feeds and flourishes. Even in this, there are ironies. Przewalski's Horse, who once roamed the Eurasian steppes until it became extinct in the wild, has been here introduced and has thrived in a zone of invisible fences of fear that keep people out.

The other region could not be more different. A coastal plain with low hills and ribbon beaches where the Pacific Ocean, in normal times, rolls to a quiet foam. River inlets, small towns and villages, fishing ports here and there, embraced by rice paddies and vegetable fields and many charming views. The taller inland hills are rugged and a vibrant green; they remain that way today. Much else of this pictorial coastline is now gone, scraped clean of buildings, trees, and human beings by the great tsunami of March 11, 2011. Irony has sprouted here too from the ruins, but with a dark face. That day when a great earthquake killed over a thousand and a tsunami took the lives of many thousands will be known for a nuclear calamity that killed no one.

Chernobyl and Fukushima are names burned into modern memory, recognized worldwide by billions. When spoken, they often become adjectives to "disaster" and "catastrophe." To many people, they define events in league with the atomic bomb. What we can say, for certain, is that Chernobyl and Fukushima are inescapably bound together as dark entries in the human imagination. Yet their connection can't be explained only in terms of what happened and why, their shared maximum seven rating on the INES nuclear accident scale,[1] or even the deceptions committed by each government. They are linked because of what facts and truths they have revealed – the data and knowledge they have generated, the informed awareness we now have of how bad things can get. The world of research has not wasted these events.

But if a great deal has been learned, most of it remains to be widely known. The level of rumor and exaggeration has continued to overshadow the results of committed study. Fear and revulsion are common mental debris and emotional smolder. Much confusion continues. This demands that we treat each incident candidly, without spin or speculation. Part of what has been learned, after all, is that each incident was both less terrible and more damaging than at first believed. For those affected, each event promised nightmares, mass radiation exposure and casualties, environmental annihilation. And as we will see, these were precisely the fears that brought more suffering to more people than radiation possibly could have.

This chapter will clarify many such elements of each accident. It draws on detailed, technical study by international organizations and research groups none of whom represent a specific government, industry, or activist perspective. A point, in fact, should be made in this regard. Conclusions based on this work are not complete but do represent the best that has been done. Affected populations, like atom bomb survivors, will continue to be monitored for decades. There are voices, however, that deny validity to the work done thus far, that would prefer to see many more people become sick, suffer, and die from radiation in order to nourish a particular position. Such voices are not included here. The politicization of knowledge about nuclear accidents defines a casualty of another kind.

Chernobyl – The What, How, and Why

Two things must be known at the beginning of any discussion about this accident. First, it could not have happened anywhere but in the Soviet Union. Second, it has been more studied than any other industrial calamity in human history.

[1] The International Nuclear and Radiological Event Scale (INES). This ranges from one, called an "anomaly" to three, "serious incident" to five, "accident with wider (than local) consequences, to seven, "major accident." A full explanation is available on the website of the International Atomic Energy Agency: www-ns.iaea.org/tech-areas/emergency/ines.asp

In February of 2003, a grouping of nine agencies under the United Nations[2] established the Chernobyl Forum, whose mission it was to gather, analyze, evaluate, and review all available data in order to produce "the most comprehensive evaluation of [Chernobyl's] consequences to date" in time for the twentieth anniversary of the event (2006). Documents that emerged from this effort covered the fields of human health, radiation impacts, behavioral responses, socioeconomic effects, and environmental impacts. Already well-known were the causes of the accident.

It began after midnight on April 26, 1986. During an ill-advised test where operators ignored plant specifications and safety, Unit 4 of the Chernobyl nuclear power facility underwent a massive power surge from a sharp increase in heat that ruptured portions of the reactor core and led to a series of steam explosions. These explosions blew open the building, exposing the graphite core to the atmosphere (thus oxygen) so that it caught fire. For ten days the fire raged and flamed, sending clouds of highly radioactive smoke and soot into the air. This went out over an area first encompassing parts of Ukraine, Russia, and Belarus. Smaller amounts were caught by the winds and carried to Poland, Scandinavia, Austria, and other parts of Europe, as far south as Greece. Soviet scientists later indicated about 180–190 metric tons of fuel and fission products were in Unit 4 at the time of the accident. Estimates of how much was borne away into the atmosphere range from a low of 6 percent to a high of 30 percent. Since it has remained too dangerous to examine the core directly, no final figure can be given. In the weeks that followed the fire, much of the airborne matter fell on the forests and farmland of the surrounding region, on the nearby town of Pripyat, on hundreds of small villages, their crops, pastureland, animals, and homes [1].

For the first two days, no announcement of the accident was made by any Soviet authority. Emergency crews, including local firefighters, were sent in to put out the fire. None were told about the danger of radiation. From above, helicopters poured sand, boron, and lead on the exploded, burning reactor, the sand being intended to smother the fire, the boron to absorb neutrons and shut down any nuclear reactions, and the lead to reduce the release of radiation. With no announcement to the public and no protective measures taking place, children in nearby Pripyat went to school as usual and played outdoors. Soccer games took place and outdoor weddings were held. People went about their business in the cool, spring weather. Those among the rescue workers who became ill could

---

[2] These include: International Atomic Energy Agency; Food and Agriculture Organization; Office for Coordination of Humanitarian Affairs; UN Development Programme; UN Environment Programme; UN Scientific Committee on the Effects of Atomic Radiation; WHO; and World Bank.

not be treated, as no hospitals were equipped for radiation sickness. The closest such medical center was in Kiev, over a hundred miles south.

A dramatic turn occurred when the weight of material dumped into the reactor chamber began to collapse the floor and supports. Beneath lay a large emergency storage pool of water for use in a loss of coolant accident. Contact between the superheated core and this pool would create an immense steam explosion and huge increase in radioactive material reaching the atmosphere. A critical valve to drain the pool did not respond; three plant workers volunteered to go into the pool, find the value and release it, which they did. All three were among those who died in the first several weeks from severe radiation poisoning.

In the meantime, Soviet propaganda did almost everything in its power to ensure the accident would be a real disaster. Instead of providing information to people in affected areas, it spent much effort decrying a "poisoned cloud of anti-Sovietism" in foreign media reports. Material about the radiation illnesses, deaths, and contamination was classified by the KGB. No one in the surrounding area was told to stop eating locally grown food or drinking milk from their own cows that had been feeding on contaminated grass. When evacuations finally began, there was chaos. Many were told they would return in a few days as radiation levels were returning to normal. Tens of thousands were taken from areas of lower to higher levels of contamination. The consistent gap between official reassurance and panicked actions added hugely to rumors that spectacular numbers of people would die, perhaps horribly. Taken together, such details tell a frightening tale of incompetence, of human blunder compounded to colossal proportions. All of which ensured that the accident would be as bad as it possibly could have been.

In fact, the accident began much earlier than April 1986. It began with the design of the reactor known as RBMK, short for *reactor bolshoy moshchnosty kanalny* or "high-power channel reactor." No other nation has ever built such technology; it would have been rejected by any regulatory body. Unstable at low power levels, it also had no containment structure, no way in an accident that damaged the core and surrounding walls to prevent the release of radioactive matter to the outside.

A brief description can help point up how truly unique was the RBMK design. Its core was a graphite pile with a large number (~1700) of vertical tubes, or "channels." Each tube, about 9 cm (3.5 inches) in diameter, held a series of tightly packed fuel rods. This arrangement allowed the fuel to heat up rapidly to very high temperatures. To take away heat, tubes were filled with water kept under pressure but still allowed to boil within the tube. Resulting steam was used to drive the turbine-generator, then cooled back into water and returned to the core. The graphite and tube structure was encased in a concrete-lined vessel that was capped by a steel cover weighing around 1,100 tons.

The cover could be removed by a remote-controlled crane to refuel the reactor even when it was operating, a distinct advantage. A mixture of helium and nitrogen gas filled the core vessel to keep out any oxygen, which, at high temperatures, could cause the graphite to catch fire.

There are two key points to note. First, there was no steel reactor pressure vessel (RPV) to sheathe the core, nor a containment shell surrounding the RPV as a second layer of protection. What existed was a single, concrete-walled vessel with a steel cap. This alone would have disqualified the design anywhere outside the Soviet Union. The RBMK was designed to be cheap, easy to build, and capable of refueling during operation. Containment would have significantly added to the cost and construction time and was deemed unnecessary by the Soviet nuclear science ministry. Second, the core design itself traded stability for larger power generation. Here, it helps to understand that the moderator (graphite) and the coolant (water) both acted to slow neutrons, but that the water also absorbed a certain portion of them as well. If, for some reason, the water *stopped* absorbing neutrons, there would be more of them available to increase the level of fission, thus the amount of heat generated. What mattered greatly was the amount of boiling inside the tubes: fewer bubbles meant more neutrons were absorbed, while more bubbles allowed more neutrons to pass through, be moderated by the graphite, and increase fission.

Once this began and wasn't quickly controlled, a runaway cycle would result. The core temperature would rise rapidly, cause more boiling, which would increase fission even more. The result would be a tremendous surge in temperature and steam production (thus pressure) inside the core tubes. These would burst, exposing the fuel and creating a steam explosion inside the vessel, blowing off the steel cover. All of the helium-nitrogen gas escapes, and with oxygen now available, a fire ignites in the graphite, the smoke carrying away exploded, partly pulverized fission products.

Such is what happened at Chernobyl. The accident was due to human error, beginning with the design and ending with poorly trained operators making poor decisions related to a bad idea for testing the reactor. The full sequence of decisions and events is too long to repeat here. Basically, operators wanted to see if, when the reactor was shut down, the continued spinning of the turbine-generator could still produce enough electricity to power the main cooling pump (imagine driving on a packed, six-lane highway, shutting off your engine, and trying to coast to the next exit across five lanes of traffic). Without getting the required permissions for such a test, they lowered the power level of the reactor using control rods and then turned off power to the turbine-generator. This reduced the flow of water to the core, causing a rise in steam production. As power levels shot up, operators tried to adjust the level of fission with the control rods but it was too late. The reaction went entirely out of control, super-heating the core, and causing a steam explosion that lifted off the 1,100-ton steel plate. The explosion was powerful enough to eject a large portion of the graphite from the core and cause fires within the reactor, surrounding building, and on the roofs of nearby buildings, while releasing a large volume of radio-active particles into the atmosphere.

Fukushima: A Different Collection of Errors

March 11, 2011, is known in Japan as "3/11." To the Japanese people, 3/11 represents a three-fold assault on the nation: the most powerful earthquake ever recorded; a tsunami event of colossal destructive, life-ending power; and a major nuclear accident that, no less than Chernobyl, was the result of multi-fold human error.

Comparison with Chernobyl, in fact, is revealing and necessary. The Soviet Union was a communist state, authoritarian to the bone; Japan is one of the world's advanced democracies. In 1986, the Soviets had the largest nuclear arsenal on the planet; the Japanese in 2011 wore the identity of the only people who had ever suffered a nuclear bombing. Where Chernobyl was entirely a nuclear accident, events at Fukushima involved a major earthquake and monstrous tsunami in addition to the resulting nuclear incident. Where dozens of workers and firemen were killed by radiation at Chernobyl in the first few months, three died at Fukushima as a result of explosions and debris, but 18,391 people lost their lives to the tsunami and more than a thousand to the earth-quake. Given such differences, we might be forgiven for believing the two events have little to do with one another.

We would be very wrong. It is in two chief areas, government responsibility and psychosocial damage that Fukushima and Chernobyl become sibling events. They meet, in other words, where the human dimension becomes most central and important.

In each case, government made key mistakes. Those related to Chernobyl began with the reactor design and ended with inept response to the accident. In Japan, the government failed in regulatory oversight by allowing the plant owner to put off safety upgrades. Both governments evacuated or relocated hundreds of thousands of people, branding large circular areas as "exclusion zones," whatever the reality of actual radiation levels. In both cases, many people could have returned home within a year or two but were not allowed to. This was especially the case with Fukushima, where people were kept in tents and other temporary housing long after dose levels had declined to near background levels. In the name of "protecting the public," officials were essentially responsible for real, not statistical, casualties. Stress, depression, anxiety, and other forms of anguish for these people, as for those at Chernobyl, had fatal results. Though the administration of Shinzo Abe finally declared that most residents would be allowed to go home by early 2017, a great many rejected this out of fear and distrust, filing lawsuits against the government for trying to pretend the danger was over and to force people to endure high levels of radiation (which never existed) [2]. One unique positive for Japan was its investment in earthquake-resistant buildings. It is amazing, by any measure, that only a thousand lives were lost in such a gigantic quake. In many nations, tens, even hundreds of thousands would have perished.

Causes of the Fukushima accident can be outlined fairly easily. As with Chernobyl, a true understanding of why it happened, including how it might *not* have happened, hold the keys to the event.

The most immediate factor was the Great Tohoku Earthquake of March 11, 2011, a magnitude 9.0 event that remains among the largest ever recorded in modern times. The quake was generated by slip along the subduction zone between the westward-moving Pacific Plate and the Okhotsk Plate, thrusting the island of Honshu about 2.4 m (8 ft) to the east. Earthquakes of such magnitude, besides being rare, do not at all disqualify Japan from having safe nuclear power plants. Nearly a dozen other power plant reactors, including the Fukushima Daini plant only 10 km to the south, as well as the reprocessing and fuel fabrication center at Rokasho, were affected by the quake but shut down as designed and avoided any loss of cooling incident.

Fukushima Daiichi was one of the largest and oldest commercial nuclear plants in Japan, with six boiling-water reactors built between 1967 and 1978. Units 1–5 used the same basic design, created by General Electric in the mid-1960s, while Unit 6 was newer. The site was a local hill overlooking the Pacific Ocean in a sparsely populated area. Height of this hill was 30–35 m (100–116 ft) above local sea level, but was mostly soil so was bulldozed down to rock at 10 m (33 ft). This was done for several reasons: to root building foundations in stable bedrock; to reduce costs by providing better access to ocean water (used in condensers that cooled steam into water); and to remain above the estimated level of flooding, related to storm surges and tsunami [3].

Regarding this last point, the engineers and seismologists who analyzed possible risks at the time (early 1960s) looked to the great 1960 Chile earthquake (magnitude 9.5), for a model of what might be expected. The tsunami from this quake, travelling 17,000 km across the Pacific, reached a height of 3.1 m (10 ft) along the coast in Fukushima Prefecture. But it was 10.7 m (35.3 ft) at Hilo, Hawaii, and as high as 25 m (83 ft) in parts of Chile itself [4].

Historical records existed for three other tsunamis, all generated by quakes near Japan, but little or no data was listed for the Fukushima area. The 1896 Meiji Sanriku quake (magnitude 8.3) produced a tsunami that killed 22,000 people and reached run-up heights of 35 m (119 ft) in Iwate Prefecture to the north, where a rugged coastline with narrow valleys funneled the waves to such heights [5]. In 1933, the Showa Quake (M8.1) caused 3,000 deaths with heights of 10–30 m (33–100 ft) [6]. Only five years later, a third quake (M7.9) had only a very small tsunami.

The first two events were well known, and the Japanese government had installed warning systems in coastal towns [7]. The problem for scientists siting the nuclear plant was that no run up data existed for the entire coastline between Fukushima and Sendai, a distance of 100 km. There were no obvious indications that high waves had ever washed over this part of the coast [8]. Much about Japan's geology was unknown at the time the plant was sited in 1961. Plate tectonics, which a decade later would identify subduction and thus the likely occurrence of large quakes and tsunami anywhere along the coast, did not yet exist.

All of which begs a rather important question. Why, during later decades, was new geologic knowledge not used to upgrade in a major way the security of Fukushima Daiichi?[3] For the answer, we can turn to the IAEA's own extensive report on the Fukushima accident, which (in rather dry language) tells us:

> The vulnerability of the Fukushima Daiichi NPP to external hazards had not been reassessed in a systematic and comprehensive manner during its lifetime. At the time of the accident, there were *no regulatory requirements in Japan for such reassessments* ... The regulatory guidelines in Japan ... were generic and brief, and did not provide specific criteria or detailed guidance ... Before the accident, the operator had conducted some reassessments of extreme tsunami flood levels, using a consensus based methodology developed in Japan in 2002, which had resulted in values higher than the original design basis estimates. Based on the results, some compensatory measures were taken, but they proved to be insufficient at the time of the accident [9]. (italics added)

So *some* reevaluation did take place by the company, TEPCO, but proved ineffective.[4] In hindsight, the whole situation will strike us as incredible, not to say reckless.

---

[3] By contrast, suggested upgrades to the Mark I containment design in Units 1–5 were released by GE in the late 1970s, and TEPCO followed through on these.

[4] According to the IAEA and information from TEPCO report, new models of tsunami run-up heights released by the Japanese Headquarters for Earthquake Research Promotion in 2002, along with another created by TEPCO scientists, had suggested much higher water levels could indeed occur. Yet TEPCO seemed to take its time in responding even to its own information. These reports were still being reviewed when the earthquake struck in March 2011.

What actual events led to the accident? Were there important errors involved here, too? Let us sketch out the scene. At the time of the quake, reactors at the plant were in different conditions. Units 1, 2, and 3 were in full operation; Unit 4 was shut down for refueling; Units 5 and 6 were in "cold shut down" (fission stopped, core temperatures lowered, very low activity) for maintenance. Though not operating, Unit 4 had a pool where spent fuel was being stored and actively cooled. Meanwhile, a total of eleven reactors at four other power plants on the Sanriku coast were in full operation.

Violent shaking of the ground lasted for more than two minutes. The force was at least 20 percent stronger (measured by ground acceleration) than any of the reactors were designed to withstand. Nonetheless all 11 reactors, including Units 1–3 at Fukushima Daiichi, shut down as designed. All eleven cores, however, also continued to generate heat due to the decay of radioactive fission products in the fuel. In every plant, emergency cooling systems started up, as did emergency power systems. Eight reactors, at Onagawa (three reactors), Fukushima Daini (four reactors), and Tokai (one reactor), suffered damage but were successfully brought into cold shutdown within four days. At Fukushima Daiichi, the emergency cooling system lost all electricity. The earthquake toppled power lines and damaged switchyard equipment, cutting all external power. Almost immediately, the emergency backup power system, consisting of diesel generators, turned on and went into action, restoring AC power to all six Units.

This situation, had it continued, would likely have allowed repairs to be made and systems to be brought back on line. Buildings at the plant had withstood the quake, reactors had shut down as designed, and all twelve emergency generators had restored power to cooling systems in all six Units. Operators had followed procedure almost entirely, though sizeable aftershocks had scared operators from performing some actions. But for a brief and fragile moment, everything seemed to be under control.

Each reactor had two emergency AC generators. One is enough to satisfy the power needs in shutdown mode, so the other was there for backup. If both went out, there was a room of batteries able to provide DC power for about eight hours. There was thus a good amount of redundancy for emergency power. The only problem was that practically all of it had been placed in underground rooms.

Forty-one minutes after the quake, the first tsunami reached the Sanriku coast. This wave was comparatively small at Fukushima Daiichi, having a run-up height of 4–5 m (13–17 ft). A seawall shaped like the prow of a ship, designed to withstand a 5.5 m (18 ft) wave, protected the plant from this first assault. Arriving ten minutes later, the next wave swelled monstrously above the first, overtopping and collapsing the seawall, then surging upslope to flood the entire plant with meters of salt water bearing mud and debris. Pumps for both the main and secondary cooling systems were smashed or choked. All basement and ground floor rooms were inundated. Units 1–4 went into black-out; emergency power died, generators and batteries ruined by salt water. The single bright spot was one diesel generator above ground able to continue supplying AC power to Unit 6 and later Unit 5. But for all other Units, operators were left blind and deaf with no way to know what was happening or what to do. As if this weren't bad enough, two workers in the basement of the turbine building in Unit 4 had drowned.

Undoubtedly operators suspected the fearful truth: reactors in Units 1, 2, and 3 were all heating up, boiling off water. While Units 2 and 3 did have some temporary emergency cooling, Unit 1 had lost all effective ability to cool. Relief valves were eventually opened to vent steam from reactor pressure vessels and prevent pressures from becoming dangerously high. But this had its own consequences. The radioactive steam went into a special water-filled chamber that, in Unit 1, eventually ruptured, letting the steam into the building. As water continued to boil away inside the reactor vessel, the fuel became exposed and its production of heat surged. Temperatures went so high the zirconium fuel rods began to glow red-hot, then burst and melt ($>1,830°C$), while also interacting with oxygen in the steam to produce hydrogen gas.

Uncovered, the fuel soon heated to $2,800°C$, where it melted into a kind of lava called "corium." Fear of a "China Syndrome" situation – melted fuel eating through the bottom of the reactor vessel and underlying floor, down to the water table, causing a steam explosion – led TEPCO and the Japanese government (now alerted to the danger) to order fire trucks on the scene to inject water into the reactor via external connections. This was achieved about 4 a.m. on March 12, with no small amount of heroic work.

But meltdown had already occurred, even before midnight on March 11. And the danger was of a different kind. The mentioned rupture in Unit 1 had allowed radioactive steam *and* hydrogen to collect in the reactor building. Unbeknownst to all, injection of water from the fire engines helped aid produc-tion of hydrogen gas, it seems. This continued to build up through the morning and early afternoon hours until it reached a sufficient concentration so that the tiniest spark would set it off. It turned out a bitter irony that, at 3:30 p.m., Unit 1 became the first of the damaged reactors to have AC power finally restored. Six minutes later, the building exploded.

The explosion showered the area with pieces of radioactive concrete, glass, steel, and plastic, while radioactive dust rose in the air, some to be carried off in the wind but most to settled over the plant as a whole. In the following three days, Units 3 and 4 would both suffer the same volatile fate, with Unit 2 undergoing a smaller explosion but a higher degree of radioactive venting. Though the specific progression of events and deci-sions differed in each case, Units 2 and 3 both underwent core meltdowns accompanied by hydrogen production, which found its way out of contain-ment and into each building. Unit 4 received hydrogen because of a pipe connection to Unit 3. One-by-one, each building blew up, releasing radio-isotopes into the atmosphere. Rain and then snow then brought them out of the sky, in particular along a narrow, northwest trending zone about 15–25 km wide and 45 km long.

No core material was ever directly exposed to the outside, as happened at Chernobyl. None of the reactor vessels was blown open, and even if they had been, the fuel itself would have been contained by the primary containment. Despite three separate meltdowns, no corium melted its way through the bottom of a reactor vessel. And while it has been often said that the GE Mark I design was not up to the task of handling a giant earthquake *and* tsunami, the accident might well have been prevented had the emergency generators been moved to a higher floor. In this very real sense, Fukushima happened because of human error, not because of a natural disaster.

Fukushima Response

The major tsunami wave arrived at 3:50 p.m. on March 11. In less than four hours, at 7:03 p.m., an official Nuclear Emergency was declared. At 8:50 p.m., the first evacuation order was given, for people within 2 km of the plant. This was soon expanded by the Prime Minister, Naoto Kan, to 3 km, and by early the next morning, when it became clear that Unit 1 was beyond control, to 10 km. Then, following the first explosion, an evacuation zone of radius 20 km was declared. Where it took three days for the Soviets to move people out of the immediate contamination zone when a clear danger existed, this happened in about eighteen hours in Japan. At the same time, the Japanese authorities did withhold much information from the public. A major example were the melt-downs at three reactors; this was kept secret for three months and only made public just before IAEA inspectors were about to visit the plant.

People living between 20 km and 30 km from the plant were allowed to stay or asked to leave on the basis of estimated dose levels. The limit was first set at 1 mSv above background – an extremely low level – in echo of what was done at Chernobyl. This proved a poor choice with major consequences. It was soon understood that 1 mSv was too restrictive (many parts of Japan have natural background levels more than 1 mSv above those in Fukushima). But when it was raised to 20 mSv/yr (2.2 µSv/hr), there was a strong public reaction, especially with regard to children, and the threshold was lowered back to 1 mSv for those under eighteen years of age. This had the impact of keeping families from returning to their homes for years longer than necessary.

Starting in 2011, a program of "remediation" was launched in the more highly contaminated area of the prefecture. It began with removal of topsoil (upper 2 inches, or 5 cm) and surface cleaning of equipment on school playgrounds, but later expanded to a far more comprehensive effort focused on Cs-137. At first, authorities used a sliding scale to decide where work should be done; in most areas, a dose level in the range of 1–3 μSv/hr, or 8.7–26.2 mSv/yr was applied. But later, the government decided on a specific figure of 0.23 μSv/hr, equal to only 2 mSv/yr. Actual work expanded from playgrounds to local towns, cities, and residences, to soil of any kind, to concrete and asphalt surfaces, swimming pools, the cleaning of houses, buildings, roads, trees, bushes, as well as the removal of fallen leaves and twigs, lawn and pasture grass, and so on. By 2016, no less than 9 billion cubic meters of "hazardous nuclear waste," much of it at dose levels below 2 mSv, had been removed. Not surprisingly, this led to struggles between local and national authorities about where all of this material should be stored, for how long, and at what cost.

When we state the facts like this, clear and cold, it makes the effort sound rational, conservative perhaps, but aimed in good faith at protecting the public. Taking a few steps back, however, the entire "remediation" effort comes into view as a stunning over-reaction on nearly every level. Dose levels were set so low as to have *created* "hazardous waste" purely by decree.

The accident also inspired the government to shut down all the country's reactors, forty-nine of them. This was another overreaction, more of a domestic political decision to demonstrate public concern than anything else. The quake and its aftershocks, as well as tsunami, would affected only a limited part of the country. Most reactors were under no immediate threat and could have been inspected and tested in small batches, leaving most online. What a total shut down meant was that Japan lost 30 percent of its electricity: its industries, businesses, homes, and economy as a whole all suffered hugely. It also meant turning off more than 95 percent of the country's noncarbon power and increasing energy imports considerably. The entire nation had to ration electricity for several years, while natural gas, oil, and coal were increased to fill the gap, raising air pollution levels and carbon emissions. By 2013, emissions had climbed to a historical maximum. Because oil and gas (LNG) prices were high during this period, Japan also spent many billions of dollars on importing these sources, showing, in reverse, the large contribution nuclear power had made to energy security. Five years after 3/11, the government has a program in progress to reopen at least half of its operable nuclear plants. The process, however, has proved difficult and slow, mainly due to local public resistance.

Impacts on the Public: A Tale of Two Accidents

Impacts from Chernobyl and Fukushima can be divided into two basic domains: effects related to radiation, and to stresses on the affected population. These are not the only areas of impact, to be sure, but they are the most relevant to our discussion here.

What follows are akin to "briefings" that cover the key findings of research organizations heavily vested in scientific and medical understanding of these events.

We should begin with the fact that the first analyses done on the accidents, right after they occurred, proved both good and bad. The forecast that local crops and milk products should be monitored carefully and continually was vital to keeping children safe from thyroid cancer in the Fukushima area. On the other hand, the estimate that Chernobyl would result in over 40,000 cancer deaths turned out to be both wildly exaggerated and, when reported by the media, very frightening. This number was based on a set of formulas that involved taking the total radiation released for each major radioisotope, dividing it by the affected population to get a radiation per person number, and multiplying the result by a risk factor. Derived from analysis of effects at Hiroshima, the approach treats a nuclear accident like a bomb explosion.

As revealed in Chapter 5, time is needed to clarify many aspects of a nuclear accident. Response to Fukushima benefited greatly from long-term information gathered on Chernobyl and the people affected. Yet, as we've seen, such benefit was curtailed by reactions that were less informed.

Chernobyl

The main area in Belarus, Russia, and Ukraine affected by fallout from Chernobyl was inhabited by some 5 million people. Well over 99 percent of these people received minor doses (<10 mSv). But the situation was different for others. Total fatalities attributable to the accident are thus far about sixty-one.[5] This includes two workers killed by the explosion and twenty-eight deaths out of 134 workers and firemen who suffered from acute radiation

---

[5] This number is slightly larger than the fifty-six fatalities mentioned in some other volumes. See, for comparison, James Mahaffey, *Atomic Awakening*. (New York: Pegasus, 2010).

syndrome (ARS). It also includes fifteen children who died from thyroid cancer during the following decade (the number is approximate due to uncertainty in identifying each cancer as due to radiation). In addition, nineteen other workers (out of the original 134) died between 1987 and 2004 from various causes like tuberculosis, cirrhosis of the liver, heart attack, trauma, and cancer. These deaths cannot be confirmed as caused by radiation, yet this cannot be ruled out either [10].

Among the workers with ARS who survived (dose levels of 1–3 Sieverts), many recovered within three years, but a sizeable number developed cataracts. Those who suffered medium to severe levels of ARS (3–6 Sieverts) frequently had significant skin damage in addition to cataracts. A number required forms of surgery later on, ten years or more after the accident, suggesting that they suffered from serious medical problems for a long time. Other illnesses related to cardiovascular and gastrointestinal sickness showed no correlation with degree of ARS and appear unrelated to radiation (smoking, alcohol use, and diet seem more important factors). Exposure for these workers was primarily external, with some probable internal doses due to inhalation of radioactive dust from the fire. No cases of ARS occurred for the general public [10].

There is no final, agreed-upon estimate for the number of people who may eventually die or suffer radiation-induced cancers and other illnesses caused by the accident. Uncertainty and debate continue about this and will do so for some time. A chief reason is that medical science cannot tell the specific origin of any particular cancer; there are no tell-tale signs for radiation or other causes, whether at the molecular or physiological level. As a result, all estimates must be based on risk models, which are probability calculations. Such models remain based on the LNT hypothesis, whose limitations were talked about in Chapter 5. The nearest thing to a current consensus comes from several reports completed within the past decade. This work can be divided into two subject areas. One covers the population most directly affected by fallout in the three nations surrounding the reactor site, Russia, Belarus, and Ukraine. The other includes this area plus thirty-seven European nations where some evidence of fallout existed.

A key report for the first area is a 2008 document by UNSCEAR [10]. It concludes that about 4,000 future deaths (total, all time) from radiation-induced cancer may occur. About 2,200 of these deaths will likely be among the roughly 600,000 emergency workers or "liquidators," especially the 200,000 or so who helped clean up the site during the first year. These people included soldiers, police, firefighters, and others brought in from all over the Soviet Union. More recent work has identified an increase of up to ~18 percent in cancer among these workers compared with what would normally be expected, but no increase in deaths [10–11]. As for the general public, another study estimates total doses over the period 1986–2005 to be quite low: 5.1 mSv in the most contaminated parts of Russia; 2.8 mSv in Belarus; 2.1 mSv in Ukraine [12]. UNSCEAR, meanwhile, concluded: "the values of inferred risks are so small that in general no discernible radiation-related increase of overall cancer incidence would be expected among exposed members of the general public" [13].

What about Europe as a whole, then? This analysis estimated a dose of 6.1 mSv for those members of the public living in the most contaminated areas. This was slightly higher than the number given above, but still (for example) below the natural background dose in Denver (US) for a year. For all those living outside these areas of highest fallout, doses were estimated at under 1 mSv. Statistical methods, in part based on the LNT model, yielded a calculation of 22,800 lifetime cancers (not deaths) that would be caused by radiation, not including thyroid cancer. This sounds like a big number. However, it applies to a total population of over 565 *million* people, of whom 194 million are normally expected to get cancer (average national rate 26 percent).

The radioisotopes I-131 (half-life: eight days) and Cs-137 (half-life: thirty years) were found to be responsible for the great majority of exposures to the public. As a short-lived radionuclide, I-131 decayed to low levels within three months. But it affected plants and pasture (cows, horses, sheep) to a high degree in the first several weeks. Cs-137 decreased more slowly at a rate that further slowed after the mid-1990s. Uptake and retention of Cs-137 was found to be quite selective: highest levels were not in agricultural soils but mostly natural ecosystems, particularly in mushrooms, berries, game animals, and, in Scandinavia, reindeer. Long-term, a problem was Cs-137 presence in milk and meat, especially beef; feeding of cattle with nonlocal forage has done much to address this. By the 2000s, radionuclide levels were very low, deemed "negligible" in terms of any further accumulated dose for the public [14]. This includes large portions of the Exclusion Zone within the 30-km diameter used for evacuations.

Dose levels for people included the following: average of 120 mSv for liquidators (dominant range 20–500 mSv); 30–33 mSv for 116,000 evacuees, with doses up to 50 mSv for those in the zone of "strict radiological control" closer to the Chernobyl plant; 9–20 mSv cumulative over two decades for residents in contaminated areas of Ukraine, Russia, and Belarus. The 5 million people that lived in areas with detectable radionuclides from the accident have been subjected to effective doses of under

5 mSv, i.e. well within the range of natural background in the region. For European nations, doses are noted as less than 1 mSv above background. No data from the accident supports an increased risk of cancer at doses below 100 mSv [12].

Roughly 100,000 people inhabit the area still designated as being under "strict control," where dose levels have been under 10 mSv/yr for nearly two decades or more. Because of this, the Chernobyl Forum recommended that such designations now be dropped, as they only serve to create unnecessary anxiety. In all contaminated areas, dose levels are dropping by around 5 percent per year. A rise and peak in leukemia cases, predicted to occur about 5–7 years after the accident, never happened. However, there is some evidence that leukemia has risen to some degree among liquidators who absorbed the highest doses. No evidence exists for either fertility problems or birth defects.

Every research group in the Chernobyl Forum identified mental health effects as "the largest public health problem created by the accident." Personal interviews have revealed that many people suffered from serious depression and anxiety and from the belief that they would contract ailments that could not be treated and that would irreparably damage and shorten their lives. Such feelings, in turn, encouraged a sense of victimization, helplessness, and a dependency on state assistance. Many people (8–13 percent of different cohorts studied) thought of or attempted suicide well into 1990s and even the 2000s [15–17]. This type of response was also true for people who were children at the time of the accident. Collapse of the Soviet Union in 1991 added to these problems the loss of many social services [18].

A human face has been put to this suffering by the Ukrainian-born writer Svetlana Alexievich, who received the Nobel Prize for Literature in 2015. In her book, *Voices from Chernobyl*, individuals like Zinaida Kovalenko recount their experiences:

They closed the wells ... Said the water was "dirty." How can it be dirty ... ? They told us a bunch of nonsense. You'll die. You need to leave. Evacuate.

People got scared. They got filled up with fear. At night, people started packing up their things. I also got my clothes ... Such sadness! It filled my heart. Let me be struck down right here if I'm lying. And then I hear about how the soldiers were evacuating one village, and this old man and woman stayed. Until then, when people were roused up and put on buses, they'd take their cow and go into the forest. They'd wait there. Like during the war, when [the Germans] were burning down the villages. Why would our soldiers chase us? [*Starts crying.*] It's not stable, our life ... They told me later there was a column of people walking. And next to that there was a column of livestock. It was war! [19]

Evelyn Bromet of the Stony Brook University School of Medicine has spent many years studying the mental health impacts of Chernobyl. She notes that these have included "depression, anxiety, post-traumatic stress disorder, general distress, and medically unexplained somatic symptoms (e.g. fatigue, severe headaches, muscle and joint pain)." Yet she also emphasizes that there are other dimensions to consider:

> The Chernobyl disaster encompassed a multitude of stressors in addition to the radiation exposure. The population in the 30 km around the plant was evacuated, but the evacuation was both delayed and chaotic. Families were sometimes separated, and pregnant women were told to have abortions. Evacuees were not welcomed by the communities where they were resettled. Evacuee adults and children were not only stigmatised because of their radiation exposure but also strongly resented because they were given new apartments ahead of local residents who had spent years on waiting lists ... Doctors attributed diseases and symptoms to Chernobyl indiscriminately ... The psychosocial fallout from Chernobyl was then compounded by the political and socio-economic turmoil following the break-up of the Soviet Union. Benefits given to evacuee children, such as annual medical check-ups and hot lunches in the schools, became bones of contention amidst widespread poverty in the general population [20].

The accident affected a population that was dominantly poor. These people raised much of their own food and were particularly vulnerable when given no information by authorities. The worst nuclear accident in history imposed its burdens on a people already oppressed, deprived of understanding, and left largely defenseless.

Fukushima

There have been no deaths, cases of ARS, or other serious injuries from radiation. Two TEPCO workers died from drowning, due to the tsunami (Unit 4), and one worker with a subcontracting company was killed in 2015 by an accident involving a head injury. As dose levels were quite low, no discernible increase in cancer incidence or mortality for the public or plant workers is expected above normally expected numbers. At the same time, over 1,600 people have died due to stresses, depression, fear, suicide, and other psychological impacts related to the evacuations, whose extent and longevity are now seriously questioned in terms of having been excessive and largely unjustified, given the levels of radiation involved.

A variety of studies have monitored and assessed radionuclides released by the accident. This work has measured radioactivity in the atmosphere, above ground, and at ground level, as well as within the upper soil layer, and has used such data in computer modeling of dose distributions. Dominant radioisotopes include I-131 and Cs-137, with smaller amounts of Cs-134. The I-131 isotope comprised about 10 percent of the total atmospheric release, with Cs-137 making up around 50 percent. Data show that in the first days after the accident began (March 11–15), wind directions were to the northwest. Both rain and snow led to the deposition of all three radionuclides in a northwest zone, oriented N30°-60°W, extending roughly 45 km from the Fukushima plant. Thereafter, prevailing winds shifted eastward, carrying the largest part of the total radionuclide release out over the North Pacific, where it was dispersed and deposited in the ocean. Small amounts were distributed around the globe within the first three weeks after March 11. Networks in Europe and North America, including Alaska and the West Coast, identified levels of Cs-137 that were an order of magnitude or more below natural background.

A large amount of radioactive water, coming from leaks in reactor cooling systems and from storage tanks set up to contain such water, found its way into the sea and into local groundwater. This has been an ongoing problem for efforts to stabilize the plant and prepare it for decommissioning. Once in the ocean, however, the radionuclides rapidly disperse. Continual monitoring of Cs-137 in sea water off Japan's coast revealed such rapid fall-off in activity with distance. Monitoring in other parts of the Pacific, plus sampling of sea life, including tuna and other species used as food, has repeatedly shown a lack of any danger. This is true for the Japan Sea, Hawaii, or along the west coast of North, Central, and South America [21].

Land deposition of Cs-137 occurred in the mentioned NW-trend zone. Within this zone, maximum dose levels of 165–550 mSv/yr, measured aerially, were in a narrow band 3–4 km wide and 28–30 km long, in a direction N55°W. Wind, rain, and surface drainage (to the ocean) continually reduced this area in size and radioactivity: by November 2011, it had decreased in area by 50 percent, with dose levels now at 100–300 mSv/yr. By November 2015, maps showing levels at 1 m (3.3 ft) above ground indicated that areas at 150 mSv/yr and higher (maximum ~250 mSv) had shrunk to a small number of localized places, except for a larger area adjacent the nuclear plant itself [22]. If Chernobyl be a guide, some local pockets of higher radioactivity will remain for decades, presumably due to binding of Cs-137 to clay minerals.

About 78,000 people were evacuated from the 20 km-radius area around the plant. A further 62,000 or so left their homes from within the 20–30 km (voluntary evacuation) zone, and in April another 10,000 were evacuated. Anyone whom the government judged might receive a dose of 20 mSv or above during the first year was ordered to leave. The dose limit set for returning home was 1 mSv above background. This meant that evacuees were only allowed to return in significant numbers starting in 2015, with tens of thousands kept away until 2017, and an unspecified number having to wait still longer. At this writing, many residents refuse to return to their homes even in the lowest dose areas. This is because of worries about lost employment, disrupted neighborhoods, distrust of government, as well as fear of radiation. In Minamisoma City, for example, which had a prequake population of 72,000 people, 86 percent were evacuated, with only 45,000 later deciding to return. Most who stayed away were young, especially parents with children under ten [23]. Many neighborhoods will be partially, even wholly, abandoned, creating a sense of desolation. Loss of young families has taken place in many parts of the prefecture.

Radiation doses determined for the general public are in the range 1–10 mSv. This applies to both external and internal exposures. UNSCEAR, in its 2014 report, concluded that:

> ... averages of effective doses to adult evacuees [were] less than 10 mSv in the first year after the accident ... In the most affected districts of the areas that were not evacuated, average lifetime effective doses to adults were up to just over 10 mSv above natural background. Individual doses could be lower or higher by a factor of about 2 to 3. The Committee estimated that perhaps 15,000 people in the highest dose bands might have received average lifetime effective doses of about 25 mSv ... However the values of inferred risks are so small that in general no discernible radiation-related increase of overall cancer incidence would be expected among exposed members of the general public [24].

Monitoring of over 200,000 people across different portions of Fukushima Prefecture, outside the evacuation zones, showed doses of under 1 mSv. In some cases, there was no evidence of any intake of radionuclides at all. The highest thyroid equivalent doses, which were determined for March 2011 when the presence of I-131 was highest, were below 10 mSv for 95.7 percent of children, with a few up to 43 mSv [25]. Data from atomic bomb survivors and from Chernobyl strongly suggest this is not high enough to raise thyroid cancer incidence above that expected for the rest of Japan.

Japanese authorities put into action a screening program that covers some 370,000 children who were 0–18 years old when the accident occurred. As of late 2016, no rise in thyroid cancers or abnormalities have been detected that can be associated with radiation from the Fukushima Daiichi accident [26]. This should be considered of no small importance, since the latency period for such cancers to appear (4–5 years, based on Chernobyl and the LSS study of atomic bomb survivors) has now passed.

An interesting result was that in all outdoor areas personal monitors gave *lower* doses than those determined by model-based interpolations. That is, statistical methods used to fill in gaps where direct measurements were lacking routinely *overestimated* dose levels by a factor of two or more. Moreover, the difference increased with increasing dose levels: for example, at an annual dose of 0.5 mSv determined from monitors, models estimated 1.1 mSv; at 1.3 mSv, the estimate ranged up to 4.2 mSv.

The same result has been found in a unique and revealing comparison between airborne and personal dosimeter surveys for Date City [27]. Located some 50 km northwest of the Fukushima plant, in the outer portion of the higher dose trend, Date was not ordered evacuated, and the local government decided to provide badge-type dosimeters to everyone who would volunteer to wear them and turn them in at certain intervals. In all, approximately 53,000 people, including children and pregnant women, supplied data to the effort, which continued from five months after the accident to fifty-one months. Because badge-type (radio-photoluminescence) glass dosimeters require no handling by the wearer, the data is considered to be free of artifacts and other problems, and to comprise the most comprehensive and internally consistent survey of individual doses since the accident occurred. The information shows that estimates of individual exposure based on airborne surveys were three to as much as five times too high. The suggestion, therefore, is that many people within the designated evacuation zones may have been exposed to much smaller dose levels and that, even by the government's low limit (20 mSv/yr), were unnecessarily ordered to leave.

Roughly 25,000 workers were involved in phases of clean up at the plant between March 2011 and October 2014. This included not only TEPCO employees but firefighters, police, and Japan Self-Defense Force (military) personnel. Among this group, over 75 percent received doses of 20 mSv or less, 98 percent less than 50 mSv, the average being about 12 mSv for the entire group. Highest doses occurred during the first year, when 175 workers exceeded the 100 mSv limit originally set. Estimated cancer risk for this group is higher than for all others, yet it is still predicted to be indiscernible in any future epidemiological studies. This refers to external exposures. Internal doses came dominantly from breathing elevated I-131 levels during the first several months inside Units 1–4. Due to inadequate training, respirators were not always used effectively. As many as 1,757 workers are estimated to have incurred thyroid equivalent doses above 100 mSv, with seventeen individuals above 2,000 mSv (2 Sieverts). Two individuals appear to have received thyroid-equivalent doses as high as 12,000 mSv (12 Sieverts). While such levels are very high, they are *not* whole body doses (which would mean almost certain death) and are estimates based on determinations of I-131 concentrations. An increased risk of thyroid cancer/disorder exists for these workers [28].

The International Commission on Radiological Protection (ICRP) suggests that in emergency situations a whole-body dose of up to 100 mSv should be considered for professional workers. Yet the Nuclear and Industrial Safety Agency, Japan's regulatory body, set the threshold at 20 mSv. This made it absolutely certain that anyone working in the reactor buildings would go above the limit, requiring either that they either be removed from work or that the limit be raised, giving the appearance of worsening conditions. The regulatory limit for workers went from 20 mSv/yr (normal operation) to 100 mSv, then to 250 mSv in the first week, suggesting that the situation was continuing to escalate in its threat, which wasn't true. For the general public, meanwhile, a dose limit of only 1 mSv above normal background was set. This was so low that it ensured large areas of Fukushima Prefecture would appear dangerous and would need to remain evacuated for years longer than was actually necessary.

Industries that suffered most heavily from the Fukushima accident were those related to food, especially agriculture and fishing. These also happen to be important sources of employment in the region. Thus impacts on them had large and negative economic consequences. Such impacts, particularly on agriculture, came from two main sources: 1) the remediation program, which involved removing topsoil, pasture grass, and any crops displaying radioactivity; and 2) radioactivity and dose limits set by the government for locally grown food, including milk and water. The first of these we have already discussed above. The second we mentioned in Chapter 5 on radiation, where we noted that activity limits for foods were first dropped to half of ICRP recommended levels[6], then lowered by an order of magnitude.[7] The result was to keep a majority of locally grown or raised food off the market.

Repeatedly, therefore, to counter perceptions of irresponsibility, the Japanese authorities imposed threshold dose limits that were overly conservative, even damagingly so. They were so low, in fact, as to be easily exceeded, thus creating needless prohibitions, false "emergencies," misperceptions of threat, and, of course, heightened anxiety. This becomes all the more important when we consider that for this accident, as for Chernobyl, the most serious health impacts were due to evacuation and later psychological stress. To drive this truth home, it helps to read what happened to 840 medical patients abruptly moved from the 20-km exclusion zone on March 14:

---

[6] To review, international levels were 1000–1200 Bq/kg^2. These were first dropped to 500 Bq/kg^2 for meat/eggs/fish/grains/vegetables, and 200 Bq/kg^2 for dairy products and water.

[7] Final regulation values were: drinking water 10 Bq/kg^2; milk 50 Bq/kg^2; other foods 100 Bq/kg^2; with a new category of infant foods set at 50 Bq/kg^2.

Medical personnel did not accompany the patients during transportation. Bed-ridden patients were laid down on the seats, wrapped in protective gowns. During transportation, some patients suffered trauma by falling from the seats of the vehicles . . . As the situation at the damaged plant became more volatile, the evacuation became more rushed . . . Late at night on March 14, patients were required to leave the buses because admitting hospitals or facilities could not be found and the vehicles were required elsewhere. Eventually, the patients were temporarily housed at a meeting room of the Soso Health Care office in Minamisoma city, with no heaters or medical supplies . . . 27 patients with severe medical problems such as end-stage renal failure or stroke were transported more than 100 km to Iwaki city. At least 12 of them were confirmed dead at 0300h on March 15, ten of whom seemed to have died in the vehicles during transportation. Later, it was reported that more than 50 patients died either during or soon after evacuation probably owing to hypothermia, dehydration, and deterioration of underlying medical problems [29].

Such unintended but fatal results reflected the lack of a clear plan for how to evacuate such people. But its immediate cause was fearful overreaction – the emotional and behavioral chaos imposed by the assumption of a mortal threat that was never there.

This, however, was only the beginning. Certainly, when we speak of stress, depression, post-traumatic stress disorder associated with 3/11, for a significant number of people this came from experiencing first the earthquake, then tsunami, and finally evacuation. For older residents who had spent most of their lives in this quiet, rural area, the combination of events could easily have resulted in shock. Demographically, the region is older than most of the country. It also has comparatively high rates of smoking, alcohol consumption, cancer, hypertension, and suicide, as well as smaller incomes and higher unemployment [30]. Such characteristics could well have increased the degree of physical and psychological vulnerability to 3/11 and to evacuation.

By 2015, at least 1,656 individuals had died or taken their own lives among evacuees. Some surveys that examined areas outside the evacuation zone put the total number of stress-related deaths much higher, at around 3,000 [31]. Most of these people were over sixty-six years of age. Causes of death were variable, including stroke, heart attack, and unspecified illness. Often mentioned are the ill effects of divided families and neighborhoods, changes in diet, loss of ordinary comforts, increased levels of pain, shift to higher health risk behaviors, all tied to staying for years in shelters or other temporary housing, without work or sense of purpose. Studies of evacuated people show that large numbers of both adults and children (14–24 percent of all evacuees), as well as emergency workers, have suffered from depression and PTSD [32–33]. Less studied so far are problems that may have come from stigmatization, both with regard to personal identity and treatment by others. Such difficulties are well known for atom bomb survivors; *hibakusha* have faced entrenched forms of discrimination, not least for jobs and also for marriage (like people elsewhere, the Japanese have continued to mistakenly believe that genetic damage from bomb radiation will cause birth defects for many generations). This has been true to such a degree that *hibakusha* have constituted a kind of distinct minority group within Japanese society as a whole [34]. How much of this may come to bear upon the Fukushima evacuees isn't clear, yet in a number of ways it has clearly begun [35].

One final and related impact of the Fukushima accident has been the unprecedented volume of global media coverage it received. This is due, of course, to the full advent of the Internet and social media: Fukushima is the first nuclear accident to fully "benefit" from this. Viewed overall, Internet communication tended to add an exponent to the ill-informed, misleading, and sometimes hysterical side of coverage. As close observers of such coverage between March 2011 and December 2014, the authors of this book noted the following developments: websites, articles, blog posts, and more portraying the accident as lethal to the Japanese public, as contaminating the Pacific Ocean and Japan Sea, as sending clouds of deadly radioactivity to the Americas, generating cancers in naval ship crews, creating deformed sea life, and producing a dangerous rise in global radiation levels. The sheer volume and relentless repetition of such material tended to overwhelm Internet searches, making it very difficult for Internet users to acquire accurate information. Other voices appeared in order to counter the flood of misinformation, but with only partial success. It must be said, too, that the wide range of misinformation was itself helped by both the lack of accurate information from TEPCO and the Japanese government and the setting of very low dose limits.

While Internet media offered many advantages for helpful communication during the crisis, its disadvantages were also made clear. No accountability is required to put material on the web; any group or individual can do this and brand themselves with a title like "natural news" or "global research." Moreover, material put on the web remains in place unless taken down. Over time, it has come to be replaced in search engines by legitimate sources, but this took years and is far from complete.

What Have We Learned?

A good deal of information has been presented on the two most serious nuclear accidents that have yet taken place. The reason for this is to provide support for what can be learned from these incidents. It is possible, in fact, to list some of the "lessons" in simple and straightforward terms:

1. Large-scale nuclear accidents are far less dangerous than has been believed or expected. It remains a challenge for the public and officials to accept this truth and to act accordingly.

2. The primary enemy of public safety in a nuclear accident is fear of radiation. Terror and panic by both the public and officials lead to poor decisions, chaotic policies, and long-term mental health problems that destroy a great many lives.

3. To date, the major form of cancer caused by nuclear accidents is that of the thyroid, normally a highly treatable form. Resulting from ingestion of I-131, it can be prevented by distributing iodine pills and testing the supply of milk from cows in contaminated areas.

4. Chernobyl and its impacts were the result of an oppressive, totalitarian system that cared more for technology and authority than safety and human life. It is likely to remain the worst such event in history. Fukushima supports this idea.

5. Both accidents proved the consequences of official overreaction and chaotic evacuations. Overreaction involved setting unnecessarily low dose limits, which had dire effects and increased public fear. Worries about causing panic led officials to suppress information and lie to the public. Information is vital in any accident. Censorship will be discovered, creating much anger and distrust.

6. All nuclear power programs should require regular review of plant facilities in light of new geologic, climate, or other knowledge relevant to the site. Upgrades suggested by such knowledge should be required, monitored, and inspected.

7. Chernobyl and Fukushima, as well as several smaller accidents (including Three Mile Island), provide evidence that core meltdowns do not lead to a "China Syndrome," i.e. molten fuel burning its way through the reactor vessel, building foundation, and into the Earth.

8. Inspections of nuclear power plants should be performed by an independent organization of qualified personnel with no direct connection either to nuclear companies or the government. Inspectors would not be volunteers but would be paid out of a fund supplied by contributions from industry and government.

9. This same body could also act as an expert source for information about nuclear power and related issues. It could answer any questions from the media, educators, or general public. This would include serving as an information center in case of an accident, whether in the country itself or elsewhere.

10. These two accidents reveal beyond any doubt that something is deeply amiss in how nuclear power is now understood. Far more fear and worry have been inspired by these two events than the *thousands* of nuclear weapons that remain deployed today.

The Idea of "Normal Accidents": Relevant Today?

Are nuclear power plants so complex that they are doomed to fail at some point? Can we say that this is proven by the accidents that have happened so far?

In 1984, a highly influential book by the sociologist Charles Perrow answered in the affirmative, based on a detailed study of the third famous nuclear incident of the past forty years. *Normal Accidents: Living with High-Risk Technologies* emerged from its author's work on the President's Commission to Investigate the Accident at Three Mile Island (TMI) [36]. Perrow also took up airplane crashes, dam failures, accidents at sea, and recombinant DNA research, but his true target was indeed nuclear power viewed through the 1979 accident at TMI.

Located near the city of Harrisburg, in a fairly well-populated rural area, the TMI plant suffered a malfunction that led to a succession of escalating problems resulting in a partial meltdown. These could not be properly diagnosed by operators because of inadequate instrumentation. Actions they took first made things worse before later ending the crisis. Simply, the first malfunction led to a rise in coolant temperature, triggering the control rods and shutdown of the reactor. A relief valve then failed to close (no instrument showed this, a design flaw) so that coolant water drained away, exposing the core. About half the fuel melted but was contained by the reactor vessel. Buildup of hydrogen gas in the vessel, a source of much worry, was vented, never constituting a real threat due to lack of oxygen (a design feature).

TMI has been considered a major incident by official reports, media coverage (up to the present), and public memory. It is often mentioned in the same breath as Chernobyl and Fukushima. But this reflects the level of anxiety and confusion that were generated, not its radiological realities. By this count, TMI bears no comparison to Fukushima, and certainly none to Chernobyl. The accident was almost fully contained: the only release was nonthreatening radioactive noble gases. There were no injuries and no threat, either to workers or the public. The highest dose recorded anywhere was 12 mSv, directly over the stack where gases were vented. In the surrounding area, doses were less than 1 mSv above natural background.

Yet in other ways, TMI does recall the two big accidents. It brought a similar level of fear, confusion, misinformation, and imagery of mass mortal threat. Though air and soil tests revealed no threat, this information – key as it was – found itself drowned in a deluge of chaotic press releases, speculative (sometimes hysterical) reporting, rumor, antinuclear claims, and more. No mass evacuation was ordered (pregnant women and preschool age children within

5 km of the plant were advised to leave). Yet more than 140,000 people fled the area, creating further chaos and feeding national fear. Government representatives citing low doses became objects of accusation and ridicule. Yet there were positive impacts, too. Improvements in technology and training, emergency preparation, and inspection were all put in place, and a sharing of best practices among nuclear plant operators began [37].

Not all of this is covered by *Normal Accidents*. The book, unfortunately, did not count such factors as media coverage or public reaction as central parts of the accident. The focus, instead, was technological and organizational. Two characteristics were identified as sealing the fate of major accidents. One was "interactive complexity," where a system has a great many individual parts that depend on each other for proper operation. The other was "tight coupling," meaning "processes happen very fast and can't be turned off" so an initial problem escalates and "operator action or the safety systems may make it worse" [38]. Some systems like this can be simplified and rendered more controllable. Some cannot. Those that cannot, like nuclear plants, have accidents that are "normal" because they are an *inherent property* of the system itself.

The idea of "normal accidents" fit well a period when technology was a target of much doubt and criticism. But as we have seen, both Chernobyl and Fukushima were the result of human error from the beginning. Design of the RBMK reactor, lack of safety culture, and a badly conceived system test were pivotal at Chernobyl. For Fukushima, the real problem was regulatory failure; if all emergency generators had been ordered to higher locations, the accident would almost certainly have been avoided. Similar factors apply to other nuclear accidents, including such examples as Wind Scale (where UK authorities were reckless in rushing construction when the designers had limited knowledge of how the graphite moderator would behave) and Kyshtm (another example of Soviet carelessness). The idea of normal accidents does not help us understand these events; on the contrary. What it leaves out *entirely* is what turns a TMI, with no casualties, into a "disaster." As we have learned, it is not the release of radiation, but the disastrous response to it.

Normal Accidents boldly predicted there would be more TMIs, even a growing number of them. There weren't. The author stated there hadn't been enough time by 1979, only about twenty years, for the real risks and failures of commercial nuclear power to become manifest. Thirty-five years later, only two accidents have occurred, and designs for new, advanced reactors include major simplifications, such as passive safety systems.

History has not been kind to the normal accident idea. Nor should it be. Nuclear accidents are no more a matter of destiny than are bad decisions or sociological theories. However welcome at the time it appeared, the normal accident concept has since been strongly debated. Theories that allow for even the most complex, coupled systems – the International Space Station or Large Hadron Collider, for example – to achieve high reliability have been found more illuminating in many circumstances [39]. Ultimately, but also locally and practically, human beings bear the responsibility both for the calamities they create and the advances they are able to make.

Some Perspective

For decades, "Texas City" was synonymous with "disaster" across the US. In 1947, a ship carrying 2,300 tons of ammonium nitrate caught fire in this crowded port town, dense with commercial docks, oil refineries, and chemical plants. People eagerly came out to watch the fire, entranced by the unusual glow. When the ship exploded, the force hurled chunks of metal and concrete miles into the air, destroying two planes flying overhead and shooting debris into oil and chemical storage tanks that exploded, doubling the devastation. Over 570 people were killed, with at least 5,000 injured, many with serious burns. Another 113 remain "missing": no identifiable parts were ever found. The entire town was leveled, with thousands homeless.

Only ten years earlier, in New London, Texas, a natural gas leak went undetected for days beneath a large new school (built with money from the giant East Texas Oil Field nearby). Ignited by a stray spark during morning classes, the gas exploded, lifting the building into the air and blowing it apart, so that the walls and roof collapsed inward, crushing everyone inside. Out of 500 students and forty teachers, 300 were killed – over 260 children – with many more badly injured. The disaster led to laws requiring an odor be added to natural gas (mercaptan).

We could go on. There are other high fatality accidents to note in the oil and gas industry. These, moreover, don't even begin to compare with the death (plus disease) numbers related to coal mining accidents. Staying with the US (for now), between 1910 and 1950 over 90,000 lives were lost in coal mines [40]. In the worst such accident, at Monogah, West Virginia, at least 500 men and boys were killed by a massive explosion that ripped through major shafts hundreds of feet underground.

Texas City, New London, Monogah. All remain among the worst industrial accidents in US history. Yet their names are virtually unknown today outside of their immediate areas. Instead, the almost universally recognized calamity remains Three Mile Island, a "catastrophe" where not a single person was injured, where no significant contamination of the surrounding area took place, and where the public was never seriously threatened.

More than a few Russians recall the Ufa train disaster of 1989, where up to 800 or more lost their lives, including many children. Neither is Japan a stranger to appalling deaths from industrial accidents, as in the Mitsui Miike coal mine tragedy of 1963, where 460 people died, or the horrific department store fires in Osaka, 1972 and Kumamoto, 1973, that together killed nearly 300. When the word "disaster" is invoked, however, both countries are known to the world and to their own people for accidents whose core threat, radiation, brought far fewer casualties. We might well wonder if there might be something wrong with this picture.

References

[1] World Nuclear Association Chernobyl Accident 1986 (Internet), (June 2016). Available from: www.world-nuclear.org/information-library/safety-and-security/safety-of-plants/chernobyl-accident.aspx

[2] M. Fackler, 4 Years after Fukushima Nuclear Calamity, Japanese Divided on Whether to Return (Internet), *New York Times* (August 8, 2015). Available from: www.nytimes.com/2015/08/09/world/asia/japan-fukushima-nuclear-disaster-iitate-return-plan.html?_r=0

[3] International Atomic Energy Agency (IAEA), *The Fukushima Daiichi Accident: Technical Volume 2, Safety Assessment* (Vienna: International Atomic Energy Agency, 2015), 2.1–2.2.

[4] United States Geological Survey, Historic Earthquakes: Chile (Internet). Available from: http://earthquake.usgs.gov/earthquakes/world/events/191960_05_22_tsunami.php

[5] S. W. Kieffer, *The Dynamics of Disaster* (New York: W.W. Norton, 2013), 127–134.

[6] N. Mori and T. Takahashi, The 2011 Tohoku Earthquake Tsunami Joint Survey Group, Nationwide Post Event Survey and Analysis of the 2011 Tohoku Earthquake Tsunami, *Coastal Engineering Journal*, 54:4 (2012), 1–27.

[7] E. Corkill, Heights of Survival (Internet), *Japan Times* (June 12, 2011). Available from: www.japantimes.co.jp/life/2011/06/12/life/heights-of-survival/#.VrwKNRgrJiV

[8] N. Mori and T. Takahashi, The 2011 Tohoku Earthquake Tsunami Joint Survey Group, Figure 6.

[9] *The Fukushima Daiichi Accident: Report by the Director General.* (Vienna: International Atomic Energy Agency, 2014), p. 49.

[10] UNSCEAR, Health Effects Due to Radiation from the Chernobyl Accident (Internet) (New York: United Nations, 2008), pp. 47–220, Appendix D, *Sources and Effects of Ionizing Radiation*, Vol. II, Scientific Annexes C, D, and E. Available from: www.unscear.org/unscear/en/publications/192008_2.html

[11] V. V. Kashcheev et al., Incidence and Mortality of Solid Cancer Among Emergency Workers of the Chernobyl Accident: Assessment of Radiation Risks for the Follow-Up Period of 1992–2009, *Radiation and Environmental Biophysics*, 54:1 (March 2015), 13–33.

[12] E. Cardis et al., Estimates of the Cancer Burden in Europe from Radioactive Fallout from the Chernobyl Accident, *International Journal of Cancer*, 119:6 (September 2006), 1224–1235.

[13] UNSCEAR, *Sources, Effects and Risks of Ionizing Radiation: UNSCEAR 2013 Report* (Internet), vol. 1. (New York: United Nations, 2014), p. 252. Available from: www.unscear.org/unscear/en/publications/2013_1.html

[14] L. R. Anspaugh, Environmental Consequences of the Chernobyl Accident and Their Remediation: 20 Years of Experience, *Chernobyl: Looking Back to Go Forward Series* (Vienna: International Atomic Energy Agency, 2008), pp. 43–76.

[15] E. J. Bromet and J. M. Havenaar, Psychological and Perceived Health Effects of the Chernobyl Disaster: a 20-year Review, *Health Physics*, 93:5 (2007),516–521.

[16] K. Loganovsky et al., The Mental Health of Clean-Up Workers 18 Years After the Chernobyl Accident, *Psychological Medicine*, 38:4 (2008), 481–488.

[17] E. J. Bromet et al., Suicide Ideation, Plans and Attempts in Ukraine: Findings from the Ukraine World Mental Health Survey, *Psychological Medicine*, 37:6 (2007), 807–819.

[18] G. Contis and T. P. Foley, Jr., Depression, Suicide Ideation, and Thyroid Tumors Among Ukrainian Adolescents Exposed as Children to Chernobyl Radiation, *Journal of Clinical Medical Research*, 7:5 (2015), 332–338.

[19] S. Alexievich, *Voices from Chernobyl*, trans. K. Gessen (Normal, IL: Dalkey Archive Press, 2005), p. 29.

[20] E. J. Bromet, Mental Health Consequences of the Chernobyl Disaster. *Journal of Radiological Protection*, 32: 1 (2012), N71-N75, N72.

[21] K. Buesseler, Radiation from Fukushima (Internet), Woods Hole Oceanographic Institution. Available from: www.whoi.edu/page.do?pid=83397&tid=3622&cid=94989

[22] Extension Site of Distribution Map of Radiation Dose, etc. (Internet), *Japanese Ministry of Education, Culture, Sports, Science and Technology (MEXT)*. Available from: http://ramap.jmc.or.jp/map/eng/

[23] K. Ishikawa, Y. Kanazawa, S. Morimoto, and T. Takahashi, Depopulation with Rapid Aging in Minamisoma City after the Fukushima Daiichi Nuclear Power Plant Accident, *Journal of the American Geriatric Society*, 60:12 (December 2012), 2357–2358.

[24] UNSCEAR, *Sources, Effects and Risks of Ionizing Radiation*, p. 252.

[25] IAEA *Director's Report*, pp. 121–126.

[26] D. Normile, Mystery Cancers are Cropping Up in Children in Aftermath of Fukushima (Internet), *Science*, 351:6277 (March 4, 2016), 1022–1023. Available from: www.sciencemag.org/news/2016/03/mystery-cancers-are-cropping-children-aftermath-fukushima

[27] M. Miyazaki and R. Hayano, Individual External Dose Monitoring of All Citizens of Date City by Passive Dosimeter 5 to 51 Months after the Fukushima NPP Accident (series): 1. Comparison of Individual Dose with Ambient Dose Rate

Monitored by Aircraft Surveys, *Journal of Radiological Protection*, 37 (2017), 1–12.

[28] UNSCEAR, *Sources, Effects and Risks of Ionizing Radiation*, pp. 9–11.

[29] K. Tanigawa, Y. Hosoi, N. Hirohashi et al., Loss of Life After Evacuation: Lessons Learned from the Fukushima Accident (Internet), *The Lancet*, 379:9819 (March 10, 2012), 889–891; 890. Available from: www.thelancet.com/journals/lancet/article/PIIS0140-6736%2812%2960384–5/fulltext

[30] ODOMON (Internet), *Statistics Japan* (2016). Available from: http://stats-japan.com/

[31] S. Fukiwara and S. Tabuchi, Three Years After: Stress-Related Deaths Reach 2,973 in Tohokyu (Internet), *Asahi Shimbun* (March 7, 2014). Available from: http://ajw.asahi.com/article/0311disaster/life_and_death/AJ201403070057

[32] H. Yabe et al., Psychological Distress After the Great East Japan Earthquake and Fukushima Daiichi Nuclear Power Plant Accident: Results of a Mental Health and Lifestyle Survey Through the Fukushima Health Management Survey in FY2011 and FY2012, *Fukushima J. Med. Sci.*, 60:1 (2014) pp. 57–67.

[33] International Atomic Energy Agency the Fukushima Daiichi Accident: Technical Volume 4 – Radiological Consequences (Internet) (2015), pp. 163–166. Available from: www.pub.iaea.org/MTCD/Publications/PDF/AdditionalVolumes/P1710/Pub1710-TV4-Web.pdf

[34] R. J. Lifton, *Death in Life: Survivors of Hiroshima* (Durham, NC: University of North Carolina Press, 1991).

[35] J. Shigemura and R. K. Chhem (ed.), *Mental Health and Social Issues Following a Nuclear Accident: The Case of Fukushima* (New York: Springer, 2016).

[36] C. Perrow, *Normal Accidents: Living with High-Risk Technologies* (Princeton: Princeton University Press, 1984).

[37] B. A. Osif, A. J. Baratta, and T. W. Conkling, *TMI 25 Years Later: The Three Mile Island Nuclear Power Plant Accident and Its Impact* (University Park, PA: Pennsylvanian State University Press, 2004).

[38] Perrow. *Normal Accidents*, p. 4.

[39] N. Leveson, N. Dulac, K. Marais, and J. Carroll, Moving Beyond Normal Accidents and High Reliability Organizations: A Systems Approach to Safety in Complex Systems, *Organizational Studies*, 30: 2–3 (February/March 2009), 227–249.

[40] Centers for Disease Control and Prevention, US Department of Health and Human Services, Number of Fatalities and Fatality Rate (5-year aggregates) in the Mining Industry by Commodity, 1911–2010 (Internet). Available from: www.cdc.gov/niosh/mining/statistics/allmining.html

7

Godzilla's Children: Origins and Meaning
of Nuclear Anxiety

Angst macht den Wolf grösser als er ist.

(Fear makes the wolf bigger than he is)
German proverb

Nuclear Anxiety: An Introduction

Fear, we are told by psychologists, is a natural response to dangerous situations. Yet we know from experience that fear takes many forms, and its causes may be dangers that are real, possible, or imaginary. There are things, that is, which attract far more dread than they deserve, about which we are excessively afraid. Consider these lines, for example:

> Radiation has an evil aura, which is partly physical and partly perceived, but both are equally real. The physical aspect is the irradiated particles which release energy in the process of decay, which can damage living tissue. The perceived aspect is the feeling of being surrounded by an invisible danger that we know can harm us but that we do not understand.[1]

Such is a kind of fear that can reduce us to children. The cause seems beyond control and knowledge, untouchable, metaphysical ("evil"). We are powerless, mere "tissue," in its grip. It seeks only to harm us for unknown reasons.

Within the 30-km evacuation zone around the Fukushima plant, radiation levels have fallen even below where experts say it is safe for a majority of people

---

[1] This quote comes from page 8 of a report published in 2000 by the UN Office for the Coordination of Humanitarian Affairs. Titled *Chernobyl: A Continuing Catastrophe*, it was written by nonscientists and much criticized for its poorly informed text, which made many untrue statements. It was later rewritten in part to try and address some criticisms – the first few words of the above quote were changed to "Radioactive contamination is an invisible aura."

to go home. Many tens of thousands, however, refuse to return. This is true even if their neighborhoods were not seriously damaged by the earthquake or touched by the tsunami. They are afraid of radiation, and they do not trust what the government or the experts say. Many are more persuaded by badly informed, even paranoid predictions of death and pervasive cancer. Fear and distrust greatly increase their victimization, in other words, depriving them of their homes, adding great mental stress and possibly medical problems to their lives, and making them vulnerable to misinformation that feeds their fear in turn.

Such anxiety about radiation, we know, exists in many countries. Though studied and written about, most extensively by Spencer Weart in his fascinating book *The Rise of Nuclear Fear* (2012) [1], focusing on popular culture in the twentieth century, there remain important questions about the contours of this fear and its meaning. It has been often observed that there are ready connections to the horrors of Hiroshima and Nagasaki. Yet, as Weart demonstrates, this is far from the whole story. Radiophobia is a social construction with several roots whose influences have evolved over time and been attached to events, movements, repeated media coverage, and ideas subsequent to the atomic bombings. Can nuclear anxiety, then, have a more complex, even sociohistorical basis? Might it be linked, for instance, to deep worries about the nature of society itself, its destructive tendencies, its powers of control and silent violence, its denial of individual importance?

Consider: among all energy technologies, nuclear is the only one bathed in perceptions of risk and danger – risk, that is, to human life first and foremost, but also to all other living things at every scale of the biosphere. Not even coal is granted such a level of hazard. Nuclear power is also the energy source with the greatest disparity between how experts view risk and how the general public perceives it. An example involves nuclear reactors and nuclear weapons: where experts view these as separate, much of the public sees them as two faces of the same perilous knowledge. This suggests that, even beyond Hiroshima and Nagasaki, nuclear power has come to be invested with certain anxieties related to war, e.g. an insidious enemy, unseen threats, death on a vast scale, military-style secrecy, and mortal vulnerability of the citizenry and the self.

Studies about risk perception have not avoided research in this area. The work of Paul Slovic, in particular, has been illuminating in its emphasis that risk tends to be understood emotionally and personally. In the late 1970s and 1980s, he showed that people are most intolerant of risks that make them feel small, helpless, and preyed upon. In Slovic's words, such risks are "involuntary [(unchosen)], unknown to those exposed ..., uncontrollable, unfamiliar, catastrophic, severe (fatal), and dreaded" [2]. Adding to such perceptions were risks whose impacts are delayed and whose benefits seem to be small or inequitably distributed. It seems clear that, in general terms, these characteristics remain true in 2017.

What are the terms commonly used to talk about a nuclear accident, for example. They include: "nuclear peril" and "nuclear nightmare," "nuclear disaster" and "nuclear calamity," "nuclear catastrophe," even "nuclear holocaust," when discussing either weapons or power plant accidents. It is a discourse that suggests all things "nuclear" are equally capable of ultimate threat. Other common words: radiation is "spewed" (like deadly vomit); it creates a "cloud" or "plume" that spreads over a vast area (no possibility of escape), resulting in massive "contamination" that produces either "heavily contaminated" or "moderately contaminated" but never "lightly" or "insignificantly contaminated" food, water, towns, forests, soil, etc. Looked at in total, this is a kind of speech that tends to move from the signs of crisis to the sintered edges of cataclysm. Indeed, we have no discourse to talk about an incident where nothing perilous happens; we can only speak in denials, e.g. "no dangerous radiation resulted" or "no threat to the public." A phrase like "only safe levels of radiation occurred" makes no sense.

Nuclear power, we should remember, began with unfortunate historical timing. Born in the midst of war, it was sheathed in military secrecy, then darkened by the atomic bombings, thereafter to wear the shadow of the Cold War and annihilation. As a civilian industry, nuclear power came about in late 1950s and early 60s, the same years that public concern rose to a peak over the issue of fallout from nuclear testing, expressed in fears regarding milk contaminated with Strontium-90 (Sr-90). The year 1962 saw hugely heightened anxiety due to the Cuban Missile Crisis. This coincided, moreover, with publication of Rachel Carson's *Silent Spring* (1962) and the early awakening of the environmental movement. Though known for its indictment of pesticides and other chemicals, Carson's enormously influential work began with a different kind of threat:

> There once was a town in the heart of America where all life seemed to live in harmony with its surroundings. The town lay in the midst of a checkerboard of prosperous farms, with fields of grain and hillsides of orchards where, in spring, white clouds of bloom drifted above the green fields ...
> Then a strange blight crept over the area ... Some evil spell had settled on the community: mysterious maladies swept the flocks of chickens; the cattle and sheep sickened and died. Everywhere was a shadow of death ... In the town the doctors had become more and more puzzled by new kinds of sickness ...
> In the gutters under the eaves and between the shingles of the roofs, a white granular powder still showed a few patches; some weeks before, it had fallen like snow upon the roofs and the lawns, the fields and streams. No witchcraft, no enemy

action had silenced the rebirth of new life in this stricken world. The people had done it themselves [3].

Carson wrote her book at the peak of the controversy over fallout. Her model for pollution she made clear in saying "chemicals are the sinister and little-recognized partners of radiation in changing the very nature of the world" [4].

What we discover in Carson's words and in later anti-nuclear claims is that fear of nuclear power has never been irrational. It is not like a form of mild but perennial panic, like that toward terrorists or child molesters. Nuclear anxiety has its own rationality, one that draws together certain suspicions, uncertainties, and unknowns into a semi-coherent image of threat. This is also apparent from surveys conducted in the US showing correlation between a decrease in nuclear opposition and various issues, such as a possible energy crisis [5]. Fear of nuclear power, as we will see, often depends on worries about other aspects of our civilization, political, environmental, economic, and social.

Of course, there is another dark pillar of anxiety: cancer. This is the disease that radiation produces, and is assumed to produce almost like a contagion. The connection is real, and the medical community has established that many forms of the disease have been produced by high dose exposures, though the link even there (and at low doses, especially) is made complex by many factors related to smoking, diet, other lifestyle aspects, exposure to pollutants, and, of course, individual genetics. But nearly all of this is either imperfectly known or else is quickly forgotten when any news of a "radiation leak" arrives. The logic involved holds that radiation equals cancer.

The connection, in fact, should not be underestimated in terms of its force. Until very recently, and for many people it persists, a diagnosis of cancer was equivalent to a death sentence. It defines a disease imbued with enormous dread, even terror, as well as qualities of punishment (for bad lifestyle choices), malevolence (the body taken over), and, with regard to tumor cells, contamination. Thus, a certain fearful logic can be seen operative here as well: the same radiation produced by the most terrifying weapon ever conceived will generate the deadliest and most incurable of diseases. WWII helped install a militarized discourse for cancer, such that it became common by the 1950s to speak of a "crusade against cancer," the need to "fight back" against the disease, and to "wipe it out" [6]. This discourse became official when President Nixon declared a "War on Cancer" in passing the National Cancer Act of 1971. It proved a war that, as the 1970s dragged on and death tolls rose ever higher, could not be easily won, or won at all. It was a war, moreover, like nuclear weapons and radiation, that humans had brought upon themselves.

The connections between cancer, radiation, and war were not merely compelling on a factual basis, in other words. They shared a common set of omens. Many causes for cancer have been attributed to contaminants in the environment, carcinogens generated by society that invade the body from the air, food, and water. Radiation is precisely this kind of agent. Indeed, at a subfactual level, there exists a crude and angst-filled equation involved: radiation means cancer, and cancer, whatever the current ability to do battle against it, means a damaged self who, all too often, must stare death in the face.

Perception and Proportion

One thing must be settled. Is it really true that the common fear of radiation, especially regarding nuclear power, waste, accidents, etc., is out of all proportion to the actual risks that sixty years of civilian reactors have revealed?

The answer is an unqualified "yes." Moreover, the mismatch is easy to show. This does not mean invoking risks related to personally chosen (voluntary) actions like smoking, motorcycles, handguns, base jumping, crocodile wrestling, etc. The comparisons that make sense are with other energy sources.

Nuclear anxiety, for example, generally ignores the incomparable consequences for the public that have come from coal, some of which we have previously mentioned. In the US, abundant study has determined that as many as 3,000–13,200 premature deaths per year are due to particulate matter from coal-fired power plants [7], with many thousands more suffering cardiovascular and respiratory impacts. Though widely reported, this information has led to no national outcry or protest movement. Imagine, however, if a single nuclear incident in the US killed as many as 3,000 people, or for that matter, half that number. What would be the public and official reaction? By the number given above, coal has taken 30,000–130,000 American lives in a decade – roughly the same number as were killed at Hiroshima. For decades, older plants without full pollution controls continued to operate due to "grandfathering" under the 1971 Clean Air Act, partly due to pressure from members of Congress from coal-rich states. Thus, Big Coal and government collaborated to preserve lethal power plants. Meanwhile, not one death due to radiation is recorded for the public in six decades of civilian reactor operation.[2]

On the global stage, however, the US is a bit player in coal casualties. Worldwide, lives lost and irreparably damaged can only be compared to the

---

[2] A few deaths have occurred in military nuclear facilities and among workers at commercial plants, mostly in nonnuclear accidents (electrical, steam), but the total is small (<20), especially for a major industry, and has involved no member of the general public.

victims of a major war. More than one million people die prematurely each year in China and India from coal use in power plants, factories, and homes. Dozens of other developing and emerging nations that rely on coal for power without full pollution controls, such as South Africa, Turkey, and Indonesia, add many thousands more to the toll [8]. Even in Europe, coal pollution takes more than 22,000 lives every year [9]. None of this includes the millions more whose lungs are damaged from living in polluted cities, towns, and homes. With children especially, the long-term effects remain unknown and delayed. For all the benefit it has brought society over time, coal has commanded a horrific price.

What, then, of Fukushima and Chernobyl? Having discussed these in detail in Chapter 6, we can see that their impacts bear no comparison with what has just been said about coal. In the case of Fukushima, there have been no radiation-related deaths, diseases, or serious injuries in five years, and none are expected to be discernible among the public. With Chernobyl, the consensus figures include 56 deaths and 4,000–6,000 cases of thyroid cancer (99 percent survival rate), with fifteen deaths among these cases. Up to 4,000 (0.7 percent) cancer deaths are estimated to be possible for 600,000 people under study. Among the total 572 million people (Europe and Former USSR) potentially affected by fallout from the accident, experts have estimated 22,800 radiation-induced, nonthyroid cancers may occur – in addition to the 194 million cases that would normally be expected [10]. By far the worst impact is in the realm of mental health, the levels of depression, post-traumatic stress disorder, and other forms of psychological distress born from misperceptions and myths about the perils of contamination due to radiation [11].

But if the worst nuclear accident in history cannot compare with the annual human cost of coal use, it is also dwarfed by other energy-related disasters. In 1975, a large dam in a project to control flooding and generate power along the Ru River in China failed during a sustained deluge [12]. Like many of China's major dams built in the 1950s, Banqiao Dam was an earthen structure and when overtopped it quickly eroded, then collapsed. At least 26,000 people were drowned, but another 145,000 died from epidemics due to water contamination and famine. Nearly 11 million were affected by illness and homelessness. None of this includes the mental health effects that follow a disaster of this kind, with so many families lost and towns annihilated. Dam failures, meanwhile, have not stopped happening and could well rise in number, as climate change continues to produce more episodes of extreme precipitation [13] in northern temperate zones. This brings us back to the US where the American Society of Civil Engineers, in its "Report Card for America's Infrastructure," has identified over 4,000 deficient and 2,000 "high-hazard" dams [14].

Despite this, "safety" is a term urgently applied only to nuclear power, even by the nuclear industry, in obedience to public fears. There is even more irony here than we might first realize. It can be legitimately said, after all, that in substituting for many additional coal plants in the 1960s and 70s (before pollution controls were advanced) nuclear plants in the US have quite literally prevented many thousands of premature deaths. For China and India, where plans are underway to greatly expand both nuclear and renewable power, millions of more lives will be helped. Once we accept the human cost of coal and potential cost of hydro, it is no longer possible to single out nuclear power for presumed dangers to the public.

Other issues? Evacuated lands and waste disposal do not alter the picture. As noted in Chapter 6, evacuations have been guesses based more on overreaction than hard data. Much of the Chernobyl Exclusion Zone (30 km diameter from the reactor) has safe levels today (<10 mSv/yr), except for a number of "hot spots," and has become the largest wildlife refuge in Europe, with flourishing ecosystems. But it is also stigmatized land, infected with fear. For comparison, we might consider the amount of land removed from habitation that dam reservoirs have created worldwide, with millions of people forcibly relocated. Coal fires that burn in many nations – the US, UK, China, India, Indonesia, Australia, South Africa, Poland, Germany, Mongolia [15] – have also put huge areas worldwide off-limits, with toxic fumes killing off vegetation and animal life.

As for nuclear waste, by industrial standards the total global volume is small, even tiny. At roughly 240,000 tonnes (264,000 tons) of spent fuel, it would occupy a single acre of land piled to about 50 ft (15 m) – roughly a single Walmart store. This volume represents sixty years of operation, with more than 400 reactors online since 1990. All this waste could be easily stored underground in a single site. The total, in fact, might be compared to the more than 28 million tons of other hazardous waste generated by the US alone *per year* (nuclear = 0.02 percent of this total), the majority of which *is* disposed of underground [16]. Given the strict regulations governing how it is packaged and contained, nuclear waste is far less dangerous than dozens of chemicals injected underground in aqueous solutions.

Deep anxiety about nuclear power simply lacks concrete support. Three major accidents in more than half-a-century, only one with radiation fatalities numbering less than sixty, does not define a precarious technology. If it did, no use of fossil fuels or hydropower would be acceptable. Renewables, too, would be the object of major worry, even outrage, due to thousands of accidents, hundreds of fatalities, and, in some nations, secrecy about such incidents [17].

Rephrasing the nuclear record as one of "low-frequency, high consequence events," as some have done, is a clever way to make things sound ominous. "What if" scenarios can always be rendered extreme. But this game works for any energy technology. A massive explosion at an urban refinery could kill thousands from the blast, fire, and fumes. Wind turbines can be blown over in a "low-frequency, high consequence" weather event, crushing homes. An electrical fire in a turbine (many have occurred) could drop sparks to ignite a wildfire or forest fire that spreads to homes, farms, entire neighborhoods, schools. And so on.

So we come to an interesting conclusion. One of the safest baseload sources is soaked in worries about "safety." Only for nuclear has it been said that an accident anywhere is an accident everywhere. We might even go further. An accident in any plant, of whatever age or design, is an accident in all plants that will ever be built. Nuclear fear holds that the technology cannot be remediated or re-engineered or reconceived or made safe under any circumstances, no matter what powers of human innovation are brought to bear. The problems are absolute. And this tells us that the technology itself is not really the issue.

Pandora's Touch: A Brief History of Fear

The first public protest against a nuclear power plant happened in the US during a crucial period. This was the late 1950s, the historical moment when the Western world first became seriously concerned about radiation in the form of fallout and, by association, "atomic power." It was when radiation entered the American consciousness linking together nuclear war, weapon testing, and power generation.

For much of the 1950s, Americans saw radiation as bathed in complexity. It was unconnected to daily life, a scientific matter. Yet many were also aware, if only vaguely, that something was wrong. A 1956 poll showed 69 percent of respondents felt "no fear" at all about nuclear power, but another 20 percent already *did* fear the "peaceful atom" [18]. More than a few remembered the *Lucky Dragon* incident of 1954, when Japanese fisherman had been sickened by fallout from the Bravo test at Bikini Atoll. This had been widely reported and helped spark a growing movement in the US to end weapons testing.

In May of 1958, the Soviets declared they would stop atmospheric testing in October, essentially forcing (by moral example) the US to accept a moratorium and to begin negotiations on a test-ban treaty. In the intervening five months, both nations rushed to test as many weapons as they could (the US tested seventy-seven, more than twice any previous year). By early 1959, levels of

Strontium-90 – the radionuclide of greatest concern, due to its appearance in milk – began to rise across the US The fact showed up in medical studies, then in a *Consumer Reports* (CR) article, "The Milk All of Us Drink and Fallout," proving elevated Sr-90 levels in milk from fifty cities. The article caused something of a sensation and made the Atomic Energy Commission, with its assurances that fallout was harmless, appear misleading and irresponsible [19]. Repeated and expanded upon by other news outlets, the fallout "threat" became widely known, helping contribute to the first controversy over a nuclear plant, just then underway.

In fact, the strongest and most influential document giving credibility to such worries was a report by the National Academy of Sciences, *Biological Effects of Atomic Radiation: A Report to the Public* (1956). Written for a lay audience, the report became a reference for educated readers, nonnuclear scientists, medical professionals, academics, and journalists. Though not the final word on its subject, it was the first and most authoritative for more than a decade. Long-term, "no scientific assessment has had a broader impact on the development of biological thinking in nuclear policy in the United States and abroad ... " Its conclusions "stood the test of time ... informing decisions about nuclear testing, radioactive waste, and the development of civilian atomic energy in subsequent decades" [20]. It was a key document establishing the linear no-threshold (LNT) model and thus radiation protection policy up to the present.

BEAR 1, as it is known, the first in a series of related reports by the NAS over the next several decades, was meant as an independent, objective assessment in a realm that had begun to worry the public and about which scientists had made conflicting statements. The AEC and some physicists like Edward Teller claimed that fallout from the Nevada tests created no threat. But it was clear that a shroud of secrecy lay over any details about nuclear-related information. To a degree, this was inevitable. The AEC was the direct descendant of the Manhattan Project. It had a dual role: the development of nuclear weapons *and* both R&D and promotion of civilian atomic energy. It had divisions on biomedical and environmental research, as well as on fallout monitoring [21]. But combining military and civilian responsibilities in a single agency was never a good idea. Priority fell to military considerations, further elevated by the Korean War (1951–53), with the civilian side always limited by "national security considerations." The wartime culture of confidentiality surrounding all things nuclear carried into the post-war era.

AEC Chairman Lewis Strauss aggressively defended this policy time and again. He foolishly claimed that the crew of the *Lucky Dragon* could not possibly have been harmed by fallout from the Bravo test. Other incorrect statements he made, as a nonscientist seeking to protect the testing program, seemed not just overly defensive to many scientists, but deceitful. A dismissive and imperial tone only added to the impression. Indeed, along with his vendetta against J. Robert Oppenheimer, whom he accused of communist sympathies, and his open distrust of other Manhattan Project physicists who now called for nuclear disarmament, Strauss' repeated denials of any need to worry about fallout deepened misgivings about the AEC.

It also helped intensify the position of Hermann Muller and other geneticists who saw a direct relation between radiation and genetic damage. The relation had come from Muller's Nobel Prize-winning work on x-ray effects in fruit flies. Muller had no problem making the leap from *Drosophila melanogaster* to *homo sapiens* despite scant evidence. To be sure, he had made the jump ten years earlier, in his Nobel speech. Now, as one of the leading authors of the BEAR 1, he pressed his case as if it were solid fact.

BEAR 1 was a summary work by six committees. These dealt with radiation in the areas of genetics, pathology, food and agriculture, meteorology, oceans and fisheries, and radioactive waste. Billed as a review of what was then known, it was something far more. Battles were fought between the geneticists and AEC scientists over the meaning of radiation. On the whole, the geneticists won. We see this in the very first paragraph: "Whenever atomic energy is released, there are released with it certain invisible but powerful radiations . . . [W]hen these radiations strike living things they cause important changes that are often harmful . . . [and] may be passed on to succeeding generations" [22]. The report states that it will provide "only scientific data." Yet immediately afterward, we are told: "Behind any discussion of radiation must necessarily loom the specter of full-scale atomic war." No qualification is offered; *all* human-made radiation is a peril haunting today's world. What, then, of atomic war and atomic power?

> [S]o far as radiation is concerned the two aspects are not entirely unrelated. In the first place, when a world-wide atomic power becomes fully developed, its accumulated waste products might represent more radiation than would be released in an atomic war. Of course, this radiation will be imprisoned, not broadcast. But the point underscores the magnitude of the coming problem.
>
> Secondly, it becomes clear in this report that even very low levels of radiation can have serious biological effects. In several instances the size of the effect turns out to depend directly on the amounts of radiation. Thus, *many of the disastrous consequences of atomic war are clearly implied in this investigation of peacetime problems.* (p. 2, italics added)

Throughout the text, this connection is repeatedly made. When the reader is told "man has been lucky," the reference is not to the lack of nuclear war but instead to nuclear power and the idea that man is "dealing with an enormous new force whose potential effects he has only dimly understood" yet has so far escaped disaster (p. 2). Again and again, we are informed that any biological damage from peacetime nuclear activity has been "negligible" and that "radiation problems, if they are met intelligently and vigilantly, need not stand in the way of the large-scale development of atomic energy" (p. 3). But then, only a few lines later, we are greeted by this trembling news:

> Everyone is subjected to the natural background radiation which causes an unavoidable quantity of so-called spontaneous mutations. Anything that adds radiation to this naturally occurring background rate causes further mutations, and is genetically harmful.
>
> There is no minimum amount of radiation which must be exceeded before mutations occur. Any amount, however small, that reaches the reproductive cells can cause a correspondingly small number of mutations. The more radiation, the more mutations.
>
> The harm is cumulative. The genetic damage done by radiation builds up as the radiation is received, and depends on the total accumulated gonad dose received by people from their own conception to the conception of their last child. (p. 3)

Such views were not universal. Many physicians and radiologists felt that there actually was a threshold range below which radiation did not cause harm, that the "no minimum" didn't accurately represent the human response. This view, and the debate it represented, was suppressed by the geneticists. Still, they were urged by AEC scientists on the committees to recommend exposure limits that the government could use to keep people safe. This was done, and it established a pattern – using dose limits to protect the public instead of risk calculations based on exposure. Yet Muller and the geneticists had their revenge. The idea that any exposure, no matter how tiny, bore a mutation risk dominated the report, and it gave rise to some striking imagery:

> A population that is exposed, generation after generation, to an increased amount of radiation will experience a rising death rate and a falling birth rate because of harmful mutations . . . If in this process the death rate comes to exceed the birth rate, the population will decline and eventually perish. At present we are extremely uncertain about the level of this fatal threshold . . . This is one reason why we must be cautious about increasing the total amount of radiation to which the entire population is exposed. (p. 19)

Society seemed to be hurtling ahead with a technology for which it was not ready. "Past experience gives only a pale intimation of what is to come." (p. 30), the NAS says. Storage of waste and a core accident "spread[ing] disastrous quantities of radioactivity over thousands of square miles" (p. 32) must be anticipated. Nations could well be imperiled if "nuclear plants spring up ad lib, over the earth" without adequate control and planning. "A large part of the information that is needed to make intelligent plans is not yet at hand. There is not much time left to acquire it" (p. 32).

BEAR 1 therefore ends not with a bang or whimper but a warning. What the NAS produced was more akin to the "Dreadful Atom" than a "Peaceful Atom." This was particularly true of the section written by geneticists. Their dire conclusions were the ones chosen to appear in the *New York Times* the day after BEAR 1 came out. An introductory article with the headline, "Scientists Term Radiation a Peril to Future of Man," left little doubt about the key message: "atomic radiation, no matter how small the dose, harms not only the person receiving it but also all his descendants" [23].

In plain language, BEAR 1 articulated and even dramatized many of the fears that would come to surround nuclear power. Beyond the inevitable harm that radiation would do, these included: the potential for massive contamination of soil and food, the certainty of lethal nuclear waste in vast quantities, the need for vigilant oversight, and the vision that humanity had unleashed a force it could not fully control.

What seems shocking about all this is that, despite such messages, Lewis Strauss and the Eisenhower Administration thereafter used the NAS report to argue for a *lack* of any real risk from nuclear testing. This could not help but intensify distrust of the AEC still further, especially among scientists, including many who had participated in the NAS work itself. Instead of solving the controversy over radiation (fallout), BEAR 1 gave it new vigor. Public figures, such as Nobel Laureate Linus Pauling, who helped create and lead the social movement against weapons testing, drew from the report. By 1959, when the movement was reaching its peak, Pauling was among a number of scientists estimating hundreds of thousands of children born worldwide with "gross physical or mental defects" and nearly a million "embryonic and neonatal deaths" [24].

Today we know that many of the worries expressed by the NAS were overblown or wrong. BEAR 1 was written at an early stage when a great deal remained unknown. Predictions made that a great many birth defects and stillbirths were inevitable from atmospheric testing proved wholly incorrect. Rather than a rapid surge in stillbirths after 1950, US data shows precisely the opposite, a spectacular and continuous drop from 18 per 1,000 pregnancies to only 8 by 1980 [25]. A second idea based on the Muller model that proved untrue had to do with radiation exposure to reproductive cells, especially in men. Fallout was supposed to cause a jump in genetic mutations that would raise defects in later generations. The supposition was mostly speculative, and no surge in birth defects happened. Rather, it was soon learned that the real danger from radiation exposure to the male reproductive system was something quite different: sterility.

Similarly, it was later found that birth defects do not simply increase with increasing exposure. This has been negated by the lack of birth defects in the children born to atomic bomb survivors, as discussed previously (Chapter 5). Data from animal studies, on the other hand, suggests that any risk for such defects or miscarriage is highest in the first two weeks after conception, at dose levels over 200 mSv, thereafter rising from 500 mSv to over 1,000 mSv, where cell death occurs [26]. The information on atomic bomb survivors implies that such levels are low and that their use by the medical community reflects a desire to be conservative in order to ensure the public is protected.

Studies in the 1990s and 2000s, meanwhile, have shown that, with important exceptions, fallout from atmospheric testing was halted (1963) before any significant risk accumulated for the global population. Determinations by UNSCEAR of the annual worldwide dose from such tests show a peak in 1963 of about 150 μSv (0.15 mSv), falling to 5 μSv (0.05 mSv) by 2000 [27]. Such levels are a small fraction of natural background (2.4 mSv global average). On the other hand, risk estimates and cancer incidence remain debated (and highly contentious) in the US for those most affected by test fallout. So-called "downwinders" and military personnel who worked on atmospheric tests have been repeatedly studied. A problem is that there are uncertainties about actual doses, since monitoring at the time was far from thorough. Despite thousands of claims of personal illness and hundreds of millions of dollars in compensatory payments paid out under the Radiation Exposure Compensation Act (1990, expanded 2000), the extent of impacts is still not known [28–29]. A 2005 review by the NAS concluded that risk, especially for thyroid cancer, was real and significant for children. But for those who were adults, "it is unlikely that onsite participants and the downwinders . . . are at significantly increased risk."[3] [30] Current thinking, therefore, is that testing did not endanger the American public as a whole, as BEAR 1 suggested it did.

Perhaps the most potent disproof of the geneticists' position returns to their grim forecast about a population subject to growing levels of radiation. They would presumably suffer rising death rates and falling birth rates. But from 1970 to 2010, when total background dose levels grew by 3–4 mSv, thereby doubling for many nations due to expanded use of medical imaging, death rates fell as much as 50 percent [31]. Fertility rates, meanwhile, declined in the US

---

[3] This discussion does not include risks for uranium miners and other workers nor for Marshall Islanders exposed to high levels of fallout radiation, especially from the Bravo test of 1954.

and Europe during the 1960s and 70s, but then stopped and flattened out over the next forty years [32].

What we learn, then, by comparing BEAR 1 to current knowledge can be summed up in a single line: radiation is much less harmful than was believed in the 1950s and 60s, and perhaps less than is generally believed today. BEAR 1 is therefore extremely important itself for yet another reason. It shows that nuclear anxiety did not begin with the public but with the scientific community. It began not only with those who worked on the Manhattan Project and who understood what radiation was, who were shaken by the deaths of Harry Daghlian, Jr. and Louis Slotin, both of whom had been careless with a plutonium bomb core [33], and deeply sobered by the bombings in Japan. Radiation worries were even stronger among those in the life sciences, genetics especially.

These researchers, after all, came to the study of radioactivity from a different direction, namely the damage it could do to biological systems. Their fears for humanity made sense from this vantage. And the best way to solidify their viewpoint, they seem to have concluded, was to obey the government's need for threshold dose limits to protect the public but to establish these on the basis of their own no-threshold theory. This would at least help keep the limits so low that the public would be guaranteed a high level of safety. That their own worries about radiation might have been excessive, requiring more research to confirm, didn't occur to them. That exceedingly low dose limits might one day add credibility to a widespread public terror about radiation and the thought of a nuclear accident of any scale was even further from their imagination at the time. This may be saying too much for the prosecution. But in a fundamental sense, radiation had gained an official sensibility – a sensibility that countered everything the "peaceful atom" was supposed to bring to society.

Bodega Bay and the Pattern of Protest

Debate and concern over the effects of fallout began to fade after the Limited Test Ban Treaty went into effect in 1963, forbidding above-ground testing. But the fears articulated by BEAR 1 did not die away with them. On the contrary. They had already found a new controversy in which to bloom.

This, the first protest against a nuclear power plant, took place at Bodega Bay, a sleepy and scenic fishing town of about 350 people some 45 miles (60 km) north of San Francisco and the site of Alfred Hitchcock's 1963 film, *The Birds*. In 1958, the California utility, Pacific Gas and Electric (PG&E), proposed building a power plant on a rocky headland bordering the bay, using eminent domain to acquire the land. It did not say what kind of plant it would build; it didn't announce this for three years.

Opposition began immediately from residents whose land was to be taken. It soon spread to others in the town who saw a large industrial installation as ruining the area's pastoral beauty. Hearings before the California Public Utilities Commission ended with such concerns being dismissed. Residents were assured that PG&E's scientists and engineers had everything in hand, and that the project would go forward. All requests for further hearings were denied. This lack of concern for the people who would be most directly affected did not sit well. Opposition changed to outrage.

In fact, there were two motives behind the plant. The state wanted more electricity to boost economic development, especially in the north. PG&E hoped to establish leadership in a brand-new market of nuclear power generation. The Utilities Commission and PG&E had discussed the idea of a power plant at Bodega Bay prior to any hearings. Though fairly common at the time, this kind of prelicensing exchange would soon be the target for accusations of collusion between regulating and regulated entities.

The protestors decided to expand their methods and recruit support from a variety of groups and individuals. Over time, and especially after it was announced that the power plant would be nuclear, the role of women proved pivotal. They were most effective in drawing into discussions and media conversations the national concern over fallout. What would happen if the nuclear plant had an accident? Couldn't it contaminate the milk from northern California's dairy farms and poison children and families in surrounding areas [34]?

The enlarged opposition formed their own body, the Northern California Association to Preserve Bodega Head and Harbor. Activist spokespeople from San Francisco, University of California, Berkeley, conservation groups, and local towns began writing letters to major media outlets. In 1962, the group took its case to the AEC itself when PG&E made a formal application for the power plant. But the protestors discovered that only those with "recognized expertise" were allowed to speak. This did not include members of the general public.

At this point, the nature of the controversy shifted. Because the plant was nuclear and because, as became clear, it would be sited only a thousand feet from the San Andreas Fault, the real issue was public safety. Scenery was no longer the point; the heart of the matter was radiation. There could be no guarantee that a major earthquake, such as the 1906 San Francisco quake that had caused movement in Bodega Bay, wouldn't happen and cause an accident that would spread contamination over large portions of northern California. A succession of geoscientists, producing a series of analyses, yielded conflicting conclusions [35] but, in the end, seemed to support PG&E's position that the plant could be built to withstand a large quake [36]. Part of the problem was that the nature of the San Andreas was not understood at the time. Plate tectonics did not yet exist, and the reality of the fault as an active boundary between two of the Earth's largest plates was unknown. No nuclear plant would be sited in such a location today.

Opposition to the plant was by now a movement, with hundreds of supporters and allies in newsrooms. The argument continued to evolve: no longer did it focus only on the possibility of accidents but spoke about how, during normal operation, the plant would likely leak radioactive gases into the air and fluids into the ocean, damaging the coastal environment for birds and sea life. Sited right on the ocean, from where it would draw water, the plant could also injure fish, whether through discharging hot waters or radiation-laden waste, and thus ruin local livelihoods. Thus the image of a nuclear plant had become a persistent generator of life-threatening contamination. To drive the point home, the Northern California Association published a pamphlet on fallout and how dangerous radioactive "particles" find their way into cow's milk and thus adults and children. In June of 1963, a group of followers released 1,500 helium-filled red balloons each with a message: "This balloon could represent a radioactive molecule of strontium 90 or iodine 131." Landing sites for these missives ranged from hotels and businesses in downtown San Francisco to dozens of farms and towns tens of miles to the east.

A key leader of the opposition, David Pesonen, later explained, "I had a feeling of the enormousness of what we were fighting; it was anti-life." And further, "I had an epiphany. I began to think that there really was evil in the world. PG&E had a single-mindedness that didn't involve people's well-being" [37]. Pesonen contacted the US Department of the Interior, whose Secretary, Stewart Udall, an avid environmentalist, sided with the protest once he learned how close the plant site was to the fault. This led to much further media coverage, with the result that the governor, Edmund (Pat) Brown, also weighed in on the side of the protesters. Newspaper accounts then took up the full weight of the seismic issue, radiation safety, and the David vs. Goliath theme.

Then, in 1964, the giant Sherman Earthquake in Alaska (9.2 magnitude) devastated Anchorage and large sections of coastline. Governor Brown commented on camera: "This nuclear danger is so great that you can't take any chance whatsoever" [38]. He requested PG&E abandon their plans. By late 1964, the regulatory staff of the AEC had decided that there was not enough evidence to prove that the plant could be built and operated safely. A phrase from one of the later geologic reports can be understood as defining the AEC position: "Because we cannot prove that the worst situation will not prevail … we must recognize that it might" [39]. PG&E withdrew its application.

In all, the struggle had taken more than six years. It did not set loose the antinuclear movement in full form, but it did achieve something nearly as significant. It put in the spotlight many of the core elements that the movement would come to employ and depend upon when it arrived. One of them, of course, was the existential threat posed by radiation. Time and again, the opposition "raised the specter of an earthquake disaster being compounded in unfathomable dimensions by a nuclear catastrophe" [40]. This brought the stakes of the controversy to the highest level, invoking nuclear technology as having the power to pollute the very air, land, and water on which all life depends. "Nuclear" became synonymous with death. The connection made in the BEAR 1 report was made here too: a nuclear power plant held the same potential for catastrophe as a nuclear bomb.

Such fears were blended with a second kind. This came from the perception (not wholly inaccurate) of corporate and government powers acting in a despotic way. Public concerns had been dismissed in favor of experts who worked *for* these same powers. Profit had seemingly been placed above public well-being. Such was not democracy; it verged on the very type of oppression found in the Soviet Union.

These perceptions gave powerful support to a righteous anger. Such anger in turn gave justice to an emotional, symbol-laden, and accusatory rhetoric of great effect. Casting the authorities (PG&E, Utilities Commission, AEC) as "enemies" against nature and the public had a real impact in magnetizing support. For those confused by the facts, a demonizing rhetoric cast everything into a sharp, simplified, energizing light. If it tended to ignore the facts themselves, this did not prevent it from being effective against the restrained, often technical and bureaucratic language employed by the other side. This technocratic discourse found itself repeatedly outmatched. It lacked any real means to address attacks delivered from a (presumed) moral high ground, borrowing from some of democracy's most sacred principles.

Lessons from a Clamshell and a Physicist

The Bodega Bay protest thus brought together growing fears and concerns that had begun to emerge in the early Cold War period. Starting with nimby distress about the local environment, it swelled to anxieties about radiation and about the nature of postwar society. The controversy was only one in a number of other siting protests in the early 1960s. But it was the first to establish the basic issues and rhetoric that would soon evolve into signatures of the antinuclear movement.

Over the next decade, distrust of major institutions deepened as realities like the Civil Rights movement, Vietnam War, and Watergate became major national issues.

There were new fears as well, brought by the environmental movement, many of whose activists saw radiation, nuclear waste, and heated waste water as among the worst forms of pollution. The presumed dangers of radiation were further elevated by apprehensions about the overweening power of major institutions, the indifference and greed of corporations, the broken legitimacy of government agencies, and the combined effects of all this to impose on the public a new technology linked to weapons with the power to destroy life on an unbearable scale. Antinuclear groups therefore emerged to resist what was perceived to be an all-out assault on nature, public health, and political liberty. Such groups as the Clamshell Alliance, Abalone Alliance, Greenpeace, and Friends of the Earth (FOE) made this clear in their platforms and statements. Accidents were inevitable, they said. Nuclear energy was too formidable to be controlled by human beings. Nuclear plants were similarly too complex, sure to break down and bring threat to millions.

The political side to all this had a particular edge. Nuclear power demanded greatly concentrated forms of economic and governmental power. Only huge corporate entities, with strong political allies and large-scale government support, could build a fleet of reactors. Government statements from the 1950s to the early 1970s that as many as a thousand reactors would be built in the US therefore promised a new, highly centralized society where individual and communal freedom would be first curtailed and then wiped out. We can see much of this in the manifestoes of the more influential anti-nuclear groups that emerged in the 1970s such as the Clamshell Alliance, founded in 1976 to halt construction of the Seabrook Nuclear Plant in New Hampshire. In its "Declaration of Nuclear Resistance," the Alliance states that "Nuclear power is dangerous to all living creatures and to their natural environment. The nuclear industry is designed to concentrate profits and the control of energy resources in the hands of a powerful few, undermining basic principles of human liberty." It then declares:

- That there is a direct relationship between nuclear power plants and nuclear weapons ... The export of nuclear reactors makes possible the spread of nuclear bombs to nations all over the world ...;
- That the centralized nature of nuclear power takes control of energy from local communities and strengthens the monopoly of the utilities ...;

– That the dangers of nuclear power are intolerable. They include release of "low-level" radiation – a cause of cancer and genetic disorders; the creation of deadly radioactive waste which must be completely isolated from the environment for 250,000 years; the destruction of our lakes, rivers, and oceans by thermal pollution; and the possibility of a catastrophic meltdown. No material gain ... worth the assault on life itself that atomic energy represents [41].

Without doubt the most influential "manifesto" of this kind, both in the US and Europe, was a 1976 article in *Foreign Affairs* magazine written by a young physicist and member of FOE, Amory Lovins. Today an ageing icon of the antinuclear movement, Lovins wrote "Energy Strategy: The Road Not Taken?" as a dense, sophisticated, and visionary argument for the idea of a "soft energy path." This meant, in today's parlance, an energy system based on renewable and clean coal technologies locally distributed and controlled. Nuclear power, like fossil fuels traditionally used, belonged to the more risky, costly, and environmentally damaging "hard path," defined by large-scale power plants. Brilliant and far-reaching, with its recommendations about energy efficiency, conservation, new technologies, and even climate impacts, the article is often seen as borne out by forty years of subsequent history. Yet, looked at with a dry eye, Lovins' essay isn't really about energy; it is a piece of social philosophy. As the author says, the most pressing issues about energy strategy "are not mainly technical or economic but rather social and ethical. They will pose a supreme challenge to the adaptability of democratic institutions and to the vitality of our spiritual life" [42]. Put differently:

> Siting big energy systems pits central authority against local autonomy in an increasingly divisive and wasteful form of centrifugal politics ... In [such a] world, your lifeline comes not from an understandable neighborhood technology run by people you know who are at your own social level, but rather from an alien, remote, and perhaps humiliatingly uncontrollable technology run by a faraway, bureaucratized, technical elite who have probably never heard of you. Decisions about who shall have how much energy at what price also become centralized ... For all these reasons, if nuclear power were clean, safe, economic, assured of ample fuel, and socially benign, it would still be unattractive because of the political implications of the kind of energy economy it would lock us into [43].

Nuclear power, in short, was a true enemy of the people. It had inherent evils and could not be made acceptable under any circumstances. In blunt terms, it represented a kind of "technological authoritarianism" [44]. It was thus far more than a new technology haunted by the ghosts of a former war. It was, in fact, the bearer of a dread spirit that would always work its will against an ethical, democratic social order. And, no less, as the words of the Clamshell

Alliance tell us, it will spread weapons of mass destruction abroad while contaminating, sickening, and killing citizens at home. In a very real way, therefore, nuclear power counted as a form of suicide for modern civilization.

If ordinary citizens did not see things in quite so dramatic a fashion, the anxieties they absorbed were often no different in kind. These were worries that tended to focus on physical threat, on the possibility of nuclear catastrophe, the buildup of deadly nuclear waste, and the suspicion that nuclear power plants were constantly releasing radiation invisibly into the air, soil, and water. Behind these apprehensions of harm, however, lived a question: how could such a dangerous technology ever have been nurtured by US scientists, by the US government, and by US companies? Were US citizens being treated like fodder, asked to accept anything these authorities decided was "in the national interest"? Thus, the sense that there might be something wrong in the halls of power could not be separated from the feeling that a risky technology was now spreading throughout the landscape.

The 1970s were the peak of antinuclear protests, to which the media often gave sympathetic coverage. It was the time that celebrities got involved as spokespeople against nuclear power (e.g. Jane Fonda, Martin Sheen, Jack Lemmon). National organizations with scientific credentials, such as the Union of Concerned Scientists (UCS), Natural Resources Defense Council, and Sierra Club, also sided against nuclear as a dangerous technology. Apparently the UCS were the ones to discover (in AEC files) and bring to media attention the term "China Syndrome" [45]. This idea, with its arresting image of glowing fuel melting its way through the floor and deep into the Earth, became well-known even before the movie of the same name. The film made "China Syndrome" a household word, entering theaters only twelve days before the TMI accident in 1979. What it stood for, however, went beyond a major meltdown. As a metaphor, it signified a runaway technology able to seriously damage the Earth. one created by human beings yet with an ultimate power that lay beyond human control.

Antinuclearism in Europe

Similar fears to the American case had developed across the Atlantic by the mid-1970s. Antinuclear movements pursued different strategies in different countries, responding to specific political structures and opportunities [46]. Nearly all of these began like the Bodega Bay controversy, in local opposition to a power plant or facility site. By the early 1970s, however, with the rise of larger political concerns, this early scatter of protest came together as a

collection of groups aimed at national resistance. The impact of these movements varied considerably. Yet they also shared a common angst about nuclear
power and what it represented. While there isn't room here to review the
diversity of detailed reactions, a few comments can be made that are helpful
to understand the larger situation in Western democracies.

In some European nations, the debates and protests rose to an intensity
surpassing what was seen in the US. Part of the reason for this come from the
truth that the European situation was very different, in essential ways. The
continent had suffered immensely from two terrible wars perpetrated by state
power, military escalation, and the willing participation of science-based
industries. Unlike the US, European states were on the front lines of the Cold
War and understood that they could easily become the first nuclear battleground. During the 1950s and 60s, "a complex interplay between Cold War and
WW II experiences influenced the debates about the dangers of nuclear fallout
and of nuclear weapons" in countries like Britain, France, and Germany [47].
This was most true for Germany, where NATO forces had emplaced tactical
nuclear weapons. Still more, state control of German technological effort had
resulted in such innovations as mustard gas in WWI and Zyklon B used in the
gas chambers. There is much significance in the fact that German antinuclear
groups regularly employed terms such as "police state." Such points hardly
explain the full complexities of opposition to nuclear power; established
political parties, probusiness and industry groups, and labor unions all supported expansion of Germany's nuclear program. Yet the country remained
split in two by the Cold War and German lands occupied by American and
Soviet militaries. Grassroots efforts by antinuclear groups that associated
reactors and weapons had an added layer of fearful meaning.

On the other hand, a different kind of history existed for France. The French
government was able to keep strict control over nuclear development, as a
state-level response to the oil crisis of 1973, and official procedures did not give
much room for public feedback. But a more important factor seems to have
been national pride. French scientists had discovered radioactivity and made
some of the most important discoveries in the early twentieth century. These
contributions were a source of national pride and prestige, and the government
made skillful use of this to gain support among the general public [48]. It did
not prevent protest, however; far from it. In July 1977, a march by tens of
thousands against the Superphénix breeder reactor involved the throwing of
Molotov cocktails and a major clash with police causing the death of a
protestor. Even so, the massive public resistance involving all ages and classes
of people that happened in Germany did not sweep over *La patrie*. France and
Germany, side-by-side, represent the two ends of a spectrum in Europe's

overall response to nuclear power. Where many French people tolerated or even embraced it (though France had its own antinuclear movement), the Germans developed a profound fear and distrust shared by many levels of society and that formed a primary set of beliefs helping power the Greens to a position of major influence in the German government.

Britain presented another case of a movement with unique national aspects. Unlike Germany but similar to France and the US, Britain developed and tested its own nuclear weapons, and early protests during the 1950s and 60s opposed the British government and military's contribution to the rising global level of fallout radiation. Britain also saw a significant fire at the Windscale Nuclear facility in 1957, and though no evacuations were called and no negative health effects for workers were reported, it led to confiscation of milk from nearby areas for several months and thus to much public concern. There were demonstrations against the dumping of low- and intermediate-level waste at sea, which Britain and a number of other European nations (Belgium, France, Switzerland, Germany, Sweden, Netherlands) had also done. But a larger amount of fear was aimed at the US and Soviets, due to the arms race and constant threat of war [49]. Journalists and public leaders when discussing nuclear events in America often employed religious terms, e.g. nuclear energy as a "demonic power" providing "weapons of the apocalypse." German headlines about the *Lucky Dragon* incident read like a menu of black magic: "Under the Spell of Planetary Danger," "The Horror at Bikini," and "Peace by Terror" [50]. These were images that did not vanish after atmospheric testing stopped.

They appear in what is perhaps the most famous antinuclear book ever published in Europe, *The Nuclear State: Progress in Inhumanity* (1977), written by the Austrian journalist and author Robert Jungk. Having earlier published works on the Manhattan Project and the after effects of Hiroshima, Jungk was a powerful voice, a leader in the Austrian antinuclear movement, and hugely respected. *The Nuclear State* (*Der Atomstaat* in German) went into multiple editions and was translated into a number of languages before the end of the decade, especially after the TMI accident. It was an impassioned warning that took antinuclearism to an extreme new height:

> With the technical exploitation of fission has come a daring leap into an entirely new dimension of violence. First directed against military opponents, today it endangers its own citizens. For "atoms for peace" has no principal difference from "atoms for war." The declared intention to use fission only for constructive aims changes nothing with regard to the hostile nature of this new energy source. Efforts to control the risks can only partly manage the dangers. Even proponents must admit that there can be no success in eliminating them entirely ... This grip on the future, the fear of vast damage caused by runaway nuclear power, will be the greatest conceivable

burden for humanity, whether as an ineradicable trail of poison or the shadow of an eternal anxiety [51].

The book contains stories about oppressive treatment of nuclear workers, theft of nuclear material, and other nasty transgressions. Most of them were based on rumor, but this did not stop them from being easily believed. *Atomstaat*'s larger message was entirely of its time. They expressed what Lovins and most nuclear opponents feared but in more feverish, histrionic language. Jungk warns that a "totalitarian technocratic future" had already begun. Since uranium resources were small (or so it was then thought), nations would be forced to reprocess all spent fuel, generating huge amounts of plutonium whose surveillance, protection, and use would demand the tactics of a totalitarian state. Europe and the US were approaching a point of no return; Orwell's *1984* loomed ahead.

Last Years of the Cold War to the First Years of the New Century

But for the general public in most Western nations, fear that democracy would be annihilated by the nuclear embrace never penetrated very far. This was especially true in the US where the experience of fascism and other forms of authoritarian state power did not exist. In the early 1980s, moreover, the election of Ronald Reagan to the presidency brought to the fore conservative political rhetoric about reducing and limiting government power, weakening its role in daily life. The one exception was national defense. A renewal of aggressive language toward the Soviets and an enormous buildup of military strength had a potent effect in bringing back fears of nuclear war, with inevitable effects on views about nuclear power.

If much of the public was confused about exactly how much anxiety should be spent on nuclear plants, Three Mile Island helped them focus on danger and thus safety. Yet "safety" by this time had acquired a number of meanings. It not only involved fallout from an accident, but the possibility of nuclear plants leaking radioactive gases and waste water. The issue of nuclear waste and its disposal had also become a topic of national concern. But TMI also made sure that people understood the nuclear industry and its government defenders couldn't fully be trusted. An accident had now happened and would likely happen again, only with worse consequences. A raft of new safety regulations by the Nuclear Regulatory Commission did not mollify these sentiments. It did, however, increase the time and cost still further for building new plants, thus "proving" that the technology was hugely expensive and more complex than any other type of energy production. Studies of public attitudes at this time showed a marked fall in acceptance of nuclear power to levels even below those of the 1970s. They also revealed that people knew little about the technology and what they did know was mostly wrong [52].

It pays, at this point, to look again at the warnings found in the BEAR 1 report. How many of these might have made their way into common understanding, even though, factually speaking, they proved incorrect? Let us list them:

1. Radiation is harmful. Any exposure produces damaging biological change. Such changes are cumulative and likely to be passed on to succeeding generations.
2. Nuclear weapons and nuclear power are two sides of a single coin, equally capable of producing cataclysm.
3. Nuclear power is a source, first and last, of radiation (dangerous), not of electricity (benefit, basis for modern life) or heat (widely useful) or new isotopes (useful for medicine, industry).
4. Nuclear reactors, because of the great dangers they pose, require the highest level of planning, control, and vigilance. They will always be a major burden on society.
5. Nuclear waste defines a threat as great as nuclear war. Enormous volumes of highly lethal waste will accumulate due to routine reprocessing of spent fuel.
6. Nuclear power represents a technology for which society is not ready; it might not be handled adequately and safely even by the most advanced nations.

To a significant degree, every one of these causes for anxiety were part of the "common knowledge" about nuclear power at the end of the 1970s. The only exception is perhaps the second part of #5. Recall from Chapter 4 that the US halted all reprocessing for civilian reactors in 1977; thus, there was no massive buildup of high-level waste. At the same time, most of the public did (and does) believe that *all* nuclear waste is highly lethal for thousands of years (recall: this is only true for high-level waste; the great majority is low- and intermediate-level whose radioactivity decays to less than hazardous levels in thirty to fifty years). One fear not listed above but added in the 1970s was that nuclear power would lead directly to proliferation. This worry was not without reason. The Non-Proliferation Treaty (1968) allowed all signatory nations to have the full complement of nuclear technology, including reprocessing and the ability to produce plutonium. But pressure from the US which halted all civilian reprocessing in 1977, helped ensure the technology was not exported all over the world. Between 1955 and 1995, as many as a dozen governments began and then ended weapons programs. By 1990, only four states – India, Pakistan, Israel, and South Africa – had actually built weapons. Over the next decade, four gave them up: Ukraine, Belarus, and Kazakhstan, which inherited weapons from the Soviet Union, and South Africa.

There were other specific worries that had grown up in the 70s, particularly related to terrorism. These, too, made sense, given the rise in terrorist attacks and their vicious targeting of ordinary people, as shown by the Rome and Vienna airport attacks. Yet by the early 1980s, the renewed intensity of Cold War conflict under the more hawkish Reagan administration brought fears of nuclear war back to center stage for the US public and much of the world. Influential writings affecting and articulating this primal worry returned to the kind of imagery used three decades earlier when imaginings about the end of the world drew directly on the atomic bombings in Japan. Inevitably, this came back to the angst about radiation. We find, it for example, in the most widely read and discussed work on nuclear war in the pre-Chernobyl era, Jonathan Schell's *The Fate of the Earth* (1982):

> In general magnitude, the energy of radioactive emissions greatly overmatches the strength of the chemical bonds that hold living things together. The vulnerability to radioactivity of genetic material, in particular, is well-known. It is perhaps not surprising that when cosmic energies are turned loose on a small planet overwhelming destruction is the result [53].

Schell's book was generally well-informed by a basic understanding of nuclear science, but he repeats here the error of the Muller hypothesis, now (and still today) part of the common wisdom. We see, too, that such understanding did not prevent him from making statements that easily abandon science for the apocalyptic imagination. The author even invokes a situation where bombs and reactors interact, where a weapon is dropped on a nuclear power plant. The result, at this point in history, is predictable:

> The intense but comparatively short-lived radiation from the weapon would kill people in the first few weeks and months, but the long-lived radiation that was produced both by the weapon and by the power plant could prevent anyone from living on a vast area of land for decades ... It can be put down as one further alarming oddity of life in a nuclear world that in building nuclear power plants nations have opened themselves to catastrophic devastation and long-term contamination of their territories ... [54]

Thus, we are back in the embrace of BEAR 1. Those nations who built nuclear plants endanger themselves no less than if they built weapons. They are doubly at risk. *Fate of the Earth* indicts government for having interpreted "national interest" as the need to imperil all of humanity. A reader emerging from its pages would likely have experienced both a renewed dread and a touch of reassurance – the latter, because so much of the common fear about radiation and all things nuclear had been confirmed.

Such confirmation was brought to a peak several years after by the accident at Chernobyl in 1986. Studies on public opinion consistently show a particular fall in acceptance of nuclear power after Chernobyl (followed by an increase from the late 1990s until the Fukushima accident in 2011) [55]. Lack of clear information about the incident from the Soviets allowed Western media to indulge in rumor and speculation and, without appreciation for the problematic RBMK design, to draw comparisons and "lessons" applicable to Western nuclear plants. Newspaper reports, using unconfirmed statements by local residents, spoke of thousands dead [56], whether in the streets of nearby towns or in piles being bulldozed into mass graves. Other stories discussed the innumerable birth defects that would take place all across Europe. *Time* magazine wrote of "an ominous pall of radiation [that] had spread across Eastern Europe and toward the shores of the Mediterranean." It cited a Johns Hopkins medical professor who speculated that residents as far away as sixty miles would suffer "significantly increased deaths from leukemia and other forms of cancer during the next thirty years" [57]. Evacuees (mainly women and children) transported to European cities were swept with Geiger Counters before being allowed to deplane. In many parts of Europe, pregnant women and young children were asked to remain indoors as much as possible. Few assurances by experts about low radiation levels were trusted. Fear became its own reward.

Antinuclear groups flamed into action. Millions had been exposed to high levels of radiation, they said; hundreds of thousands of cancers would result. In Germany, the Greens held mass protests with the message "Chernobyl is Everywhere!" For years afterward, studies appeared in reputable journals and newspapers claiming radiation effects would be even worse than imagined even thousands of miles distant from the accident [58]. Internet sites put up in the 1990s and 2000s continue to support such ideas and images and to feed a mythology of devastation that has grown up about Chernobyl concerning everything from mutant animal species to hideously deformed people.

The greater impact of the Chernobyl accident in Western nations was to essentially end nearly all plans for expansion of nuclear power programs. In a sense, the accident achieved what anti-nuclear groups had failed to do – stop the technology from moving forward. But in another way, antinuclearism had done its part to help institutionalize exaggerated fears in the public mind. Together with the culture of secrecy and misrepresentation created by government in the 1950s, the antinuclear angst over radiation found an apotheosis in a true disaster created by Soviet totalitarianism.

In the decades since 1986, public acceptance of nuclear power fell for a while, but then, by the early 2000s, rose again as climate change became a major issue, oil prices surged, and energy once more became a topic of much concern. A new generation, too young to have been deeply affected by Chernobyl, had grown up never experiencing a major accident. That, of course, changed in 2011 with Fukushima,

Is Nuclear Anxiety a Global Phenomenon?

The answer is almost certainly yes. But this "yes" is not simple. Again, there isn't space to do more than to cover a few main points about this. Moreover, the literature on public attitudes outside the OECD is limited at this point. Yet significant things can be said, including observations on the Chinese public.

It is important to stress that climate change has given nuclear power a new context, one that is recognized worldwide. This context is compelling and seems to have weakened the fear of nuclear energy in some portions of the population of many countries. But again, there is much diversity here (as we should expect). Every nation has its own profile of nuclear anxiety, related to its history and culture. Why, for example, does nuclear have such low approval ratings in Greece (<20 percent) yet such high ratings in China (>70 percent)? How did such ratings change after the Fukushima accident?

For our purposes, the second question is particularly important. Fukushima had a significant impact, without a doubt. A sizeable fraction of people world-wide who learned of the event became more fearful of nuclear power as a "risky technology." Such is hardly surprising. Not only has the advent of the Internet made for an audience far larger than what existed at the time of Chernobyl, but the Internet allows for the most exaggerated, misleading, and fraudulent material to be put online and to remain there interminably. There has been no lack of such material. Websites have claimed to show monstrous forms of sea life due to contamination or that the West Coast of North America is being "fried" by gamma rays. Scientific maps of tsunami height across the Pacific have been deceitfully relabeled as indicating the spread of radiation (which somehow stops abruptly at coastlines). Fortunately, as with Chernobyl, this material has been somewhat counteracted by legitimate material. But without external guidance, the confused or unwary viewer is likely to have his or her fears reaffirmed.

A 2011 international poll taken in forty-two countries showed a preaccident approval of nuclear power at 52.7 percent and a postaccident figure of 45.4 percent [59]. This seems important, but doesn't quite indicate a "collapse" in worldwide support. There was, however, a wide range in these figures. Some countries – Japan, China, Egypt, Iraq, Bangladesh – showed a decrease of more than 12 percent, while a larger number declined by 5 percent or less. More importantly, among those nations with approval ratings of 55 percent or higher before the accident – Bangladesh, Bulgaria, Cameroon, Canada, China, Czech Republic, Egypt, Finland, France, India, Iraq, Japan, South Korea, Netherlands, Nigeria, Pakistan, Romania, Russia, Tunisia, US and Vietnam – only four fell below 50 percent afterwards (Cameroon, Canada, Netherlands, Romania), with the US dropping from 58 percent to 50 percent.

Such numbers suggest that much of the drop in public approval may prove temporary. This kind of pattern, a rapid loss of approval in the immediate wake of an accident followed by a more gradual return toward former levels of acceptance, has been observed for TMI and Chernobyl in Western nations [60]. There are some indications that this has happened in developing countries too, and will continue if no other nuclear accidents occur. The possibility is echoed by government plans for new reactors, which have grown worldwide from 540 in February 2011 (under construction, planned, and proposed) to 575 in September 2016.

In China, public fears about nuclear power plants increased after 2011, but did so in interesting ways. Antinuclear protests occurred at several locations and were responsible for the government halting a uranium fuel fabrication plant in 2013 near the city of Jiangmen in Guangdong Province [61]. Opinion surveys since 2002 have shown consistent support for the government's nuclear power program, with one exception: people do not want to see a power plant built in their own local area. Though little information is provided to the public about nuclear plans and operations, people appear to trust the government much more than they do nuclear companies, even though some of the latter are state-owned. This probably reflects the generally poor view many Chinese have of industries as being interested in profit too often at the expense of public safety [62]. Other research confirms that nimbyism, not antinuclearism per se, has grown in the post-Fukushima era. Yet it also suggests that the anxiety behind this can be lowered "if the government transmits more information about the nuclear power programs and provides several channels for comments such as government hotlines and websites, which [can] help to involve the public in the nuclear power projects" [63].

Whether such faith will continue in China remains an open question. It seems noteworthy that the greatest source of public protest to date has been industrial pollution. High on the list of complaints has been the terrible air quality in China's cities due to the overwhelming use of coal. As we have noted several times in other chapters, China's nuclear power program is specifically intended to reduce this coal dependence. China's leaders are also well aware that electricity stands a good chance of powering a growing portion of transportation before long. This would further reduce air pollution levels, thus related disease and premature death. These are potent arguments to defeat anxieties over a form of energy that has never taken the life of a member of the Chinese public.

Concluding Statement: The Consequences of Nuclear Fear

Often has it been said that feelings of fear about nuclear power have their origin in Hiroshima and Nagasaki. The suggestion is that subsequent history hasn't been very important. Nuclear reactors will always be bombs in disguise. They were conceived in war, created in secrecy, and revealed to humanity in the horror of a weapon. Yet even this statement, with its pitiless poetry, tells us that that history cannot be deleted from the matter. If some part of nuclear fear continues to reside in the primal image of the mushroom cloud, there are today other elements that have come to make this fear more complex, involving a mixture of physical and symbolic ingredients. Nuclear fear is more than fear of nuclear power.

The most historically developed anxieties do indeed exist in Western and Westernized populations. To the fear of physical harm and delayed cancer must be added worries about genetic defects, nuclear waste, environmental damage, excessive cost, and proliferation. Though, in the US most of these fears were present in the 1956 BEAR 1 report by the National Academy of Sciences, it took time for them to fully emerge in the public mind. Accidents at TMI, Chernobyl, and Fukushima, was required for this to happen. But when looked at in terms of their symbolic reach, these trepidations have their own story to tell. To be sure, it is not a happy one. It is a story of modernity gone astray. It tells about the egregious crimes that society has committed – "society" in the form of runaway government, military power, and corporate profiteering – against individual well-being, against the natural world, against democratic laws and values, in favor of conflict, war, and the search for ever-more terrible means to generate death on a mass scale. Encoded in the dread of nuclear power is a disbelief in, even rejection of, modernism itself as an effort to advance society, technologically, ethically, and politically.

Which brings us to one final element of nuclear angst: the mistrust of modern institutions. As we have seen, this began in the 1950s during the fallout controversy and early protests against nuclear plant sites. A decade later, in an era when the legitimacy of government and other traditional authorities was under attack, these earlier perceptions returned and bloomed into a social movement. Nuclear power was then given a malevolent social reality. It was conceived as a political threat, commanding an erosion of democracy, as well as damage to the natural environment, and the spread of nuclear weapons. If the public failed to buy all of this, it was still nagged by images of a technology far riskier than it should be. Such images were then confirmed and confirmed again by accidents. These events, because so few in number, were immensely significant. They provided opportunities by which the public became more vulnerable to fear-inspiring imagery. Anti-nuclear advocates could drive home their messages, while the media helped regenerate questions about "safety" with the discourse of "disaster." In the wake of TMI, that portion of the public who thought a nuclear plant could explode like a weapon jumped from a third to well over half [64].

Through all of this, fear was the enemy of fact. Distrust and suspicion – for which authorities themselves were largely to blame early on – have reduced the willingness to accept that nuclear power is less of a threat than many other industries. Over time, news outlets have done more to frighten people than to inform them about what the risks and problems actually are. The popular imagination has been trained, in a sense, to be unknowing and to feel most at home in anxiety about all things nuclear.

Nuclear anxiety culminates in the fear of radiation. We have taken note of this many times in this book, and for good reason. It is possible to understand this fear as officially sanctioned, to a certain degree, by the linear no-threshold (no safe dose) hypothesis, going back to the Muller model (any dose is harmful) and therefore to the BEAR 1 report – the most authoritative document written for the public in the early post-war decades. But in today's world, after so many years of research and much advanced understanding, it is greatly exaggerated, extremely distorting, and also enfeebling. Even in the case of a small, contained accident, many people in nearby towns and neighborhoods will feel vulnerable, uncertain, and helpless. They will likely feel skeptical toward statements by those in charge to the effect that no danger exists, that radiation levels are too low to be a concern (there is *always* reason for concern!). They will feel these things more than if a tanker truck carrying chorine gas or sodium hydroxide crashed and spilled its contents on a downtown street.

Fear of radiation is an institution of belief. It has a central role in the history of nuclear power, as one of the core factors that have limited the use of this power source and that have distracted attention from the staggering damage to human life and the global environment for which coal use is responsible. It is no exaggeration to say that nuclear fear, with radiophobia as its sharper edge, has been a wonderful gift to the coal industry, granting it a much longer lease than it otherwise would have had. In this context, we should pause on another fact. So distorting has nuclear fear been that it can make people wonder whether coal power or nuclear power is more of a threat to public safety – to place on the same level, that is, an energy source that kills over a million people worldwide every year and a source that kills no one.

So where does this leave us? The answers are not difficult to see. First, the view that nuclear power defines an especially dangerous and risky technology has no basis in fact, none whatsoever. This is also true for the dread of radiation. More than enough time has passed and research accumulated to say this with iron confidence. To shake loose the grip of dread, knowledge and familiarity are needed, a degree of understanding about nuclear matters (which this book hopes to provide). Indeed, it is no accident that a large gap exists between scientists, who tend to favor expanding nuclear power, and the nonscientist public, which does not [65]. In this regard, we might note that antinuclear activists don't need to challenge nuclear scientists, the IPCC, or other professional scientific organizations. Nor do they need to produce peer-reviewed papers or perform detailed research on the biological effects of low-level radiation. All they need to do is frighten people, spread doubt, create uncertainty.

Second, nuclear fear has repeatedly been the origin of the worst public health effects associated with nuclear power, a conclusion repeatedly confirmed by professionals from a variety of nations and institutions (unrelated to the nuclear industry). This, too, is clear from past accidents. It has been psychological risk that can be blamed for the overwhelming majority of casualties. Exaggerated fear of radiation also ensures that a so-called "dirty bomb" – or for that matter any use of radioactive material by a terrorist group or individual – would be certain to generate panic on a massive scale, no matter what its actual danger.

Third, as a pose retained in the twenty-first century, antinuclearism is further than ever from fact, from global reality, and from the needs that climate change and lethal pollution have placed upon humanity. Those who see nuclear power as a major threat to human health and the environment do not have truth on their side when we examine the historical record and when we make comparisons to other energy sources, *including* renewables.

Fourth, and most troubling, nuclear anxiety demands many victims. For nuclear power to be truly worthy of fear, many people must die. If "only" fifty-six lives have been lost from Chernobyl and none from Fukushima, this is wrong. There must be hundreds, thousands. If experts estimate "only" a few thousand for Chernobyl, the worst accident in history, this is not enough. There must still be more, there *will* be more, and to try and deny this is to be part of a cover up. For, in order that there be a "catastrophe," the body count must pile high. Such is the paradox of entrenched antagonism to nuclear: in defending human safety, it must create many deaths; in protecting the environment, it must push colossal damage; in the name of public welfare, it must terrify the greatest number.

In the end, nuclear fear has become an obstacle to the future. It will not help us deal with the growing global peril of climate change, a very real threat that has already begun to destroy many lives. If it is believed that our capacity for innovation was never equal to harnessing a technology like nuclear power to a reasonable level of safety, then there is scant hope we will ever succeed in a project so vast and complex as decarbonizing the world's energy system. Fortunately, such incapacity is a myth. "I refuse to believe our ingenuity is unequal to the task," Alvin Weinberg said in 1995. He pointed out that for forty years no nuclear weapon had been used on another nation, despite a world full of intense and relentless conflict. That frame has advanced another generation. It is time to exchange fear for a more productive response.

References

[1] S. Weart, *The Rise of Nuclear Fear* (Cambridge, MA: Harvard University Press, 2012).

[2] P. Slovic, Perception of Risk and the Future of Nuclear Power (Internet), *Physics and Society Newsletter*, 23:1 (January 1994), 1–5; 2. Available from: www.aps.org /units/fps/newsletters/1994/january/ajan94.html#a1

[3] R. Carson, *Silent Spring* (Greenwich: Fawcett, 1962), pp. 1–2.

[4] Ibid., pp. 3.

[5] J. W. Stoutenborough, S. G. Sturgess, and A. Vedlitz, Knowledge, Risk, and Policy Support: Public Perceptions of Nuclear Power, *Energy Policy*, 62 (2013), 176–184.

[6] S. Sontag, *Illness as Metaphor* (New York: Farrar, Strauss, Giroux, 1978).

[7] Clean Air Task Force, The Toll from Coal: An Updated Assessment of Death and Disease from America's Dirtiest Energy Source (Internet) (September 2010). Available from: www.catf.us/resources/publications/view/138

[8] M. Ives, Indonesia Coal Mining Boom is Leaving Trail of Destruction (Internet), *Yale Environment 360* (December 17, 2015). Available from: http://e360.yale.edu/ feature/indonesian_coal_mining_boom_is_leaving_trail_of_destruction/2941/

[9] Coal Dust Kills 23,000 per Year in EU: Report (Internet), *Phys.org* (July 4, 2016). Available from: http://phys.org/news/2016–07-coal-year-eu.html

[10] T. J. Jorgensen, *Strange Glow: The Story of Radiation* (Princeton: Princeton University Press, 2016), p. 365.

[11] J. M. Havenaar, E. J. Bromet, and S. Gluzman, The 30-Year Mental Health Legacy of the Chernobyl Disaster, *World Psychiatry* 15:2 (June 2016), 181–182.

[12] E. Fish, The Forgotten Legacy of the Banqiao Dam Collapse (Internet), *The Economic Observer* (February 8, 2013). Available from: www.eeo.com.cn/ens/ 2013/0208/240078.shtml

[13] Intergovernmental Panel on Climate Change (IPCC), Climate Change 2014: Synthesis Report, Summary for Policymakers (Internet). Available from: www.ipcc.ch/pdf/assessment-report/ar5/syr/AR5_SYR_FINAL_SPM.pdf

[14] American Society of Civil Engineers (ASCE), Dams – 2013 Report Card for America's Infrastructure (Internet). Available from: www.infrastructurereport card.org/dams/

[15] R. Gens, Global Distribution of Coal and Peat Fires (Internet), *Interactive World Map of Coal and Peat Fires, Elsevier*. Available from: http://booksite.elsevier.com /brochures/coalpeatfires/interactivemap.html

[16] EPA, Quantity of RCRA (Resource Conservation and Recovery Act) Hazardous Waste Generated and Managed (Internet). *EPA's Report on the Environment, US Environmental Protection Agency*. Available from: https://cfpub.epa.gov/roe/indi cator.cfm?i=54

[17] Summary of Wind Turbine Accident Data (Internet), *Caithness Windfarm Information Forum*. Available from: www.caithnesswindfarms.co.uk/ AccidentStatistics.htm

[18] J. S. Walker, Reactor at the Fault: The Bodega Bay Nuclear Plant Controversy, 1958–1964 – A Case Study in the Politics of Technology, *Pacific Historical Review*, 59:3 (August 1990), 323–348, 324.

[19] T. Jundt, *Greening the Red, White, and Blue: The Bomb, Big Business, and Consumer Resistance in Postwar America* (New York: Oxford University Press, 2014), pp. 97–98.

[20] J. D. Hamblin and A Dispassionate, Objective Effort: Negotiating the First Study on the Biological Effects of Atomic Radiation, *Journal of the History of Biology*, 40:1 (March 2007), 147–177; 149.

[21] Records of the Atomic Energy Commission (AEC) (Internet), *Guide to Federal Records, US National Archives*. Available from: www.archives.gov/research/ guide-fed-records/groups/326.html#326.3.3

[22] National Academy of Sciences (NAS), *The Biological Effects of Atomic Radiation: A Report to The Public*, 9 Washington, D.C. 1956), 1.

[23] A. Leviero, Scientists Term Radiation a Peril to Future of Man, *New York Times* (June 13, 1956).

[24] L. Pauling, Genetic Effects of Weapons Tests, *Bulletin of the Atomic Scientists* (December 1962), 15–18.

[25] Eunice Kennedy Shriver National Institute of Child Health and Human Development, National Institutes of Health, US Department of Health and Human Services (NIH), How Common is Stillbirth (Internet). Available from: www.nichd.nih.gov/health/topics/stillbirth/topicinfo/Pages/how-common.aspx

[26] S. Reinou, J. Y. Bae, and K. J. Lim, Fear of the Unknown: Ionizing Radiation Exposure During Pregnancy, *American Journal of Obstetrics and Gynecology*, 206:6 (June 2012), 456–462.

[27] UNSCEAR, Report of the United Nations Scientific Committee on the Effects of Atomic Radiation to the General Assembly (Internet) (2000). Available from: www.unscear.org/docs/reports/gareport.pdf

[28] B. Vastag, Scientific, Political Debate Continues on Methods for Estimating Fallout Exposure, *Journal of the National Cancer Institute*, 97:17 (September 2005), 1240–1242.

[29] N. A. Dalager, H. Kang, and C. M. Mahan, Cancer Mortality Among the Highest Exposed US Atmospheric Nuclear Test Participants, *Journal of Occupational and Environmental Medicine*, 42:8 (August 2000), 798–805.

[30] Committee to Assess the Scientific Information for the Radiation Exposure Screening and Education Program, Assessment of the Scientific Information for the Radiation Exposure Screening and Education Program (Internet), *US National Academy of Sciences, National Research Council* (2005), 108. Available from: http://nap.edu/catalog/11279.html

[31] Centers for Disease Control and Prevention, National Center for Health Statistics (CDC, NCHS), Data Brief No. 88 – 75 Years of Mortality in the United States, 1935–2010 (Internet) (March 2012). Available from: www.cdc.gov/nchs/products/databriefs/db88.htm

[32] United Nations Department of Economic and Social Affairs, Population Division (UNPD), World Fertility Data 2015 (Internet). Available from: www.un.org/en/development/desa/population/publications/dataset/fertility/wfd2015.shtml

[33] A. Wellerstein, The Demon Core and the Strange Death of Louis Slotin (Internet), *The New Yorker* (May 21, 2016). Available from: www.newyorker.com/tech/elements/demon-core-the-strange-death-of-louis-slotin

[34] T. R. Wellock, *Critical Masses: Opposition to Nuclear Power in California, 1958–1978* (Madison: University of Wisconsin Press, 1998), pp. 17–67.

[35] R. L. Meehan, *The Atom and the Fault: Experts, Earthquakes, and Nuclear Power* (Cambridge, MA: MIT Press, 1984).

[36] J. S. Walker, Reactor at the Fault: The Bodega Bay Nuclear Plant Controversy, 1958–1964: A Caser Study in the Politics of Technology, *Pacific Historical Review*, 59:3 (August 1990), 323–348; 330–331.

[37] J. Daly, Nuclear Fault Line – Bodega Head (Internet), *Sonoma Magazine*. Available from: www.sonomamag.com/nuclear-fault-line/

[38] Walker, p. 344.

[39] Meehan, p. 13.

[40] Walker, p. 348.

[41] Clamshell Alliance, Declaration of Nuclear Resistance (Internet). Available from: www.clamshellalliance.net/legacy/2010/03/06/declaration-of-nuclear-resistance-revised-version-adopted-november-1977-at-the-clamshell-congress/

[42] A. B. Lovins, Energy Strategy: The Roads Not Taken? *Foreign Affairs* (October 1976), 65–96; 95.

[43] Ibid., pp. 92–93.

[44] J. Byrne and S. M. Hoffman, Nuclear Power and Technological Authoritarianism. *Bulletin of Science, Technology, and Society*, 7:3–4 (1987), 658–671.

[45] Weart, pp. 189–190.

[46] H. P. Kitschelt, Political Opportunity Structures and Political Protest: Anti-Nuclear Movements in Four Democracies, *British Journal of Political Science*, 16 (1986), 57–85.

[47] H. Nehring, Cold War, Apocalypse and Peaceful Atoms: Interpretations of Nuclear Energy in the British and West German Anti-Nuclear Weapons Movements, 1955–1964. *Historical Social Research*, 29:3 (2004), 150–170; 154.

[48] G. Hecht, *The Radiance of France: Nuclear Power and National Identity After World War II* (Cambridge, MA: MIT Press, 2009).

[49] R. E. Peierls, Britain in the Atomic Age, *Bulletin of the Atomic Scientists (June* 1970), 40–46.

[50] Nehring, p. 155; Note 22.

[51] R. Jungk, *Der Atomstaat: Vom Fortschritt in die Unmenschlichkeit* (Hamburg: Rowohlt rororo, 1977), pp. 9–10.

[52] S. M. Nealey, B. D. Melber, W. L. Rankin, *Public Opinion and Nuclear Energy* (Lexington, MA: D.C. Health, 1983).

[53] J. Schell, *The Fate of the Earth* (New York: Knopf, 1982), p. 12.

[54] Ibid., pp. 60–61.

[55] T. Bolsen and F. L. Cook, Public Opinion on Energy Policy: 1974–2006, *The Public Opinion Quarterly*, 72:2 (2008), 364–388.

[56] D. Fairhall and M. Walker, USSR Finally Admits Chernobyl Disaster (Internet), *The Guardian* (April 30, 1986). Available from: www.theguardian.com/world/ 2006/apr/24/russia.ukraine

[57] J. Greenwald, Deadly Meltdown, *Time*, 127:19 (May 12, 1986), 38–45, 41.

[58] J. T, Dahlburg, Chernobyl: Grim New Assessment – Fallout Study says 'Hundreds of Times' More People May Have Suffered Fatal Exposure Than Had Been Thought (Internet), *Los Angeles Times* (April 14, 1992). Available from: http:// articles.latimes.com/1992–04-14/news/mn-170_1_fatal-exposure

[59] Y. Kim, M. Kim, and W. Kim, Effect of the Fukushima Nuclear Disaster on Global Public Acceptance of Nuclear Power, *Energy Policy*, 61 (2013), 822–828.

[60] C. de Boer and I. Catsburg, The Impact of Nuclear Accidents on Attitudes Toward Nuclear Energy, *The Public Opinion Quarterly*, 52:2 (1988), 254–261.

[61] Limiting the Fallout (Internet) *The Economist* (July 20, 2013). Available from: www.economist.com/news/china/21582016-rare-protest-prompts-government-scrap-plans-build-uranium-processing-plant

[62] G. He, A. P. J. Mol, L. Zhang, and Y. Lu, Public Participation and Trust in Nuclear Power Development in China, *Renewable and Sustainable Energy Reviews*, 23 (2013), 1–11.

[63] C. Sun and X. Zhu, Evaluating the Public Perceptions of Nuclear Power in China: Evidence from a Contingent Valuation Survey, *Energy Policy*, 69 (2014), 397–405; 403.

[64] W. L. Rankin, B. D. Melder, T. D. Overcast, and S. M. Nealey, *Nuclear Power and the Public: An Update of Collected Survey Research on Nuclear Power* (Seattle: Battelle, 1981), p. 128.

[65] Pew Research Center, Major Gas Between the Public, Scientists on Key Issues (Internet) (July 2015). Available from: http://www.pewinternet.org/interactives/ public-scientists-opinion-gap/

8

Why *Not* Nuclear? Points and Counterpoints

Overview

Reasons why people oppose nuclear power are diverse, though not overly so, and deserve an explicit place in this book. They also deserve to be addressed and answered, to the degree possible. Such answers need to be straightforward, understandable, and backed by verifiable information. Such is the goal of this chapter. In most cases, the claims made against nuclear power stem from anxieties that have been wrongly called irrational or unfounded. As we have discussed at some length in Chapter 7 fears over nuclear power grow from complex origins with deep historical roots that cannot be denied or dismissed.

The antinuclear position is also a position regarding the nature of society itself. On emotional grounds, it wishes to rid social reality of a contaminating threat. Thus its appeal is powerful, gripping, and distinct. We have seen its return in the wake of Fukushima, with a renewed potency caused in no small part by the nearly infinite repetitions offered by the Internet. But on truth grounds, like the many horrors claimed about Fukushima itself, the antinuclear position fails. It fails because it largely relies on rejections of both history and science and does so for ideological reasons, as it must.

Antinuclearism has not changed its main claims in forty years. This offers a certain clue. Opposition seizes on what it considers problems that are inherent in the technology, that were born with it under Stagg Field and revealed at Hiroshima, and that will always be there, no matter how or how much the technology may evolve. Some of this can be understood as a result of ideas about society, as noted. Nuclear power defines a highly concentrated, centralized form of energy production; it matches a social reality of large cities, industries, business and consumer networks, hospitals, and more, with urbanized forms of life. It is antithetical to the world desired by those who wish for a "softer" path, one based on smaller-scale, localized existence, a scale that can be accommodated by renewable technologies without any need for massive infrastructural supports. This, however, is not the reality that most of the world lives in or is headed toward. Urbanization, bringing an ever-greater density of human life and need, is the long-term – centuries long – direction in which humanity has been moving, where it is arriving.

The stakes today for antinuclearism are far higher than they were in the 1970s and 80s. As repeated many times in this book, climate change and coal use are both real, proven threats on a global scale. Such are realities established by scientific work. Any argument for ending a major source of noncarbon energy must therefore be based on more than worry. Fears frozen from the past will not help humanity deal with the future.

One of the authors of these pages has spent a good deal of time over the past ten years talking with health physicists, radiation biologists, nuclear engineers, and others involved in radiation studies and nuclear power. He has benefited greatly from these talks, in a number of ways. But it has also been a sobering experience. This is because many experts feel a degree of fatalism, not to say exhaustion, in terms of exaggerated concern regarding their chosen field. One individual, who works for the US Centers for Disease Control, framed it like this:

> I rarely talk about my work, or about radiation, Chernobyl, etc. What many people feel they know about these things, probably from decades of news hysteria and other sources, is too misinformed, so they don't want to hear what I have to say, not really. It would take many hours to correct any part of this. And you'd be climbing a steep hill the whole time. By the way, you can't use my name.

This chapter is an attempt at such correction, or at least a beginning of one. Each of the claims addressed will likely be familiar to some, but the responses will not be, at least not all of them. We, the authors, have worked hard to be objective, aware that this is an ideal intellectual condition not entirely available to human beings. Yet our attempt has been honest and aimed at providing a way to avoid both the resignation and stoicism evident in the quotation above (name withheld).

Dangerous and Accident Prone

Nuclear power is a dangerous and accident-prone technology. Chernobyl and Fukushima show that radiation from an accident is a major threat to the public, responsible for many deaths and huge numbers of cancers, while also raising the threat of birth defects.

What the historical record shows: In the sixty years that civilian reactors have continually operated, there have been three incidents identified as "major accidents": Three Mile Island (TMI), Chernobyl, and Fukushima (they are discussed in more detail in Chapter 6). These involved five operating reactors out of a world average of 312 over the sixty-year period.

To date (2017), at least 4,000 cases of thyroid cancer and fifty-six deaths can be directly attributed to radiation from Chernobyl. No radiation deaths or serious injuries occurred at Three Mile Island or Fukushima. About future deaths, there is much uncertainty, as there are only statistical estimates of possible fatalities. The two most credible estimates for Chernobyl are 4,000 and 14,000, about half of either figure being workers who helped stop and clean up the accident. After three decades, there had been an increase of cancer among these workers of up to 18 percent compared to the general public, but no increase in deaths. Regarding the general public, "there is no scientific evidence of increases in overall cancer incidence or mortality rates or in rates of non-malignant disorders that could be related to radiation exposure," according to UNSCEAR [1].

No future deaths or cancers are expected from Three Mile Island. Early estimates for latent fatalities associated with Fukushima ranged up to 1,000 [2], but the more recent and thorough study by UNSCEAR concluded: "the values of inferred risks are so small that in general no discernible radiation-related increase of overall cancer incidence would be expected among exposed members of the general public" [3].

Lifelong study of atom bomb survivors, meanwhile, has shown no increase in birth defects associated with radiation exposure. Belief that such defects are inevitable led hundreds of young women in several European nations to have abortions as a result of the Chernobyl accident.

For comparison (industrial accidents): Toulouse, France, 2001 – AZF chemical (nitrogen fertilizer) factory exploded, killing twenty-nine, severely wounding 800, and injuring another 2,000. Up to 20,000 homes, apartments, and offices were damaged, while three hospitals, sixty schools, and a university had to be evacuated and abandoned "until further notice" [4].

Piper Alpha, North Sea, 1988 – North Sea oil production platform that underwent a series of explosions and massive fire that killed 167 and injured at least a dozen. Acute psychological trauma has affected the fifty-nine survivors. The event is considered a national tragedy in Scotland and commemorated as such [5].

Bhopal, India, 1984 – Release of toxic methyl-isocyanate gas from a large chemical plant. Estimated 3,800–10,000 dead in the first few days, 15,000–20,000 premature deaths in next two decades, over 100,000 injured. A large number of congenital birth defects are associated with the accident. Hundreds of babies with such problems continue to be born each year [6–7].

Texas City, Texas, 1947 – Cargo vessel loading ammonium nitrate catches fire, explodes, and creates a chain reaction of fires and explosions in oil storage tanks and chemical plants. Between 580 and 800 people were killed and over 5,000 injured, including many young children. Hundreds of homes, businesses, factories, and other facilities were destroyed. Considered the worst industrial accident in US history [8].

Measured against such industrial accidents, Three Mile Island and Fukushima fail to qualify as "disasters" or "major incidents" with regard to radiation impacts. Such terminology does not apply, and, in fact, its routine use can be said to belittle true disasters where many were killed and injured. Placed beside Bhopal and Texas City, the terrors of TMI and Fukushima can only appear misplaced. Chernobyl must be considered in a different category. However, nearly all of its proven fatalities resulted from the incompetent response of authorities (first responders not told of radiation danger, not given any protective clothing). For documented health impacts, the greatest threat has come from fear-based reactions, both by affected people who suffered from mental health impacts and by ill-advised reaction from authorities. Panic evacuations and lack of proper information and care given to the public led to more than a thousand deaths in the case of Fukushima and many thousands at Chernobyl, where fatal and long-term psychological problems ensued, like suicides, unnecessary abortions, and life-shortening depression.

Three significant incidents, only one of which had fatalities, does not qualify a technology operated on the scale of nuclear power as "accident prone" or "risky." The truth is closer to the opposite. This becomes very clear when comparison is made to accidents in other major industries. Fossil fuel, chemical, textile, mining, and forestry industries all have fatal accidents on a yearly basis. Thousands of people die *every year* in coal mine accidents, and more than a thousand times the same figure die prematurely due to coal-related pollution. It is notable that the three countries which suffered major accidents have continued to use nuclear power, while some that have never undergone such a major accident have turned away from it.

Accidents Contaminate Huge Areas

Nuclear accidents contaminate very large areas with dangerous, even fatal, levels of radiation, requiring large evacuations. Contamination makes it impossible for these people to return home, not just for years but for decades, or even forever.

What research has found: Radioactive contamination from Chernobyl, which released the largest amount of radionuclides from any accident, was highest over an area of about 50,000 km^2 (19,300 mi^2), affecting roughly 5 million people. More than 95 percent of these people received doses of under 1 mSv per year. This is less than natural background levels, which average 2.4 mSv worldwide.

Inhabitants of the most contaminated villages in Russia, Belarus, and Ukraine wore dosimeters for a month each year, starting about the fifth year after the accident. Mean recorded doses ranged from 1.5 to 2.5 mSv/yr in the first year of measurements, dropping to 1.0–1.5 mSv/yr by year eight [9]. For certain "critical groups," such as foresters, herdsmen, and field-crop workers, who spent much time outside, these levels were typically 1.3–1.7 times higher. Thus, no levels were ever above 4.25 mSv, and at that level for only a year or two. By 2004, doses had fallen to below 1.0 mSv/yr even in areas with residual Cs-137 in soils [10]. Radioactivity of locally produced foodstuffs, from both collective and private farms, had fallen to permissible limits by 1995 or sooner. Overall, about 40 percent of evacuees could have returned home within two to four years (data are lacking to be more precise) and more than 85 percent within a decade. While there do remain some "hot spots," these are known and can (and should) be remediated using proven methods. Meanwhile, the Chernobyl site has become a tourist attraction.

Environmental impacts included adverse effects up to a distance of 20–30 km during the first year. Substantial recovery of both plants and animals was observed by the next growing season. More complete recovery took several years, yet involved immigration into the area so the original ecology was modified. A few plant species (pines) showed more long-term damage. Within a decade, however, the 4,300 km^2 (1,660 mi^2) Chernobyl Exclusion Zone was abundantly populated by animal species, some of which had recovered from prior hunting (e.g. wolves). By the late 1990s, the area served as one of Europe's largest wildlife preserves; this included the successful introduction of Przewalski's Horse in 1998, a species nearly extinct in the wild [11–12].

In the case of Fukushima, authorities set an upper dose limit of 1 mSv/y above natural background to determine when and where people could return. Such a low value ensured many areas would remain off-limits for years. Today (2016), areas where people are not yet permitted to live have dose levels as low as 8–10 mSv/year.

For comparison (contaminated areas): Coal fires in underground mines, waste piles, and coal seams number in the thousands worldwide, being especially concentrated in areas of historical mining. Such fires cause major land subsidence, producing sinkholes, vents, surface fractures, and other features that create instability and that allow escape of highly toxic, even lethal, gases and particulate matter. Gases include carbon dioxide, methane, and carbon monoxide, and carry mercury, arsenic, selenium, and lead. Fires burn for decades, centuries, even millennia, and are extremely difficult to put out. Because they contaminate air, soil, and water, destroy much of the immediate environment, and are poisonous, these fires have forced the permanent evacuation of towns, villages, and agricultural areas amounting to tens of thousands of square kilometers in more than a dozen countries [13–14]. Such countries include the US, Australia, India, South Africa, and, above all, China. Coal fires can be ignited naturally, by lightning or forest fires, but many are caused by humans. Unsurprisingly, they are a large source of greenhouse gases.

Acid mine drainage (AMD) is a global environmental problem of massive proportions. Highly acidic waters, enriched in heavy metals, drain from abandoned mines and waste rock piles poisoning ground water, lakes, streams, rivers, and wetlands, killing most or all aquatic life and preventing use by people. Sulfuric acid results from the interaction of moisture, oxygen, and sulfide minerals, such as pyrite (FeS_2) in coal and base metal sulfides in ores. Levels of acidity, especially from coal mines, can be very high (pH range: 2–3) and damaging. In the US alone, there are tens of thousands of mines that have been producing AMD for a century or more. The US Forest Service has estimated that up to 50,000 AMD mines exist on lands it manages, impacting as many as 10,000 miles of streams [15]. Large portions of western and east-central Pennsylvania, including more than 3,200 miles of streams and associated ground water, are heavily polluted by AMD. Here, and in historical coal mining districts worldwide, surface and ground water is off-limits to human use, resulting in permanent depopulation.

In sum, levels of dangerous contamination due to nuclear accidents are miniscule and short-lived compared with the impacts of coal fires, coal mines, and AMD. Loss of once-inhabited and inhabitable land from these realities is invisible to the general public, perhaps seen (if and when it is mentioned) as a regrettable by-product of industrialization.

Waste Disposal Is an Unsolvable Problem

Disposing of nuclear waste remains an unsolved problem. Such waste has been building up for decades and is dangerous for hundreds of thousands of years. No one has found a way to dispose of it safely and every year this toxic legacy grows, threatening future generations.

What the historical record shows: There is a known and proven way to dispose of nuclear waste, just as there is a known and proven way to dispose of other highly toxic industrial wastes. Billions of gallons of wastes are routinely stored every year in underground geological settings. This is done using disposal wells spread across the US, for example, and has been ongoing for many decades. Such wastes, moreover, include material that is deadly to human health. Examples include: sodium/potassium cyanide in mining; acetone, formaldehyde, ethylene oxide, and toluene from petrochemical, pesticide, and textile industries; and biomedical wastes with infected human blood, diseased organs, and other pathogen-bearing tissues and fluids. Nuclear waste is not the most hazardous material produced by contemporary society.

It is also small in volume compared to what is produced by other industries: the 240,000 metric tons of spent nuclear fuel accumulated worldwide over sixty years would cover a soccer field to a depth of about 60 ft (18 m) [16]. By comparison, petroleum refineries in the US alone produce several times this amount of hazardous waste every year. Also, more than 200,000 tons of waste ash and scrubber sludge annually comes out of a single large (700 MW) coal-fired power plant [17].

Spent nuclear fuel from a light-water reactor (LWR) is both hot (>1,000°C) and highly radioactive from short-lived fission products when it is first removed from the core. It is in an extremely lethal form and, like other such industrial wastes, is treated before being sent to storage. For spent fuel, this means being allowed to cool down and become less radioactive. It involves transferring spent fuel to a cooling pool of circulating water for up to five years. At that point, dose levels from gamma radiation at about one meter from a fuel assembly are in the range of 10–20 Sv/hr, so that direct, unprotected exposure would be fatal in about ten to fifteen minutes. Dose levels fall continually but are still 1 Sv/hr after ninety to one hundred years, so the fuel remains dangerous if not contained.

These figures might be compared with the stored volume and lethality of certain chemical materials and wastes. A good example is formaldehyde, fatal if inhaled in any quantity, causes skin lesions on contact, and produces serious eye and respiratory irritation and injury. Such impacts can begin at air concentrations as low as 0.1 parts per million. Thousands of tons are annually produced for a range of uses but also as a waste product and as unused surplus in need of disposal. Petroleum refinery wastes, for example, which are produced for much of each year include: benzene, toluene, xylene, dioxin, mercury, selenium, vanadium, lead, chrome, solid wastes and sludge, with toxic organics and heavy metals, in addition to liquid wastes.

The Tale of Yucca Mountain: To date, Finland is the only country to select a geological repository for nuclear waste, to complete and approve a design for it, and set aside the funding. As discussed in Chapter 3, it will be excavated to about 1,500 ft (455 m) below ground in granite. The geology and engineering aspects are not challenging, given that such underground excavation has been routine in the mining industry for decades. There are today mines more than eight times as deep as Finland's planned repository.

The challenge has always been of a different nature. In 1982, the US Congress passed, and President Reagan signed, the Nuclear Waste Policy Act into law. This required that the US Department of Energy (DOE) identify a number of candidate sites for a permanent geological repository, these to be divided about equally east and west of the Mississippi River. In the end, there would be one eastern and one western site, one of which would open by a deadline of 1998. DOE in 1983 selected nine sites in eight states west of the Mississippi. Two years later, eight candidate sites in seven states were chosen for the eastern region. The Act specified that the public should be involved in the process, so DOE sent out its draft reports on each candidate site for comment.

Coming within just a few years of Three Mile Island, there were storms of protest in every eastern state. Citizen organizations formed, including scientists and local leaders. Members held public meetings, published letters, wrote editorials, appeared on television and radio. In the face of such opposition and a mid-term election, the government backed off. President Reagan ended up approving three western sites: Deaf Smith County, Texas; Hanford, Washington (site of plutonium production for weapons); and Yucca Mountain, Nevada. Washington argued it should be exempted, as it already had military waste from Hanford to deal with. Texas opted out using its political influence, in a year when the Republican Party was battling to keep a majority in Congress. This left Yucca Mountain, in a state with little Congressional power, a small population, and a lot of desert. In 1987, an addendum to the earlier 1982 Act was passed specifying Yucca as the single chosen site. This became known in policy circles as the "screw Nevada" decision [18].

Further actions, however, stalled in the 1990s. The site was still opposed by anti-nuclear groups. The EPA had difficulty deciding on final standards for the repository, while nuclear companies and utilities began suing the DOE for not meeting the 1998 deadline for opening a repository. By the early 2000s, over $10 billion had been spent on scientific evaluation of the Yucca site, and Congress had approved the project, with most scientists supporting it as well. But in 2011, President Obama shelved the plan. By this time, Nevada had acquired influence in the form of Senate Majority leader Harry Reid, who declared he would not allow his home state to become "America's nuclear waste dump." Needing Reid's support against a hostile Republican opposition, Obama deactivated the Yucca Mountain project. In its 2011 review of the failed thirty-year effort to create a repository, the US General Accountability Office plainly noted that "social and political opposition . . . not technical issues, is the key obstacle," and, with a touch of understatement, that "consistent policy, funding, and leadership" were much needed [19].

EPA radiation standards for Yucca Mountain were finalized in 2008. They extended to 1 million years – longer by an order of magnitude than *homo sapiens* have existed. For the first 10,000 years, an effective dose limit above natural background was set at 0.15 mSv per year. For the period extending from 10,000 to 1 million years, a limit of 1 mSv/yr (reduced from a previous 3.5 mSv/yr) was established [20].

This might seem conservative. It is actually something else. Traveling to Albuquerque, Santa Barbara, or Denver and staying for twelve months would likely raise one's dose level at least ten times the limit for Yucca Mountain (first 10,000 years). Since the 1980s, background radiation for the US public has doubled. It has gone from an average of 3 mSv/yr to 6 mSv/yr, due to the use of medical imaging (cancer incidence has decreased since that time) [21]. The increase is *twenty* times the 10,000-year limit for Yucca Mountain and three times the million-year figure. The Yucca Mountain standards make sense only as an embodiment of terror inspired by the idea that any level of radiation is harmful. Such fear even turns the eye and mind away from the most obvious fact in blatant support of underground storage: for over fifty years, nuclear waste has been stored successfully, in ever increasing volumes, *above ground*.

For comparison (waste storage): Each year, approximately 9 billion gallons of industrial waste, including hazardous material, are injected underground into geologic zones in the United States. A significant percentage of such material includes highly toxic, even lethal and carcinogenic fluids (benzene, formalde-hyde, chloroform, cyanides, corrosives, lead- and mercury-containing waste) from the chemical, pesticide, metal production, printing, and petroleum refin-ing industries, among others. Deep injection wells for this purpose are classi-fied as "Class 1" by the US Environmental Protection Agency (EPA), with Class 2, 3, 4, and 5 reserved for less toxic and non-hazardous substances. Regulations for Class 1 wells have been increasingly tightened over time, covering specifications on siting, construction, operation, inspection, testing, reporting, and record keeping [22]. Rules dating from the 1990s stipulate that hazardous material must be judged safely contained for at least 10,000 years. Geologic zones into which waste is injected range up to 12,000 ft (3,640 m) deep and must be located well below any aquifers. These zones are made of porous rock bounded both above and laterally by non-porous, impermeable "sealing" rock of significant thickness.

Thus, the US (and some other nations too) already has many permanent geologic repositories for hazardous waste. In 2016, there were about 800 Class 1 wells operating in ten states. EPA indicates about 17 percent (136) of these wells receive especially toxic materials to be injected (Class 1HW). While there have been significant leakage problems reported for Class 2 wells (many of which were drilled between 1930 and 1950 and abandoned), especially related to oil field brines, this is not true for Class 1HW, which show a very small number of violations of federal and state regulations [23].

Aging Nuclear Plants Are a Growing Threat

The US and Europe have many nuclear plants that are now old and approaching or already past their design lifespan. They are therefore becoming more dangerous, more prone to accidents, and more liable to fail. This is a legacy we simply can't leave to the next generation.

What the historical record shows: Nuclear plants were not designed to have life spans of thirty to forty years. In the 1960s, 70s, and 80s, there was not enough information or experience to know how long a plant might last. The mentioned age-range, as a licensing period, was chosen for *financial* reasons, to provide enough time for all loans from the original investment to be repaid. Thus, saying that a thirty-seven-year-old plant is "nearing its age limit" or that one operating for forty-two years is "over aged" has no substance [24].

In 2016, the average age of nuclear power plants worldwide, not counting China, was twenty-nine years. In the US and Europe, averages are higher, at thirty-five and thirty-one years, respectively. These averages are well-known in the nuclear industry. The age of plants has caught no one off-guard. Nearly every component and system can be replaced, and in older plants many have been. The TMI and Chernobyl units were young (<10 yrs) when their accidents happened. The fault lay with human error. Such fault was also true for Fukushima, which was older but withstood a giant earthquake well beyond its design resistance. A massive tsunami was not considered in the design or siting at all. Neither was a dysfunctional regulatory environment.

The only major component of a nuclear plant that is not generally considered replaceable is the reactor vessel, though Russia has performed such replacement several times. Early on, there was little understanding of how long the vessel might remain an effective shield to neutrons. Because of this, test reactors were built to examine how various vessel alloys responded over time to high levels of neutron radiation and heated, pressurized water. This research has shown that long-term neutron bombardment makes the metal more brittle, thus able to crack under extreme circumstances, and that contact with heated water and steam can cause corrosion if certain chemicals are present in the water [25]. These facts, too, are well-known and taken into account with regard to monitoring and inspection of reactors [26]. In this respect, Fukushima had the good effect of urging worldwide reviewing, inspecting, and upgrading of nuclear plants. Such effort has been part of the growing trend to relicense plants that pass all tests and inspections.

By the mid-1990s, the IAEA began issuing advice on how to manage both ageing power plants and research reactors, and since then it has made available a number of reports and recommendations [27]. The industry, moreover, continues to discuss and share best practices, and ageing is one focus of this. Much thought, now based on experience, has gone into understanding how nuclear plants age. There is systematic study of what scientific, technological, and management factors need to be closely addressed. This goes directly to the heart of the matter about extending the acceptable life of such plants.

No power plant lasts forever. It now seems that relicensed reactors will come to the end of their useful days for economic, not safety, reasons. A sixty-to-eighty-year lifespan will surely tempt practical and economic limits. Eight decades is a long time for technology to advance, become more efficient, productive, cost-effective. So it is for Gen III+ and, soon, Gen IV reactors. While advanced nations are busy relicensing older plants, emerging and developing countries are building new plants with new technology.

For comparison (ageing infrastructure): In many countries, the oldest sites for generating electricity are hydropower stations. The number of such stations that involve sizeable dams is not known exactly but must be very large. Hydropower generated nearly 18 percent of global electricity in 2015, nearly twice that of nuclear power.

Second only to China, the US has over 85,000 dams of varied sizes, 9,300 of which are classified as large and 2,400 of which are involved in hydropower generation [28–29]. A large number of the total are considered old and in a state of deterioration. In fact, the average age of US dams in 2016 was more than fifty-three years, with some major hydroelectric stations, like Hoover Dam, over seventy years old [30].

The fact has been noted by the American Society of Civil Engineers. Every four years, the Society produces its "Report Card for America's Infrastructure," evaluating the condition and safety of essential structures for daily life, such as roads, bridges, airports, waterways, and dams. In its 2013 version (the most recent at the time of this writing), US dams were awarded a "D" grade. In the report's own language:

> Thousands of our nation's dams are in need of rehabilitation to meet current design and safety standards. They are not only aging, but are subject to stricter criteria as a result of increased downstream development and advancing scientific knowledge predicting flooding, earthquakes, and dam failures [31].

Put differently, dams built fifty years ago had more lax standards for their primary vulnerabilities – flooding and earthquakes. Many are almost certainly in no state to withstand major floods or seismic events. This includes a significant (but unspecified) number of dams classified as "high-hazard," which means that their failure would result in deaths, injuries, property damage, and more. A total of 13,991 high-hazard dams is given in the report, a disturbing number to say the least [31].

The great majority of US dams are built of earth, not cement. They are more subject to erosion, liquefaction, and collapse. A number of states with high earthquake risk have many high-hazard dams, like California (807 such dams), Nevada (149), Utah (252), and Washington (227). Such dams hold back waters that would, upon release, claim many lives. Events of this kind have not been rare in the past sixty years.

In 1972, for instance, a major failure occurred in the Buffalo Creek Valley, West Virginia. A coal-waste impoundment dam collapsed, flooding the towns below, killing 125 people. In November of 1977, after a period of unexpectedly heavy rains, an embankment dam on Toccoa Creek above Toccoa City (Georgia) collapsed, sending masses of water through the grounds of a local college and surrounding area, causing the deaths of thirty-nine students. The dam, in fact, had begun life as a small hydroelectric plant around the turn of the twentieth century. It then grew in size through much of the 1900s before being covered over and turned into an earthen barrier in 1957, after which it entered a period of neglect and decay [32]. Unlike nuclear power plants, that is, many dams are not subjected to regular inspection or updated safety codes or relicensing requirements or public demands for accountability. They are simply allowed to degrade and turn fatal.

Uranium Mining Has a High Environmental Cost

Nuclear power cannot be separated from the dangers and environmental costs of uranium mining, which threatens watersheds and the public at a high level.

What the historical record shows: Objections to uranium mining, as a particularly harmful kind of extraction, tend to focus on the radioactive nature of the ore and waste. With regard to worker health, criticisms point to practices that no longer exist in most nations due to advances in safety and ventilation. Yet accusations regarding environmental damage are often accurate, due to problems created in the past that have yet to be remediated. Unfortunately, as with hard rock mining in general, there are many older, abandoned and improperly reclaimed mines. These *should* be the target of concern and public criticism, as they are definite sources of toxic pollution. But they do not reflect uranium mining today, which is strictly regulated in most exporting nations.

The period from the 1920s to the early 1970s, when uranium extraction grew rapidly, saw rising rates of lung cancer among underground workers and little concern for environmental stewardship. Especially in the first few decades of the Cold War, mining was almost exclusively done under military contracts for stockpiling uranium, and worker safety and pollution were secondary considerations. With the advent of civilian nuclear power, mining was largely privatized. Growing awareness of problems by workers' unions, local communities, and the public led to major changes. Use of ventilation to provide constant air circulation through a system of ducts, pipes, powerful fans, and air filtering (required for hard rock mines in general and many coal mines as well) were a key improvement. International exposure limits were also established and, in most countries, enforced by law. By the mid- to late-1990s, worker exposure to radiation, in the form of radon and "radon progeny" (decay products of Rn-222), had fallen to where it was similar to that in many homes. Workers ever since have been monitored on the job.

Overall, a degree of special attention given uranium mining during the past several decades has made it one of the most regulated and lesser polluting types of mining worldwide when best practices are followed [33]. While this is not always done, it *has* become the norm in a number of the world's primary uranium suppliers, including Australia, Canada, the US, and, increasingly, Kazakhstan, Namibia, Niger, and China.

Several methods of hard rock mining are employed to extract uranium, each suited to specific geologic settings and each having advantages and drawbacks [34]. Open pit mines are employed when an ore body is close to the surface, within about 300 ft (90 m) or less. Large amounts of soil and rock are removed and set aside in piles, which today are often back filled into the pit and covered with a meter or more of clay, then new soil, and finally native plants. Where waste rock piles are allowed to stand for years without any impoundment, environmental damage can be locally severe. Such damage does not come from radioactivity, however, as the volume of radionuclides is usually quite small, but from heavy metals and other pollutants dissolved and washed out of the waste rock. Pollution of this kind was serious and widespread in the past.

Underground uranium mining may be used when ore is too deep for an open pit. The most dangerous overall, underground mines have seen huge improvements in the past thirty years, as noted. After ore is brought to the surface, as with open-pit ore, it is sent to a milling operation, usually close by. Milling pulverizes the ore, mixes it with water to produce a slurry, then adds sulfuric acid or a strong alkaline solution to dissolve out the uranium, which is precipitated as uranium oxide and dried into yellow cake (U_3O_8). The waste, essentially a watery sand-silt slurry, commonly contains 85 percent of the original radioactivity in the ore (in the form of small amounts of radium and thorium), as well as heavy metals. It is pumped to a tailings pond behind a dam. Prior to the 1980s, there were few regulations for such ponds. Dam leakage, stability problems, and flooding led to contamination of ground and surface water in more than a few cases. As for radiation, studies of people who lived for decades near one of world's largest unremediated sites show low levels of 1–2 mSv/y, with rare examples up to 6 mSv/y [35].

Today, a detailed design for tailings disposal and treatment must be submitted as part of a site license application, with companies held responsible for carrying it out. Chemically neutralizing and physically stabilizing this waste is now common practice. A variety of dewatering techniques are used and the consolidated waste buried by clay or silt (a radon barrier) and capped by local topsoil and plants. Large-scale programs to clean up tailings sites using such techniques have been carried out in the US, Australia, Brazil, China, the EU, and former Soviet republics [35]. Efforts in the US strongly suggest that the most difficult part of such remediation has to do with contaminated waterways, such as creeks and rivers.

In recent years, the desire to avoid a large environmental footprint, with its costs and liabilities, has increased the use of In-Situ Leaching (ISL). This method applies when uranium is hosted in a porous sandstone or conglomerate (lithified gravel) containing moveable but non-potable water. Target zones have ranged from 330 ft (100 m) to 3,000 ft (900 m) or deeper. In all cases, the geologic setting includes impermeable shale or other rock types above and below the ore body. Solvent is injected into the ore zone and allowed to move slowly through the rock, often for several or more years. The mineral-rich fluid is then pumped to the surface in production wells. Uranium is chemically removed and the solution prepared for reuse. The solvent fluid is either weakly acidic (usually sulfuric acid) or alkaline (sodium carbonate).

In the US, Canada, Australia, and Kazakhstan, plus several other countries, it is required that ISL be performed in remote areas, distant from where people live. Another requirement, with some exceptions, is that water quality be restored to a baseline condition chosen before the project began. This may involve injecting clean (or original composition) water with chemical agents to eliminate any further leaching capability. The goal is to ensure any former use of such water (e.g. for agriculture) can be resumed. While this has not always been achieved, regulations for ISL and other uranium extraction methods have continued to be reviewed and updated to improve remediation. Documented violations in the US, according to the NRC, which has oversight of ISL projects, have been minor [36].

Overall, the challenges and uncertainties related to uranium mining and milling are similar to those of all hard rock extraction projects. Very rarely do they present special, elevated risks or threats when modern practices are used. Studies of decadal public exposure to older, unremediated sites show that dose levels are typically 1–2 mSv/yr. Measurement and modeling of air exposures, particularly in arid and semi-arid settings, also indicate low dose levels [37]. Lung cancers among uranium miners today are overwhelmingly due to mining conditions that ended by the 1990s in most countries. This can be missed, however, because a fair amount of later research, even into the 2010s, continues to use data from that earlier time period. The most serious damage associated with uranium mining is the same as that for mining in general: waste waters pregnant with heavy metals and other toxins flowing from abandoned mines, waste rock piles, and tailings. It is the remediation of these sites that continues to be a challenge for governments and companies.

For comparison (other types of mining, water use): Uranium extraction does not produce the most toxic mining waste. Nor is it the only type that leaves behind radionuclides. More hazardous, both in the short- and long-term, are operations to mine and process mercury, asbestos, nickel, and a number of other sulfide minerals. Mercury is highly toxic even at very small concentrations in ground and surface water, as well as in wind-blown dust. Asbestos continues to be mined in a number of countries, including Brazil, Russia, China, and Kazakhstan, and exported to many others, especially in Asia [38].

Mining and smelting of sulfide ores, moreover, create solid, liquid, and particulate waste that, when allowed exposure to the environment, result in aggressive devastation to local landscapes. This is adequately shown by such examples as the Sudbury complex in Canada and Norilsk in Russia.[1] Mining

---

[1] These are both nickel mining areas well-known for their impacts. Today, however, they present a striking contrast: while Norilsk largely continues older practices that have destroyed much of the local environment, the famous "moonscape" and orange streams of Sudbury have been progressively reclaimed to a green landscape due to a combination of local government and company efforts.

and processing of gold, moreover, often involve host rock rich in heavy metals. None of these examples, even in combination, however, can compare with the level of pollution, toxic waste, acid mine drainage, fires, explosions, and unparalleled human cost from coal mining.

Radioactive waste, meanwhile, is generated by the extraction, milling, and refining of rare earth metals. These metals commonly occur in association with thorium and, less often, uranium, and their decay products, in deposits of the phosphate mineral monazite ($[Ce,La]PO_4$). The presence of radionuclides in rare earth waste rock has become a source of public concern and opposition [39]. While rare earths have many uses, among their primary applications today are in renewable energy technologies, particular wind turbines and solar panels, as well as in hybrid and electric cars. Thus, to a degree, these technologies share responsibility for radionuclide-bearing mining waste.

Nuclear Plants Use and Contaminate Vast Amounts of Water

Nuclear power plants use enormous amounts of water, far more than any other kind of power generation. Moreover, they also produce huge volumes of radioactive waste water that has to be disposed of. Fukushima shows how bad this can get.

What the historical record shows: Let's take the second claim first. Water becomes radioactive in a nuclear power plant by one of two ways, neither of which requires hazardous material disposal. In a BWR, water circulates through the reactor core and boils to steam, driving the turbine, then is passed through filters and recycled to the core. This water, while in the reactor vessel, comes in contact with fast neutrons, some of which are absorbed by the oxygen (H_2O) to create nitrogen-16 (N-16). This isotope is quite radioactive but has a half-life of only 7.2 seconds. It was an original concern in the 1950s that such radioactivity would make the BWR design infeasible. But the assumption was proven wrong by testing. Steam in a BWR has significant radioactivity when produced but loses it rapidly, in a minute or less. The N-16, moreover, constitutes around 95 percent or more of water radioactivity in a BWR nuclear plant. Another source of radioactivity comes from neutrons striking the walls of the steel reactor vessel, which produces radionuclides of iron, nickel, and cobalt in very small quantities. There is also some diffusion of fission products through the fuel cladding, and there may be tiny leaks as well. These waters are not allowed to buildup high levels of radionuclides but are cleaned and treated well before this can happen.

For a PWR, the dominant radionuclide is tritium (half-life 12.4 years). This is produced from neutrons being absorbed by boron, which reacts to create helium and tritium. The boron is added to the cooling water as boric acid (recall: boron is a good neutron absorber) to help control the fission reaction and its effects on materials. Tritium is weakly radioactive and produced in small quantities – so small that the NRC in the US allows diluted tritium-bearing waters to be released locally under controlled and monitored condition [40]. Dose levels for the public determined from "a significant tritiated water spill" in 2005 at a plant in Illinois (Braidwood) were 0.001 mSv/yr, more than a thousand times less than natural background [40–41].

Like other steam-based power plants, nuclear stations clean their water before it is reused. Besides any buildup of radionuclides, this is done to avoid water becoming corrosive, able to damage internal materials of the plant itself. Impurities, including radionuclides, are removed by one or more proven methods, including filtration, ion exchange, other chemical treatment, reverse osmosis, or others [42]. After treatment, water must meet strict regulatory criteria to be reused. If it doesn't, it is sent to onsite "liquid rad waste" treatment. Nuclear plants, meanwhile, are designed to have emergency supplies of water available at all times and to prevent leaked water from escape beyond plant boundaries. The Fukushima case is an entirely different situation, since the core is damaged and water is directly exposed to the partly melted fuel. Here, water must be removed after one cycle and stored in tanks onsite. In fact, rad waste treatment facilities were brought in, and, as of 2016, stored water had been largely cleansed of radionuclides except tritium, with decisions still pending about whether to discharge it to the ocean (full information provided to the public) [43–44].

As for water use by nuclear plants, it is not true that they need enormous volumes compared to other industries or energy sources. Some context is helpful. Water use is by far the largest in the agriculture industry. Even in wealthy nations, over 70 percent of all water goes to this sector, with total energy production second, at about 15 percent [45]. When talking about water needs by power plants, it's important to distinguish two basic systems. In one system, water is used to create steam that runs the turbine-generator, producing electricity. During plant operation, water cycles from the boiler to the turbine, then to the condenser, and back to the boiler. Such "process water" (as it's called) is reused many times and may need topping off now and then due to minor losses. A second system goes to cool the steam back into liquid water. Its main job, in a manner of speaking, is to carry away heat from the power generating unit as a whole. In almost every case, it uses much larger volumes than the process water. How much larger depends on the cooling system.

A *once-through* system takes water from a local source, circulates it through a network of pipes in the condenser where it absorbs heat from the steam, and then sends it back to the source, warmer than before. Such a system is simple, direct, and requires a minimum of energy use. In a *closed-loop* (also: *recirculating*) system, water goes through the condenser but is then sent to a cooling pond or tower; when it has lost enough heat, it is recycled to the condenser. Thus, closed-loop systems use far less water, up to two orders of magnitude less, but have higher levels of evaporation. Once-through cooling was widely used in the past, due to simplicity and lower cost. But because it carries heat directly into the local environment and can have detrimental impacts, the majority of power plants built since the 1970s have been closed-loop [46].[2] Most countries with nuclear power have implemented a maximum temperature for water returned to its source.

Actual water use can be measured in several ways. For comparison among different types of power plants, it is common to use volume per unit electricity generated. Fossil fuel plants, partly because they lose some of their heat through waste gases (smoke stacks), tend to use less water than nuclear plants. But the differences are not large. According to a summary by the IEA, withdrawals for once-through nuclear plants are in the range of 90,000–200,000 l/MWh, compared to 80,000–400,000 l/MWh for fossil plants (highest numbers for lower efficiency coal plants). For closed-loop systems, numbers (l/MWh) for nuclear are on the order of 1,500–16,000, while fossil fuel plants vary from about 1,000 up to 15,000 [47]. Overall, total water use for fossil fuel plants is somewhat lower but overlaps that for nuclear power plants [48].

Such figures help answer only part of the issue about water use, however. While roughly half of all power plants in the US, including 60 percent of nuclear stations, have once-through cooling, this reflects the age of such facilities. Since the mid-1980s, closed loop systems have been typical. A major question therefore concerns what type of systems will be used in the hundreds of new power plants to be built in developing nations? Many of these nations will be facing challenges of water availability as the climate warms, droughts increase in many areas, and heat waves become more frequent and intense. Will power plants be forced to compete with agriculture for water?

Today, options are more numerous. Hybrid systems exist, with a combination of once-through and closed loop via cooling towers. These have flexibility in

---

[2] A third option, known as *dry cooling*, involves high-powered fans that use air as the primary medium for removing heat. While this type of cooling system is employed in coal plants, the added power demands and expense make it unlikely the method will find much use for large nuclear plants. It could well find widespread use if small modular reactors become commonplace.

terms of balancing cost, efficiency, and environmental impacts. At the same time, plans for making nuclear power stations into cogeneration facilities would reduce and disperse cooling needs. This would involve directing waste heat to desalination, industrial processes, hydrogen production, and more. There have also been innovations in water sources. Using graywater (lightly used waste water) is one such idea. Palo Verde Generating Station near Tonopah, Arizona, largest nuclear plant in the US (3.9 GW capacity, run at 95–98 percent capacity factor) is located in the desert and for cooling receives partially treated municipal waste water via pipeline from Phoenix, about thirty-six miles away. Palo Verde uses a close loop system that discharges no water to the environment except by evaporation. As a single plant, it operates at low cost (<$0.03/kW), generates 35 percent of Arizona's total electricity, and exports power to California and Texas (relicensed in 2011 till the late 2040s) [49]. Cooling water does not need to be potable quality, and the Palo Verde example should provide a precedent for the use of partially treated waste water in nuclear (and other power) plants in developing nations.

Achilles Heel of Nuclear: Cost

The Achilles heel of nuclear is cost. Huge delays and cost overruns are typical. Early plants were so expensive that half of them were cancelled. The world simply can't afford nuclear as a way to fight climate change.

What the historical record shows: Sixty years of commercial power production reveals that there are no clear universals when it comes to the economics of nuclear power and certainly no fixed destinies. Differences local, national, and regional are the rule. This includes differences in the level of government involvement, in the nature of electricity markets, in approaches to licensing, and, not least, methods of financing nuclear plants. Moreover, much of this is in the process of change and re-evaluation today.

To be sure, there do exist general realities. Nuclear plants are expensive to build compared to most other projects for power generation, and they have always been so (see Chapter 4). But there is complexity here. New nuclear plants of 1.1–1.4 GW capacity have been built in China and South Korea for $3–5 billion, compared to $5–9 billion in Western nations [50]. A new (advanced) coal plant of 1.0 GW capacity, meanwhile, will cost $2–4 billion in both regions. Prices for nuclear fuel comprise a small part of the total costs, typically 15 percent or less. For fossil fuel plants, fuel costs are commonly

40 percent or more of total plant expense. Moreover, oil, gas, and coal prices are far more volatile and unpredictable compared to uranium.

When comparing different technologies, it is common practice to use what is called the "levelized cost of electricity" (LCOE). This is defined as the cost of building, operating, and maintaining a power plant for a specified cost recovery period, usually 30–40 years, estimated in the form of dollars or euros per unit of electricity (kWh or MWh). LCOE comparisons regularly differ, due to assumptions made by their estimators; thus it is best to use figures from a source with no political or financial attachment to any of the technologies involved. The following are 2015 estimates, in 2013 $/MWh, from the US Energy Information Administration, a statistical branch of the Department of Energy [51].

New Nuclear	95.2
Conventional Coal	95.1
Advanced Coal	115.7
Combined Cycle Gas	75.2
Hydropower	83.5
Wind Onshore	73.6
Wind Offshore	196.9
Solar PV	114.3 (with government subsidy)
Solar Thermal	220.6 (with government subsidy)

By such accounting, nuclear is far from the costliest technology. Still, it is not among the cheapest either, and because so much of its total cost is accrued up front, it has specific financial demands. Largest of all is the cost of capital,[3] or, differently said, the terms on which loans are made for building a new facility. Because investors in Western nations tend to view nuclear plants as riskier than other power sources, the cost of capital is high. This cost (loan servicing) has to be covered during the entire period of construction when no revenue is coming in. If there are delays, extending construction for years, servicing the cost of capital can more than double the total expense of the project. In Europe and the US, such delays have been common.

The reasons are several. But before looking at some of them, it helps to realize that LCOE figures, like those presented above, leave out some crucial elements. They do not include grid integration costs, nor the costs of new transmission (power lines), both of which become significant as the amount of

---

[3] "Cost of capital" can be defined as the rate of return needed to convince an investor to make a particular investment. The investor, that is, expects the investment to grow by a certain minimum percentage, e.g. whether 3 percent, 5 percent, or 10 percent. The market will determine this percentage; thus, if a project is seen as risky compared to alternatives, the percentage will be higher, i.e. a higher minimum return will have to be offered to attract investment. This level of return must be paid during the period of construction and adds to the construction cost.

variable power from renewables has to be accommodated. LCOE doesn't account for how reliable a source might be or how much electricity it is actually able to produce. Nuclear power, for example, has 9 percent of the total power generation capacity in the US, but it generates more than 19 percent of the country's electricity in any given year. In current power markets, no value is given to this kind of dependability. Nor does the market reward nuclear in any way for being a noncarbon source. Government, however, has been generous with its subsidies for wind and solar in recent years, which, between 2003 and 2015 totaled over \$70 billion in direct support and tax credits. In truth, government has often supported new industries with varied levels of support, as a way to help them survive and advance. This was certainly the case with nuclear too, which benefited from billions of dollars in federal R&D funding during the first several decades of its existence. Yet the reason for supporting renewables today is their noncarbon nature, their ability to lower climate changing emissions and air pollution from the power sector, the largest contributor to such emissions in the realm of energy use. Nuclear performs the same function and does it far better at present than wind and solar combined, accounting for more than 62 percent of noncarbon electricity in the US in the late 2010s. The point is that both renewables and nuclear should be given value for their contribution to the cause of lowering emissions.

But, as noted, nuclear suffers for bigger reasons. The tendency in much of the West to use a different, first-of-kind design for each new plant or small group of plants has been one factor. That a standardized design will reduce costs, especially after the first several plants are built, was proven by France in the 1970s and 80s, which built more than thirty-five reactors based on a single design. As China and South Korea have found, costs can continue to fall as systems for manufacturing, testing, and delivering components become more tightly organized and interrelated, making construction almost modular.

In the US, especially, the largest causes of delays have been poor estimates of actual costs, frequent regulatory changes, and opposition by local communities and antinuclear groups. The combination of these factors had their effects well before and after the TMI accident (see Chapters 4 and 7). This history along with the fear generated by Chernobyl and Fukushima, is embodied in the cost of capital for nuclear plants today. It also appears in the fact that very few new plants have been built in the last twenty-five years, not only in the US but in Europe too, a lack of experience that means new Gen III and III+ plants will face first-of-kind challenges.

All of this ignores the critical benefits that nuclear power offers, economically speaking. Nuclear plants remain operable longer than any other source of electricity except hydropower, which is less constant and has far greater environmental impact. With relicensing, a 1-GW nuclear plant can deliver enough noncarbon power to run a city of 750,000 people for sixty years or more. Moreover, nuclear is superior to every other source in terms of its footprint, i.e. land use (MW per acre or hectare). If we consider this in the context of climate change, a deeper meaning emerges: nuclear gives us the most zero-carbon electricity for the smallest amount of planetary impact. These factors represent real value in terms of social, environmental, and economic benefit, but they are not decisive. They do not ensure that nuclear plants will be profitable in every case – not in Western nations, that is. Before we see why, though, a few other points must be made.

Unless there is a carbon tax or other method of putting a price on carbon, natural gas doesn't have to pay for its impacts on climate change. Nuclear power, on the other hand, does pay for the waste it generates. Solar and wind also benefit by not having to include in their price of electricity the cost of backup power they have most often required.

Nuclear plants are not inherently "too expensive." A great deal depends on type of market (regulated or deregulated) they compete in, government policies affecting that market, and the cost of raw materials and labor. Such a claim, moreover, ignores a great many realities in the energy industry, which routinely builds the largest, most expensive infrastructure anywhere: oil refineries, LNG plants, major pipelines, large hydropower dams. Any one of these will cost billions of dollars today (at this writing, several LNG projects underway in Australia are priced at over $30 billion each). Such projects regularly see delays and cost overruns and need decades to achieve profitability. Large-scale renewable energy projects are not necessarily cheaper either. The Noor Solar Facility in Morocco, a 580 MW-capacity installation priced at $9 billion with a five-to-six-year build period, is only one example [52]. This is twice the cost for half the power and roughly fifteen times the amount of land of a new nuclear plant with one reactor in China, South Korea, or Russia.

Historical Trends at Present

Yet it is also true that nuclear power is faced with serious economic challenges in certain Western countries. These challenges are due to a distinct set of historical circumstances: 1) cheap, globally abundant natural gas; 2) deregulation in electricity markets; 3) government partiality toward renewable energy; 4) nearly three decades without a new nuclear plant having been built; and 5) lack of new demand for electricity. These factors work in combination. Deregulation means short-term competition among sources, favoring the cheapest option today or next week, not over the long-term, which is where nuclear tends to excel and also where solar-thermal would need to compete were it not heavily subsidized in the short-term. Deregulation, however, becomes something else – a deformed market – when certain sources are chosen for special financial support by government. Nuclear must therefore compete on a highly uneven playing field against gas that has become very cheap and subsidized renewables whose costs keep falling.

As always in the energy universe, there are other complexities. In the US, over-abundant gas supply exists due mainly to the fracking boom. This gas has remained within the domestic market, meanwhile, because the country doesn't have enough LNG (liquefied natural gas) export terminals. By 2016, the first few terminals began to come online, and more should be ready in coming years. This could reduce the amount of oversupply, but it could also lead to more new supply being created too, as prices rise, so the outlook is uncertain. How long gas will remain cheap is unknown, and the same goes for the rest of the world. Nothing is written in stone. The entire situation makes it more difficult for investors to justify a large-scale, long-term investment without more government support. No surprise, therefore that in the US and Europe, new reactors are being built by utilities that are still regulated (e.g. Southern Company in Georgia) or where forms of government participations and foreign equity are involved, as in England (Hinkley Point C reactor) and Finland (Hanhikivi plant).

Deregulation, meanwhile, has had mixed results and is far from the standard, even in US states. Competition among different sources and short-term profit-ability are the aim of liberalized markets, with the goal being that the cheapest option wins out. Regulated markets are where the government assumes control over power supply and price, as it does over key services like water or sewage, essentially guaranteeing utilities a profit, investors a return, and customers a reliable supply. In place until the 1980s and 90s, such markets were based on the idea of electricity as a public good, something too important, too fundamental, to be treated as a commodity by market forces, where prices can fluctuate a great deal and be the subject of manipulation. Deregulation uses the idea that competition will increase efficiencies (companies streamlining to lower their costs) and benefit consumers with lower prices. A chief effect is the premium placed on near-term price, which downplays or ignores the value of long-term reliability, stability, and other benefits that come from a source like nuclear power. At the same time, however, governments have continued to provide support for certain sources to keep prices lower than they would be if market forces were left in control. There are tax write-offs for oil and gas, loan guarantees and liability caps for nuclear power, and, more recently and at a higher level, subsidies granted to wind and solar in the name of reducing carbon emissions.

Nuclear suffers economically where it is given few or no incentives for being a noncarbon source. Between 2008 and 2015, advanced nations invested $1.15 trillion in renewables, with nuclear receiving two orders of magnitude less [53]. This seems problematic at the very least if reducing emissions from carbon energy sources is truly a primary goal. Hesitation on the part of Western nations to promote their chief source of noncarbon power may change, however, as new precedents are being set.

The UK, for example, has a national energy plan that marks a major departure from the past [54]. In part, this plan involves phasing out coal and replacing most of its existing nuclear plants with new generation reactors largely financed from abroad. The UK has found renewables, particularly offshore wind, to be expensive on a per-MW basis and unreliable without a backup source. As domestic sources of natural gas from the North Sea are in decline, expanded nuclear will substitute for these too, thereby reducing future imports (particularly from Russia). In brief, nuclear and renewables together will replace a large part of fossil fuel power generation, reducing emissions nearly 60 percent by about 2030 and greatly improving energy security. The plan is motivated by three overriding priorities: climate change, national security, and affordability. This last will be fulfilled by having foreign nuclear companies (e.g. Toshiba, GE-Hitachi) finance as much as 60–100 percent of the plants they build and thus have majority ownership. It provides a new model for other Western nations that allow for such levels of foreign equity (as of now, the US doesn't). Undoubtedly there will be complexities and challenges with this approach, but it does add new possibilities for future new builds.

There are other signs, too, that EU nations are rethinking their hesitancy to maintain and expand their nuclear fleet. In 2016 Sweden repealed a tax on nuclear power that had been in place since 1984 and allowed for the construction of new plants at existing sites, as older plants retire [55]. Recent reports written for the European Commission and for individual nations, such as Belgium have strongly emphasized the necessity of maintaining and expanding nuclear power for the sake of reducing emissions and air pollution [56–57].

As often noted, a true market-based approach to lowering emissions would be a carbon tax, not subsidies for selected sources that insulate them from competition [58]. Such a tax would need to be high enough to move the mix of sources away from fossil fuels. This would help support *all* noncarbon sources (though some more than others) [59]. But it would also raise electricity prices for consumers, something governments are less fond of doing. Instead, economically speaking, the "pain" for higher prices is made indirect by financial supports like rebates, government loans, special tariffs, and more, granted to wind and solar power [60]. The aim, of course, is to make these sources competitive at an early stage. Yet the effect is to make nuclear plants less competitive and thus, when they close and are not replaced or are replaced by natural gas plants, to erase much of the gain made by renewables. As noted in Chapter 7, nuclear is too large a baseload source to be easily replaced by wind and solar, so coal or gas generation has to be added. This has happened repeatedly [61].

In early 2017, the nuclear firm Westinghouse filed for Chapter 11 bankruptcy. Starting in 2005, the Japanese company Toshiba had become the firm's parent company, and shortly thereafter Westinghouse applied to the NRC for licenses to build four new reactors using its own AP1000 design. These were the first US plants approved since 1978. To build them, Westinghouse chose a company (Shaw Group) that had purchased the well-known construction entity, Stone & Webster, which had built many nuclear plants in the 1970s but had since shifted to other project areas due to the lack of any new reactor orders. Two of the AP1000 plants are sited in South Carolina (Summer 2 and 3), the other two in Georgia (Vogtle 3 and 4). Begun in 2012, the plants were well behind schedule at the end of 2016 and several billion dollars in the red. The three main reasons for this were: 1) the need to have many components manufactured overseas and shipped to the US; 2) design changes forced by new NRC regulations after the Fukushima accident and, most of all; 3) Westinghouse chose very poorly but revealingly a company that, despite its earlier achievements, could no longer successfully build a nuclear plant. After three decades, the manufacturing capability, supply chains, human capital, and project management experience no longer exist as they once did. Westinghouse, meanwhile, will not disappear. Neither will the AP1000, two of which are nearly complete in China at the Sanmen and Haiyang sites.

The final historical factor, falling or flattening demand, may turn out to be the most significant of all. From its beginnings in the late nineteenth century until the early 2000s, Europe and the US were the global center of electricity generation and use. Their demand grew especially rapidly, at 4 percent a year, in the post-WWII era. This long-term pattern ended and even turned negative after 2007. Reasons for this are not entirely understood, but relate to better efficiency (e.g. in lighting, heating, computer equipment) and the shift away from power-hungry industries like steel, metal refining, car/ship building, and textiles, among others. Little or no growth in demand obviously means less need for new power generation. Market space depends on shut down of existing plants using other sources. In Western countries, this will mostly be coal plants and, in a few nations, oil-burning facilities, with gas-fired plants a target for closure in the long-term. The opportunity for nuclear will therefore depend a great deal on the factors we have discussed above, government policy most of all.

In the developing world, where the greater part of the nuclear future seems likely to reside, these factors do not much apply. Markets here are regulated, with governments and state-owned companies directly involved in power plant decisions. While some amount of private investment can and does take place in new nuclear plants, this is usually in the form of a joint venture with a state-owned firm. The situation tends to be different than that in the West, since a different set of priorities, directly related to government needs, dominate. Energy security, reliability of supply, amount of power, and level of emissions will be among these, the first few more important than the last.

In nations with a centrally planned economy, financing costs are usually absorbed by the government. There is far less concern about profit levels, though this can vary depending upon whether a domestic or foreign government firm is in charge of building and running a plant. Nations like China, Russia, and India have benefited from repeated use of standardized designs and cheaper labor. Developing countries, moreover, are not often subject to public protests and large-scale opposition. What stands out most as a determining factor, however, is the level of government support.

A recent, well-considered review of the economic situation for nuclear and renewables concludes that both "face significant challenges." Falling cost for renewables will slow due to the rising costs of infrastructure and labor. Nuclear, as we've said, has financing challenges in many western nations due to investor worries about delays, regulatory changes, public opposition. Some level of government support is necessary for both, if they have to compete with fossil fuels in markets with no carbon pricing [62]. This strikes a rather cautious, warning tone. Such is common among energy analysts and has a firm rationale (avoid favoritism, appear objective). The above urges us to think that noncarbon energy will struggle for some time.

But there is another way to see things. A gray diagnosis tends to ignore something of critical importance – the dynamism of energy markets and government policy. Rapid and large-scale changes can and do happen. Between 2004 and 2008, oil and gas prices shot to decadal highs, then dropped and held steady from 2011 to 2014, and then collapsed in late 2014. Volatility and dynamism are inherent in these markets. Meantime, the Fukushima accident in 2011 seemed to mark the arrival of nuclear twilight in the West; a host of nations declared plans to roll back their programs, retire plants early, and cancel new ones. Other nations, China included, called a halt to new construction until thorough inspections could be done of all existing plants. A year later, sixty-four reactors were under construction and planned new builds had grown to more than 160. Between 2012 and 2016, the global reactor fleet went from 432 to 450, with China bringing online six or seven reactors every year. By late 2016, as many as thirty-nine new reactors were planned for North America and Europe [63].

Nuclear Reactors and Weapons Are Too Closely Linked

Nuclear reactors work by the same process as bombs, so accidents create the same level of death and contamination. Power plants have generated tons of plutonium, enough for thousands of weapons, that are a constant temptation to terrorists, proliferation, and to those who would steal and sell nuclear material to the highest bidder.

What the historical record shows: Nuclear reactors and weapons are both based on the process of nuclear fission. There would seem to be an undeniable connection, therefore, between civilian and military uses of nuclear energy. But there are fundamental differences. For a weapon, the design and materials and high enrichment level are all aimed at maximizing the production of neutrons in order to create a runaway fission reaction. In a reactor, the aim is to precisely control neutron production and the rate and amount of fission. Fuel is only slightly enriched (3–5 percent), and there is *no* possibility for a nuclear explosion. The mushroom cloud has no relation to an accident at a power plant.

Among TMI, Chernobyl, and Fukushima, only the Chernobyl accident had anything directly to do with fission. The detonation and fire were due to a steam explosion caused by an increase in the rate of fission and resulting heat production. TMI and Fukushima were meltdowns related to decay heat in highly radioactive fission products in the fuel that had become uncovered from loss of coolant. Explosions at Fukushima were produced by hydrogen gas from a chemical reaction between the overheating fuel and its cladding.

Early fears that a reactor accident would produce impacts as devastating as a bomb have been disproven by the three events just mentioned, the most serious in six decades. Initial models predicting thousands of deaths from radiation and cancer in the first decade at Chernobyl were entirely wrong, as well as later estimates that such deaths would occur within thirty years. Also shown to be false, in this case by a major study of the National Cancer Institute in the US, is the idea that living near a nuclear power plant increases the risk of cancer incidence or mortality – in other words, that such a plant is responsible for insidious yet large-scale disease and death over time [64].

Yet there do exist possible connections between reactors and weapons that must be mentioned. These connections have to do with the production and utilization of weapons-usable fuel. One side of this involves the production of plutonium via the reprocessing of spent power plant fuel. This plutonium, stockpiled as "reactor-grade" material, contains a number of Pu isotopes but can be used to make a weapon. Such a weapon using reactor-grade plutonium was tested in 1962 by the US military and found to have significant explosive power (<20 kilotons; exact yield still confidential) [65]. Due to the isotopes it contains, reactor-grade plutonium is considerably more radioactive and gives off more heat than weapons-grade (>90 percent Pu^{239}), and this fact makes it a good deal more difficult to handle and also complicates both the design and manufacture of a weapon. A number of nations today reprocess spent fuel: France, Japan, Russia, the UK, Pakistan, India, and China. The total global stock of reprocessed plutonium from civilian reactors is about 267 tonnes (294 tons) and has been increasing at about 1 percent to 2 percent a year since 2010. If freely handed out to bomb makers able to deal with the higher radioactivity, this total could yield up to 53,000 weapons (~5 kg/bomb).

But it can also be used as fuel in two forms: as blended with LEU to make mixed-oxide (MOX) for use in existing light-water reactors, or as plutonium fuel in fast neutron reactors (FNR). According to the World Nuclear Association, MOX is widely used in the EU and Japan, with about 2,000 tonnes (2,200 tons) burned since the 1980s [66]. As for FNRs, there are only a few currently operating, mostly in Russia. Yet major plans are underway to expand their use in China, South Korea, India, and possibly Japan, as well as Russia. Indeed, three of the six designs chosen for future development by the Generation IV International Forum are fast reactors. Such reactors, we should recall, can burn not only plutonium but all actinides in spent fuel, thus reducing both the volume of waste and the time it remains radioactive (from hundreds of thousands of years to a few centuries). FNRs have been controversial because of their ability to breed plutonium fuel as well as burn it. No FNR or MOX fuel facility exists in the US. Thus, other options must be found to reduce civilian plutonium. One possibility, already discussed, is to dilute the plutonium with inert material to where it can be stored in the Waste Isolation Pilot Plant (New Mexico), the country's working geologic repository for intermediate and low-level waste.

At the same time, 267 tonnes (294 tons) of reactor-grade plutonium is volumetrically very small, especially compared to lethal chemical materials and waste stored at many sites. It could fit in a room no more than about 9 m^2 (100 ft^2), piled to a height of about 1.5 m (5 ft). Even were we to combine it with the 140 tons or so of military plutonium, the total would still fit easily in a two-car garage. Thus, it should not be difficult to safeguard. That no major theft or loss has occurred does not by any means tell us all is fine and well. Terrorism has proven that the past is no secure guide to the future when it comes to levels and techniques of violence. Yet of all pathways to a bomb, plutonium from civilian reactors is surely among the most challenging, due not only to its radioactivity and heat but the sophistication of the bomb technology needed compared with that for a uranium weapon. Far simpler would it be to seek out HEU (which is not used in civilian power reactors) or to get hold of a tactical (small-scale) weapon.

Finally, there are many reasons why a nuclear power plant cannot be called a "dirty bomb waiting to happen." Reactors worldwide are protected by armed personnel, usually from the military, with automatic weapons and strong security protocols. In the US, since 9/11 the NRC has ensured that nuclear plants can withstand an impact from a commercial airliner, and the same is true in many parts of the world. Terrorists or others wishing to get their hands on radioactive material would hardly need to attempt a siege on a power plant. In any city, there are bound to be a dozen or more hospitals and clinics with significant amounts of radioisotopes used for diagnosis and therapy, places that are not guarded by military personnel.

Conclusion: Beyond Myth

This chapter does not seek to white wash the nuclear domain. Nuclear has its difficulties; it is far from flawless in any sense. Like all large-scale industries, especially those in energy, it must strive to do better, much better in fact. Will there be future accidents? It is a definite possibility. But to single out nuclear power, above fossil fuels especially, as *the* menacing source of modern energy makes no sense. For a variety of reasons, people have learned to fear nuclear power far more than they have learned to understand it. As a magnet for anxieties about the nature of society and more, nuclear power has managed to instill fear in many people while, at the same time, providing safe and necessary power to a great many others (more all the time). As this chapter shows, however, calling this form of energy inherently too "dirty, dangerous, and expensive" or "obsolete" simply doesn't stand up to scrutiny. The claim doesn't do very well when compared with the truths of history, radiology, engineering, hydrology, or economics.

Today there exists a belief that nuclear and renewables should be separated, posed in opposition. The world's noncarbon sources in power generation must occupy rival sides of a "clean and green" barrier. Such will not help us deal with the real, proven threats of climate change and particulate pollution. It is common, no doubt, for passionate proponents of either nuclear or renewables to overstate their case and to put forward enthusiastic, even inebriated, estimates of what might be achieved if only the world were to favor their chosen technology above all others. But billions of wind turbines and solar plants or many thousands of nuclear reactors are not realistically in the cards.

There is a truth here, however, that needs to be clarified. Any such vision of an energy future is also a vision of society: if a world dominated by renewables is one based on distributed (dispersed) supply and therefore smaller cities and localized communities, a social space where nuclear plants prevail over other sources is one of more centralized, large-scale authority embodied in cities of medium to mega size. These are broad generalizations, to be sure, but they hold when we look a bit deeper.

Note again the tendency in many Western nations to give considerable financial and policy privilege to wind and solar power and to downplay any central role for nuclear in a noncarbon future. There is a striking message here, hiding in plain sight. It is this: lowering carbon emissions and advancing a noncarbon future that will mitigate climate change are not the ultimate goals at issue. Indeed, climate change itself is not the fundamental motive. Instead, the underlying aim appears more ideological – to employ renewable energy as the builder of a new society, one that is "clean," ethically superior, without risk, washing away a past that has been a denial to all these good things for more than two dark centuries. To reach this new era of energy purity, climate change is less a core reality than a needed, motivating force; it will get us there sooner.

We might well call all this a kind of grand vision for a better world, except for one thing. It defines an absolutist idea. As much as it promotes one domain of energy use, it banishes and forbids all others. All else must be demonized as "dirty," dangerous, and threatening. The realities of energy diversity in technology, national needs, distribution of resources, and the simple fact that fossil fuels are enormously rich sources of energy and will require many decades to replace, are all pushed to the side and ignored. A pure future has no place for "competitors." Indeed, the renewables-only vision has a political quality that might sound familiar. We may ask: is there a corresponding mirror-image view, equally inflexible, on the other side? Yes, there is: antinuclearism must be understood as the fundamental cause of global warming; without it, the world could have been powered decades ago by a noncarbon source.

Once we are out of uniform for absolutist causes and truly serious about climate change and lethal pollution, it becomes apparent that renewables and nuclear are wholly compatible. Moreover, they are both in a similar state of technological advance. New utility scale solar plants and wind turbine technologies that have emerged in the past decade are matched, in a sense, by new reactor designs that range greatly in size, structure, fuel, and financing. Both domains will continue to advance, as they must, to reduce the overwhelming dominance of fossil energy and thus to provide a better balance of sources for the rising demands of developing nations.

References

[1] United Nations Scientific Committee on the Effects of Atomic Radiation (UNSCEAR), The Chernobyl accident – UNSCEAR's assessments of the radiation effects (16 July 2012). Available from: www.unscear.org/unscear/en/chernobyl.html

[2] F. N. von Hippel, The Radiological and Psychological Consequences of the Fukushima Daiichi Accident, *Bulletin of the Atomic Scientists*, 67:5 (2011), 27–36.

[3] United Nations Scientific Committee on the Effects of Atomic Radiation (UNSCEAR), Sources, Effects and Risks of Ionizing Radiation: UNSCEAR 2013 Report, Vol. 1 (Internet) (2014), 252. Available from: www.unscear.org/unscear/en/publications/2013_1.html

[4] M. Simons, French Search for Cause of Chemical Plant Explosion (Internet), *The New York Times* (25 September 2001). Available from: www.nytimes.com /2001/09/25/world/french-search-for-cause-of-chemical-plant-explosion.html

[5] The Night the Sea Caught Fire: Remembering Pipe Alpha (Internet), *The Scotsman* (13 June 2008). Available from: www.scotsman.com/lifestyle/the-night-the-sea-caught-fire-remembering-piper-alpha-1-1433754

[6] R. Ramesh, Bhopal: Hundreds of New Victims are Born Every Year (Internet), *The Guardian* (29 April 2008). Available from: www.theguardian.com/world/2008/apr/30/india.pollution

[7] E. Broughton, The Bhopal Disaster and Its Aftermath: A Review. *Environmental Health*, 4:6 (May 10 2005), www.ncbi.nlm.nih.gov/pmc/articles/PMC1142333/

[8] H. W. Stephens, *The Texas City Disaster, 1947* (Austin: University of Texas Press 1997).

[9] UN Chernobyl Forum, Environmental Consequences of the Chernobyl Accident and their Remediation: Twenty Years of Experience (Internet), *Report of the UN Chernobyl Forum Expert Group "Environment"* (August 2005), 103–105. Available from: www-pub.iaea.org/mtcd/publications/pdf/pub1239_web.pdf

[10] Ibid., pp. 168.

[11] J. Wendle, Animals Rule Chernobyl 30 Years After Nuclear Disaster, *National Geographic* (18 April 2016).

[12] UN Chernobyl Forum, Environmental Consequences, pp. 135–137.

[13] USGS, Emissions from Coal Fires and Their Impact on the Environment (Internet). *US Geological Survey, Factsheet 2009–3084.* Available from: https://pubs.usgs.gov/fs/2009/3084/pdf/fs2009-3084.pdf

[14] C. Keunzer and G. B. Stracher, Geomorphology of Coal Seam Fires, *Geomorphology,* 138:1 (2012), 209–222.

[15] Reclamation Research Group, Acid Mine Drainage and Effects on Fish Health and Ecology: A Review (Internet), *US Fish and Wildlife Service, Anchorage Fish and Wildlife Field Office* (2008). Available from: www.pebblescience.org/pdfs/Final_Lit_Review_AMD.pdf

[16] World Nuclear Association (WNA), Storage and Disposal of Used Fuel and Separated HLW (Internet). *Radioactive Waste Management, (WNA)* (October 2016). Available from: www.world-nuclear.org/information-library/nuclear-fuel-cycle/nuclear-wastes/radioactive-waste-management.aspx

[17] Union of Concerned Scientists. Environmental Impacts of Coal Power: Wastes Generated (Internet). Available from: www.ucsusa.org/clean_energy/coalvswind/c02d.html#.V27AZ-crJ_w

[18] J. S. Walker, *The Road to Yucca Mountain* (Berkeley: University of California Press, 2009).

[19] US General Accountability Office (GAO), Commercial Nuclear Waste: Effects of a Termination of the Yucca Mountain Repository Program and Lessons Learned, *(GAO)*, GAO-011-229 (April 2011), 1.

[20] US Environmental Protection Agency, Public Health and Environmental Radiation Protection Standards for Yucca Mountain, Nevada (Internet). Available from: www.epa.gov/radiation/public-health-and-environmental-radiation-protection-standards-yucca-mountain-nevada-40

[21] National Cancer Institute, US National Institutes of Health, Incidence (Internet). Available from: http://progressreport.cancer.gov/diagnosis/incidence

[22] US Environmental Protection Agency, Underground Injection Control (UIC), Class 1 Industrial and Municipal Waste Disposal Wells (Internet). Available from: www.epa.gov/uic/class-i-industrial-and-municipal-waste-disposal-wells

[23] A. Lustgarten and K. K. Schmidt, State-by-State: Underground Injection Wells (Internet), *ProPublica* (20 September 2012). Available from: http://projects.propublica.org/graphics/underground-injection-wells

[24] US Nuclear Regulatory Commission (NRC), Backgrounder on Reactor License Renewal (Internet). Available from: www.nrc.gov/reading-rm/doc-collections/fact-sheets/fs-reactor-license-renewal.html

[25] P. Voosen, How Long Can a Nuclear Reactor Last? (Internet), *Scientific American* (20 November 2009). Available from: www.scientificamerican.com/article/nuclear-power-plant-aging-reactor-replacement-/

[26] K. L. Murty, *Materials' Ageing and Degradation in Light Water Reactors: Mechanisms and Management* (Philadelphia: Woodhead Publishing, 2013).

[27] International Atomic Energy Agency (IAEA), Ageing Management (Internet). Available from: www-ns.iaea.org/standards/documents/topics.asp?sub=200

[28] International Commission on Large Dams Number of Dams by Country Members (Internet). Available from: www.icold-cigb.org/GB/World_register/general_synthesis.asp?IDA=206

[29] Office of Energy Efficiency & Renewable Energy, US Department of Energy, Types of Hydropower Plants (Internet). Available from: http://energy.gov/eere/water/types-hydropower-plants

[30] US Army Corps of Engineers, National Inventory of Dams (Internet), *CorpsMap*, Available from: http://nid.usace.army.mil/cm_apex/f?p=838:12:18949907211654

[31] American Society of Civil Engineers, Dams (Internet), *2013 Report Card for America's Infrastructure*. Available from: www.infrastructurereportcard.org/a/#p/dams/conditions-and-capacity

[32] Federal Investigative Board, The 1977 Toccoa Flood Report of Failure of Kelly Barnes Dam Flood and Findings (Internet), *US Geological Survey* (21 December 1977). Available from: http://ga.water.usgs.gov/publications/ToccoaFIBReport/body3.html

[33] Nuclear Energy Agency, Organization for Economic Cooperation and Development, Managing Environmental and Health Impacts of Uranium Mining (Internet) (20 June 2014). Available from: www.oecd.org/green growth/managing-environmental-and-health-impacts-of-uranium-mining-9789264216044-en.htm

[34] New Mexico Institute of Mining and Technology Uranium—How Is It Mined? (Internet), *New Mexico Bureau of Geology and Mineral Resources*. Available from: https://geoinfo.nmt.edu/resources/uranium/mining.html

[35] IAEA, The Long-Term Stabilization of Uranium Mill Tailings (Internet), *International Atomic Energy Agency Report TECDOC-1403* (August 2004), 20. Available from: www-pub.iaea.org/MTCD/publications/PDF/te_1403_web.pdf

[36] US Nuclear Regulatory Commission (NRC), In Situ Recovery Facilities (Internet), Available from: www.nrc.gov/materials/uranium-recovery/extraction-methods/isl-recovery-facilities.html

[37] United Nations Scientific Committee on the Effects of Atomic Radiation (UNSCEAR), Sources and Effects of Ionizing Radiation – Volume I: Sources (Internet), *UNSCEAR 2000 Report to the General Assembly, with Scientific Annexes* (2000), 181–182. Available from: www.unscear.org/docs/publications/2000/UNSCEAR_2000_Report_Vol.I.pdf

[38] US Geological Survey (USGS), Asbestos: Statistics and Information (Internet). Available from: http://minerals.usgs.gov/minerals/pubs/commodity/asbestos/

[39] S. H. Ali, Social and Environmental Impact of the Rare Earth Industries, *Resources*, 2014:3 (February 2014), 123–134.

[40] US Nuclear Regulatory Commission (NRC), Backgrounder on Tritium, Radiation Protection Limits, and Drinking Water (Internet). Available from: www.nrc.gov/reading-rm/doc-collections/fact-sheets/tritium-radiation-fs.html

[41] Health Physics Society, Tritium, Fact Sheet (Internet), (March 2011). Available from: http://hps.org/documents/tritium_fact_sheet.pdf

[42] Office of Nuclear Energy, US Department of Energy Cooling Water Issues and Opportunities at Nuclear Power Plants (Internet). Available from: http://energy.gov/ne/downloads/cooling-water-issues-and-opportunities-us-nuclear-power-plants

[43] Treatment Ends of Contaminated Water at Fukushima Daiichi, While No Full Face Mask Area Is Expanded Greatly (Internet), *Japan Atomic Industrial Forum* (3 June 2015). Available from: www.jaif.or.jp/en/treatment-ends-of-contaminated-water-at-fukushima-daiichi-while-no-full-face-mask-area-is-expanded-greatly/

[44] K. Mathiesen, Is It Safe to Dump Fukushima Waste into the Sea? (Internet), *The Guardian* (13 April 2016). Available from: www.theguardian.com/environ ment/2016/apr/13/is-it-safe-to-dump-fukushima-waste-into-the-sea

[45] International Energy Agency (IEA), Chapter 17: Water for energy (Internet), *World Energy Outlook 2012*, (November 2012). Also available as an excerpt: www.worldenergyoutlook.org/media/weowebsite/2012/WEO_2012_ Water_Excerpt.pdf

[46] US Energy Information Administration (EIA), Many Newer Power Plants Have Cooling Systems That Reuse Water (Internet), *Today in Energy*, (11 February 2014). Available from: www.eia.gov/todayinenergy/detail.cfm?id=14971

[47] IEA, Chapter 17: Water for energy, Table 17.4.

[48] J. Meldrum, S. Nettles-Anderson, G. Heath, and J. Macknick, Life Cycle Water Use for Electricity Generation: A Review and Harmonization of Literature Estimates, *Environmental Research Letters*, 8:1 (March 2013), 1–18.

[49] R. Peltier, Top Plants: Palo Verde Nuclear Generating Station, Wintersburg Arizona (Internet), *Power* (1 November 2015). Available from: www.powermag .com/palo-verde-nuclear-generating-station-wintersburg-arizona/

[50] J. Conca, China Shows How to Build Nuclear Reactors Fast and Cheap (Internet), *Forbes* (22 October 2015). Available from: www.forbes.com/sites/jamesconca/ 2015/10/22/china-shows-how-to-build-nuclear-reactors-fast-and-cheap /#113fb9444d0b

[51] US Energy Information Administration (EIA), Levelized Cost and Levelized Avoided Cost of New Generation Resources (Internet), *Annual Energy Outlook 2015*, Available from: www.eia.gov/forecasts/aeo/electricity_generation.cfm

[52] A. Neslen, Morocco to Switch on First Phase of World's Largest Solar Plant (Internet), *The Guardian* (4 February 2016). Available from: www .theguardian.com/environment/2016/feb/04/morocco-to-switch-on-first-phase-of -worlds-largest-solar-plant

[53] Frankfurt School of Finance and Management, Global Trends in Renewable Energy Investment 2016 (Internet), *Frankfurt School-UNEP (United Nations Environment Programme) Collaborating Centre for Climate and Sustainable Energy Finance* (2016). Available from: http://fs-unep-centre.org/sites/default/ files/publications/globaltrendsinrenewableenergyinvestment2016lowres_0.pdf

[54] World Nuclear Association (WNA), Nuclear Power in the United Kingdom (Internet), (October 2016). Available from: www.world-nuclear.org/information-library/country-profiles/countries-t-z/united-kingdom.aspx

[55] Sweden Abolishes Nuclear Tax (Internet), *World Nuclear News* (10 June 2016). Available from: www.world-nuclear-news.org/NP-Sweden-abolishes-nuclear-tax-1006169.html

[56] European Commission Publishes Report on the Future of Nuclear in the EU (Internet), *NucNet* (4 April 2016). Available from: www.nucnet.org/all-the-news /2016/04/04/european-commission-publishes-report-on-the-future-of-nuclear-in-the-eu

[57] Belgium Needs Nuclear and Renewables, Report Finds (Internet), *World Nuclear News* (10 October 2016). Available from: www.world-nuclear-news.org/EE-Belgium-needs-nuclear-and-renewables-report-finds-10101610.html

[58] E. Hung and K. B. Medlock III, Why America's Clean Energy Plans Need to Embrace Nuclear Power (Internet), *Forbes* (31 March 2016). Available from: www.forbes.com/sites/thebakersinstitute/2016/03/31/environmental-policy-nuclear-power-carbon-tax-and-a-portfolio-approach-to-reduce-co2-emissions/#ef57063266d6

[59] U. Irfan, The Nuclear Option Could Be Best Bet to Combat Climate Change, (Internet), *Scientific American* (3 June 2016). Available from: www.scientificamerican.com/article/the-nuclear-option-could-be-best-bet-to-combat-climate-change/

[60] A. Powell, Whither Solar Power? (Internet), *Harvard University Center for the Environment* (24 May 2016). Available from: http://environment.harvard.edu/news/huce-headlines/whither-solar-power

[61] A. Robson and J. Lovering, In Most Cases, Closing a Nuclear Plant is All Pain and No Gain (Internet), *Third Way* (30 June 2016). Available from: https://medium.com/@ThirdWayTweet/in-most-cases-closing-a-nuclear-plant-is-all-pain-and-no-gain-135911655b8e#.l3c17eody

[62] H. Khatib and C. Difiglio, Economics of Nuclear and Renewables, *Energy Policy*, 96:C (2016), 740–750.

[63] World Nuclear Association (WNA), World Nuclear Power Reactors & Uranium Requirements (Internet), *Information Library*. Available from: www.world-nuclear.org/information-library/facts-and-figures/world-nuclear-power-reactors-and-uranium-requireme.aspx

[64] National Institutes of Health, No Excess Mortality Risk Found in Counties with Nuclear Facilities (Internet), *National Cancer Institute Fact Sheet*, (19 April 2011). Available from: http://dceg.cancer.gov/about/organization/programs-ebp/reb/fact-sheet-mortality-risk

[65] US Department of Energy, DOE Facts: Additional Information Concerning Underground Nuclear Weapon Test of Reactor-Grade Plutonium (Internet), *Office of Public Affairs*. Available from: www.ccnr.org/plute_bomb.html

[66] World Nuclear Association (WNA), Mixed Oxide (MOX) Fuel (Internet), (August 2016). Available from: www.world-nuclear.org/information-library/nuclear-fuel-cycle/fuel-recycling/mixed-oxide-fuel-mox.aspx

9

Global Energy and Nuclear Power: The Next Thirty Years

Energy Trends: A Changing World

The lights never go off in Chicago, Paris, or Tokyo. From space, the illuminated circuit boards of these cities are as well-defined as if traced out on a map. Every district and avenue appears. When resolution is sufficient, we can even descend to individual neighborhoods, where street lamps send cones of light onto sidewalks, cars, lawns, and streets. Not so in Lagos, Dhaka, or Mumbai. In these places, great megacities of the developing world, large portions at night are dark. Millions live here with little or no power. In 2017, the whole of Nigeria, with over 170 million people, had less electricity than San Francisco. Worldwide, more than a billion people are without access to this most fundamental form of modern energy. Another two billion have only intermittent access, which is therefore unreliable and often unpredictable.

Such realities also form part of the context for nuclear power in the twenty-first century. Global energy, in fact, has entered a new era of its own. Here are a few trends to show that this is so:

– Humanity's demand for energy will keep rising to 2050 and beyond. Virtually *all* this growth will be in developing nations. The 200-year era when Western nations dominated modern energy production and use has now come to an end. This defines a major historical change.
– In 2016, more than 85 percent of global marketed energy still came from fossil fuels, especially oil and coal, the most carbon-rich sources. Consumption of these sources, along with natural gas, has continued to grow due to rising demand in developing nations.

- The most rapid growth area will continue to be electricity. Coal remains the largest fuel for power, at over 40 percent of global generation. Though declining in some nations, its total use is rising. The lowest impact noncarbon sources are nuclear power and renewables. After twenty years of rapid growth, renewables are a mainstream source supplying 7 percent of world electricity in 2016.
- Because of technological advances unlocking unconventional oil and gas from shale and other tight reservoirs, the world now faces the possibility of immense fossil fuel abundance. This is even more the case if coal is included, as its reserves are larger (energy content) than conventional oil and gas combined.
- Climate change impacts, already responsible for yearly deaths and damage on a significant scale, will increasingly urge a shift toward noncarbon energy. This shift will also be compelled by lethal pollution from coal use and by demand for energy security.
- All of these realities need to be seen against the fact that the world continues to urbanize.[1] In 2007, half of humanity lived in cities for the first time in history. By 2040, nearly 70 percent will. The future of energy lies in cities most of all, especially those of the developing world.

None of these points is controversial. They can all be found, in one form or another, in expert analyses of world energy and its future [1–4]. What they speak of is a redrawing of the world energy map. This does not mean a "revolution" is in the offing. Looked at in global terms, the most epochal change is the shift in the center of world energy demand from wealthy to developing nations. The implications of this shift are enormous, especially for the long-term. But such implications are also debated and in part uncertain. This is true, above all, for the one sector of energy use that we (and most of the world) are most interested in.

It is in the electricity sector where the highest level of debate occurs. Forecasts predict that fossil fuels will continue to run the greater part of the world in 2040, including power generation. By then, natural gas and coal are predicted to be used for 60 percent of electricity production [5]. Gas use will presumably more than double, while coal use falls, at least in some places. Forecasts, in fact, see this fuel declining significantly over the next several decades, but only in advanced nations. In developing

[1] Before roughly 2010, rural and urban populations were both increasing overall, with the rate of increase for rural areas slowing and for urban areas rising. For discussion of this and related population trends, see: *World Urbanization Prospects: The 2014 Revision*. New York: United Nations, Department of Economic and Social Affairs, http://esa.un.org/unpd/wup/highlights/wup2014-highlights.pdf

nations, it is predicted to *increase* as much as a third [6]. Coal, it seems, will remain a major challenge for a lower-carbon world. While China will slow or even halt its vast coal dependence, this will be exceeded by new consumption elsewhere – in India, Southeast Asia, Africa, and Latin America [7]. Though claims have been made that such growth in coal use can be curtailed by either natural gas, renewables, or nuclear power, it is all but certain given the scale of use today that replacing coal will require a combination of all these options.

In the lands of energy, realism is a required starting point. For emerging and developing economies, the two most carbon-rich fuels, oil and coal, are typically default choices. Why is this true? Oil still has no real alternatives in transport, especially on land. Coal, however, has many competitors – natural gas, hydro, solar, wind, and nuclear – so its advantages must seem strong to governments and firms in developing nations. They do. It is cheap, abundant in many countries, and has simple infrastructure needs. It lacks the price volatility common to natural gas, the site limitations of hydropower, and the weather-dependency of hydro, wind, and solar. Some of this might be countered if there were a price put on carbon, e.g. through taxes. But such efforts are rare in developing nations, where the goal has mainly been to increase electricity at the lowest cost. Government policy is thus hugely important. This is especially true in countries with large coal reserves – China, India, Indonesia, South Africa, Russia, Turkey, Kazakhstan, Poland, Vietnam, Colombia, among others. All these nations have committed to reducing carbon emissions. They are all signatories to the 2015 Paris Climate Agreement. It is far from certain, however, how much they are willing to turn away from the cheapest, most abundant fuel within their own borders.

Energy realism also requires that we deal with the question of whether renewable energy can solve the coal problem. Wouldn't that be the best solution? There are many who believe it is, and that governments every-where must concentrate policy and investment on a "green energy revolution." Since the late 1990s, wind and solar have grown at a remarkable rate. From tiny beginnings, they have risen to supply about 7 percent of global power by 2017 (mainly in advanced nations). How fast is this? Between 1950 and 1970, natural gas grew from about 2 percent of global electricity supply to 12 percent. Meanwhile, in the two decades after the first oil crisis (1973–1993) nuclear power rose from less than 1 percent to over 18 percent. This begs the question of why renewables haven't done better.

Status and Outlook for Renewable Energy

Renewables, like nuclear power, had their time of troubles. That they are now part of the energy mainstream defines an extraordinary turnaround from the past. The first oil crisis brought a period of high investment focused in part on renewables, especially solar. Leading such investment was the US, which devoted billions of dollars to energy R&D. This, however, was snuffed out after 1980 by the Reagan Administration and by government leaders in other nations who also favored "market forces" and "small government." Because of this, an entire generation of experts in renewable energy was mostly lost. Today, more than three-and-a-half decades later, the tables have reversed: solar and wind power exist in 160 nations, based on progress that has mostly been made since 2000.

This being said, renewable technologies have not had enough time to mature to where they can run the show. Indeed, it would be naïve to expect that they could. Attempts to push them into such a global role are both disloyal to fact and unfair to the technologies themselves. The reasons are several. Major challenges faced by these sources in the early 2000s have not been fully solved. Among them: high cost, low efficiency, large footprint, low predictability, short life span, and variable generation (intermittency). A wrinkle also comes from the almost universal tendency in developing nations to smile at wind and solar but embrace hydropower as a renewable source.[2]

Space is limited to discuss all these points in detail. Only a few key realities can be mentioned. Costs, to be sure, have fallen enormously. But in 2017, forms of financial assistance like loan guarantees, feed-in tariffs, renewable-only auctions, and outright subsidies remain the rule. This is especially true for utility-scale solar, purported to be the game-changer to help eliminate coal. While it is true that other sources receive government support in various forms, that for renewables has been especially high and has not yet succeeded in making them fully competitive. This will almost certainly change; progress in cost reduction will continue, though materials and labor may place a limit on this. A problem here is that the expense of integrating solar and wind into the grid isn't often included in cited costs. Neither is the necessity for backup

---

[2] The debate over whether hydropower, especially involving large dams, should be considered "renewable" is unresolved. Because dams disrupt river and delta ecosystems, plus increase carbon emissions due to drowned and decaying vegetation, many experts now prefer to treat hydropower as a separate category. Others, however, focus more exclusively on the energy aspects of hydro, claiming these are renewed by natural processes. An objection to this is that periods of serious drought, which have increased and will increase more due to climate change, can greatly lower and even eliminate the energy production of hydro stations. It is for both reasons that this book does not include hydro in the "renewables" category.

sources of power that fill in when sun and wind aren't available. At present, nations like Denmark and Germany that have installed large amounts of renewable capacity can keep things stable by drawing on the regional European grid, which has much reliable power from other countries that utilize nuclear, natural gas, and coal.

Discussions of efficiency, meanwhile, point to actual performance. The essential metric is capacity factor (CF), the amount of power produced as a percentage of total installed capacity. In 2016, the average CFs for various technologies were as follows: 10–20 percent for solar photovoltaics (PV), i.e. solar panels; 20–30 percent for solar thermal (concentrated solar power); 25–30 percent for wind; 35–45 percent for hydropower; 45–60 percent for fossil fuels (coal and natural gas); 45–60 percent for biomass; 65–75 percent for geothermal; and 80–90 percent for nuclear power [8]. Not surprisingly, low CF means that wind and solar need large amounts of land to generate power at utility scale. This gives them a comparatively large environmental footprint. An example: a 3,500-acre (1,400 ha) nuclear plant with 5.6 GW capacity can be matched in capacity by building fourteen solar-thermal plants, *each* needing around 3,000 acres (1,200 ha) to produce 400 MW.[3] If we now consider CF, we find the nuclear plant will be typically run at 90 percent of total capacity, producing 5.04 GW. To match this, at a CF of 30 percent, another 12.5 solar plants would be needed, making twenty-six-and-a-half in all.

Another consideration are the sites for solar. They cover the ground with panels or heliostats (special mirrors) and so remove it from other uses. They change the local ecology by blocking sunlight and require clearing of plants, rocks, and other natural material. Wind farms need even more land, but allow for other uses like agriculture. They aren't universally appreciated for their aesthetics, and in some areas they have required the cutting of trees and building of roads. This doesn't make them environmentally disastrous or anything like it. But they do have real impacts. Consider Sweden's Markbygden Wind Farm in the northern part of the country, largest in Europe [9]. Planned for 1,100 turbines (~4 GW capacity) spread over 450 km² (111,200 acres, 174 mi²), the project has involved road construction and tree clearing in an area of reindeer herding by indigenous Sámi people, who strongly oppose it [10]. Such problems aren't unique. Markbygden Wind Farm, a key project for Sweden's plans to lower emissions, taps into deep-seated, long-term grievances by the

---

[3] The two projects here compared are the Barakah Nuclear Power Station in the United Arab Emirates (see this book, Chapter 9) and the Ivanpah Solar Generating Station in the Mojave Desert of Southern California (details: http://www.nrel.gov/csp/solarpaces/project_detail.cfm/projectID=62

Sámi against loss of land to government and industry. As wind farms increase in scale, their land needs bring them inevitably into conflict with certain groups. No less than natural gas or coal plants, wind and solar farms are industrial facilities. Their land challenges involve more than simple nimbyism.

What about low predictability in power production? This can be partly solved by day-ahead weather forecasting. Related methods, based on computer modelling and known as "ensemble forecasting," rely on massive amounts of data, in turn reliant on good historical weather and climate information [11]. Such methods can be quite accurate, though never without uncertainties. But with their data and computing needs, they are largely confined to advanced nations and will be a challenge elsewhere for some time.

As for lifespan, testing by the US National Renewable Energy Laboratory (NREL) indicates a "useful life" for photovoltaics of twenty-five to forty years and wind turbines, twenty to twenty-five years [12]. These are estimates, of course; solar and wind farms using twenty-first century technology are still young. Not until the mid-late 2020s will there be enough data to accurately evaluate lifespan, by which time, the technology will have advanced. Solar panels degrade due to chemical changes in their material, particularly where large temperature variations occur. They are usually given a twenty-twenty-five-year warranty, but NREL tests show that in temperate climates they can probably last forty years.[4] Even so, their longevity does not entirely compete with fossil fuel, hydro, and nuclear plants. These have proven lifespans of thirty to sixty years and more. New nuclear plants are designed for sixty to eighty years, while a growing number of older plants with forty-year design life have been relicensed for sixty years. Wind turbines, meanwhile, are subject to mechanical stresses that wear rotors and internal parts, reducing performance. Their lifespan is commonly judged to be twenty to twenty-five years, with the former number deemed more likely as an average. While some studies have shown an average lifespan lower than this, in the range of thirteen to fifteen years, this is not considered accurate for the industry as a whole. Nonetheless, replacing turbines or solar panels at twenty-year intervals would more than double and possibly even triple costs during the lifetime of a nuclear plant. Such frequent replacement also challenges the idea of a sustainable energy system built of renewable sources alone.

---

[4] Panel degradation can vary from about 0.2 percent per year to over 1 percent, with severe climates (desert, subarctic) or stormy years causing the most rapid decline in performance and annual decline tending to increase with time. Commercial solar companies provide product warranties of twenty to twenty-five years for 80 percent or higher of a panel's rated power. The figure of 80 percent is generally taken as beginning of "failure," since the panel may not be able to achieve its rated capacity any longer.

Variability has been one of the biggest concerns for integrating renewable power generation. Major up and down fluctuations in power, caused by the intermittent nature of sun and wind, require major adjustments for grid stability. The most common way to deal with this is "curtailment," an approach used since the birth of the grid itself. It means cutting power from one or more sources when a surplus occurs. It is done by temporarily turning off some solar panels or wind turbines or other sources, like natural gas or hydro, both of which can be raised or lowered quickly. Whatever source is curtailed loses money, however, so there can be challenges. Avoiding curtailment might be achieved by upgrading the grid, building more transmission lines, and improving interconnectedness; this way, renewable power could be spread to different geographic areas [13]. Adding "smart grid" technology that allows for demand-response rebalancing on a moment-to-moment basis is another approach [14] and is slowly happening. New storage technologies that allow power generated during hours of good wind and sun to be retrieved later are yet another answer to variability. But commercial (affordable) solutions on a utility scale are still lacking. As a result, large wind or solar plants needed reliable back-up, usually from gas or nuclear generation. The idea of using connections within and among regional grids to gain coverage at all hours – for example, selling surplus wind power generated in Denmark to Spain, where a deficit exists, or sending solar power generated in Central Asia to Europe, where it is night – is an ad hoc solution whose reliability still can't be guaranteed without a huge amount of over-capacity (there will still be good and bad days even regionally).

None of these methods is a cure. A fundamental point is that renewables introduce new burdens for any grid system. The more these sources grow in scale, the more accommodations must be made. To be sure, this was always to be expected with intermittent sources. Moreover, some of the adjustments required by renewables will only make the grid better, much better in fact, if we are talking about transmission, interconnection, and "smart" technology. But while some of this makes absolute sense, there is always the matter of who will pay for it, which returns us to the larger context.

Rich, technologically advanced countries have the resources to do some of this. Most developing nations do not. From the viewpoint of these nations, renewable sources begin by costing more, producing less power, needing more land, lasting a relatively short time, and requiring special adjustments. Grids in these countries are often limited, ageing (first built in colonial times), and fragile. There may be frequent breaks in transmission (Pakistan), widespread theft of power (India), near-annual storms that cut power (Southeast Asia).

Renewables can solve none of these evils and may even contribute to them. Very often grids must be improved before renewables can be added and integrated. Cost again rears its head.

Advances have been made by solar micro-grids, built for villages or other small communities. In some cases, these have been quite successful, as in East Africa, while in other areas, like India, success has been mixed [15–16]. There is hope that such efforts will help millions in rural areas rise out of energy poverty and "leapfrog" traditional sources. But micro-grids can do little for the megacities and other urban areas where the vast majority of people in developing nations will be living by 2040. In these places, trillions of dollars are needed to build and power the full-scale grids required [17].

For more than a decade, Germany has pursued an ambitious plan to heighten the role of renewable energy. Known as *Energiewende* (Energy Shift), its ultimate goal is to increase renewables to 80 percent of all energy use by 2050. Fukushima led to public pressure on the government to close nine of its seventeen nuclear plants, thus about 10 percent of all power, with the remaining eight to be closed by 2022. National goals were then set at 35 percent of all power from renewables by the year 2020. This was never going to be possible. Officials soon realized Germany's industrial economy couldn't do without its main sources of reliable power, nuclear and coal. Thus, a choice had to be made. A strong tradition of antinuclearism made this easy, but brought difficult consequences. Expanding coal use to fill the gap left by nuclear closures meant that a zero-carbon source was traded for the most polluting, high-emitting fuel. Most of the coal at issue, moreover, was lignite, or "brown coal," whose emissions are worst of all. Most lignite comes from vast open-pit strip mines that release huge amounts of methane, thus increasing the climate impact. The overall effect is that Germany's decline in emissions stalled (no overall decrease between 2011 and 2015) [18]. The government refused to admit that shutting nuclear plants had any negative impact and, to save face, tried to slap a "climate fee" on the very coal plants it had chosen to keep open. This lit a firestorm in trade union protests; the fee was withdrawn [19]. Meantime, due to heavy subsidies for renewables, German households have been paying more than twice as much for their electricity as their neighbors, the French, who have made nuclear the core of their power system [20].

No doubt the Germans will recover and begin to reduce emissions in earnest again, though they stand little chance of achieving their goals for 2020. The gap created by shutting down nine reactors was not so huge after all. But let us be frank. They grew renewables at the expense of nuclear while not significantly reducing either coal in particular or fossil fuels in general. This shows that renewable energy is no less politicized than nuclear power; in some ways, it is more so. As we have mentioned elsewhere in this book, renewable energy is about much more than climate change. It is also about a social vision of cleaner, less industrialized, smaller scale civilization. In this regard, we might note that Germany defines one of the very few nations in the world that might be able to make *Energiewende* work. It has the resources, the expertise, the social and political consensus to do so. But equally important, its electricity demand has largely peaked, it has no megacities, and its population is the least urbanized of any large nation in Western Europe. This means that it is not a model, not for many wealthy nations but not at all for the developing world.

Despite hopes and dreams that a "green energy revolution" will take over the world in a few short decades, no serious analysis today shows anything like this happening. The most non-hydro renewables are expected to do by 2040 is about 15 percent to 20 percent of world power generation, and even this will not be easy to achieve. Moreover, it will likely be heavily concentrated in wealthy nations, including China and possibly (and ironically) oil-rich places like those in the Persian Gulf. Not, however, in Africa, South and Southeast Asia, much of Latin America, where the demand for power will grow. Renewable energy needs more time before it is ready to run a significant part of the world. It is certainly not the lone answer to climate change. No such answer exists, except perhaps human extinction. Yet impelled by the sense that the world is running out of time, encouraged by the progress that has so quickly been made in the renewable domain, many will continue to find in renewable sources a solution that doesn't exist and whose perception requires exaggerating their capabilities. In this way, more is being asked of these technologies, and claimed on their behalf, than they can deliver.

The healthiest, most profitable way to look at renewables today is as an essential part of humanity's noncarbon energy shift (*Unverkohlenwende*). This places them together with nuclear power, a certain amount of hydropower, biogas, and geothermal power (a hugely undervalued renewable source), all of which can deliver baseload electricity. Diversity of source types make for a more robust, dependable, and adaptable energy system. Proposals for using renewables only lead to impossible ideas about dealing with climate change, air pollution, energy poverty, security, and urbanization all at once. One such idea, for example, involves hundreds of millions of rooftop solar arrays, millions of wind farms, many tens of thousands of wave-energy systems (whose technology is not yet commercialized), and more [21]. Such plans are no more realistic as actual roadmaps than the notion of the world building a hundred or more nuclear reactors per year to mid-century. Scenarios like these are perhaps most worthy for revealing how much actually needs to be done to decarbonize our energy systems. In real-world terms, however, they are fantasies, no more helpful to achievable goals than proposing that everyone in the world stop eating meat and grow their own food. If the world is truly serious about climate change, lethal pollution, and bringing electricity to a great many who do not yet have it, practical solutions are needed that emerge from something other than computer models.

Demand for Electricity: Choice of Sources

Most of the world is energy poor. This isn't a relative statement. There are few chances for a country to advance economically if its people remain bound to the burning of wood and animal dung. Energy poverty is real, objective, and comes with inexorable effects in the domains of food, water, disease, life expectancy, and opportunity. Most of all, energy poverty means lack of reliable power. Consider for a moment what electricity can bring: light, at all times and without indoor pollution; clean water that is pumped into homes, not hauled from a well kilometers away; appliances to clean, wash, sanitize, cook (again, no indoor pollution); modern hospitals, medicines, and healthcare; computers and digital information and all this means; modern schools and equipment; refrigeration to preserve food, liquids, and medicines; entertainment and contact with the greater world.

In most areas of energy poverty, women and girls are the energy providers. According to WHO, more than two billion of them are the ones who must collect wood and other biomass for the home, build fires, tend them, cook over them, heat and dry with them, and therefore breathe their smoke and waste gases, especially indoors. They are also the ones, therefore, most impacted by the particulate matter and other pollutants. They are more vulnerable to lung cancer, chronic obstructive pulmonary disease, stroke, and suppressed immune systems. Reliable power is thus something more than an improvement in lifestyle for these people: in sufficient quantity, it is a kind of liberation into better health and welfare. Adding to this is the situation in sub-Saharan Africa, where one of the most frequent killers of women is cervical cancer. Caused by the human papillomavirus (HPV), this kind of cancer has a high survival rate if it is diagnosed early, for example by a Pap Smear, and treated by radiation therapy often combined with chemotherapy. It can also be prevented by a vaccine known as Gardasil, which, like many vaccines, must be refrigerated for storage.

Energy poverty, especially power poverty, cannot be solved by microgrids, village solar, or diesel generators. It requires massive amounts of supply, much of it available at all hours of every day (modern healthcare is impossible without this). In truth, there are not many sources able to provide this kind of baseload supply.

At this point in history, the countries where poorer people live, and where hundreds of millions of other people live who are less poor and on the verge of joining the global middle class, have governments that are deciding what fuels will power their future. Much advice has been given, not least from western nations via the historic 2015 agreement at COP21 [21]. But, as we have repeatedly said, there are other issues for developing nations when it comes to energy choices.

Decision makers in these nations have focused on three principal options for power generation: coal, natural gas, and nuclear power. While they also include renewables in their calculus, these sources (wind and solar mainly) have thus far been given a secondary role. The reasons are fairly straightforward and come back to what has been said above. Most nations in the global south have greater solar resources than wind, and solar technologies remain expensive, especially at utility scale. They also require a great deal more land than other sources yet do not deliver as much power per acre or facility. With the possible exception of biomass (which has its own environmental challenges), renewables can't satisfy the fundamental need in these nations for power that is reliable at all times.[5] Finally, the fragile, often undeveloped state of national grids in these nations make it much more difficult to integrate variable sources [22].

To date, in fact, coal has been the default for electricity, especially in Asia. To understand why requires that we view things from the desk of policy makers in these countries. First, we are dealing with limited capital. Power plants are among the most costly facilities to build, so we need to invite foreign financing whose investors will want low-risk projects. Globally speaking, coal remains the cheapest, most abundant fuel with a secure international market and delivery system. On this basis alone, the attractions are strong. Coal plants can also be built quickly (two to four years), at fairly low cost, and with one key advantage: their fuel being delivered by rail and road, thus infrastructure that already exists in many cases. Against such considerations, then, climate and pollution concerns are weighed. Countries are building their power systems at a time, as we've mentioned, when the social and environmental costs of coal still have little effect on the market price. Carbon taxes or cap-and-trade systems exist in a number of nations, true enough,. Yet most of these efforts have been in wealthy nations. Moreover, most have been tenuous, temporary, or priced so

---

[5] Some nations, due to their geology, could develop geothermal resources for reliable generation. This, however, is the exception and, in any case, has not been favored by foreign investors nearly as much as wind and solar.

that the disincentives for using coal aren't strong enough to make a large difference. Pricing carbon thus far has not been sufficient to weaken the many attractions of coal we have described [23].

The only noncarbon source able to reasonably satisfy most of these attractions is nuclear power. And here we mean advanced nuclear, Gen III and later. Hydropower and geothermal can do this too, but these resources do not exist for all countries; hydro, moreover, is vulnerable to periods of drought. Nuclear, above other options, is the nonfossil source most able to replace coal, indeed all fossil fuels, in large-scale power generation. Renewables then have the ability to meet demand in distributed areas where smaller-scale generation is more appropriate, e.g. rural areas, towns, smaller cities. This returns us to the matter of urbanization.

The best solution yet found for poverty is economic development. Such development has always been concentrated in cities. Asian countries today, from Korea to Cambodia, reveal a pattern of rising GDP/capita with increasing percentage of the population living in urban areas [24]. Until now, the growth of cities has meant a growth in fossil fuel use. The question of whether this will be true in the future has immense importance. By mid-century, around 6.5 billion people will be urbanites. They will live in expanded older cities, in new mega cities (>10 million), in smaller secondary cities (0.5–3 million), and still smaller and newer cities of 50,000 to 500,000 [25]. Urban growth will make for urban diversity. Such diversity, with its evolving blend of traditional, new, and unexpected city types, will come with surging power demands, as digital technology becomes ever-more central to daily life [26]. The task of the present is to ensure these demands will be met in different ways than in the past.

Nuclear Power Today – An Overview

In the decades between 1965 and 1986, the number of civilian nuclear reactors rose from a mere handful to 424. By the 90s, however, following the Chernobyl accident, the industry had gone into a "brown out" phase, where it would remain for over two decades. Many orders for reactors were cancelled, and new builds essentially stopped, with a few notable exceptions (France). After 1990, the number of reactors grew less than 5 percent, reaching 435 in 2010.

The lack of new reactors meant a rise in coal use for the US and an end to its rapid decline in Europe. US emissions, which had been fairly consistent since the early 1970s, grew by thirty percent between 1986 and 2006, with a sixty-percent increase from the power sector alone. Had public fear not helped kill the growth of nuclear power, there could be two-and-a-half or three times as many nuclear plants in OECD nations, whose total emissions would be forty to fifty percent less. With the introduction of wind and solar on a significant scale after year 2000, the world would have easily dealt with climate change, preventing a two degrees C increase in average near-surface temperatures.

Nonetheless, nuclear managed a positive outcome. To meet power demands, the CF of existing plants was gradually raised from around 60 percent in 1990 to over 90 percent by the early 2000s, thus preventing even greater use of coal. Had only half of the 120 reactors cancelled in the wake of Three Mile Island been built, coal in the US could have been a fraction of what it became in 2007, when it produced 50 percent of all electricity [27].

Another effect of the nuclear brown out was a drop in funding for related R&D and a halt in bringing to market newer, advanced reactors. Even in 2010, the great majority of plants worldwide were based on technology more than thirty years old. But even more important, the turn away from nuclear meant a huge loss in human capital – scientists and engineers trained for the nuclear industry who left the field. Many colleges and universities in advanced nations ended their programs in nuclear engineering, dismantling scholarships, labs, and research reactors they had used for training [28–29].

But in other parts of the world, 2010 proved a key moment. That year, the number of new reactors being built went above sixty, the highest figure since the 1980s. This number fell after the Fukushima accident in 2011, but quickly rebounded to over seventy by 2014 [30]. The bulk of these new builds were in China, India, South Korea, and Russia. Yet among the 170+ planned reactors listed in 2014, many were in nations that did not yet have nuclear programs, like Bangladesh, Egypt, Indonesia, Jordan, and Turkey. By 2016, companies from Japan, South Korea, Canada, France, Russia, and China were competing for shares of a global market that promised to reach over $700 billion by the mid-to-late 2020s [31]. Russia's state-run firm, Rosatom, was particularly success-ful in gaining new contracts and agreements with dozens of nonnuclear nations [32]. This has led some observers to fret over a coming "Russian nuclear empire" [33] or, in a less dramatic key, a new period of nuclear diplomacy with Russia in a particularly strong position. Whether Moscow will be able to fund all these projects or not seems a question worth asking, to say the least. Not in doubt, however, is the strong interest in these nonnuclear nations to build nuclear plants.

Looking again at reported figures for future reactors, we find a total of 542 planned and proposed in May of 2017, with an additional sixty under construction. Over 80 percent of these reactors are in non-OECD countries (without Russia, it is 70 percent). A list that includes nations both actively pursuing and strongly interested in a nuclear program would look like this:

– *Middle East and North Africa*: Turkey,* United Arab Emirates,* Saudi Arabia,* Qatar, Kuwait, Yemen, Israel, Syria, Jordan,* Egypt,* Tunisia, Libya, Algeria, Morocco, Sudan.

– *SubSaharan Africa*: Ghana,* Nigeria,* Senegal, Niger, * Kenya,* Uganda, Tanzania, Namibia, Zambia, South Africa+.

– *Latin America*: Cuba, Chile, Ecuador, Venezuela, Bolivia, Peru, Paraguay.

– *Central and South Asia*: Azerbaijan, Georgia, Kazakhstan,* Mongolia, Bangladesh,* Sri Lanka

– *SE Asia*: Vietnam, Indonesia,* Philippines, Thailand,* Laos, Cambodia, Malaysia,* Singapore, Myanmar.

– Europe: Albania, Serbia, Croatia, Portugal, Norway, Belarus+, Poland,* Estonia, Latvia, Ireland [34–36].[6]

At present, nuclear accounts for 22 percent of power generation in Europe and the former Soviet Union, and 18 percent in North America. In no other region of the world is it above 4 percent. In the whole of East Asia, it is a mere 3.6 percent [37]. The total figure of 449 operable reactors in late 2016 included: 290 (65 percent) pressurized light-water, seventy-eight boiling light-water (18 percent) and forty-nine (11 percent) pressurized heavy-water reactors. There are also twenty-nine graphite-moderated reactors and three fast breeders, the longest running (since 1980) in Russia, the most recent (since 2014) in China. The average age of all operable reactors is twenty-five years. Age, in fact, is not a great concern, as many existing plants have been upgraded and uprated, able to be run at higher capacities. As a result, they have been re-licensed from forty to sixty year lifespans, a trend that will continue (as noted previously, the forty-year "design life" was assigned for financial reasons, not engineering ones).

Meanwhile, the average national share of nuclear in electricity generation is about 25 percent. Figures range from 77 percent for France down to 3 percent for China and Brazil. If we look at a simple plot of such percentages, from low to high, we see an interesting pattern: a group at 2–6 percent, followed by a jump to a second group at 16–20 percent, then another jump to 30–38 percent, and then a final leap from 42 percent to 77 percent. What this suggests – and a detailed look at national nuclear programs confirms this – is that each distinct group defines a set of limits having to do with economics, political challenges, domestic energy resources, and public acceptance. As we will see below, this is well borne out by China, which has relied on domestic coal above all else. For Brazil, where more than three-quarters of electricity comes from hydropower, the vulnerability this poses to climate change, especially after a drought in the

---

[6] *Country that has decided to begin a nuclear power program.
+Country that currently has nuclear power program

early 2000s caused major power shortages, has altered policy toward more nuclear. For Iran (2 percent) and South Africa (5 percent), international politics have been determining factors, but so have domestic resources, natural gas in Iran and coal in South Africa. Iran, however, would prefer to save its natural gas for export, while South Africa, in the midst of an electricity crisis, is pursuing policies to diversify its sources and utilize more of its abundant uranium. All of these nations have plans to double or even triple their nuclear programs.

Until recently, Europe, Japan, Canada, and the US were the world leaders in reactor technology. This title is fast passing to Asian nations like South Korea and China. In 2014–15, Europe had a total of 129 operating reactors, representing 28 percent of all electricity generated in the EU and *50 percent of its low/ zero carbon electricity* [38]. But in 2017, only four of the sixty-five new reactors under construction worldwide were in the EU (France, Finland, and Slovakia). As in the US, with ninety-nine operating reactors and five being built, the outlook for any major expansion is mixed. Opportunity certainly exists; hundreds of coal plants will likely be closed by 2025 [39]. But while the climate argument for nuclear gained strength in the 2000s, it stalled and even reversed in some countries after Fukushima.

Much attention has been given the small number of countries that have decided to phase-out nuclear power. Such attention has greatly exaggerated the importance of such decisions, as if they represented a global trend. In fact, the very opposite seems at least as likely. Germany's position we have already reviewed. Italy and Austria voted after Fukushima to remain nonnuclear, while Spain (seven reactors, 20 percent of power generation), Switzerland (five reactors, 38 percent), and Belgium (seven reactors, 50 percent) have decided on no new builds, including replacements for existing reactors – but with the possibility of relicensing. Sweden (47 percent electricity production from nuclear) had earlier determined to begin a nuclear phaseout in 1980, after Three Mile Island. But in 2010 Parliament repealed the decision. The country is determined to close its four oldest reactors by 2020 and, as of 2016, has no plans to build any new ones. Its five other reactors, however, are licensed to operate until the 2040s. By any measure, the most extensive plan announced for reduction in nuclear power has been put forward by none other than the French. In 2015, after much debate (and as a lead up to the COP21 Paris climate talks), the French government passed the Energy Transition for Green Growth Act, mandating a rise in renewable-generated electricity (wind and solar primarily) to 40 percent by 2030 and a lowering of nuclear to 50 percent by 2025 [40]. Put forward by François Hollande's Socialist Party government, the plan must be said to have an uncertain future under future administrations. It is based in part on technologies that do not yet exist: mass storage of wind/solar generated power; cheap offshore wind power; low-priced and higher efficiency solar PV. and proposes to shut down a large part of the country's existing zero-emissions power generation.

France's new policy, however, is representative in some ways. In most advanced nations, nuclear must now compete not only with natural gas (extremely cheap in North America), but with aggressive preference given wind and solar. Total upfront expenses of siting, insuring, licensing, financing, and then building a new nuclear power station in the West are on the order of $5–$8 billion, higher when delays happen. Such costs are far lower in Asian nations, where cooperative arrangements between government and industry are able to help keep new plants in the range of $3–$5 billion and at times even lower (see Chapter 8). Deregulated markets in the West also make it more difficult for nuclear to compete, given investor's demand for more near-term profits and the subsidies given to renewables (we see also the discussion of costs in Chapter 8). Certainly there are ways to reduce costs for nuclear plants in Europe and the US, for example by the repeated use of one design for multiple power plants and related modular construction. Yet an even more important option involves new, flexible financing options based on major investment from abroad in partnership with European firms. Nations that have shown interest in such investment include China, South Korea, Japan, and Russia. Such options for Asian nations to help build power plants in wealthy states of the EU marks another part of nuclear power's globalization.

At the last, the strong turn to renewables and away from nuclear power by a handful of European nations will not become a model for the rest of the world, least of all developing countries. If there are difficulties in betting on renewable technologies and prices that do not yet exist, the real problem lies in conceiving renewable and nuclear energy as antagonists. Efforts to find compatibility between renewables and nuclear will do much more to lower emissions world-wide than a showdown between the two noncarbon sources with the greatest capability to reduce emissions

Energy Security: Why So Important?

Defining "energy security" is both challenging and simple. It has typically meant having an adequate supply of energy sources from reliable suppliers at affordable prices [41]. Such a definition applies to importers, not exporters (who want reserves in hand, reliable demand, and prices neither too high nor too low). But that seems acceptable, given that most of the world's nations *are* importers. Added to the definition today, meantime, is the need to avoid environmental and climate harm to the degree feasible. Energy supply should therefore be sufficient, reliable, affordable, and nondamaging.

Yet, if truth be our goal, we would admit that few nations have been consistently loyal to such principles. Instead, they have tended to follow a more crude and naïve logic: maximize domestic resources, minimize imports. We might recall US President Jimmy Carter's famous words in 1977 that dealing with an energy crisis was "the moral equivalent of war." He was referring to the 1973 oil crisis, and he believed – as did a great many others – that he was not exaggerating the case. His solution was a national program for conservation and expanded development of America's own conventional and unconventional sources [42]. Carter expressed what many nations still pursue as a goal, based on the idea that energy is a zero-sum game. Imports mean unwanted dependence, insecurity in an insecure world. In this view, the only real security is total self-reliance, life on an island, surrounded by walls. It is a view that may appear odd, after decades of globalization. It is also absurdly self-centered and ignorant of economic reality. Backing out of international markets, trade relationships, multi-lateral networks into energy isolation hardly writes a formula for security. On the contrary. Interconnection with other nations, interdependence with capable partners, is what brings higher stability and resilience. Europe's own Continental Synchronous Grid provides a good example, serving more than 400 million people in 24 nations that are able to back each other up to varying degrees. The Nordic regional grid is another example, with Norway, Sweden, Finland, and partly Denmark able to make up for each other's limits and insufficiencies. Indeed, these regional networks have been absolutely essential to the buildup of intermittent renewable energy in Germany and Denmark, among others.

How, then, does nuclear power fit in to this frame? The formula of angst does not apply. Nuclear plants provide very large amounts of noncarbon electricity that can be relied upon and therefore helps stabilize national and international grid networks. They are the workhorses of any system and thus add much security. There is another dimension to this. For most developing nations, the technology, the fuel, even in some cases the engineers and operators are (will be) all imported, and yet this very fact makes nuclear power more secure. Launching or expanding a nuclear program today follows a process that engages international help and oversight at every step. None of the 168 nations belonging to the IAEA are left to create such a program on their own. A core document, *Milestones in the Development of a National Infrastructure for Nuclear Power* (updated 2015) lays out the basics of how a nuclear program should begin and assures any government that international expertise will be available to assist in all aspects so that everything is done correctly [43]. It makes clear the commitments to the public, the international community, contracted partners, and to the IAEA itself, that must be accepted and fulfilled. It helps familiarize officials with the economic dimensions, the nuclear fuels market, and related safeguards. And, in the wake of Fukushima, the IAEA system also ensures there is a plan in place for responding to an accident. Thus, with regard to energy production, the level of security is very high, indeed perhaps higher than for any other source.[7]

What about world uranium supplies? These are not a concern. There is no OPEC of uranium; nor will there be. Largest proven resources are to be found in Australia, Canada, Kazakhstan, South Africa, Niger, the US, and Brazil, hardly a group likely to forge a cartel. As for resources, uranium is discussed in terms of "reasonably assured resources" (RAR) and "inferred resources" (IR). The numbers involved are never fixed and final; they depend on price, technology, and interpreted geology. "Reasonably assured" means that portion of a deposit that has a high possibility of being extracted at a profit, using today's prices and technology. "Inferred," on the other hand, extends this up to a higher price limit. Every few years, the Nuclear Energy Agency (NEA) and the IAEA put out a thick report known as the "Red Book" that details world uranium statistics. The 2016 version shows that since the late 1990s, both RAR and IR have grown considerably, due to new exploration and re-evaluation of known deposits [44].

None of this includes the possibility of extracting uranium, and thorium as well, from sea water. The approach has been the subject of much recent research, particularly in the US. Current technology has developed an advanced, reusable absorbent material for uranium that could be deployed directly in the ocean without any need for pumping or filtering of seawater [45]. Capabilities at present are on the order of 1 kg uranium extracted for every 167 kg of absorbent over a period of about 55–60 days. Not yet commercial, absorbent technology will remain an R&D target in the US and possibly several other nations (the general approach can be used for other metals as well). The main idea underlying such work is to make nuclear power fully sustainable for the long-term. Given such a context, in fact, uranium, and thorium as well, qualify for the term "renewable," since erosional debris carried by rivers continually resupply the oceans with these (and other) metals to the tune of millions of tons per year.

Despite all this good news, however, some observers point to one possible security concern. Russia's state-run company, Rosatom, is an integrated

---

[7] Discussion of security issues related to nuclear weapons and related materials are not discussed here. They are taken up in full in Chapter 11 where nonproliferation is covered in detail.

nuclear monopoly, meaning that it does everything from create fuel to build and operate reactors. Rosatom is not a dominant supplier of fuel; its share of the global market (6 percent in 2014) pales in comparison to companies in Kazakhstan (32 percent), Canada (16 percent), and Australia (11 percent). The concern is with Rosatom's plan to be the world leader in reactor exports. This includes a bold, unique and, for some, worrying approach known as "build-own-operate" (BOO). Under this arrangement, Rosatom would finance the building, operating, and decommissioning of reactors. It would also provide and reclaim the fuel, while selling the electricity at a long-term guaranteed price, sharing profits with the host country. Also included is the training of local engineers in how to operate and maintain a power station, thus in a sense completing both the fuel cycle and human capital side.

The idea seems aimed at countries without an existing nuclear program and who might have trouble financing one. Russia (Rosatom) has other financing arrangements that it has used with China, Belarus, and Hungary, including long-term loans, shared ownership, and direct payment. Rosatom has routinely demanded that its fuel be part of the deal. Altogether, Russia offers a diverse portfolio of financing options, a potent sign of flexibility in a new era of nuclear globalization. It is the BOO, however, that tends to scare observers. This is because it can nuclearize pretty much *any* nation, including those in conflict zones or with anti-Western regimes. Thus far, nothing like this has occurred. In December 2015, Rosatom stated it had orders for thirty-four reactors in thirteen nations, at a cost of about $5 billion each [46]. The countries included Turkey, Vietnam, Belarus, India, China, Bangladesh, Armenia, Finland, and Jordan, with other agreements (not contracts) signed by Egypt, Nigeria, Indonesia, Algeria, and Myanmar. Moscow's control over Rosatom does suggest political entanglements for any nation solely dependent on a BOO arrangement. The solution, of course, is to avoid such mono-dependence.

Realistically, Rosatom's eyes are likely to be far bigger than its wallet. This is particularly true as long as Russia remains under economic sanctions for its annexation of Crimea. But the mismatch between ambition and capital would still exist even if sanctions were lifted. But whether Russia can carry out such a program or not doesn't really matter. It will have robust competition from other exporters, not least China, which does have the capital to move things forward. Chinese plans to build nuclear power plants as part of the country's new "One Belt, One Road" program, aimed at areas from Pakistan to Europe, are at least as ambitious and likely better funded [47].

Nuclear Power Today: Case Studies

China

In its untamed rush to industrialize, China has played the part of Faust on a grand stage. Beginning in 1978s, when China's leader, Deng Xiaoping, first declared "to get rich is glorious," the country began to modernize its economy, turning to its coal reserves as the dominant energy source. As China's economy grew, so did its coal use, by orders of magnitude. In 1985, consumption stood at about 700 million tons per year. A decade later it had more than doubled to 1.5 Mt, surpassing even the US But in the 2000s, coal consumption tripled in a single decade, reaching 4 billion tons per year in 2013 [48], roughly equal to the rest of the world combined. Despite rising amounts of hydropower, natural gas, and wind/solar, coal accounted for over 70 percent of electricity consumed.

Air pollution in both urban and rural areas was already a serious problem in the 1990s. To keep prices of electricity and goods low, Chinese industries and companies were allowed to burn cheaper, low quality coal without pollution controls. This largely continued for years after 2000, when the country went into high gear for heavy industrialization. Chinese cities were soon choked with thick, dense smog for many months of the year. In January, temperature inversions caused such smog to spread over all of eastern China, covering millions of square kilometers in the North China Plain where more than 600 million people live. Rising public outrage forced the government to take measures against the problem, yet the declared "war on pollution," achieved only minor improvement [49–50]. From 2000 to 2015, cardiovascular and respiratory diseases rose rapidly, prematurely ending as many as 10 million lives [51–54]. China's Faustian bargain has traded public health and the environment for "energy security."

It is within this frame that China's turn to nuclear power should be understood. In May of 2017, the country had thirty-six operable reactors (~4 percent of electricity production), twenty-one under construction, another forty-two planned, and 174 more proposed, a total of 273 [55–56]. This is more than twice the number the US had in 1997, when its reactor fleet was at a maximum (107). China's plan is to have about 135 reactors operating by 2030, expanding capacity from about 29 GW up to 150 GW. This will require bringing online six to seven new reactors each year. But this could well be a minimum. The total could be quite a bit larger if small- and moderate-capacity reactors (300–700 MW) and small modular designs (<100 MW) are built. The majority of China's reactors, according to stated plans, will employ Gen III and III+ technology and will thus represent a new nuclear era.

Yet China also seeks to be an unrivalled testing ground for new reactor designs, including Gen IV technologies. Its program includes building a series of demonstration reactors, in collaboration with scientists and engineers from other nations, which, if successful, will then be scaled up to full size. At this writing, four pilot Gen IV reactors have already been built or are in construction (2016). The first was tested as successful in 2011, when the China National Nuclear Corporation connected to the grid its fast-breeder reactor, known as CEFR (China Experimental Fast Reactor). Built with Russian help, this small-scale, 20 MW unit employing a pool-type design and liquid sodium coolant has been tested at full power and is considered a key project for future development [57]. Recall that sodium-cooled fast reactors (SFR) are one of the Gen IV technologies able to burn spent fuel (actinides in U-Pu metal matrix). At a larger scale are two new plants employing high-temperature gas-cooled reactors planned for 2017–2020. Using pebble bed fuel, these cannot suffer melt down or large releases of radioactive material. The first plant, in Shandong province, includes two 105-MW reactors, while the second, in Jiangxi province, will be larger, producing 600 MW for the grid. Both plants, like the SFR, will serve as pilots for commercial units and for export. China has already signed a preliminary agreement for gas-cooled reactor technology with Saudi Arabia [58].

Smaller scale designs define yet another focus. China has an interest not only in small modular reactors (SMR) but also, following Russia's lead (and using its assistance), floating nuclear power plants. Several different designs and sizes of SMRs are planned, including 140 MWe, 100 MWe, and 60 MWe versions. In 2014, China's Atomic Energy Authority and Russia's state-run firm Rosatom signed an agreement to build several or more floating nuclear plants with cogeneration capability (process heat for local industry, buildings, or desalination) [59]. For many nuclear engineers, an especially important SMR project will be China's molten salt-cooled reactors (MSR), one of which is intended to demonstrate the thorium-uranium fuel cycle. These are planned as a direct result of collaboration between the US Oak Ridge Laboratories and the Shanghai Institute of Applied Physics, where the reactors are being built. Plans include completion and testing of both prototypes by about 2020 and then construction of full-scale commercial plants by 2030 [60]. Thorium MSR technology has a particular appeal, since it not only reduces nuclear waste enormously, but fulfills China's own fundamental concept of energy security. That is, thorium enjoys high abundance in the country as a "waste" product of rare earth metal processing, China being the global leader in the export of these metals.

Observers of the Chinese nuclear program have mentioned a long-term goal of up to 350 GW capacity or more by mid-century [61]. Nuclear now constitutes a mere 3.6 percent of total power generation; were this to rise to the current average in nations with nuclear, 25 percent, and China's power demand to rise only 50 percent by 2050 (from 1,360 GW capacity to 1,950 GW), this would mean a growth in nuclear power capacity to roughly 510 GW. In either case, China could easily have 400–500 power reactors operating [62] by mid-century, with a global export market for Gen IV technology as well. This scale of expansion may sound extraordinary, even radical. Yet it accords well with the original government-industry plan for nuclear power in the US, which proposed building as many as 1,000 reactors in an overall system that was to use breeder reactors as the domestic fuel source for plutonium-consuming power plants able to provide nearly all US electricity for centuries.

In brief, China has already begun to act as the world's proving ground for advanced reactor technologies. But perhaps the most striking thing to the western eye in this program isn't its scale, complexity, or expense. It might be the simple fact that China routinely includes nuclear power in the same "clean energy" category as wind, solar, and other renewables. That a country soon to become the global leader in nuclear power views noncarbon energy in this way might offer a worthwhile view to follow.

Turkey

With a population nearing 80 million and few domestic energy resources other than coal and hydropower, Turkey finds itself in a challenging position. Energy consumption more than doubled between 2001 and 2015, and similar growth could continue for another decade or even two. People have been moving into cities at a high rate, with the urban population rising from around 60 percent to more than 73 percent during this same time period [63]. The most urgent demand is for electricity. Lack of sufficient power has restrained economic growth, and Ankara's goal to become one of the world's top twenty economies is unthinkable without dramatic increases in the power supply.

Since the country has little oil or gas, it has to import up to 98 percent of these sources. They are a source of real insecurity. Turkey's coal reserves are mainly lignite, whose use has surged. In spite of higher emissions and air pollution, the government plans to exploit this further for electricity. Hydropower, the other domestic source, is also slated for expansion. Only half of the economic resource for hydro has been developed, but even so it will not be able to provide more than about 25–30 percent of all electricity by the mid-2020s [64]. In the past, Turkey focused on the use of natural gas too, only recently turning toward renewables and nuclear. Growing use of wind and solar power is planned, but this will require upgrading the transmission system to handle the variability in power levels. Though the grid is now connected to the Continental Europe system, it has some major challenges made clear in 2015 by a major blackout, caused by local oversupply, that affected nearly the entire country.

Natural gas, meanwhile, has become the country's largest energy source, which is not to the government's liking. Imports have grown more than 100 percent since the early 2000s, sending much currency out of the country. Dependence on pipelines from Iraq and Iran have led to disruptions due to insurgent sabotage. At such times, Turkey has turned to Russia to make up the loss, finding itself by 2015 dependent on Russian imports for nearly 60 percent of all gas. New insecurities then arrived, when the shooting down of a Russian plane over Turkish airspace in 2015 led Moscow to retaliate by raising prices and threatening to cancel a major new pipeline ("Turkish Stream") [65].

Ankara understands the nation's energy predicament and has set new goals to favor energy security. It defines such security as broadening its sources of imports to spread geopolitical risk and increasing its level of energy self-reliance. It has stated such goals in more specific terms: diversify supply routes and source countries, raising levels of energy efficiency, growing the share of renewables, and launching a large nuclear program [66]. The most rapid development, however, has focused on building new coal power plants, which has outstripped everything else. Ankara gave its support to eighty new plants in 2015, all of them intended to burn domestic lignite [67]. Few plants have pollution controls, and growing air problems in many towns and cities has prompted major medical organizations in the country to state their concerns over public health [68].

Turkey's air pollution, in fact, has reached levels that are among the worst in the OECD. While verifiable data is not available for all years, existing information suggests that as many as 30,000 people die prematurely due to particulate matter and ground-level ozone (the latter from vehicles) [69–70]. Large portions of the country have $PM_{2.5}$ and PM_{10} readings in the 50–100 $\mu g/m^3$, well above safe levels designated by WHO. Ankara and Istanbul, with a combined population of over 20 million people, have figures in the range of 60–200 $\mu g/m^3$, considered to be unsafe [71]. At this writing, natural gas accounts for about 45 percent of the country's total power generation, with hydro and coal each providing 25 percent and renewables (wind, solar, geothermal, and biowaste) another 4 percent. High dependence on gas imports from Russia are a situation the government would like to change. Turkey's other main sources of natural gas include Iran (20 percent), Azerbaijan (10 percent), and Algeria (8 percent) [72].

Not lost on officials are concerns regarding these other suppliers. Most pressing are two geopolitical realities. First is a highly uncertain future for the Persian Gulf region, due to violent extremism and existential conflict between Iran and Saudi Arabia, plus other Gulf Sunni states (Kuwait, Qatar, UAE). Second is the so-called frozen war between Azerbaijan and Armenia, with continued fighting over the enclave of Nagorno-Karabakh. An outbreak of hostilities in either region would be extremely damaging to energy security.

Added to these realities are the nuclear power programs of Iran, Jordan, and United Arab Emirates, plus agreements signed by the Saudis and by Egypt to separately explore starting nuclear energy programs. This makes it imperative for a growing regional power like Turkey to begin such a program itself. Finally, Turkey has uranium resources. Reasons for Turkey to pursue nuclear power are therefore many and irrefutable. Indeed, they stand as a potent example for why this energy source is now expanding outside the West. These reasons can be summarized like this: an urgent need for electricity; growing pollution levels; a commitment to lower emissions; geopolitical uncertainties among import suppliers; and Turkey's own ambition to secure its place as a regional power. Without doubt, these are potent arguments. They are arguments, moreover, that do not lack relevance in other parts of the world.

In fact, Turkey made efforts to begin a nuclear power program decades ago. For various reasons, however, attempts in the 1970s, 80s, 90s, and 2000s never succeeded, though some progressed quite far. What did emerge was the choice of two sites that remain attractive because of access to water, lack of earthquake activity, and small population. These sites – Akkuyu on the Mediterranean Sea (Mersin Province) and Sinop, a headland on the Black Sea (Sinop Province)— are now designated for nuclear plant construction. A third site is at Igneada (Kirklareli Province), also on the Black Sea and close to Istanbul. The government's goal is to have 100 GW online by the 2030s.

Akkuyu would be first. An agreement was signed with Rosatom in 2010, based on BOO terms. Four PWRs are to be built, with 4.8 GW total capacity to be online before 2025. The reactors are to be VVER-1200, a Russian Gen III+ model that benefits from post-Fukushima design ideas, including seismic upgrades that make the unit able to withstand a 9.0 quake. The VVER-1200 also has enhanced containment, both active and passive safety systems, and backup generators located in individual buildings to prevent simultaneous malfunction. There is also equipment to eliminate hydrogen gas buildup and, in case of a meltdown, to catch and contain the core melt itself.

The contract, meanwhile, includes a fifteen-year power purchase agreement at a fixed price (12.35 US cents per kWh). This is for half of the electricity generated, the rest to be sold by Rosatom on the open market. The plant is estimated to be paid off in fifteen years, after which Rosatom will pay the Turkish government 20 percent of all profits from the continued sale of electricity. Actual construction will be carried out not by Russian contractors but mostly by Turkish firms that should be able to complete about 90 percent of the buildings and half of the interior installations. Ground for the first Akkuyu reactor was broken in mid-2015, but then work was halted. Later in the year, Rosatom announced it was interested in selling up to a 49 percent share in the project. Reasons were conflict between the Turkish and Russian governments (noted above) and the sad state of the Russian economy, due to low oil prices and economic sanctions [73].

Sinop, on the other hand, was awarded to a joint venture involving Mitsubishi Heavy Industries (Japan) and Areva (France). A Japanese company was chosen due to the greater earthquake risk at Sinop, which lies roughly 80 km from the North Anatolia Fault, an active structure similar to the San Andreas Fault. Like Akkuyu, the plant will include four PWRs, each with 1.15 GW capacity (~4.5 GW total). A Gen III+ design known as ATMEA1 will be used for all four units. Advances in this design include: long operating time between refuelings, both passive and active safety systems, and the ability to raise or lower power output rapidly (load-following), at 5 percent per minute. As with all Gen III+ light water designs, it prevents hydrogen buildup and catches/contains any core melt [74]. Contract terms are a BOT (build-operate-transfer) arrangement, with Japanese and French construction, a French utility to operate, and the Turkish Electricity Generation Corporation (EUAS) to own 49 percent. Financing by the joint venture will involve 70 percent debt and 30 percent equity, with each reactor predicted to cost around $4–5 billion. A twenty-year agreement has a Turkish utility selling the power at an average price of 10.8 cents/kWh [75].

For the third site, Igneada, Turkey has signed an agreement with the State Nuclear Power Technology Corp. of China. This firm plans to employ Westinghouse technology to build four more PWRs, with a total capacity of over 5 GW. These will have similar advanced systems to those of the ATMEA1 and VVER-1200.

Each of the three sites, if built, will add large amounts of reliable power to the grid at key locations not far from industries and cities. Like the UAE at its Barakah power station, Turkey is helping to set a precedent for nations with large power needs in concentrated areas. Multiple reactors of one design at a site greatly simplifies the process of evaluating, approving, licensing, and building a power station. It saves a good deal of land, which means cost and, often, public concern. The vulnerability of multiple reactors to a single natural event, like an earthquake, or attack, has been taken into account. It bears repeating that such considerations are rarely applied to oil refineries and oil/gas storage areas; nor are they routinely applied to hydropower dams.

Ghana

In late 2015, a group of eminent leaders called the Africa Progress Panel came together to discuss the continent's worrisome situation regarding energy, health, and climate change. Well over 800 million people, they noted, live either without power or with so little it barely lifts them above subsistence. The introductory words of the report these leaders assembled on the subject are striking in their clarity of what is at stake:

> Nowhere are the threads connecting energy, climate and development more evident than in Africa. No region has made a smaller contribution to climate change. Yet Africa will pay the highest price for failure to avert a global climate catastrophe. Meanwhile, the region's energy systems are underpowered, inefficient and unequal. Energy deficits act as a brake on economic growth, job creation and poverty reduction, and they reinforce inequalities linked to wealth, gender and the rural-urban divide [76].

All of these points come together in the sub-Saharan nations. It is stunning to think that in 2015, the forty-eight nations of sub-Saharan Africa, with 850 million people, had no more than 90 GW total at their disposal. This is the amount for just 27 million people in two US states, Illinois and Pennsylvania. Half of the 90 GW, moreover, is concentrated in South Africa, the one country with nuclear power [77]. Use of the term "energy deficit" in the passage above is diplomatic. Africa lags the rest of the world in many factors of development, from manufacturing to medicine, and at the base this is a poverty of modern energy, above all electricity. After acquiring independence in the 1950s and 60s, most sub-Saharan nations remained non-industrial, dependent on traditional wood and charcoal. Hydropower was the main power source developed by colonial occupiers, with smaller amounts of oil and coal power. The beginnings of rapid economic development in the 1990s led to major advances but ran into a wall by the 2010s, as demand for electricity wholly outstripped supply.

Choices facing sub-Saharan nations are clear but not simple. To grow their electricity base to a level that has some chance of meeting actual demand, while keeping energy security and affordability in sight, they find themselves faced with choosing between hydropower, coal, and nuclear. Wind and solar are targeted by nearly every country but cannot provide the reliable baseload needed for economic development and urban centers. Nations with oil and gas have other options, particularly gas. Yet this requires an extra realm of infrastructure, such as pipelines, storage tanks, and more.

Ghana counts as fortunate. Though GDP per capita remains fairly low ($4,300 in 2015), it has abundant natural resources, including natural gas, and hydropower. Yet it is looking to begin a nuclear power program as part of the solution to its long-term needs. Ghana had early plans along nuclear lines. This was in 1961, only four years after the country's independence from Britain. Ghana's first president, Kwame Nkrumah, sided with the Soviet Union and China in the Cold War, and an early agreement with the Soviets was to provide a research reactor and training of engineers. The project came to a sudden end in 1966 due to a military coup. A second attempt in the early 70s, involving a small research reactor from Germany, met the same fate. Only after a new Constitution was approved in 1992 did interest in nuclear power revive. A research reactor was finally built in 1995 by the China Institute of Atomic Energy and, though quite small, has served as a training and research center ever since.

Ghana has depended on hydropower for the majority of its electricity. Three dams were built in the 1950s and 1960s, the largest on the Volta River with a capacity of 1.04 GW. Starting in the late 1990s, however, drought began to affect river discharge, decreasing the amount of power. An oil-fueled plant was built in 2000 to address the problem, but a more prolonged dry period set in after 2003, creating a crisis. Two smaller (~200 MW) thermal plants, one burning oil, the other gas, were constructed between 2007 and 2010, but these too were not enough to match demand. Realizing a more long-term solution was needed, the government took up the nuclear idea once more in 2007. By this time, the country produced roughly 1.8 GW of grid power, with the industrial sector consuming 60 percent of this and the residential sector another 35 percent [78]. Only 55 percent of the population had power for most or all of the day, with another 30 percent at half a day, and 15 percent only an hour or two. Diesel generators were widely used off-grid, but fuel became expensive starting in 2010 when world oil prices rose to around $100 per barrel.

A motive to increase the use of natural gas came on the wings of offshore oil and gas discoveries in Ghanaian waters in the late 2000s. This has provided Ghana with the potential for significant new export revenue and rise in domestic energy production. But development in this direction has been slow and halting. Foreign investment in new generation has been difficult to acquire. Meanwhile, mechanical problems have affected hydro generators and, reportedly, the oil-burning power plant, adding to the power shortage [79]. Much discontent spread among the populace, as electricity prices were raised and inflation went over 18 percent, stalling the rapid rise in GDP and living standards [80]. Though Ghana has been one of the half-dozen or so sub-Saharan countries to make real progress in bringing electricity to its people, it has been unable to sustain such improvement and carry it further. The country's population (28 million) continues to grow rapidly and to urbanize, adding to power. The country benefits from resources like gold, bauxite (aluminum), and timber but here, too, development has been held back or restricted because of the power shortage. A number of industries, businesses, and commercial enterprises have been unable to operate consistently without reliable electricity, putting many out of work.

The government has announced ambitious goals since 2000, intended to move more than half the population out of subsistence lifestyles dependent on fuelwood [81]. But such goals have proven difficult to achieve. Several new dams and the Nzema solar (PV) plant of 155 MW capacity, plus rooftop solar programs, will help [82]. Officials have also established plans (2016) to install new capacity from wind and biomass, raising nonhydro renewables further. But with power demand rising at 7 percent to 8 percent a year, these additions will not be enough, despite happy predictions.

A study of three baseload sources at different capacity levels was done in 2008, comparing hydro, natural gas, and nuclear. The results showed generation costs, measured in cents per kWh, as follows: hydro, 6.9–11.4; natural gas combined-cycle, 5–5.5; and nuclear, 4–6. The nuclear estimate relates to a Westinghouse model AP 600, a small-to-moderate size reactor with 600 MW capacity, chosen because a larger unit would surpass the capabilities of the existing grid. Thus, the reactor is viewed as a first step, with larger units to come later as the grid expands. The AP 600 is a Gen III pressurized water reactor with a sixty-year life, enhanced, passive safety features, and a simplified overall design that allows for quicker construction and easier operation and maintenance, thus lower costs. Refueling can be done on an eighteen- or twenty-four-month cycle, with only seventeen days downtime, allowing the plant to operate for more than 93 percent of each cycle. Westinghouse designed the reactor in the late 1990s and received final approval for it from the US Nuclear Regulatory Commission in 1998 [83].

At this writing, Ghana has made major progress in building a nuclear program, with IAEA guidance, in terms of a regulatory framework and human capital. This is being done in preparation for its first reactor, now planned for 2018–2020. By 2016, Ghana had in place legal infrastructure, as well as an emergency preparedness system, approved by the IAEA. Also in collaboration with the IAEA, Ghana has established a Graduate School of Nuclear and Allied Sciences to train masters and PhD students. Training is able to take advantage of the noted research reactor as well as a new ion beam accelerator for analyzing minerals and other materials. Students and workers have also been chosen for IAEA fellowships and training courses.

It seems evident, in other words, that Ghana is serious about becoming the second sub-Saharan state with a commercial nuclear power plant. But just as much, it is pursuing a path in which nuclear, hydro, solar/wind, and natural gas all work together to lower emissions and prevent use of coal. More than two decades of successful democratic government and political stability provide needed support for the fulfillment of this effort. Its success would no doubt add to the ambitions of other nations in the region who are contemplating their own programs or already have them underway.

Conclusions: The Need for Noncarbon Energy

China and Ghana represent two ends of a spectrum. Their core goals overlap quite closely, which is why they can be seen as part of a continuum. They wish to create sustainable energy systems, in electricity most of all, with "sustainable" defined not as an absolutist, fossil fuels-only or renewables-only condition, but rather an evolving balance of sources that rises toward noncarbon dominance. For both countries, nuclear power will be a key part of this and will do more as well. It will create new international connections and also obligations to work cooperatively in the new global nuclear order. It will bring scientific and technological benefits, not only in power generation but in medicine and industry. It will also advance both nations in the realm of human capital.

The state of the world guarantees that the global energy future will not be like the past. It must change, and it is in the process of changing now. The danger is that it will change on the basis of ideas that limit what can be actually done about climate change.

We now face the possibility of untold abundance in fossil fuels, a truth that has arrived exactly at the moment when the world must lower its addiction to carbon energy. A counterbalance comes from the reality that renewable energy has moved firmly into the mainstream, at long last, and will continue to expand. They now have a presence in 75 percent of the world's nations. It is for these reasons that their capabilities should not be exaggerated. Renewables are helping lead an energy transition, but they cannot do it alone. Nuclear power is the other and larger counterweight to carbon overdependence.

Undoubtedly the "return to coal" defines the most troubling aspect of the new energy era. This fuel, well known for its toxic effects, has declined in most western nations. Yet, because it is cheap and abundant in many nations, its global use soared over the past two decades. And while it has become common to blame China for this, such a view greatly oversimplifies the reality. Dozens of other nations have increased their use as well. This is why forecasts predict a continued rise in coal use in the developing world, with a peak not coming until 2030 [84]. Such a rise would mean massive amounts of carbon added to the atmosphere, lethal levels of air pollution in many countries, and millions upon millions of premature deaths and future illnesses. In every way, coal is the costliest of all energy options. But for nations that are poor and without energy resources, it will be a temptation. The only thing capable of persuading officials to make a different choice is another option that is also affordable but that offers superior benefits in security, emissions, and generated power.

We have seen in China, Turkey, and Ghana examples of nations making such a choice. Profoundly different in levels of development and natural resources, these countries have selected the nuclear option for the climate, pollution, security, and power advantages it offers. China's aggressive turn to hydro, renewables, and nuclear power speaks to the reality of a major nation in severe environmental crisis. This is the true reason why China can be model to other nations. Turkey's situation is one of coal use and geopolitical uncertainty; nuclear power addresses both issues. Ghana begins with more basic needs but intends to "leapfrog" coal by choosing nuclear and renewables. Ghana's lesson is that hydropower as a renewable base-load source by nature is vulnerable. Drier conditions are now forecast for large areas of the planet, including parts of India and Pakistan; North, West, and Southern Africa; Turkey and the Caucasus; the Caspian region; and much of South America [85]. Hydropower, in other words, can render a society less energy secure.

Nuclear power provides a superior option, but also one that does not rule out any other low/noncarbon alternative. A nation that elects to build a large-scale wind farm along with a Gen III+ nuclear plant is not breaking any rules or playing "a double game." Only those who view such choices as a matter of green ideology rather than serving human needs would see things differently. This conclusion can be denied but not refuted. A new nuclear order, based on advanced technology and emerging from cooperative diplomacy and international collaboration, will prove itself indispensable to humanity's long-term energy transition.

References

[1] BP, Energy Outlook to 2035 – 2016 Edition (Internet). *British Petroleum.* Available from: www.bp.com/en/global/corporate/energy-economics/energy-outlook-2035/energy-outlook-downloads.html
[2] Exxon, Outlook for Energy: A View to 2040 (Internet), *ExxonMobil* (2016). Available from: http://cdn.exxonmobil.com/~/media/global/files/outlook-for-energy/2016/2016-outlook-for-energy.pdf

[3] US Energy Information Administration (EIA), International Energy Outlook – Report DOE/EIA-0484 (Internet), *Department of Energy* (2016). Available from: www.eia.gov/forecasts/ieo/pdf/0484(2016).pdf

[4] International Energy Agency IEA, World Energy Outlook 2016 (Internet). Available from: www.iea.org/newsroom/news/2016/november/world-energy-out look-2016.html

[5] BP, Energy Outlook to 2035.

[6] US Energy Information Administration (EIA), International Energy Outlook, 2016 (Internet), *Department of Energy* (May 2016), Table 5.1. Available from: www.eia.gov/forecasts/ieo/pdf/0484(2016).pdf

[7] International Energy Agency (IEA), World Energy Outlook 2015, (November 18, 2015), 278.

[8] US Energy Information Administration (EIA), Electric Generator Capacity Factors Vary Widely Across the World (Internet), *Department of Energy* (8 September 2015). Available from: www.eia.gov/todayinenergy/detail.cfm?id=22832

[9] Markbygden (Internet), *Svevind*. Available from: https://svevind.se/Markbygden

[10] Sámi Opposition to Giant Wind Farms (Internet), *Eye on the Arctic, Radio Sweden (News in English)* (November 25, 2010). Available from: http://sverigesradio.se/sida/artikel.aspx?programid=2054&artikel=4176996

[11] I. Roulstone and J. Norbury, *Invisible in the Storm: The Role of Mathematics in Understanding Weather* (Princeton, NJ: Princeton University Press, 2015).

[12] National Renewable Energy Laboratory (NREL), Useful Life (Internet), *US Department of Energy, Office of Energy Efficiency and Renewable Energy*. Available from: www.nrel.gov/analysis/tech_footprint.html

[13] E. Martinot, Renewables: Global Futures Report (Internet), *Renewable Energy Policy Network for the 21st Century and Institute for Sustainable Energy Policies* (2013). Available from: www.martinot.info/REN21_GFR_2013.pdf

[14] L. Bird, J. Cochran, and X. Wang, Wind and Solar Energy Curtailment: Experience and Practices in the United States (Internet), *National Renewable Energy Laboratory, US Department of Energy, Office of Energy Efficiency and Renewable Energy* (March 2014). Available from: www.nrel.gov/docs/fy14osti/60983.pdf

[15] F. Pearce, African Lights: Microgrids are Bringing Power to Rural Kenya (Internet). *Yale Environment 360* (October 27, 2015). Available from: http://e360.yale.edu/feature/african_lights_microgrids_are_bringing_power_to_rural_kenya/2924/

[16] F. Pearce, In Rural India, Solar-Powered Microgrids Show Mixed Success (Internet), *Yale Environment 360* (January 14, 2016). Available from: http://e360.yale.edu/feature/in_rural_india_solar-powered_microgrids_show_mixed_success/2948/

[17] International Energy Agency (IEA), Electricity Transmission and Distribution – IEA ETSAP Technology Brief E12 (Internet), *Energy Technology Systems Analysis Program* (April 2014). Available from: http://iea-etsap.org/web/Highlights%20PDF/E12_el-t&d_KV_Apr2014_GSOK%201.pdf

[18] M. Darby, German CO2 Emissions Rise 1 Percent in 2015 (Internet), *Climate Home* (March 14, 2016). Available from: www.climatechangenews.com/2016/03/14/german-co2-emissions-rise-10-million-tonnes-in-2015/

[19] C. Schwägerl, Brown Coal Wins a Reprieve in Germany's Transition to a Green Future (Internet), *The Guardian* (July 7, 2015). Available from: www.thegu ardian.com/environment/2015/jul/07/brown-coal-wins-a-reprieve-in-germanys-transition-to-a-green-future

[20] When the Wind Blows (Internet). *The Economist*, (November 28, 2015). Available from: www.eia.gov/todayinenergy/detail.cfm?id=19951

[21] M. Jacobson and M. Delucchi, Providing All Global Energy with Wind, Water, and Solar Power, Part I: Technologies, Energy Resources, Quantities and Areas of Infrastructure, and Materials. *Energy Policy* 39 (2011), 1154–1169.

[21] Analysis: The Final Paris Climate Deal (Internet), *Carbon Brief* (December 15, 2015). Available from: www.carbonbrief.org/analysis-the-final-paris-climate-deal

[22] M. C. Thurber, Coal, Gas, or Nuclear: Asia's Inconvenient Energy Choice (Internet), *2016 Summit Working Paper, Pacific Energy Summit, National Bureau of Asian Research*. Available from: http://www.nbr.org/research/activity.aspx?id=696

[23] BP, Statistical Review of World Energy 2016 (Internet). *BP*. Available from: www.bp.com/en/global/corporate/energy-economics/statistical-review-of-world-energy.html

[24] The World Bank Group East Asia's Changing Urban Landscape (Internet), (January 2015), Figure 1.1. Available from: https://openknowledge.worldbank.org/handle/10986/21159

[25] International Organization for Migration *World Migration Report 2015* (2015).

[26] J. Beal and S. Fox, *Cities and Development* (London: Routledge, 2009).

[27] L. Parker and M. Holt, Nuclear Power: Outlook for New US Reactors (Internet), *CRS Report for Congress, Congressional Research Service*, (March 9, 2007). Available from: www.fas.org/sgp/crs/misc/RL33442.pdf

[28] R. Twombly, Undergraduate Enrollment Drop Threatens Nuclear Science (Internet), *The Scientist* (October 12, 1992). Available from: www.the-scientist.com/?articles.view/articleNo/12531/title/Undergraduate-Enrollment-Drop-Threatens-Nuclear-Science/

[29] M. Wald, Nuclear Programs are Losing Ground on Campus (Internet), *The New York Times* (28 June, 2001). Available from: www.nytimes.com/2001/06/28/us/nuclear-programs-are-losing-ground-on-campus.html

[30] World Nuclear Association (WNA), World Nuclear Power Reactors & Uranium Requirements (Internet). Available from: www.world-nuclear.org/information-library/facts-and-figures/world-nuclear-power-reactors-and-uranium-requireme.aspx

[31] C. T. Whitman and S. Cheney, Why the US Should Export Nuclear Power (Internet), *Fortune*, (October 22, 2015). Available from: http://fortune.com/2015/10/22/nuclear-energy-technology-u-s-russia-china/

[32] Russia: Exporting Influence, One Nuclear Reactor at a Time (Internet). *Stratfor* (7 October 2015). Available from: www.stratfor.com/analysis/russia-exporting-influence-one-nuclear-reactor-time.

[33] I. Armstrong, Russia Is Creating a Global Nuclear Power Empire (Internet), *Global Risk Insights* (October 29, 2015). Available from: http://globalriskin sights.com/2015/10/russia-is-creating-a-global-nuclear-power-empire/

[34] World Nuclear Association (WNA), Emerging Nuclear Energy Countries (Internet), (February 2016). Available from: www.world-nuclear.org/informa tion-library/country-profiles/others/emerging-nuclear-energy-countries.aspx;

[35] R. Luke, Africa Banking on Nuclear Power (Internet), *OilPrice* (October 1, 2015). Available from: http://oilprice.com/Alternative-Energy/Nuclear-Power/Africa-Banking-On-Nuclear-Power.html

[36] International Atomic Energy Agency (IAEA), Country Nuclear Power Profiles (Internet). Available from: https://cnpp.iaea.org/pages/index.htm

[37] World Development Indicators: Electricity Production, Sources, and Access (Internet), *World Bank*. Available from: http://wdi.worldbank.org/table/3.7

[38] Electricity Production and Supply Statistics (Internet), *Eurostat*, (May 2015). Available from: http://ec.europa.eu/eurostat/statistics-explained/index.php/Electricity_production_and_supply_statistics

[39] Institute for Energy Research Impact of EPA's Regulatory Assault on Power Plants (Internet), (October 2014). Available from: http://instituteforenergyresearch.org/wp-content/uploads/2014/10/Power-Plant-Updates-Final.pdf

[40] G. De Clercq, French Industry Body Backs Ambitious Renewable Energy Targets (Internet), *Reuters* (April 15, 2016). Available from: http://uk.reuters.com/article/france-renewables-idUKL5N17I3ES

[41] International Energy Agency (IEA), What is energy security? (Internet). Available from: www.iea.org/topics/energysecurity/subtopics/whatisenergysecurity/

[42] President J. Carter, Proposed Energy Policy (Internet), (April 18, 1977). Available from: www.pbs.org/wgbh/americanexperience/features/primary-resources/carter-energy/

[43] International Atomic Energy Agency (IAEA), The IAEA Milestones Approach (Internet). Available from: www.iaea.org/NuclearPower/Infrastructure/milestone/index.html

[44] International Atomic Energy Agency (IAEA), Uranium 2016: Resources, Production and Demand (The Red Book) (Internet). Available from: http://www.oecd-nea.org/ndd/pubs/2016/7301-uranium-2016.pdf

[45] Oak Ridge National Laboratory Advances in extracting uranium from seawater announced in special issue (Internet). (April 21, 2016). Available from: www.ornl.gov/news/advances-extracting-uranium-seawater-announced-special-issue

[46] World Nuclear Association (WNA), Russia (Internet). (April 2016). Available from: www.world-nuclear.org/information-library/country-profiles/countries-o-s/russia-nuclear-power.aspx

[47] China's Nuclear Plant Makers Seek New Markets Along the Ancient Silk Road into Asia, Europe, Africa and Middle East (Internet), *South China Morning Post* (4 April 2016). Available from: www.scmp.com/news/china/economy/article/1933488/chinas-nuclear-plant-makers-seek-new-markets-along-ancient-silk

[48] US Energy Information Administration, Department of Energy (EIA), China (Internet). Available from: www.eia.gov/beta/international/analysis.cfm?iso=CHN

[49] E. Saikawa, China's War on Air Pollution (Internet), *China Currents* 13:2 (October 14, 2014). Available from: www.chinacenter.net/2014/china_currents/13-2/chinas-war-on-air-pollution/

[50] E. Economy, *The River Runs Black: The Environmental Challenge to China's Future*, 2nd edn. (Ithaca, NY: Cornell University Press, 2010).

[51] M. Moore, China's 'Airpocalypse' Kills 350,000 to 500,000 Each Year (Internet), *Telegraph* (January 7, 2014). Available from: www.telegraph.co.uk/news/worldnews/asia/china/10555816/Chinas-airpocalypse-kills-350000-to-500000-each-year.html

[52] D. Levin, Study Links Polluted Air in China to 1.6 Million Deaths a Year (Internet), *The New York Times* (August 13, 2015). Available from: www.nytimes .com/2015/08/14/world/asia/study-links-polluted-air-in-china-to-1-6-million-deaths-a-year.html?_r=0

[53] M. Lelyveld, China Cuts Coal Mine Deaths, But Count in Doubt (Internet), *Economy Watch, Radio Free Asia* (March 16, 2015). Available from: www.rfa .org/english/commentaries/energy_watch/china-coal-deaths-03162015103452.html

[54] C. W. Yap, China's Coal Addition Brings Scourge of Black Lung (Internet), *Wall Street Journal* (December 15, 2014). Available from: www.wsj.com/articles/chi nas-coal-addiction-brings-scourge-of-black-lung-1418593741

[55] World Nuclear Association (WNA), World Nuclear Power Reactors and Uranium Requirements (Internet). Available from: www.world-nuclear.org/information-library/facts-and-figures/world-nuclear-power-reactors-and-uranium-requireme.aspx

[56] IAEA, China, People's Republic of (Internet). *Power Reactor Information System, IAEA.* Available from: www.iaea.org/pris/CountryStatistics/CountryDetails.aspx? current=CN

[57] Chinese Fast Reactor Completes Full-Power Test (Internet), *World Nuclear News* (December 19, 2014). Available from: www.world-nuclear-news.org/NN-Chinese-fast-reactor-completes-full-power-test-run-1912144.html

[58] R. Martin, China Could Have a Meltdown-Proof Nuclear Reactor Next Year (Internet), *Technology Review* (February 11, 2016). Available from: www.techno logyreview.com/s/542526/china-details-next-gen-nuclear-reactor-program/

[59] World Nuclear Association (WNA), Nuclear Power in China (Internet), Available from: www.world-nuclear.org/information-library/country-profiles/countries-a-f/ china-nuclear-power.aspx

[60] R. Martin, China Details Next-Gen Nuclear Reactor Program (Internet), *Technology Review* (October 16, 2015). Available from: www.technologyreview.com/s/542526/ china-details-next-gen-nuclear-reactor-program/

[61] A. Topf, China's $1 Trillion Nuclear Plan (Internet), *Oil Price* (December 27, 2015). Available from: http://oilprice.com/Alternative-Energy/Nuclear-Power/ Chinas-1-Trillion-Nuclear-Plan.html

[62] J. Conca, China Shows How to Build Nuclear Reactors Fast and Cheap (Internet), *Forbes* (October 22, 2015). Available from: www.forbes.com/sites/jamesconca/2015/ 10/22/china-shows-how-to-build-nuclear-reactors-fast-and-cheap/#53437c8b4d0b

[63] CIA, Turkey: People and Society (Internet), *The World Factbook, US Central Intelligence Agency* (2016). Available from: www.cia.gov/library/publications/ the-world-factbook/geos/tu.html

[64] International Hydropower Association, Turkey (Internet). Available from: www.hydropower.org/country-profiles/turkey

[65] N. Pakhomov, Gas Wars: Turkey Tries to Push Russia Aside (Internet), *The National Interest* (December 18, 2015). Available from: http://nationalinter est.org/feature/gas-wars-turkey-tries-push-russia-aside-14665

[66] Turkey's Energy Strategy (Internet), *Ministry of Foreign Affairs, Republic of Turkey* (2016). Available from: www.mfa.gov.tr/turkeys-energy-strategy.en.mfa

[67] D. Carrington, Is It Too Late to Stop Turkey's Cold Rush? (Internet), *The Guardian* (August 6, 2015). Available from: www.theguardian.com/environ ment/2015/aug/06/is-it-too-late-to-stop-turkeys-coal-rush

[68] Air Pollution and Health in Turkey: Facts, Figures, and Recommendations (Internet), *Health and Environment Alliance* (February 2015). Available from: http://env-health.org/IMG/pdf/150220_factsheet_air_and_health_turkey_en_final.pdf

[69] J. Lelieveld, J. S. Evans, M. Fnais, et. al., The Contribution of Outdoor Air Pollution Sources to Premature Mortality on a Global Scale. *Nature*, 525: 7569 (September 17, 2015), 367–372.

[70] O. Çapraz, B. Efe, and A. Deniz, Study on the Association between Air Pollution and Mortality in Istanbul, 2007–2012, *Atmospheric Pollution Research*, 7:1 (January 2016), 147–154.

[71] Air Pollution in Turkey: Real-time Air Quality Index Visual Map (Internet), *World Air Quality Index Project*. Available from: http://aqicn.org/city/turkey/marmara/istanbul/kadikoy/

[72] EIA, Turkey (Internet), *US Energy Information Administration, Department of Energy*. Available from: www.eia.gov/beta/international/analysis.cfm?iso=TUR

[73] N. Sahin, Rosatom to Sell 49 Percent of Akkuyu Nuclear Plant Due to Financial Issues (Internet), *Daily Sabah* (April 27, 2016). Available from: www.dailysabah.com/energy/2016/04/28/rosatom-to-sell-49-pct-of-akkuyu-nuclear-plant-due-to-financial-issues

[74] ATMEA, Status Report 99 – ATMEA1 (Internet), *Status Report for Advanced Nuclear Reactor Designs*. Available from: www.atmea-sas.com/ATMEA/liblocal/docs/ARIS%20ATMEA1.pdf

[75] 2 Japanese Companies Aim to Fund 30 Percent of Turkish Nuclear Project (Internet), *Nikkei Asian Review* (June 8, 2015). Available from: http://asia.nikkei.com/Business/Deals/2-Japanese-companies-aim-to-fund-30-of-Turkish-nuclear-project

[76] African Progress Panel, Power, People, Planet: Seizing Africa's Energy and Climate Opportunities (Internet), *African Progress Report* (2015), 14. Available from: http://app-cdn.acwupload.co.uk/wp-content/uploads/2015/06/APP_REPORT_2015_FINAL_low1.pdf

[77] International Energy Agency (IEA), Africa Energy Outlook (Internet), *World Energy Outlook Special Report*, (2014). Available from: www.iea.org/publications/freepublications/publication/WEO2014_AfricaEnergyOutlook.pdf

[78] Energy Commission of Ghana, National Energy Statistics, 2000–2013 (Internet), *Strategic Planning and Policy Division, Energy Commission of Ghana* (October 2014). Available from: www.energycom.gov.gh/files/ENERGY%20STATISTICS.pdf

[79] Ghana Electricity Crisis (dumsor) – The Causes, Disadvantages and Solutions (Internet), *AllAfrica* (March 5, 2015). Available from: http://allafrica.com/stories/201503051476.html

[80] Overview – Ghana (Internet), *The World Bank* (April 12, 2016). Available from: www.worldbank.org/en/country/ghana/overview

[81] Gov't Sets Ambitious Energy Targets (Internet), *GhanaWeb Business News* (August 4, 2014). Available from: www.ghanaweb.com/GhanaHomePage/business/Gov-t-sets-ambitious-energy-targets-319726

[82] Energy Commission, Ghana, 2015 Energy (Supply and Demand) Outlook for Ghana (Internet), (April, 2015). Available from: http://energycom.gov.gh/files/Energy%20Outlook%20for%20Ghana%20-%202015.pdf

[83] International Atomic Energy (IAEA), Status report 75 – Advanced Passive Pressurized Water Reactor (AP 600) (Internet), *Advanced Reactors Information System (ARIS)*. Available from: https://aris.iaea.org/sites/.%5CPDF%5CAP-600.pdf

[84] EIA, International Energy Outlook 2016.

[85] World Resources Institute, Aqueduct: Measuring and Mapping Water Risk (Internet). Available from: www.wri.org//our-work/project/aqueduct

10

The New Context: Global Climate Change

How We Got Here

The historic energy source was, of course, wood. Blazing wood fires warmed many a hearth throughout human history. This began to change in some locations during the sixteenth century, accelerating in the eighteenth century and hugely increasing after the onset of the industrial revolution around 1800. Before this energy needs were modest. Wood provided heat. The muscles of horses and other animals helped till the soil and provide short and medium distance transportation. For medium and long distance travel the power of wind enabled sails on ships to carry humans to every corner of the world. Water and wind provided the simple machines that ground the grain and pumped water for human consumption.

Coal has been known and used for three thousand years or more. But until relatively recently its use was marginal. It is the most plentiful fuel among the fossil fuel family and has the longest and most varied use. It has been put to limited use as a heating source since the time of the caveman. The Romans used it perhaps beginning around the time of the Common Era at least in some locations. London in the sixteenth century slowly began to switch to coal from wood as a heat source because as the city grew the area around it became deforested and wood became more and more expensive to transport. By the eighteenth-century coal became widely used in London, even among the rich who could afford bringing in wood for fuel from long distances, because it burned more cleanly and hotter than wood charcoal. But with the advent of the Industrial Revolution the overwhelming need for energy to operate the machines that were being invented caused coal to become a dominant world-wide supplier of energy.

In North America while the Hopi Indians in the southwestern United States had used coal for heating, cooking, and baking pottery, it was not widely used until its "rediscovery" by explorers in the seventeenth century. Commercial coal mines began operations in the 1740s in Virginia. During the first half of the nineteenth century coal was used to power steamships and railroad locomotives in the United States and elsewhere. Other uses for coal began to be found. By 1875 coke (made from coal) began to replace charcoal as the primary fuel for blast furnaces to make steel. In the 1880s coal was first used to generate electricity. But long after homes were being lighted by electricity produced by coal-fueled power plants; many of these homes were heated by coal-powered furnaces and had cooking stoves operated by coal. The electrification of America took a very long time and was not completed until the 1950s, some seventy years after it began in the 1880s [1].

By the late nineteenth century a new form of fuel began to catch on, petroleum, and later on a derivative, natural gas. By the end of the century oil processed into gasoline was powering the horseless carriage, the automobile. Henry Ford developed the assembly line of mass production; automobiles (or cars) became cheap. With the low-cost automobile and the spread of electricity modern industrial society in Europe and North America, later followed by Asia, was changed forever. Power plants were becoming larger and larger, until massive coal plants were widespread and hydroelectric dams, producing electricity by water pressure, were located in many places. The airplane soon appeared, consuming more petroleum made into airplane fuel, and the automobile connected cities making suburbs possible and thereby creating even more demand for energy. The economy, the society, became to a large degree fossil fuel-powered. Over a number of decades most of the rest of the world caught up with North America and Europe so that the world economy, became highly reliant on fossil fuels to produce the necessary energy to maintain the huge cities and burgeoning economies dependent on ever-increasing sources of power [2].

This brief overview of energy history is meant as background to a central point. Global climate change, as we have discovered, has originated from profound changes in the nature of civilization. These are changes that have come, in large part, from the growth and evolution of modern carbon energy. Such should not be taken as an accusation or indictment of the last 200 years but as a simple fact. Carbon energy is one of the bases for modern society as a whole, including all of its benefits and capabilities, including those allowing for change today. First coal, but even more oil and gas, are very rich sources of energy, and it can be viewed as inevitable that humanity would have at some point progressed to them from wood and animal dung. This is no less true than the truth that we must now evolve to the next, more advanced stage of energy generation and use, employing technology more than combustible natural resources. Such a transition will happen. Indeed, it is now well underway. We have noncarbon forms of energy production that are being used and advanced right now and will be in coming decades. We will certainly have other noncarbon forms in the future.

The context for this evolution is not innovation but global threat. Climate change is not something to "believe in" or "question" but to accept (or foolishly deny), like the heat of a stove when turned on. Levels of concern and anxiety that now exist range a good deal. Some experts express considerable alarm, while others are less fearful. A great majority of the scientific community is significantly worried, however, and has become more so with time. As these people are the ones who study, observe, analyze, discuss, and therefore live with climate change on a daily basis (we might compare them to the indigenous peoples of the Arctic, for whom global warming constitutes an exigent reality, even a presence), it makes sense to review what they are saying.

What follows, then, is a review of the relevant information that has come from scientific work, plus a selection of quoted material from it and from the writing of others who have been in close contact with such work. Nuclear power, though we do not discuss it very much here, has climate change as its new context. Such is also true for every other kind of energy source. But for nuclear, as for renewables, this context defines the possibility for rejuvenation in some nations, growth in others, and expansion into altogether new parts of the globe.

The Role of Carbon Energy

In 2014 coal combustion was the source of 29 percent of the energy produced world-wide, oil 31 percent, and natural gas 21 percent. Thus, more than 80 percent of the world's energy, fueling economies and societies worldwide, came from fossil fuels [3]. If we turn to electricity, we see that coal was used for no less than 41 percent of global power generation, far more than the next largest share, 22 percent for natural gas [4]. In short, a full century-and-a-half after the first power plants were built, the world still relies on the same core fuel for its most crucial form of energy, a fuel whose carbon emissions and levels of pollution are also highest of any source known.

Coal plants in the United States are the nation's top source of carbon dioxide (CO_2) emissions, while coal mines are the origin of significant methane emissions. In 2015 utility coal plants in the US sent into the atmosphere 1.4 billion tons of CO_2, with a typical plant generating some 3.5 million tons per year. Coal generated 34 percent of the electricity in the United States in 2015, down from 45 percent only five years earlier, but it remains the single largest air polluter [5]. In 2015 there were 427 operational coal plants in the United States with an average capacity of 540 megawatts [6].

A typical 500 megawatt coal plant in the United States produces per year:

- 3.7 million tons of carbon dioxide, the principal greenhouse gas;
- 10,000 tons of sulfur dioxide gas, the main cause of acid rain;
- 10,200 tons of nitrogen oxide, a major cause of smog;
- 500 tons of small particles which can damage lungs;
- 220 tons of hydrocarbons, another cause of smog;
- 720 tons of carbon monoxide, a poisonous gas and contributor to global warming;
- 120,000 tons of ash and 193,000 tons of sludge, the ash and sludge consist of many pollutants and toxic chemicals; and
- 225 pounds of arsenic, 114 pounds of lead, 4 pounds of cadmium, and many other toxic heavy metals, contaminating many lakes and rivers [7].

World electricity use is expected to more than double by the year 2030, and under current grid configurations much of that increase will be provided by the burning of greater amounts of coal. Every year a single 500-megawatt coal-fired plant sends up into the sky the same amount of carbon dioxide as do 750,000 cars. Coal combustion is responsible for a major share of the world's man-made carbon dioxide. Anyone who has been to China in recent years was exposed to the immense amount of air pollution that pervades most of eastern and its many cities China. As noted previously, such pollution is dangerus and even lethal. The smog it produces is so intense that it crosses the Pacific and creates a significant portion of the air pollution in California. Approximately 40 percent of the world's electricity is generated by coal, 22 percent by natural gas, and 4 percent by oil combustion. These fossil fuels pour huge quantities of soot, smoke, toxins, radionuclides, carbon dioxide, methane, and other gases into the atmosphere every day. Such greenhouse gases are creating climate change in the form of global warming widely interpreted to be responsible for lethal heat waves, violent storms, and rising sea levels that may come to threaten large parts of human civilization. It is understood that alternative energy sources much be developed and deployed in the very near future in order to achieve a predominately carbon free energy production sector to counter this alarming trend.

But how can we ever cut back on fossil fuels when our entire way of life depends so intimately on them? The US in 2016 consumed about 20 million barrels a day of a resource that powers just about every form of transportation.

To import the oil it demands, the United States in the past has sent hundreds of billions of dollars to the Middle East. Due to the development and wide use of fracking technology, much of the oil used in the United States is now being produced domestically. But, despite new car technologies such as hybrids, electric, and natural gas vehicles, consumption has not declined more than a few percent in the past decade. At the same time, US consumption of coal has declined considerably during this same time period but has been replaced mainly by natural gas, another fossil fuel. Though gas yields only about half the carbon and very little of the pollution that coal does, on a per-unit of energy basis, its use has grown to the point where, by 2016, its total emissions exceeded those from the country's 430 operating coal power plants. Yet, as we discussed in Chapters 1 and 8, coal has left – and very much continues to generate – a lethal legacy for many of the world's nations, including the US.

In the twenty-first century when these ill effects of fossil fuel use, especially coal and oil, are well known, and when technologies exist to greatly reduce them, there would seem no need whatsoever for this to continue. Yet it does for reasons we noted in Chapter 9 – economics, energy security, the desperate need for electricity, among them. Climate change has become an urgent global problem at the same historical moment that a majority of the world's poorer nations have launched major programs of modernization, but also before they have either the capital, technological capability, or the market incentives to employ what wealthy nations have developed to deal with the effects of carbon energy use. This includes pollution controls; stricter pollution regulations; energy-efficient architecture, transportation and agriculture; conservation; and intelligent, long-term energy planning that could all make a big difference locally and globally.

Most of this adds to costs or restricts behavior. Thus, it has been often rejected or ignored. But that is changing, as the impacts of climate change have become more clear and serious. There are enough resources to create a variety of realistic solutions tailored to local needs in developing nations, and innovations have already brought improvements. But the total effort has been far from sufficient. The world's economic situation has remained difficult and challenging, not least for wealthy nations whose economic growth has been weak or uncertain since the global financial crisis of 2008. There are serious challenges, therefore, to rapidly lowering carbon emissions. Yet the information we review here leaves little doubt that this must be done. The laws of physics do not alter when wealth is lacking. Nor do they recognize any political party or country.

On July 12, 2016, the obituary of a highly distinguished scientist and government servant, William Web Lowe II, appeared in the *Washington Post*.

He spent many years at government installations at Los Alamos, New Mexico and Hanford, Washington. He was a chemical engineer, and through his work both inside and outside the US government he made a central contribution to the introduction of nuclear electric power plants in the United States and abroad. He died at the age of ninety-five, rich in life, loved by his family with five children, three stepchildren, and fourteen grandchildren. In the 1950s he and some of his colleagues at Hanford "speculated that if concentrations of carbon dioxide in the earth's atmosphere increased so would the earth's temperature." Soon thereafter, when Charles Keeling's measurements of the CO_2 concentration in the atmosphere were reported, Lowe was among those who understood that the documented increases in this concentration would continue and create instability in the Earth's climate. In a paper he published in 1979, Lowe stated that "by burning fossil fuels at then current and projected rates, the human race was conducting a most dangerous uncontrolled experiment and that the effects on weather patterns and sea level could be catastrophic" [8].

Since the beginning of the Industrial Revolution, humans have released approximately 545 billion metric tons of carbon into the atmosphere, which converts to 2 trillion metric tons of carbon dioxide. Annual emission releases worldwide now amount to around 10.5 billion metric tons of carbon per year, so in just four decades we can double the amount of the last 220 years [9]. If nothing else, this might give us pause.

Our Climate Situation and Its Impacts

Climate scientists believe that, before industrialization, global mean temperatures had not varied more than 1.8 degrees Fahrenheit (F) (or 1.1 degrees Celsius [C]) within the past 10,000 years. Of course over the millennia temperatures varied considerably but not much during the period of human civilization – until now where it is increasing at an unprecedented rate. According to the National Aeronautics and Space Administration (NASA) and the National Oceanic and Atmospheric Administration (NOAA) the average annual temperature for the globe between 1951 and 1980 was around 57.2 degrees F or 14 degrees C. In 2015, the hottest year on record, the global mean was 1 degree C warmer than this base period [10]. Then the year 2016 broke that record. In 2015, scientists warned that the world average temperature was nearly 1 degree C above preindustrial levels, halfway to the level which could lead to dangerous climate change and halfway to the limit set in the December 2015 Paris accord on climate [11]. But on March 12, 2016, NASA released data confirming that the world average temperature was 1.35

degrees C above preindustrial levels. The 1951–1980 baseline that NASA uses is actually about 0.3 degrees C above preindustrial levels and thus February 2016 was the first month that global average temperature passed the 1.5 degrees C above the baseline mark of the preindustrial level [12]. So the numbers being used are technically a little lower than the actual temperature above the baseline, which is nonetheless rising faster than predicted.

The Paris Agreement set 2 degrees C above preindustrial levels as the target for holding the warming of the earth in check and all signers pledged a special effort to try to hold the increase to 1.5 degrees C in order to try to save island states. The February, 2016 level of 1.35 degrees C just a few months after Paris is perilously close to (and actually slightly above) the 1.5 mark. Climate change/global warming is here, now, beyond any doubt. Just a few of the symptoms of this are already here as follows:

Waves of Extreme Heat – In the summer of 2010 in Russia the mercury soared to 38°C (100°F), the highest on record and stayed very high for four weeks. Smoke from peat and forest fires blocked out skyscrapers and clogged lungs, a witches' brew of heat, smog, smoke, and nearby fires settled over Russia. It is estimated that perhaps 56,000 Russians died as a result of this heat wave. At least nineteen nations that summer hit all-time temperature peaks including Finland, 37.2°C (99°F); Niger, 48.2°C (118.8° F); and Saudi Arabia, 52°C (125.6°F). In 2011 seven more countries reached all-time highs including Pakistan at 53.5°C (130.3°F) [13]. Russian leaders had long viewed global warming science with suspicion. President Dmitry Medvedev had referred to it in early 2010 as "some kind of tricky campaign made up by some commercial structures to promote their business projects" but quickly changed his tune that summer stating in July that "what's happening with the planet's climate right now needs to be a wakeup call to all of us" [14].

Floods and Droughts – The roots of both flooding and drought lie in the physical process known as evaporation. As global warming heats up the world's oceans, water molecules near the surface become more energetic and more water vapor is created. Thus, the air around the world contains more water vapor leading to heavy rainstorms and flooding. Changes in ocean temperatures can bring changes in atmospheric circulation that bring wetness or dryness to various parts of the world. The best examples of an ocean-caused change are El Nino and La Nina which significantly hike the prospects for drought in large areas of the world. And warmer temperatures generally promote more evaporation making droughts more severe where they do occur [14]. Floods and droughts have killed millions since 1900; this is only going to accelerate and became worse as climate change advances.

Sea Ice and Glacial Melt – As the vast ice areas of the Arctic and the Antarctic melt, along with the Greenland ice cap and glaciers everywhere, the levels of the sea around the world will inexorably rise. And among the by-products of the melting Arctic, one in particular stands out as a serious threat to humanity. Trapped within the permafrost – especially in the Arctic – are billions of tons of methane clathrates (or hydrates) 150 times more concentrated than methane. Thus the melting of the permafrost as the planet warms creates the risk of the release of vast amounts of methane, potentially dwarfing the existing greenhouse gases which could cause global warming to go far beyond current projections. Methane only lasts in the atmosphere about ten to twelve years so a release would have to be colossal to contribute permanently and significantly to global warming, but there are possibilities for it to happen in the longer term [15].

Sea Level Rise – Logically, the rise in sea levels could eventually put all coastal cities around the world underwater. The rise will be gradual but during the last warming period between two glacial eras about 100,000 years ago sea levels were twenty to twenty-six feet above current levels. During this period the earth was only slightly warmer than today [16]. The *New York Times* reported on September 4, 2016, that the entire east coast is threatened by significant and regular flooding. Scientists have warned for decades that eventually global warming would imperil the United States' coastline. These are no longer theoretical judgments. The inundation of the coast has begun. The sea level has increased to the point where a high tide and a vigorous wind is all it takes to send water pouring into streets and homes. The US military has developed plans to try to head off future threats to its bases near the coast but funds for these projects have been blocked by Congress. A Republican Congressman from Colorado, Ken Buck, recently called one military proposal part of a "radical climate change proposal." In 2013 scientists reached a consensus that there would be no more than a three feet general sea rise by 2100; now they are saying six or seven feet [17].

Destructive Storms: Hurricanes, Typhoons, and Others – The Atlantic saw a major burst in destructive storms in 2010; for example, five of the year's six hurricanes reached Category 3 status – twice the usual number for an entire season; and the huge late season storm known as Sandy ravaged large sections of New Jersey and New York [18]. There could be far more of these in the future due to the increased energy in a warmer ocean.

Forest Loss – On September 9, 2016, the *Washington Post* reported that in the last twenty years big contiguous swaths of wilderness, especially forests, which often serve as key carbon sinks and are very important to the fight against climate change have been lost. When these areas are degraded they lose their carbon to the atmosphere and of course can no longer serve as sinks to draw carbon from the atmosphere. Some types of forests now have no significant wilderness areas left [19].

Views from the Front

Climate Change is a rapidly expanding existential threat to humanity. As a consequence, civilization as we know it and have known it for millennia faces the greatest danger to its continued existence that it has yet faced. Climate Change – or as it was originally termed, Global Warming – largely fueled by the ever-increasing emission of carbon into the atmosphere from the beginning of the Industrial Revolution defines what increasingly looks to be a slow motion catastrophe for most of the world. The planet will of course survive and human civilization will continue to exist, but not in the same places and perhaps not in forms that we would recognize.

Approximately half a decade ago in his book *Harmony* – backed by British science – the Prince of Wales said, "As far as climate change is concerned, there is now a strong consensus that in order to avoid the worst consequences of what we have put in train, it will be necessary for us to limit global average temperature increase to no more than two degrees Celsius above the average temperature prevailing at the end of the pre-industrial period – that is, in the late eighteenth century" [20]. This is, of course, the objective of the Paris Agreement on Climate Change adopted by 195 countries in December 2015. World average temperature is already halfway there – measurably above what it was ten years ago – at one degree above the preindustrial norm, itself a highly significant change and, as said, early in 2016 it was recorded at 1.35 degrees C above this baseline. The Prince goes on to say:

> Temperatures even three degrees above the pre-industrial average have not been seen since the Pliocene Period, some three million years ago. At that time sea levels were up to 25 metres higher than now. The last time our planet saw a comparable four degrees of warming was millions of years before then, and five degrees perhaps some 55 million years ago, at the beginning of the Eocene. At that time the earth was virtually ice-free, with the average sea level some 75 metres higher than now. Animals such as marine turtles that today we associate with the tropics and sub-tropics lived at polar latitudes. A world that is on average four degrees warmer than now would be very different and would undoubtedly bring very major upheavals and create major risks for all of humanity.
>
> I recently visited the Met Office Hadley Centre for climate research at Exeter, in Devon, England, where scientists confirmed to me that a four-degree temperature

increase during the second half of this century is to be expected on the basis of "business as usual" emissions should we not act now. However, it would be higher than this with the worst-case scenario for the end of the twenty-first century suggesting it is conceivable by then that average global temperature will rise over six degrees. To put that into perspective, a rapid six-degree temperature increase is what some scientists believe to have brought about the mass extermination that marked the end of the Permian Period some 250 million years ago. That six-degree increase is estimated to have taken some 10,000 years to occur and it took life on Earth tens of millions of years to recover from that catastrophic episode of global warming. Back then the climate change was probably caused by volcanic activity: this time the warming is caused by power stations, deforestation, cars, farms and factories. If we don't do something about these sources of global-warming gases very quickly, then we could, the most recent projections show, trigger six degrees of warming not over 10,000 years, but in less than a century [21].

In the first of two recent major reports by the World Bank on Climate Change, published in 2012, concern over the risk of warming to four degrees above preindustrial levels was expressed. The Report "Turn Down the Heat: Why a 4°C Warmer World Must be Avoided," the World Bank endorsed report said:

Recent greenhouse gas emissions and future emissions trends imply higher 21st century emission levels than previously projected. As a consequence, the likelihood of a 4°C warming being reached or exceeded this century has increased, in the absence of near-term actions and further commitments to reduce emissions. This report reaffirms the International Energy Agency's 2012 assessment that in the absence of further mitigation action there is a 40 percent chance of warming exceeding 4°C by 2100 and 10 percent chance of it exceeding 5°C in the same period.

The 4°C scenario does not suggest that global mean temperatures would stabilize at this level; rather, emissions scenarios leading to such warming would very likely lead to further increases in both temperature and sea-level during the 22nd century [22].

A second such report was published in June 2013. It forecasts the possibility of global warming to levels over 6°C in later centuries and had this to say about the nearer term:

... while the global community has committed itself to holding warming below 2°C to prevent "dangerous" climate change, and Small Island Developing States (SIDS) and Least Developed Countries (LDCs) have identified global warming of 1.5°C as warming above which there would be serious threats to their own development and, in some cases, survival, the sum total of current policies – in place and pledged – will very likely lead to warming far in excess of these levels. Indeed, present emission trends put the world plausibly on a path toward a 4°C warming within the century [23].

Thus, in summary, Paris established a plus 2°C limit, but 3°C is already built in, so below 4°C appears to be the real line to hold. Plus 5°C prevailed for about 170,000 years during the PETM, 55 million years ago, when mean sea level is estimated to have risen a minimum of about 5 m. Such a rise today would inundate millions of square km of inhabited coastline, especially in North America, Europe, the Arctic, and Asia.

In a report recently released by the US Global Change Research Program, it is stated that: "The burning of coal, oil and gas, and clearing of forests have increased the concentration of carbon dioxide in the atmosphere by more than 40 percent since the Industrial Revolution, and it has been known for almost two centuries that this carbon dioxide traps heat" [24]. The report also asserts that "The amount of warming projected over the next few decades is directly linked to the cumulative global emitting heat-type gases and particles. By the end of this century, roughly 3°F to 5°F [1.8°C to 3°C] rise is projected under a lower emissions scenario... and a 5°F to 10°F [3°C to 6°C] rise for a higher emission scenario assuming continued increases in emissions, predominately from fossil fuel combustion..." [25].

In March of 2014 the United Nations Intergovernmental Panel on Climate Change (IPCC) published its comprehensive, thirty-two-volume Fifth Assessment Report. The Chairman of the panel, Rajendra Pachauri, was quoted by the Associated Press as saying in reference to the Report that "It's a call for action." Without reductions in emissions, impacts from warming would "get out of control." The Working Group III Report, published as part of the Fifth Assessment, asserted that without new policies to mitigate climate change, projections suggest an increase in global mean temperature in 2100 of from 3.7°C to 4.8°C but its possible range, which includes climate uncertainty, is from plus 2.5°C to 7.8°C [26]. The synthesis Report of the Fifth Assessment contained the following observations:

> ... human influence on the climate system is clear and growing, with impacts observed across all continents and oceans. Many of the observed changes since the 1950s are unprecedented over decades to millennia. The IPCC is now 95 percent certain that humans are the main cause of current global warming ... [27]
>
> Anthropogenic greenhouse gas emissions have increased since the preindustrial era, driven largely by economic and population growth, and are now higher than ever. This has led to atmospheric concentrations of carbon dioxide, methane and nitrous oxide that are unprecedented in at least the last 800,000 years. Their effects, together with those of other anthropogenic drivers, have been detected throughout the climate system and are *extremely likely* to have been the dominant cause of the observed warming since the mid-twentieth century [28].
>
> Many aspects of climate change and associated impacts will continue for centuries, even if anthropogenic emissions of greenhouse gases are stopped.

The risk of abrupt or irreversible changes increase as the magnitude of warming increases [29].

> Without additional mitigation efforts beyond those in place today, and even with adaptation, warming by the end of the twenty-first century will lead to high to very high risk of severe, widespread and irreversible impacts globally (*high confidence*) [30].
>
> Surface temperature is projected to rise over the twenty-first century under all assessed emissions scenarios. It's very *likely* that heat waves will occur more often and last longer, and that extreme precipitation events will become more intense and frequent in many regions. The oceans will continue to warm and acidify, and global mean sea level to rise [31].

So the scientific reports indicate that in this century and the first few years of the next the average world temperature will surpass 3°C above preindustrial norms, that there is a serious risk of 4°C in the next fifty years, and that after the turn of the century the level could reach 6°C above preindustrial levels. Thus by summer 2100 the world's average may approach 6°C or 10°F above the preindustrial norm. Were this to happen, the increase in higher latitudes would be greater and possibly twice as much in the Arctic [32]. But what would this actually mean?

The impact of climate change as temperatures increase would not be limited to easily recognized significant weather events such as floods, hurricanes, tornadoes, and droughts but would include the following consequences as well:

> ...heat waves; dying forests; abnormally large wildfires; habitat destruction; accelerating rates of extinction; altered seasons and disruptions of normal seasonal ecological relationships; invasive species encroaching deeper into once-intact ecosystems; lethal diseases fanning out from the tropics; island nations about to be obliterated; disappearing sea ice and glaciers; rising seas; acidifying oceans; declining ocean plankton [food for many fish and source of over half the world's oxygen]; melting permafrost and Arctic wetlands [causing the release of trapped methane gas into the atmosphere a far greater threat to the climate than carbon dioxide] [33].

In the hypothesized year 2100 this could mean an average sea rise of four feet with the rise of the sea accelerating rapidly; a rapid decline of fish in the sea with the disappearance of plankton along with greatly increased acidification of the oceans; huge drought areas in North America, South America, Europe, and Africa with the disappearance of many farms and agricultural areas around the world due to a shortage of water; and many cities and urban areas partly or largely underwater with continued flooding and superstorm threats to areas above the waterline. Roughly 30 percent of the world's land area could be afflicted by drought at any given time. There would be large scale food crises continually. Governments would rise and fall with the availability of food and water for their populations. And constant conflict would be the norm as countries struggled to defend their shrinking arable areas [34].

Moreover, it is important to keep in mind that scientific studies with future temperature level predictions have thus far always been too conservative with actual results consistently exceeding projections. Global warming has been found to have taken place twice as fast since 1997 as previously estimated. Earlier estimates had the actual warming at .046°C to .08°C per decade whereas new results have it between .11°C and .12°C per decade. Other reports include under-estimated results because of incorrect measurements of warming in southern oceans and the effect of clouds on projections based on climate models. The report on the effect of clouds concluded that global climate projections misjudged the ratio of ice crystals to water droplets in mixed phase clouds and that this resulted in a significant underreporting of climate sensitivity. Equilibrium climate sensitivity is a measure of how the earth's surface temperature responds to changes in CO_2 levels in the atmosphere. Specifically it reflects how much the earth's average surface temperature would respond if CO_2 in the atmosphere was doubled from its preindustrial level. The preindustrial level was around 280 ppm. In 2013 CO_2 levels passed 400 ppm for the first time in recorded history. This rise shows a highly consistent relationship with fossil fuel burning. An eventual increase to 1,500 ppm in the atmosphere is foreseen [37]. In 2013 the IPCC estimated climate sensitivity to be within a range of 2–4.7°C; new estimates based on superior cloud analysis put this estimate at between 5°C and 5.3°C. This will have a dramatic effect for climate change analysis [38].

Glenn Scherer in 2012 asserted that after checking twenty years of projections he found the IPCC has consistently underestimated the pace and impacts of global warming. Examples include the IPCC estimate of the decline of summer Arctic sea ice and the rise of the sea level. The IPCC concluded in 2007 that the Arctic would not lose its summer ice before 2070 at the earliest. Researchers now say the region could see ice-free summers in twenty years. In its 2001 report the IPCC predicted an annual sea level rise of less than two millimeters per year. From 1993 through 2006 the oceans actually rose 3.3 millimeters per year – more than 50 percent above the projection [39].

So where are we now with respect to the existential threat that climate change represents? How should we think about climate change? The following thoughts are offered.

During the PBS NewsHour on September 7, 2016, National Public Radio reporters Judy Woodruff and William Brangham discussed the future of climate policy in the context of the presidential campaign with Coral Davenport of the *New York Times* and Chris Mooney of the *Washington Post*. First,

Michael Oppenheimer, a climate scientist at Princeton University, was asked to set the stage.

Michael Oppenheimer, Princeton University: If we don't start with rapid emissions reductions and substantial emissions reductions, we will pass a danger point, beyond which the consequences for many people and countries on Earth will simply become unacceptable and eventually disastrous.

Then, in the course of the discussion, Ms. Davenport said:

Coral Davenport, the *New York Times*: I would just say, the specific sort of marker that a lot of scientists and scientific institutions have put forth is the warming of the atmosphere beyond 3.7 degrees Fahrenheit, on average. That's kind of the point at which a lot of scientists say we will be irrevocably locked into a future of these climate impacts, and we're at the point right now where scientists say a lot of that is already baked in. There was a point . . .

William Brangham: There's no way we're going to stop hitting that mark.

Coral Davenport: Right. There was a point in the climate debate where it was about, how do we keep from getting there? At this point, in terms of the emissions that are already in the atmosphere and the rate of emissions now being produced today, scientists are saying, we're probably set to go past that tipping point. And the debate is really about, how do you keep it from getting far, far worse? How do you keep the planet habitable by humans? [40]

New York Times columnist Thomas L. Friedman attended the 2016 conference of the International Union for Conservation of Nature held every four years. Some 8,000 scientists, nature reserve specialists, and environmentalists participated. Friedman expressed some of his impressions in a column on September 7, 2016:

The dominant theme running through the I.U.C.N.'s seminars was the fact that we are bumping up against and piercing planetary boundaries – on forests, oceans, ice melt, species extinctions and temperature – from which Mother Nature will not be able to recover. When the coral and elephants are all gone, no 3-D printer will be able to recreate them. In short, we and our kids are rapidly becoming the Noah generation, charged with saving the last pairs [41].

Taking this idea to its end point, we might consider *Extinction Dialogs*, a conversation between Carolyn Baker, PhD, a widely published former psychotherapist and professor of psychology and history, and Guy McPherson, Professor Emeritus at the University of Arizona, published in 2015. A passage by Dr. Baker is worthy of serious contemplation:

On a planet 4°C hotter than baseline, all we can prepare for is human extinction, according to Oliver Tickell's 2008 synthesis in the *Guardian* (Tickell 2008). Tickell is taking a conservative approach, considering humans have not been present at 3.3°C above baseline. According to the World Bank's 2012 report, "Turn down the heat: why a 4°C warmer world must be avoided" (World Bank 2012) and an informed assessment of "BP Energy Outlook 2030" put together by Barry Saxifrage for the *Vancouver Observer*, our path leads directly to the 4°C mark. At the Nineteenth Conference of the Parties of the UN Framework Convention on Climate Change (COP 19), held in November 2013 in Warsaw, Poland, Professor of Climatology Mark Maslin warned, "We are already planning for a 4°C world because that is where we are heading. I do not know of any scientists who do not believe that" [42].

The threat is real and the very high level of danger is clear. Significant and committed action in the nearer term is imperative. There is no time available to wait years, perhaps decades, for the outcome and possible application of "green energy studies." The world community must move ahead massively as rapidly as possible with the only reliable technology that we have now to power cities and industrial facilities – peaceful nuclear power – combined with solar and wind power. This is the correct choice if extinction or something approaching it is to be avoided.

References

[1] A Brief History of Coal Use (Internet), *US Department of Energy*. Available from: www.fossil.energy.gov/education/energylessons/coal/coal_history.html

[2] D. Yergin, *The Prize: The Epic Quest for Oil, Money, and Power* (New York: Simon and Schuster, 1991).

[3] International Energy Agency (IEA), Key World Energy Statistics (Internet) (2016), 6. Available from: www.iea.org/publications/freepublications/publica tion/KeyWorld2016.pdf

[4] Ibid., p. 24.

[5] EIA, Carbon dioxide emissions from electricity generation in 2015 were the lowest since 1993 (Internet), *Today in Energy, US Energy Information Administration* (May 13, 2016). Available from: www.eia.gov/todayinenergy/detail.php?id=26232

[6] US Energy Information Administration, Department of Energy (EIA), *Electric Power Annual* (Internet), (November 2016). Available from: www.eia.gov/electri city/annual/

[7] Facts on the Pollution Caused by the US Coal Industry (Internet), *DESMOG*. Available from: www.desmogblog.com/coal-power-industry-united-states-facts

[8] W. W. Lowe II, Notice (Internet), *The Washington Post* (July 12, 2016), B-7. Available from: www.legacy.com/obituaries/washingtonpost/obituary.aspx? pid=180634763

[9] J. J. Berger, *Climate Peril* (Berkeley, CA: Northbrae Books, 2014), p. 223.

[10] US National Center for Atmospheric Research (NCAR), Frequently Asked Questions – Global Warming & Climate Change (Internet). Available from: www2 .ucar.edu/global-warming-climate-change/faq

[11] US National Aeronautical and Space Administration (NASA), Global Temperature, Latest Average (2015) (Internet), *Global Climate Change.* Available from: http://climate.nasa.gov/vital-signs/global-temperature/

[12] E. Holthaus, Our Planet's Temperature Just Reached a Terrifying Milestone (Internet), *Slate Future Tense* (March 12, 2016). Available from: www.slate.com /blogs/future_tense/2016/03/01/february_2016_s_shocking_global_warming_ temperature_record.html

[13] R. Henson, *The Thinking Person's Guide to Climate Change* (Boston: American Meteorological Society, 2014), p. 59–65.

[14] Ibid., p. 66.

[15] Ibid., p. 115.

[16] Ibid., p. 155.

[17] J. Gillis, Global Warming's Mark: Coastal Inundation, *New York Times* (September 4, 2016), A–1.

[18] Henson, *The Thinking Person's Guide*, p. 171.

[19] C. Harvey, In 20 Years, World Lost 10 Percent of Its Wilderness, *Washington Post* (September 9, 2016), A–3.

[20] H. R. H., Charles The Prince of Wales, T. Juniper, and I. Skelly, *Harmony: A New Way of Looking at Our World* (New York: Harper Collins, 2010), p. 44.

[21] Ibid., p. 45.

[22] The Potsdam Institute for Climate Impact Research and Climate Analytics, *Turn Down the Heat: Why a 4° Warmer World Must Be Avoided.* (Washington, D.C.: The World Bank, 2012), p. 12.

[23] The Potsdam Institute for Climate Impact Research and Climate Analytics, *Turn Down the Heat: Climate Extremes, Regional Impacts, and the Case for Resilience* (Internet). (Washington, D.C.: The World Bank, June 2013). Available from: http://ppp.worldbank.org/public-private-partnership/library/turn-down-heat-why -4°c-warmer-world-must-be-avoided.

[24] US Global Change Research Program Climate Change Impacts in the United States: Highlights (Internet), (2015). Available from: http://nca2014 .globalchange.gov/highlights/overview/overview

[25] Ibid., p. 5.

[26] O. Edenhofer, et. al., *Trends in Stocks and Flows of Greenhouse Gases and their Drivers, Summary for Policymakers, Climate Change 2014: Mitigation of Climate Change*, ed. T. Zwickel and J. C. Minx (Internet). Contribution of Working Group III to the Fifth Assessment Report of the Intergovernmental Panel on Climate Change [IPCC]. (London: Cambridge University Press, 2014), p. 10. Available from: www.ipcc.ch/pdf/assessment-report/ar5/wg3/ipcc_wg3_ar5_summary-for-policymakers.pdf

[27] R. K. Pachauri al., *Climate Change 2014: Synthesis Report. Contribution of Working Groups I, II and III to the Fifth Assessment Report of the Intergovernmental Panel on Climate Change*, ed. R. Pachauri and L. Meyer (Internet) (Geneva, Switzerland: IPCC, 2014), p. vi. Available from: http://epic .awi.de/37530/1/IPCC_AR5_SYR_Final.pdf.

[28] Ibid., p. 4.

[29] Ibid., p. 16.

[30] Ibid., p. 17.

[31] Ibid., p. 10.
[32] Berger, *Climate Peril*, p. 5.
[33] Ibid., p. 2.
[34] Ibid., pp. 5–21.
[35] D. Nuccitelli, Global Warming Since 1997 More than Twice as Fast as Previously Estimated, New Study (Internet), *The Guardian* (November 13, 2013). Available from: https://www.theguardian.com/environment/climate-consensus-97-%/2013/nov/13/global-warming-underestimated-by-half
[36] M. Slezak, The World Is Warming Faster Than We Thought (Internet), *Daily News* (October 5, 2014). Available from: www.newscientist.com/article/dn26317-the-world-is-warming-faster-than-we-thought
[37] National Aeronautical and Space Administration (NASA), The Relentless Rise of Carbon Dioxide (Internet) (2016). Available from: http://climate.nasa.gov/climate_resources/24/
[38] J. Shelton, Climate Models Have Underestimated Earth's Sensitivity to CO^2 Changes, Study Finds (Internet), *Yale News* (April 7, 2016). Available from: http://news.yale.edu/2016/04/07/climate-models-have-underestimated-earth-s-sensitivity-co2-changes-study-finds
[39] G. Scherer, Climate Science Predictions Prove Too Conservative (Internet), *Scientific American* (December 6, 2012). Available from: www.scientificamerican.com/article/climate-science-predictions-prove-too-conservative
[40] Seeing the Future of Climate Policy Under the Next President (Internet), *PBS Newshour* (September 7, 2016). Available from: www.pbs.org/newshour/bb/seeing-future-climate-policy-next-president
[41] T. L. Friedman, We Are All Noah Now, *New York Times* (September 7, 2016), A–23.
[42] C. Baker and G. McPherson, *Extinction Dialogs: How to Live with Death in Mind* (San Francisco: Tayen Lane, 2015), p. 45.

11

Launching a New Nuclear Power State: The United Arab Emirates

The Nuclear Rationale

Creation of a new nuclear power state defines an event of no small importance. In three decades, since the Chernobyl accident (1986), only one new country, Romania, has joined the "nuclear club."[1] That has changed as of 2017. But the importance of the United Arab Emirates (UAE) in this history of nuclear power is greater than might at first be surmised. Not only is it the first Arab state to acquire this energy source and to prove that it can be done safely in a region where conflict has existed for some time. It is also the nation to open a new era of expansion and to do so with a nuclear program that has been said to set a precedent for future nuclear starter states. We will discuss this new "gold standard" and what it means. But it is also instructive to know something about the story behind how it came to be, as well as the challenges it faced in becoming a reality.

Though the UAE has a particular rationale for seeking nuclear power, the findings it has come to in comparing various energy sources and the legal-political process it has successfully followed offer valuable information for other states regarding what might be expected. Neither should it be ignored that the country is beginning with four large reactors (~1.4 GW each), all of the same design, all of which have been on time and on budget.

The United Arab Emirates was founded in 1971 and includes seven states or emirates, including Abu Dhabi and Dubai. Dubai is the most populous city in the UAE but the Abu Dhabi emirate accounts for 86 percent of the land area of

---

[1] We are not including here those nations that, before 1991, were part of the Soviet Union or Yugoslavia, since they already had nuclear plants prior to the breakup of these states.

the UAE and 95 percent of its oil. The federal capital of the UAE is Abu Dhabi city.

The UAE for some time has been experiencing impressive economic growth. There is a close link between economic growth and electricity production. Electricity is essential to sustain this economic growth and to provide the social development the UAE desires for its people. Several studies were done in the mid-first decade of the twenty-first century which clearly indicated that the UAE was rapidly outstripping by its economic growth the supply of electricity that was available. This was indisputable by 2007. Everything was examined by the UAE leadership: oil, gas, coal, renewables, and nuclear. The studies were in agreement that total electricity demand in the UAE was likely to rise from the then current (in 2007) level of 15.5 GWe to a level nearly three times higher by 2020, with the beginning of the spike in demand to occur in 2017.

Wind and solar energy, while highly desirable when viewed from the standpoint of the environment, simply cannot provide the requisite large amounts of electricity. This was underscored later when Abu Dhabi established a small city on the outskirts, Masdar, which was to be operated entirely by renewables. Supplementary energy from gas generation had to be regularly supplied. Large scale hydro facilities are not feasible in the UAE and the country has no indigenous supply of coal. Coal-fired power generation thus would require significant investment in storage facilities and transportation as well as environmental control, which was likely to be ineffective to the detriment of the environment.

Gas and oil, which of course are abundant in the region, would seem to be a way out but the UAE is a net importer of natural gas. Much of the natural gas available is reinjected into oil wells to stimulate further production and the remainder has a sulfur content that is too high. And as far as oil is concerned, that is the UAE's principal export and using it for power generation within the UAE would exact a significant opportunity cost.

These issues were addressed in an analysis carried out by Government of the UAE and the conclusion was straightforward and compelling. Electricity generation from commercial nuclear power plants must be seriously considered as part of the UAE solution to its energy needs. Nuclear power is emission free, reliable, deployable, affordable (for the UAE) and long lasting. Nuclear power plants built today are expected to last up to eighty to one hundred years. Someday the oil will run out.

In addition to power generation the UAE relies entirely on electricity for its potable water by means of desalinization plants. In April 2008, the UAE published its comprehensive policy on nuclear energy. A few months before, Abu Dhabi, managing the nuclear power program on behalf of the UAE, had engaged Lightbridge Corporation (then known as Thorium Power, Ltd.) of McLean, now Reston, Virginia to advise it during the development and implementation of its program. The then-published policy on nuclear energy projected escalating electricity demand from 15.5 GWe in 2008 to over 40 GWe in 2020. Natural gas supplies were sufficient for only half of the increase. Imported coal was dismissed as an option due to environmental and energy security implications. Renewables would be able to supply only 6 to 7 percent of the needed power by 2020.

Nuclear power "emerged as a proven, environmentally promising, and commercially competitive option which could make a significant base-load contribution to the UAE's economy and future energy security." This led to the creation of a regulatory framework and the selection of a site for nuclear power reactors between Abu Dhabi city and Ruwais, at Barakah on the Arabian Gulf coast. In this published policy paper, known as a "White Paper," the UAE resolved to forgo domestic enrichment and reprocessing – the essence of what became known as the "gold standard"– and "to conclude long term arrangements . . . for the secure supply of nuclear fuel, as well as its safe and secure supply transportation and, if available, the disposal of spent fuel via fuel leasing or other emerging fuel supply arrangements." [1].

All of this was incorporated into the UAE national law as well as commitments in the White Paper: to the five principles for the UAE program of safety, security, nonproliferation, transparency, and sustainability; to explore in the future various technology options, innovative reactors, and fuel cycle technologies that exhibit enhanced proliferation resistance; and to establish an International Advisory Board to review the program twice a year and publish reports on its performance to demonstrate its complete adherence to the principles of peaceful and safe nuclear energy [2].

Political Questions

Very much in mind in those early days was the debacle of the Dubai Ports World initiative and the Government of the UAE, the overall manager of the UAE effort to establish nuclear power generation, was determined to avoid a repeat of that difficult time. The Dubai Ports World issue began in February 2006 and rose to prominence as a national security debate in the United States. Six major US ports were involved, twenty-two all told. The contracts to manage these ports were already foreign owned, held by the Peninsular and Oriental Navigation Company (P&O), a very old British firm. P&O was sold to Dubai Ports World, owned by a holding company under the direct control of the Prime Minister of the UAE government, Sheik Mohammed bin Rashid Al Maktoum. The sale was approved by P&O stockholders in February 2006, the Committee on Foreign Investment in the US (CFIUS) gave its approval shortly thereafter – having reviewed the sale since mid-October the previous year – and the takeover was completed in March 2006.

DP World had cleared this acquisition with CFIUS and after the Committee had resolved some concerns of the US Coast Guard – part of the Department of Homeland Security – about possible intelligence gaps that might occur with US ports being managed by a Dubai company that could prevent them assessing security risks associated with management. After these concerns were resolved CFIUS gave its approval to the transaction and the transfer of the leases to manage the various ports. The principal ports in the US where the management leases were transferred were: the Port of New York and New Jersey, the Port of Philadelphia, the Port of Baltimore, the Port of New Orleans, and the Port of Miami. As said, there were sixteen other US ports involved.

This matter promptly became a major political issue in the United States. Both Republican and Democratic leaders in the Congress, including the Majority Leader of the Senate and the Speaker of the House, denounced the deal and threatened legislation to block it. President Bush declared he would veto any such legislation which would have been his first. In a statement to reporters on February 22, 2006 President Bush said that "It would send a terrible signal to friends and allies not to let this transaction go through" [3]. Thus, the battle lines were drawn and the UAE found itself in the middle.

DP World had been represented in the P&O transaction by the law firm of Alston & Bird, where Robert Dole, the former senator and presidential candidate, was special counsel. He was asked to attempt to lobby Congress on its behalf against the bipartisan criticism of the transaction.

Events moved swiftly. On March 8, 2006, a House Appropriations Committee which was reviewing the transaction voted 62–2 to block the deal and Senator Schumer was part of an effort to pass a bill in the Senate to block the deal. The House Committee rejected the transfer; it said because it allowed the sale of some port operations to an Arab state company. The next day, March 9, DP World announced that it would "transfer" its management leases for US ports to an as-yet-unnamed US company. Senator Warner announced the change by DP World two hours before a critical vote on the question of whether the Senate would pass legislation to stop the transaction. Of course, all of this furor had nothing to do with actual security, as the vast majority of containers that flow daily into the United States remain uninspected and vulnerable to security threats at many points. A delegation of Republican Congressional leaders told President Bush that his veto threat would not stop Congress from blocking the deal. Mr. Bush declined to repeat his veto threat thereby signaling that he wanted a face-saving way out of this controversy. The next day the Prime Minister of the UAE – who was also the ruler of Dubai – made his decision to sell the management leases to an American company. "This was clearly not a business decision made by DP World," a senior administration official said. "It was a strategic decision made by the UAE to avoid further damage." In Dubai, a senior political official with extensive knowledge of the deliberations in the UAE said, "A political decision was taken to ask DP World to try and defuse the situation. We have to help our friends." The official who sought anonymity was referring to President Bush, who initially backed the sale, and several Republican Senators who did as well [4].

The specter of Dubai Ports World was very much present in the UAE in 2008 and 2009 as the first steps were being taken in the country's nuclear power program. There was great concern that this could happen again. And such fears were not entirely misplaced. The issue could return in any Congressional consideration of the UAE program. In 2008 the UAE made the decision that it was important to seek an Agreement for Nuclear Cooperation with the United States, known as a 123 Agreement. This is a special agreement, required by Section 123 of the US Atomic Energy Act, that involves the transfer of nuclear material or technology from the US to another nation. It is intended as a vital nonproliferation tool and opens the door to cooperation on research, training, and exchanges of various types. As of 2016, the US had such agreements with twenty-two nations, as well as the EU (via Euratom). In terms of legal process, such an agreement must first be signed by the Executive branch, then must lie before the Congress for 90 legislative days after which it becomes effective unless Congress passes in this time period a joint resolution rejecting it. So Congress has a real statutory role in approving 123 Agreements. Regarding the UAE, some new sticking points emerged. There were articles in American media that asserted the purpose of the UAE program was really to counter Iran. This implied that the UAE's real motivation was military, not peaceful, and that the country might be planning to build nuclear weapons.

Two top law firms, as well as a prominent lobbying firm, were engaged in Washington to help and advise the UAE. It looked like there might be trouble again. But then, in the last stages of an internal State Department review of the draft Agreement submitted by the UAE, someone suggested adding the "gold standard" to the text of the 123 Agreement. UAE Ambassador Yousef Otaiba promptly agreed and this converted the UAE – in a political, not actual, sense almost overnight – from an uncertain ally to the hero of Congress and a model for the world.

Success Arrives

On January 15, 2009, US Secretary of State Condoleezza Rice and UAE Foreign Minister Abdullah bin Zayed Al Nahyan signed a proposed nuclear cooperation agreement. After the signing ceremony, Secretary Rice said the deal is "powerful and timely for the world and region." But in an abundance of caution, the UAE asked that the transmission of the Agreement be delayed until the Obama administration took office, since it was to do so in just five days. It was during the first five months of the Obama administration that the change to the text was made and the "gold standard" included. The US-UAE 123 Agreement was submitted to the Congress on May 21, 2009. Ranking members of the Senate Foreign Relations Committee, Senator Kerry, the Chairman, and Senator Lugar, the ranking Republican, promptly announced their support. The Chairman of the House Foreign Affairs Committee Congressman Howard Berman said, "By signing this agreement, the United States and the UAE have taken an important step in building a long and mutually beneficial partnership to enhance nonproliferation and energy security in the region. The proposed agreement deserves the support of the Congress."

However, Representative Ileana Ros-Lehtinen, the ranking Republican, of the House Foreign Affairs Committee introduced a bill preventing the agreement from entering into force until the president certifies to Congress that the UAE has taken steps to prohibit the potential transfer of sensitive nuclear material to Iran, tightened up its export control laws, and ensured that it does not violate any US law. But this bill only attracted a few co-sponsors and was not pushed hard by anyone, even Representative Ros-Lehtinen.

So on December 17, 2009, 90 legislative days after its submission to Congress, the US-UAE 123 Agreement entered into force. Dubai Ports World was history and the UAE was and is the hero of the US Congress and a model for the world. Around this time Bahrain, Saudi Arabia, and Jordan all indicated that they would adhere to the "gold standard," but Jordan subsequently moved away from this commitment. Even though there have subsequently been several abortive attempts by Congress to legislatively require the "gold standard," it has not done so. And the executive branch pursuant to a bureaucratic argument between the Department of State (a strong supporter of the "gold standard") and Department of Energy, does not require it either. But it has permanently changed the relationship of the United States and the United Arab Emirates [5].

When Lightbridge first arrived in the UAE in 2007 to discuss the creation of a nuclear power program with UAE senior government officials, there was virtually no infrastructure for such a program. Hamad Al Kaabi, a graduate of Purdue University where he received a Master's in Nuclear Engineering, soon became an important part of the program. In 2010 he was appointed UAE ambassador to the IAEA. The UAE, in a large part as a result of Ambassador Al Kaabi's efforts, has evolved into one of the most active and influential members of the IAEA. The UAE does a lot in Vienna and the IAEA does a lot in Abu Dhabi. Working closely with the IAEA has been a central part of the UAE program.

In the spring of 2008, Lightbridge staff created a hugely detailed and comprehensive guide to the UAE in its efforts to create a nuclear power program. It is entitled "Roadmap to Success," is 500 plus pages long and essentially it is everything the UAE needed to do to establish a civil nuclear power program. Lightbridge CEO Seth Grae selected Ernie Kennedy, then a member of Lightbridge's Technical Advisory Board, to lead the Roadmap's compilation. Ernie Kennedy had led the deployment of the first reactors to South Korea two and a half decades earlier. In developing its program the UAE followed this guidebook almost to the letter. There was also a guidance plan from the IAEA which was closely followed. Before completing the draft of the Roadmap, the "Quick Start" program identified potential sites, provisionally established the Emirates Nuclear Energy Corporation (ENEC) and the Federal Authority for Nuclear Regulation (FANR) within the Executive Affairs Authority of Abu Dhabi (EAA), and prepared several technical reports.

The UAE announced that it would "offer joint venture arrangements to foreign investors for the construction of future nuclear power plants." These arrangements would be similar to existing independent water and power structures that are 60 percent owned by the UAE government and 40 percent by the joint venture partner. Thus, the UAE planned to manage its nuclear power program by means of contractor services rather than only developing indigenous expertise [6]. One reason for following this model was the calendar. To meet the UAE's projected electricity demand, the EAA desired to have the first unit operational in 2017. Essentially time was of the essence and the fastest route to nuclear power based on the principles of safety and security was the path to follow. The UAE invited expressions of interest to bid on constructing its program from nine countries. This list was soon shortened to three entities and bids were sought in mid-2009. The three bidding groups were France: Areva with EDF, GDF Suez, and Total proposing the EPR pressurized water reactor; Japan: GE-Hitachi proposing its ABWR; and the Korean consortium comprising Korean Electric Power Corporation (KEPCO) along with Samsung, Hyundai, and Doosan, as well as Westinghouse, proposing the Advanced Power Reactor (APR)-1400 pressurized water reactor (PWR) technology. The Westinghouse System 80+ design (certified in the US by the Nuclear Regulatory Commission [NRC]) has been developed into the APR-1400.

Early on Japan dropped out and the final struggle was between France and Korea. The competition was very spirited. French President Sarkozy made two trips to Abu Dhabi to lobby for the EPR. During the first visit, Sarkozy's public affairs officer announced publicly that an agreement had been reached. In December 2009 ENEC announced that it had selected a bid from the KEPCO-led consortium. This was Korea's first overseas sale of its reactor technology. In the end, Korea underbid France significantly. The value of the contract for the construction of four APR-1400 reactors to be built at one site was $20.4 billion, with a high percentage of the contract offered under a fixed price arrangement. Operational life of the reactors was to be for at least sixty years. Korea offered the lowest construction cost. Also Korea has a track record of being able to build reactors safely faster than anyone – which was important given the imminence of 2017 [7].

It was planned that an operating company would be established which would be 82 percent Emirati-owned and 18 percent KEPCO. In April 2010 ENEC submitted license applications and an environmental assessment for the preferred site at Barakah, on the coast 32 miles west of Ruwais and 180 miles west of Abu Dhabi city. The site evaluation process for the four reactors considered ten potential sites and was based on guidance from FANR with input from other agencies such as the US NRC and the IAEA. The Gulf seawater at Barakah is about 35 degrees Celsius which is a different environment than that of the first APR-1400 units Shin Kori 3 and 4 which are being built in South Korea. These two plants bring the first deployment of the APR 1400 which were to serve as the reference units for the four Barakah reactors. However, the temperature of the sea where the two Shin Kori units are based in South Korea is 27 degrees Celsius, so at Barakah larger heat exchangers are required. The construction schedule established for the four Barakah reactors is as follows:

Name	Type	MWe	Construction Start	Startup
Barakah 1	APR-1400	1,400	July 2012	5/2017
Barakah 2	APR-1400	1,400	May 2013	2018
Barakah 3	APR-1400	1,400	September 2014	2019
Barakah 4	APR-1400	1,400	September 2015	2020

Total: 5,600 MWe

In December 2009, pursuant to the commitment in the White Paper and in the UAE national law, the UAE appointed the International Advisory Board (IAB). While it is not invested with legally binding powers, it was designed and functions as an independent advisory body which reports publicly on the state of the UAE nuclear power program. It was contemplated that the IAB would publish many things in its reports but the IAB would be required in each of its biannual reports, with respect to the UAE nuclear program, to address the five core issues of the program which are:

1. nuclear safety;
2. nuclear security;
3. nuclear nonproliferation;
4. program transparency; and
5. program sustainability.

The individuals appointed by the UAE to the IAB in 2009 [8] were:

Dr. Hans Blix, Chairman
Mr. Jacques Bouchard
Dr. KunMo Chung
Ambassador Thomas Graham
Mr. Takuya Hattori
Lady Barbara Judge
Dr. Mujid Kazimi
Mr. Jukka Laaksonen
Sir John Rose

The IAB began its first report by underlining the importance of safety. The Board at the beginning stated that it views safety as a top priority [9].

Internationalism: A Key Component

More specifically, the IAB represents an unprecedented collection of internationally recognized experts in various disciplines associated with nuclear power and related technologies. The Board is chaired by Dr. Hans Blix, former Swedish Foreign Minister, Director General of the International Atomic Energy Agency from 1982–1997 and chief inspector in Iraq for the United Nations prior to the Second Gulf War. The other individuals appointed by the UAE to the IAB in 2009 were: Mr. Jacques Bouchard (France), Special Advisor to the Chairman, Centre de Saclay; Dr. KunMo Chung (Korea), former Minister (twice) of Science and Technology; Ambassador Thomas Graham (USA), former Special Representative of the President for Arms Control and Non-proliferation, currently Executive Chairman, Lightbridge Corporation; Mr. Takuya Hattori (Japan), President, Japan Industrial Forum, Inc.; Lady Barbara Judge (UK), Chairman, United Kingdom Atomic Energy

Authority; Dr. Mujid Kazimi (USA), Professor of Nuclear Mechanical Engineering, Massachusetts Institute of Technology; Mr. Jukka Laaksonen (Finland), Director General of Radiation and Nuclear Safety Authority; Dr. John Rose (UK), Chief Executive of Rolls Royce, plc.

The IAB is charged with conducting semi-annual reviews on the UAE peaceful nuclear energy program and to prepare public reports on these reviews which contain the Board's observations, findings, and recommendations. The IAB, while not invested with any legally binding powers, has been designed as an independent advisory body whose public findings will carry great weight.

The commitment to form such a body was among the original commitments made by the UAE which were included in the White Paper referenced above. It indicates the intent of the UAE to evaluate and potentially deploy peaceful nuclear energy within its borders to better the lives of its citizens. And in doing so the UAE further intends to develop this program in a way for it to serve as a model for the region and the world community [10].

Since the IAB views safety as one of the highest priorities in the establishment and development of the UAE nuclear energy program, Board members were gratified to learn at the first meeting of the Board that the UAE had thoroughly reviewed the safety requirements for its program at the very beginning. The first meeting of the IAB was in April 2010 and it could look back on the establishment of FANR in September 2009, three months before the UAE decided to accept the contract offer of KEPCO and to deploy the APR-1400 reactor as the mainstay of its program. The first briefing presented to the IAB at its first meeting in Abu Dhabi was conducted by FANR. The three principal objectives of FANR are:

1. reduce any harmful impact of the use of nuclear technology on human life or the environment;
2. keep worker and public exposure to radiation as low as is reasonably achievable; and
3. prevent any diversion of nuclear technology or materials for nonpeaceful purposes.

Dr. William Travers, formerly of the US NRC had been selected as the first Director General of FANR. He presented at this briefing a long list of FANR areas of responsibility to the Board. These included, among some other areas:

1. Site selection
2. Site preparation
3. Design of a nuclear facility

4. Construction of a nuclear facility
5. Operation and maintenance of a nuclear facility
6. Decommissioning of a nuclear facility
7. Import and export of any regulated material
8. Storage of any regulated material within the borders of the UAE
9. Disposal of any regulated material within the borders of the UAE
10. Emergency preparedness relating to any nuclear facility [11].

A briefing was also provided by the senior management of ENEC, including the CEO Mohamed Al Hammadi. It was clear that ENEC sought to make the development of a safety culture an essential element of the organization. The UAE government had made clear that it expects the ENEC management and every employee to understand that the success of the UAE nuclear program, as well as its own success, will depend upon the establishment of the highest safety conditions on both the technical and behavioral sides.

The APR 1400 is a 1,450 MW evolutionary pressurized water reactor. It is based on well-proven Korean standard nuclear power plant design but incorporates a number of new features which provide enhanced safety as well as improved economics. These were developed to meet some forty-three basic design requirements. These include at least a sixty-year projected life span and technology that provides a ten times lower probability of core damage and accidental radiation release over nuclear power plants first deployed prior to 2002. Ten years in development, it is designed to have a forty-eight-month construction time and a 20 percent cost advantage over competitive energy sources. The first APR-1400 plants were Shin Kori 3 and 4 in Korea [12]. Shin Kori 3 is the reference plant for the Barakah reactors. Shin Kori 3 and 4 were originally slated to be completed in mid-2013 but there have been equipment delays. Shin Kori 3 became operational in January 2016 and at present it appears that Shin Kori 4will become operational in early 2017.

In this first report to the Board FANR indicated that it had a mandate to plan and implement a program of nuclear security of both facilities and materials. The pre-existing Critical National Infrastructure Authority (CNIA) established its own dedicated group to work on the implementation of nuclear security. Together these two entities have developed a preliminary Integrated Security Master Plan that reflects the program's emergency security related regulatory requirements as well as the IAEA Guidelines. Also the UAE government supports numerous international nuclear security related agreements including UN Security Council Resolution 1540 and the International Convention for the Suppression of Acts of International Terrorism [13].

The IAB welcomed the UAE government commitment to refrain from developing enrichment and reprocessing capabilities. The IAB endorsed the UAE decision also set forth in the White Paper to support, as it explores future technology options, innovative reactors and fuel cycle technologies that exhibit enhanced proliferation resistance. In the view of the Board this underscored the peaceful nature of the UAE program. At this time the UAE was also well advanced toward developing with the IAEA safeguards to reflect the UAE's adherence to the Additional Protocol – an important new model agreement which was part of the obligations undertaken by all Non-Proliferation Treaty (NPT) Parties as part of the decision to indefinitely extend the NPT in 1995. Beginning with the second IAB report in October 2010, the Ministry of Foreign Affairs (MOFA) has always presented the briefing on non-proliferation and the briefer has always been Ambassador Hamad Al Kaabi, UAE Ambassador to the IAEA.

In the first IAB report, the Board took note of and agreed with the UAE government's intention that some of the first steps in its nuclear power program should emphasize the UAE's commitment to transparency in all aspects. In truth, establishment of the IAB itself was an indication of this commitment, as it meant that in its semi-annual reports virtually all of the significant details of the UAE nuclear power program would be public knowledge. In addition, the UAE directed that all government entities involved in the program coop-erate closely with the IAEA; second the government established FANR, as a fully independent agency with its own sources of long-term funding by charging its licensees and with safeguards to ensure that no member of the staff could face adverse actions because of a regulatory decision; the ENEC procurement process was designed to allow for joint venture arrangements with foreign investors; and the UAE government signed on to the Additional Protocol to its IAEA Safeguards Agreement [14]. Later on as the program matured, ENEC and FANR conducted a number of public presentations on the nuclear program.

Lastly the first IAB report also addressed the fifth program principle, sustainability. This remained the pattern for all subsequent IAB reports; all five principles were discussed in light of program activity in the previous six months. The UAE committed itself to develop essential nuclear capabilities in the national labor force and among UAE citizens with Khalifa University of Science, Technology, and Research, establishing forty scholarships to study nuclear-related disciplines in the United States, France, and South Korea [15]. The government also expressed a commitment to the develop-ment of a nuclear waste management program, finding diverse sources of nuclear fuel, and the establishment of an international nuclear fuel bank.

It was also understood from these early days that a dedicated decommissioning fund would need to be created to properly plan for the long-term future. And as, over the years, the labor force at Barakah approached 20,000 a virtual city to house and properly care for this large international work force – sixty-two nationalities in all – was built.

Success and the Lessons of Fukushima

In July 2010, ENEC received two licenses from FANR: one was a site preparation license to prepare the Barakah site for the deployment of four reactors, the second was a limited construction license allowing the manufacture in the UAE of some of the major components associated with the four units. The reactor internals themselves, of course, were being built in Korea.

In December of 2010, ENEC submitted to FANR a 9,000-page construction license application to construct Units 1 and 2, beginning with construction of Unit 1 in mid-2012 and Unit 2 almost precisely a year later. One of the strengths of the UAE nuclear power program is the successive annual commencement of construction of the four identical units almost exactly a year apart. This permits the application of knowledge gained and experience developed increasingly among the four units in a highly effective manner. Thus, the construction of each reactor becomes more and more efficient and expeditious. This type of plan in the international nuclear industry is relatively rare.

The eighteen-month FANR review involving some sixty staff and three consulting firms was completed and the license issued in mid-July 2012 and the first construction – the pouring of nuclear grade concrete – began almost immediately. Shortly after the third IAB meeting in March of 2011 the Fukushima accident in Japan took place. The UAE took immediate action in response. This included the establishment of a Fukushima task force by FANR and a request from FANR to ENEC to prepare a comprehensive report on lessons learned from the Fukushima accident. An interim report on this subject was available to the IAB at the November 2011 meeting, the fourth IAB meeting. The IAB also made a number of requests in addition to understanding the lessons learned from the accident. The Board wanted to know the vulnerability of the APR-1400 to earthquakes at the Barakah site, high water levels in the Gulf, and the extent that the elevation of the reactors and other safety critical facilities on the site will affect them. ENEC replied that the nearest to Barakah a Fukushima-type undersea earthquake could take place was on the western coast of India. The resulting tsunami would have some distance to travel and then would have to enter the Gulf through the Straits of Hormuz.

This would reduce any tsunami threat to a wave level run-up well within the safety elevation margin at Barakah. Likewise a cyclone at the time of high tides also was estimated to be well within the safety margin. Earthquakes are virtually unknown in the Arabian Peninsula and there is little historic seismicity in the Gulf itself. There is a history of earthquakes in Iran but well away from the UAE.

At the Board meeting in the fall of 2011, speaking for the government, Ambassador Al Kaabi presented the general government response on the Fukushima incident and how it might affect the UAE nuclear power program. He noted that after careful consideration the government had "decided on no change to its policy on nuclear power for the Emirates and that the results of a recent public survey indicated 85 percent of the public supported nuclear energy for the UAE. The government will, however, incorporate any lessons learned from Fukushima. ENEC has been asked to conduct a review of the reactor design in light of the accident. Accordingly the government will closely follow related international action, particularly at the IAEA, and specifically with respect to additional regulations for operation and the industry [16]." FANR at this meeting described its task force and its plan to monitor international reaction at the IAEA and among regulators in other countries. ENEC presented in its interim analysis proposals for possible adjustment to the Barakah reactor deployment, mentioning watertight doors, steps such as additional power generating locations to ensure that electric power will always be available for the site, and steps to minimize the effect of sandstorms.

On March 30, 2011, FANR requested ENEC to do an overall safety assessment of lessons learned from the Fukushima accident in Japan. This comprehensive safety assessment was to be completed by ENEC and delivered to FANR by December 31, 2011. As said, ENEC delivered an interim report as to safety to the IAB meeting at the November meeting. The overall assessment on safety was submitted on December 30, 2011, to FANR and a copy sent to the IAB in February 2012.

The ENEC safety report did not identify any design deficiencies in the APR-1400 similar to those that were the major causes of the accident in Japan. However, ENEC did identify other site design features and additional measures to increase the robustness of the Barakah nuclear power plants to prevent or cope with the potential consequences of severe natural events. In the safety report ENEC confirmed the response in its interim report that earthquakes and flooding do not represent significant dangers. Sandstorms and dust storms are expected to be present periodically at the Barakah site and appear to represent a considerably greater threat than earthquakes or high water. Fire, explosions, and oil spills have to be guarded against and loss of electrical power and loss of ultimate heat sink, and severe accident management are valid areas for review. The UAE has set up an internal process to monitor the implementation of the IAEA safety action plan. FANR conducted its own review to distinguish between issues that need to be resolved prior to the issuance of the construction license and those – such as mitigating design feature changes – that would be introduced in the course of construction. Some of the design modifications that ENEC proposed and were accepted were:

- Safety improvements against earthquakes by improving the seismic capacity of the main control room and the alternate alternating current (AAC) diesel generator building;
- Safety improvements against tsunamis such as countermeasures to respond to possible damage of the outdoor tanks;
- Safety improvements of design features against station blackout (complete loss of power) such as a cross-tie design for emergency power supply among units, installation of mobile diesel generator connections; extensions of the fuel capacity of the storage tank for the AAC diesel generator fuel; and battery duty extension;
- Safety improvement design features against severe accidents, external water insertion for the steam generators, the reactor system, and the spent fuel, also additional passive auto-catalytic recombiners installed in the spent fuel building and operating procedures and severe accident guidelines, along with the development of improved emergency operating procedures [17].

Together, ENEC and FANR carried out a complete review of the project after Fukushima, leaving no stone unturned to achieve the highest possible level of confidence.

As said, on July 17, 2012, the construction license for Units 1 and 2 was given by FANR to ENEC and the construction of the entire project was underway. ENEC submitted a 10,000-page application for a construction license for Units 3 and 4 to FANR in March 2013, based on the application for Units 1 and 2. The license was issued in mid-September 2014. Construction of Unit 3 began a week after receipt of the license, and Unit 4 construction began in early September 2015. In March 2015 ENEC submitted to FANR its operating license application for Units 1 and 2 [18]. Much analysis and many trials and partial tests of elements of the systems are involved in the run up to the granting of the operating license. The 15,000-page application for the operating license includes: a final safety analysis report; an independent safety verification and design review; details of the physical protection plan, facility safeguards plan, operational quality assurance renewal and emergency plan, as well as a probabilistic risk assessment report and a severe accident report. ENEC reported that Unit 1 was 74 percent complete and Unit 2, 51 percent complete in July 2015 [19].

At the October 2015 IAB meeting, the status of the operating license and the likelihood of commercial power production beginning at Unit 1 in July 2017 was discussed. The UAE by that time was nearing the point when commercial operations would begin. Accordingly, special attention was increasingly being given to Unit 1 while construction at the other three units continued to move rapidly ahead, helped by the knowledge and experience gained in the construction of Unit 1. In the FANR briefing, it was reported that there were a number of late report submittals by ENEC related to the operating license yet to be delivered. For example, the grid stability report and the grid availability study will be submitted to FANR at the end of September 2016. Once all the remaining necessary documents were submitted, all outstanding requests for additional information resolved, and all Safety Evaluation Reports approved by FANR, the license recommendations and the supporting documents would be sent to the FANR Board of Management. IAB Chairman Dr. Hans Blix asked what that meant for issuance of the Operating License Application. FANR's newly appointed Director, General Christer Viktorsson, succeeding Dr. Travers, replied that issuance of the license will be expected in February 2017.

In the ENEC briefing, the ENEC Chief Program Officer (CPO) gave an overview of the construction process. He explained that one of the reasons for some of ENEC's delayed responses is that the pace of material manufacturing has slowed down the program. He also noted that progress at Shin Kori 3 has also slowed, thus there will not be the years of operations there for ENEC to derive lessons learned but there should be at least one year. Commercial output there could begin in May 2016. It could be challenging for Bakarah Unit 1 to begin operations in May 2017 but there is a fair level of confidence that Unit 1 will begin generating power by the end of 2017. Speaking in October 2015, the CPO said that the overall commissioning process for Unit 1 is 12.38 percent complete. Major tests lie ahead, for example: the hot functional tests (which verify the operability of various systems under hot conditions before fuel loading); fuel loading; power ascension tests (these tests verify that the systems and components are ready to be operated at full capacity) [20].

The April 2016 meeting of the IAB was held shortly after the Paris Climate Conference, which took place in December 2015. This Conference had a specific and elevated meaning for the UAE nuclear power program. Virtually all countries came together in Paris to agree that limiting global emissions defined a necessity for the world, with each individual nation required to do its part in finding alternatives to carbon energy. The UAE's choice of nuclear power provided a way to do this rapidly and at a high level, while allowing for conservation of national resources and advancing the country's energy security as well.

FANR Director General Viktorsson in his presentation said that the issuance of the operating license depended upon ENEC's operational readiness. In FANR's view, at its current pace, it would complete review of the various required plans and reports for Units 1 and 2 by May 2017 at the earliest. FANR would then send the operating license recommendation to the its Board of Management.

Mr. David Scott opened the ENEC briefing on behalf of the Executive Affairs Authority Chairman (also ENEC Chairman), H.E. Khaldoon Al Mubarak. Mr Scott noted that, as of April 2016, the total Barakah Nuclear Power Project (BNPP) was 60 percent complete, with Unit 1 85 percent complete. The next major step before loading fuel to the reactor, he stated, was the Hot Functional Test. Later, the CPO and the ENEC Chief Nuclear Officer led ENEC's formal briefing. They stated that the current estimate was for the operating license to be issued at the end of May 2017 and for the licensed operator to begin generating power by the end of 2017. ENEC was now focused on guaranteeing project delivery, including the testing and commissioning of Unit 1, with operational readiness being shifted to the operating subsidiary. The first Hot Functional Test was to be performed sometime around September 2016. As for progress on the other three reactors, Unit 2 was largely on time, and Units 3 and 4 were a few months ahead of schedule [21].

The October 2016 meeting of the IAB opened with an address by ENEC Chairman, Al Mubarak. The Chairman stated that while ENEC was well aware of the program schedule set at the inception of the project, the number one priority for ENEC in managing the program was safety. The project will continue to move ahead rapidly while adhering to the rigorous safety standards that are in place. A major project related development had been the announcement of a joint venture between ENEC and the Korea Electric Power Corporation(KEPCO) for a "long-term partnership and cooperation in the UAE's Peaceful Nuclear Power Program," as reported by World Nuclear News on October 20, 2016. In addition to other arrangements, KEPCO will receive an 18 percent stake in the ENEC operating subsidiary, NAWAH Energy Company, with ENEC holding the remaining 82 percent. NAWAH will operate and maintain the four units at Barakah.

Also at the October meeting, the Barakah NPP was declared 71 percent complete in its entirety, including all four plants. In the briefing by FANR, the Director General stated that the license for operations was nearly complete, that FANR had conducted reviews for operational readiness and emergency preparedness. The pending license applications at that time were for: Transport of Fresh Nuclear Fuel-ENEC; Storage of Fresh Nuclear Fuel (preoperational)-NAWAH; and the operating license. ENEC needed to resolve legal issues with respect to all three of these licenses: establishing the legal identity of NAWAH and acquiring liability insurance as required by law. With respect to the operating license, the issuance of the pending report submittals and the FANR detailed review were underway. FANR expected the licensing decision to be made in May 2017.

At the ENEC briefing, its CEO made a presentation on the construction progress at Barakah. At the time of the meeting, October 2016, Unit 1 was 91 percent complete, Unit 2, 78 percent, Unit 3, 62 percent and Unit 4, 32 percent. The Hot Functional Test for Unit 1 was completed on October 12. The on-site date for fuel at Unit 1 was expected to be in the first quarter of 2017 [22].

In May 2017, ENEC announced the construction of Unit 1 was complete. The commencement of operations was delayed to 2018 to provide "sufficient time for international assessments and adherence to nuclear industry safety standards, as well as a reinforcement of operational proficiency…"[23]

The four reactors at Barakah are scheduled to be completed on time in July 2020. As indicated by the meeting summaries discussed above, the program has proceeded exceedingly well, while adhering strictly to the principles of safety, security, non-proliferation, transparency, and sustainability. The education of selected Emiratis in nuclear-related subjects are rapidly expanding, and women are being brought into the program in increasing numbers (20 percent of the total workforce, with a number working on site and a growing number of reactor operators to be when operations begin). It remains an all-important program for the United Arab Emirates, the Middle East region, and the world community, especially as the threat of climate change continues to increase. When the fourth plant is completed, a significant portion of the electricity produced within the UAE will be generated from a safe, clean, and reliable source of power – the Barakah nuclear power plants.

References

[1] World Nuclear Association Nuclear Power in the United Arab Emirates (Internet), Available from: www.world-nuclear.org/information-library/country-profiles/coun tries-t-z/united-arab-emirates.aspx

[2] International Advisory Board for the UAE Nuclear Program, First Semi-Annual Report, 2010 (Internet), *Nuclear Threat Initiative*. Available from: www.nti.org /media/pdfs/IAB-UAE_First_Semi-Annual_Report.pdf?_=1335555047

[3] Bush Backs Transfer of U.S. Ports to Dubai Firm, NBCNEWS.com (February 21, 2006) (Internet). Available from: www.nbcnews.com/id/11474440/ns/us_news-security/t/bush-backs-transfer-us-ports-dubai-firm/#.WOKrvFMrKgx

[4] D. E. Sanger, Under Pressure, Dubai Company Drops Port Deal, *The New York Times*, (March 10, 2006).

[5] The U.S. Atomic Energy Act Section 123 at a Glance, Arms Control Association. Updated March 2013, (Internet). Available from: https://www.armscontrol.org/factsheets/AEASection123

[6] World Nuclear Association, Nuclear Power in the United Arab Emirates. (Internet) Available from: http://www.world-nuclear.org/information-library/country-profiles/countries-t-z/united-arab-emirates.aspx

[7] Ibid.

[8] Advisory Board for the UAE Nuclear Program, First Semi-Annual Report, 2010. Cover page.

[9] Ibid., p. 1.

[10] Ibid.

[11] Ibid., pp. 1–2.

[12] H. G. Kim, The Design Characteristics of Advanced Power Reactor: 1400 (Internet). Available from: http://wwwpub.iaea.org/MTCD/Publications/PDF/P1500_CD_Web/htm/pdf/topic3/3S09_Hangon%20Kim.pdf

[13] International Advisory Board for the UAE Nuclear Program, First Semi-Annual Report 2010, p. 2, 4.

[14] Ibid., p. 6.

[15] Ibid., p. 8.

[16] International Advisory Board for the UAE Nuclear Program, Fourth Semi-Annual Report 2012, p. 3.

[17] International Advisory Board for the UAE Nuclear Program, Fifth Semi-Annual Report 2012, pp. 2–3.

[18] World Nuclear Association, Nuclear Power in the United Arab Emirates, pp. 3–4.

[19] Ibid., p. 3.

[20] International Advisory Board for the UAE Nuclear Program, Twelfth Semi-Annual Report 2015, pp. 2–7.

[21] International Advisory Board for the UAE nuclear program, Thirteenth Semi-Annual Report 2016, pp. 1–6.

[22] International Advisory Board for the UAE Nuclear Program, Fourteenth Semi-Annual Report 2016, pp. 1–7.

[23] Caline Malek, Construction of UAE's first nuclear reactor complete but operation delayed to 2018, The National (May 5, 2017). Available from: http://www.thenational.ae/uae/government/construction-of-uaes-first-nuclear-reactor-complete-but-operation-delayed-to-2018.

12

Nuclear Nonproliferation: What Have We Learned in Sixty Years?

The Great Chance

In June of 1988, United States President Ronald Reagan traveled to Moscow to exchange the instruments of ratification (approved by the US Senate and the Russian Parliament) of the Intermediate Range Nuclear Forces (INF) Treaty and thereby bring it into force. The forty-five-year Cold War was gradually drawing to an end ever since the epochal meeting between Reagan and Soviet President Mikhail Gorbachev at Reykjavik, Iceland, two years before. Gorbachev welcomed Reagan to Moscow, the center of the "Evil Empire" that Reagan had so strongly denounced early in his presidency. After the ceremony of the exchange of instruments of ratification, as it was a mild June day in Moscow, Reagan and Gorbachev took a stroll, arm in arm, in Red Square. A journalist approached Reagan during the stroll and asked him if he believed that this country where he now was visiting still was the Evil Empire. Looking at the reporter Reagan replied, "No. That was another time, another place" [1]. Although the Cold War did not truly end – until the conclusion of the Conventional Arms in Europe Treaty – nearly two and a half years later, this brief response by President Reagan serves perhaps better than anything as the symbol of the slow ending of the titanic struggle between East and West known as the Cold War.

And in considering what we have learned in the more than seventy years since the advent of the nuclear weapon in 1945, it may be more important to unlearn the attitudes of caution and conflict of today and try to recapture the spirit of Ronald Reagan and Mikhail Gorbachev at Reykjavik in 1986. "Reagan and Gorbachev broke the back of the superpower nuclear arms race. Reykjavik was the pivot point for this world–historic achievement. The ambition of these two men was breathtaking and contrasts painfully to

316

President Barack Obama's hesitancy and President Vladimir Putin's revanchist tendencies" [2] said Michael Krepon in his 2014 article "Reagan, Gorbachev and Reykjavik." And this contrast of hesitancy applies to many of those involved in the nuclear arms limitation effort that followed Reagan and Gorbachev.

Reykjavik which took place over two days, October 11–12, 1986, was truly one of the most remarkable meetings in history. President Reagan arrived on October 9, Gorbachev on October 10, and their first meeting was Saturday morning, October 11. The meeting was presented by the Soviets as a private meeting, to prepare for the Washington summit meeting, which took place over a year later at which the INF Treaty was signed. However, Gorbachev planned to surprise the Americans at the Reykjavik meeting and present far-reaching proposals to reduce and eventually eliminate nuclear weapon systems both strategic and tactical. The Americans who did bring a small but high-level support staff with President Reagan and Secretary of State George Shultz, were not entirely surprised. Gorbachev had come to Reykjavik a convert, a believer in the importance of the elimination of nuclear weapons. Reagan had held that view for years; many of his supporters were of the view that since he also supported a vast arms buildup in all types of weapons – including nuclear weapon delivery systems – that he didn't really believe in nuclear weapon elimination – but he did.

President Reagan's vehicle for ending the nuclear weapon arms race was the high-tech ballistic missile defense program called the Strategic Defense Initiative or SDI, referred to as Star Wars (after the movie) by his critics. Reagan was totally committed to SDI because of his belief that this program of missile defense which would include space-based systems really could provide absolute security from missile attack and therefore end the arms race. That this was a fantasy made the ultimate end of the negotiations at Reykjavik even more tragic. Gorbachev on the other hand had been able to wrest agreement from the Soviet military for his deep cuts in nuclear weapon systems proposal by committing that he would hold the line on SDI and confine it to the laboratory. In Soviet eyes SDI was actually intended to establish the technologized basis for a system of space weapons which would directly threaten them. Thus the possibility for failure was built into the meeting from the beginning. Nevertheless, the two leaders using their imagination and fired by their mutual commitment to eliminate nuclear weapons came close to reaching this goal – at least in principle.

Reagan in his opening remarks at the first meeting between the two asked which issues should they discuss first and that he was "proceeding from the assumption that both sides want to rid the world of ballistic missiles and of nuclear weapons in general. The world wants to know if we can make that happen." Truly a remarkable statement with which to open a summit meeting in a private meeting with the leader of the Soviet Union. A bit later in the discussion as Gorbachev was presenting his surprise proposal for deep reductions he also said, "We are in favor of finding a solution that would lead eventually to a complete liquidation of nuclear arms" [3].

Thus the two leaders, except for SDI, were on the same page. Gorbachev added, "Along the way to that goal, at every stage, there should be equality and equal security for the USA and the Soviet Union. ... We expect that the USA will act in the same way." Reagan replied, "We feel exactly the same way. ... You and I were optimistic at Geneva about reducing intermediate-range nuclear weapons in Europe. I can see us completely eliminating this class of weapons. We should be able to make progress on strategic weapons as well" [4].

So the stage was set. What followed was two days of discussing further and in more detail the elimination of nuclear weapons, while at the same time constantly being frustrated by Reagan's commitment to SDI, Gorbachev's need to limit it to the laboratory and Reagan's belief that the program must include testing in space otherwise the program would not be viable as Congress would never fund it.

There was a second meeting in the afternoon which included Secretary Shultz and Soviet Foreign Minister Eduard Shevardnadze. Then an all-night meeting of experts chaired by Ambassador Paul Nitze on the American side and the Chief of the Soviet General Staff, Marshal Sergei Akhromeyev on the other. There was also a second late-night meeting involving Ambassador Rozanne Ridgway and Soviet Ambassador Alexander Bessmertnykh dealing with human rights and regional issues. The meeting of experts made very significant progress coming close to an agreement on the outline of a Strategic Arms Reduction Treaty (START) Treaty and an INF Treaty.

In the bilateral discussion between Reagan and Gorbachev, with Shultz and Shevardnadze sitting in but not often speaking up, progress on everything was gradually made except for SDI. Reagan insisted that there had to be SDI testing in space and Gorbachev held fast to his position that it must be confined to the laboratory for ten years and would only be deployed on mutual agreement. Ten years would allow the two sides to solve the problems of reducing nuclear weapons. They were explicitly agreed on a formula for the INF Treaty and a 50 percent reduction in strategic weapons. But on SDI there was no movement. Off and on the meeting ground on all day.

In the afternoon meeting on the second day, Reagan after a time called for a recess so the two leaders could meet with their advisors. In the American meeting, President Reagan looked at Assistant Secretary of Defense Richard Perle and said, "Can we carry out research under the

restraints the Soviets are proposing?" Perle replied, "Mr. President, we
cannot conduct the research under the terms he is proposing ... "
The president thought for a moment and then turned to Nitze and Shultz.
They both counseled him to accept the language proposed by Gorbachev,
and suggested that they would worry about whether research could be
conducted in the laboratory later. Reagan then proceeded to accept Perle's
argument, over that of his most experienced counselors, Nitze and Shultz.
SDI was later abandoned in 1993 by the Clinton Administration, a 44-
billion-dollar failure in order to pursue a program of a ground-based
ballistic-missile defense [5].

At 5:30 p.m. a few hours before departure Reagan and Gorbachev held
their last meeting. It was back and forth again on what they were going to
do. Finally Reagan said, "Let me ask, do we mean that by the end of the
two five year periods [of agreed nuclear weapon reduction] all nuclear
explosive devices will be eliminated, including bombs, battlefield weapons, cruise missiles, sub-launched, everything? It would be fine with me if
we got rid of them all." Gorbachev replied, "We can do that. We can
eliminate them all." Shultz said, "Let's do it." Reagan said, "If we agree
by the end of this ten-year period all nuclear weapons will be eliminated,
we can send that agreement to Geneva. Our teams can put together
a treaty and we can sign it when you come to Washington." Gorbachev
agreed and then raised the caveat of confining SDI to the laboratory.
A furious back and forth followed, interrupted by emotional appeals by
Gorbachev and Shevardnadze.

GORBACHEV: "Is that your final position? If so then I think that we can end our
  meeting on that."
REAGAN: "Yes, it's final. You must understand that experiments and research
  cannot always remain within laboratory walls – sometimes it's necessary to
  go outside."
GORBACHEV: "And you understand me, too. The question of the laboratory
  for us isn't a matter of being stubborn or hardheaded. It's not casuistry.
  We're agreeing to deep reductions and in the final analysis to the
  destruction of nuclear arms. But at the very same time, the American
  side is pushing us to agree to allow them the right to create space
  weapons. That's unacceptable to us. If you agree to restrict your research
  to the laboratory, without going into space, then in two minutes I'll be
  ready to sign the treaty."

* * *

REAGAN: "It's a question of one word. If I give you what you're asking, it will cause me great damage at home."

GORBACHEV: "Let's end it there then. We can't agree to what you're asking – that's all I have to say."

REAGAN: "Are you really, for the sake of one word, going to reject the historic possibility of an accord?"

GORBACHEV: "It's not just a question of a word, but a question of principle.

If I return to Moscow and say I agreed to allow you to test in the atmosphere and in space, they would call me a fool and not a leader."

* * *

REAGAN: "It's a pity. We were so close to agreement. I think, after all, that you didn't want to reach an agreement. I'm sorry."

GORBACHEV: "I'm also sorry this happened. I did want an agreement and I did everything I could for it, if not more."

REAGAN: "I don't know when we'll have another chance like this, or if we'll be able to meet soon."

GORBACHEV: "I don't know either" [6].

What a tragic outcome! This is a story that would have interested Shakespeare. Just the American president's adherence to one program, one idea – which just a few years later was abandoned by his successor as impractical – prevented agreement between the president of the United States and the leader of the Soviet Union to eliminate nuclear weapons. It is true that the agreement if reached was likely not sustainable given the certain implacable opposition in the two capitals from politicians and bureaucracy. Likely it would have been quickly undermined and rendered a nullity. Nevertheless, just its brief existence would have set a standard which in future years could have led the United States and Russia and others to work together to pursue a program leading toward eliminating nuclear weapons worldwide over a long period of time. But since the word "space" did in fact block this near-agreement at Reykjavik today we have a situation in the second decade of the twenty-first century where there appears to be little chance of developing a process which could lead to the elimination of nuclear weapons. At least not by means of the traditional route, that is, negotiations between the United States and the Russian Federation, due to the current high level of enmity between the two states which appears unlikely to subside in the foreseeable future.

So in general the Reykjavik meeting is regarded as a failure, a missed opportunity of existential dimensions. It was this but it was also a success. For the first time the Russians accepted the principle of on-site inspection for arms control verification which opened the door for several new and important achievements in the near future which would not have been possible without agreement on this principle: the INF Treaty, the START Treaty, the Conventional Armed Forces in Europe Treaty, the Chemical Weapons Convention, and the signing of the Comprehensive Nuclear Test Ban Treaty.

The Post-Cold War Era

The Cold War ended in 1991 almost completely peacefully. The Soviet empire in Eastern Europe ended and the Soviet Union itself collapsed into the successor states with Russia inheriting the role of the surviving nuclear weapon state. The other heirs of nuclear weapons Ukraine, Belarus and Kazakhstan gave them up pursuant to the START Treaty. There was violence only in Romania, essentially change was peaceful everywhere else. Some forty-five years of the Cold War thermonuclear confrontation ended without catastrophic nuclear war which had the potential to annihilate humanity. One superpower, the Soviet Union, was destroyed, the other, the United States, survived apparently victorious but in fact gravely wounded and damaged. To this day in 2017 the United States has not recovered from the Cold War, even though the recovery from WWII was rapid and complete. Richard Rhodes comments on this:

> [After the Cold War ended] some of those in America who had promoted that confrontation with inflated threats, fearmongering, and misleading or fraudulent intelligence claimed shamelessly that the United States had won the Cold War. The world had won with the two superpowers at least partly disarmed. The Soviet Union had dissolved into its original components, a socioeconomic disaster for most of the new nations and especially for Russia, where life expectancy continued to decline, descending to a truncated 59.0 years for Russian males in 2000 and the population to plummet from a wide excess of deaths over births. The United States was left standing, seeming triumphant, but across the Cold War, nuclear weapons and weapons-related programs had cost the nation at least $5.5 trillion. Carl Sagan estimated in 1992 that other Cold War costs took the total even higher, to about $10 trillion ... What we bought for a waste of treasure unprecedented in human history was not peace nor even safety but a pervasive decline in the capacity and clemency of American life. As in the countries of the former Soviet Union, but not as severely, even American male life expectancy stalled compared to the European democracies and Japan." [7]

And what this meant was the decline of our cities and financial inability to meet the problems the cities faced: poverty, crime, riots, pollution, and rapidly expanding educational requirements. And with the schools not built, the roads not improved, the bridges not repaired, rail systems left to stagnate, and general civic infrastructure not improved the effect was incalculable. The deep budget deficits caused by stratospheric defense budgets which do not create investment in the economy, became a severe drag on our economy. General civic destitution, a decline in public services, like police, fire departments, and public libraries, appeared in many communities.

During the Bill Clinton administration a revival of sorts took place. Defense budgets had been declining for several years before and under President Clinton the defense budget was reduced by approximately $10 billion a year. But these savings largely went to deficit reduction as the deficits had been so deep during the Reagan era. And Bill Clinton did leave office with a balanced budget, with surpluses for the future as far in the future as could be seen. This situation, as is well known, was promptly turned around by his successor.

> "Far from victory in the Cold War, the superpower nuclear-arms race and the corresponding militarization of the American economy gave us ramshackle cities, broken bridges, failing schools, entrenched poverty, impeded life expectancy, and a menacing and secretive national-security state . . . " says Rhodes [8].

In summing up the advent of nuclear weapons, the Cold War and the continued inability to address the problem of nuclear weapons Rhodes concludes,

> The discovery of how to release nuclear energy was a fact, not a choice, a new understanding of the natural world. It revealed that there was no limit to the amount of energy that might be packaged into small, portable, and relatively inexpensive weapons; that there could be no defense against such weapons, each of which could destroy a city; that therefore a policy of common security in the short run and a program of abolition in the long run would be necessary to accommodate the new reality and avoid disaster. Recoiling from such inquiries, which would require negotiation, compromise, and a measure of humility, we chose to distend ourselves into the largest scorpion in the bottle. Obstinately misreading the failure of our authoritarian counterpart on the other side of the world, to our shame and misfortune, we continue to claim an old and derelict sovereignty that the weapons themselves deny." [9]

In part as a result of these policies we probably have lost for the foreseeable future our indispensable negotiating partner to proceed further down the road toward the elimination of nuclear weapons beyond the two US-Russia strategic weapon reduction agreements; the START treaty which bridged the end of the Cold War; and its follow-on, the 2010 New START treaty which is likely the last gasp of US-Russian strategic arms limitation cooperation for the foreseeable future. And this comes at a time when the world community is confronted with the greatest threat to its continued existence that it has ever faced – climate change. Peaceful energy from nuclear power – verifiably and completely separate from nuclear weapons – widely deployed and promptly brought into operation to provide reliable base load electricity, while over time fossil fuel power generation is completely eliminated, is our only true defense against this overarching threat. Renewable energy can be a useful adjunct, but only nuclear power has proved over decades that it can reliably provide base load energy to power cities. But this requires a strong world economy – especially in the US – free from large war expenditures and international cooperation of a depth and duration never before known in history.

Nations Wanting Weapons: From India to Iran

But before turning to the prospects for the NPT, the central international security instrument of our era, it would be useful to add to the discussion begun in Chapter One of the motivations for acquiring nuclear weapons and the history of nations doing so. In what follows, we review the weapon programs of the remaining states that have acquired nuclear arsenals over the decades: India, Pakistan, North Korea, and Israel. As part of this, we will briefly review potential programs in other countries.

From the beginning, India was interested in nuclear weapons. As early as 1947 India's first Prime Minister Jawaharlal Nehru was discussing the desirability of nuclear weapons. In 1948, he established the Indian Atomic Energy Commission and appointed Dr. Homi Bhabha its first Chairman. Homi Bhabha was to become known as the father of the Indian nuclear weapon program. In April of 1948 Nehru said, upon the opening of the Indian Atomic Energy Agency, "We must develop atomic energy apart from the war, [but] if we are compelled to use it for other purposes, no pious sentiments will stop the nation from using it that way" [10]. Already by 1958 India had started down the road of acquiring nuclear weapons. India purchased a 40 MW CIRUS (Canadian-Indian-US) reactor from Canada and twenty-one tons of heavy water from the United States. CIRUS was a research reactor, moderated by heavy water, and was fueled by natural uranium. It was sited at Trombay and at the same site India built a reprocessing plant to separate plutonium from the spent fuel. The reactor went critical in 1960 and the reprocessing plant was completed in 1965. The reactor and heavy water were supposed to be used for "peaceful purposes" but there were no verification arrangements made.

While Nehru was willing to pledge that the Indian nuclear activities were for peaceful purposes, he noted in 1958 that India had the capability to build a bomb "in three or four years if we divert sufficient resources in that direction." At the same time Bhabha told an English friend that he wanted India to acquire nuclear weapons and a colleague, the prominent French scientist

Bertrand Goldschmidt, recalled that "Bhabha always wanted the bomb." [11]. And indeed the facilities in Trombay became the foundation of the Indian nuclear weapon program, very greatly angering the Canadians and the Americans. The American government also supported the construction of the two light water power reactors in Tarapur to the north of Trombay but India agreed that the fuel for their reactors would be under IAEA safeguards. So even without a decision to test a bomb, India continued to accumulate plutonium and design research was done by Indian scientists so that India progressed steadily toward nuclear weapon capability. And India never signed the NPT.

The Indian program has always been shrouded in extraordinary secrecy. The Cabinet and the military have largely been shut out of it, the Prime Minister and the top atomic scientists were the only ones in the know. In 1964 as the expected first Chinese test grew closer, the pressure in India for the development of an atomic bomb increased. Bhabha began public and private efforts to pressure Prime Minister Lal Bahadur Shastri, who had succeeded Nehru upon his death in 1964, to go for the bomb. He said in London that India could develop and test a nuclear weapon within eighteen months of deciding to do so. The right-wing opposition party Jama Singh introduced a resolution calling for India to develop a bomb. The resolution was easily defeated as the Prime Minister, who favored nuclear disarmament, wanted, but in his speech he reminded Parliament that India could develop a weapon in two to three years [12].

In 1966 Indira Gandhi succeeded Shastri upon his death. In her first years she did little on the bomb program but the scientists kept moving ahead. In 1970 construction of a new research reactor began at Trombay which would provide important data for the design of India's first atomic device. The reactor began operations in May 1972 and the scientists began work on the development of an explosive device. A model of the device was shown to Mrs. Gandhi in September 1972 and she was asked whether it should be built. Reportedly she replied "Get it ready. I will tell you whether to do it or not" [13].

With this authorization work proceeded ahead to continue the development and to construct the device, interestingly known as the "Smiling Buddha." A test site was located and orders given to prepare a shaft 350 feet deep. Supposedly the Indian government was searching for water in the desert in Rajasthan.

That was all anyone knew except close aides to the Prime Minister and the top scientists. The device was brought to the site in great secrecy and was in place by May 15, 1974. On May 18, 1974, to the surprise of the United States, India conducted a single nuclear weapon test explosion. Condemned by much of the world India leaders hastily called this a "peaceful uses experiment." The Indian national security cabinet members, defense and foreign affairs, only learned of the nuclear weapon program a week before the test [14]. Why did Mrs. Gandhi do it? The war with China was in 1962 and the first Chinese test was in 1964; the Indian nuclear policy did not change at that time, only years later. Some believe that it was a warning shot at Pakistan whose leader had said that the Pakistan people will get the bomb even if they have to "eat grass" [15].

But this isn't the end of the story. On the day of the successful test Mrs. Gandhi's top scientists suggested more tests to which Mrs. Gandhi strongly objected. The nuclear explosive work was brought to a halt [16]. There was little change to Indian policy in the ensuing years. India did no more tests and did not produce "weaponized devices." After Mrs. Gandhi's assassination in 1984 her son Rajiv succeeded her. His principal interest was nuclear disarmament but with the growing threat of the Pakistani bomb he gave his secret approval in the late 1980s for weaponization work to begin [17]. In 1996 his successor, Prime Minister Rao, was planning a test but the US threatened sanctions; President Clinton called him and he backed down.

In March 1998 the Hindu Nationalist Party, the Bharatiya Janata Party (BJP)—the successor to the Jama Singh which called for an Indian bomb back in 1964 – came to power for the second time, this time with a working majority. During the campaign the BJP had issued a manifesto which among other things echoed the BJP's 1996 campaign calling for an end to "nuclear apartheid" (India's description of the NPT) and which said the party would "re-evaluate the country's nuclear policy and exercise the option to induct nuclear weapons." The BJP saw a nuclear armed India as a way of not only deterring Pakistan but of deterring another nation that represented an even greater threat – China [18].

The new government led by the BJP was sworn in on March 19, 1998. On April 6 Pakistan tested a Ghauri missile, which was capable of hitting India's major cities. Two days later the new Prime Minister Atal Behari Vajpayee called together his chief scientific aides and told them to proceed to test the nuclear devices that they had developed and which had long been ready [19]. He did this without consulting or informing his cabinet and his military leaders. Vaypayee had been told by his science advisors the day after he was sworn in that the testing of the devices was necessary in order to have confidence in the weapons. On May 11th India conducted three nuclear tests – one of which was said to be a thermonuclear device at the Pokhran test site in the desert in Rajasthan. Two sub-kiloton tests were carried out two days later. India announced it was now a nuclear weapon state.

Shortly after conducting the Pokhran tests Prime Minister Vajpayee set forth his reasons for conducting the tests in a letter to President Clinton and other leaders. "We have an overt nuclear weapon state on our borders [China], a state which committed armed aggression against India in 1962. Although our relations with that country have improved in the last decade or so, an atmosphere of distrust persists." Vajpayee continued by asserting that China was assisting "another neighbor of ours [Pakistan] to become a covert nuclear weapon state," one that had committed "three aggressions in the last fifty years" along with "unremitting terrorism and militancy sponsored by it in several parts of the country" [20]. But perhaps the central reason for Vajpayee was his belief as he explained to a reporter for India Today on May 25th, "The greatest meaning of these tests is that they have given India 'Shaki' [a Vedic concept of the liberation of energy], they have given India strength and they have given India self-confidence" [21]. India with the bomb would soon be taking its rightful place among the great powers for it was "India's due" as Vajpayee told Parliament, "the right of one-sixth of humankind" [22]. In these words one hears clear echoes from the British and French cases. In other words, the real objective of the tests was great power status for India. There was also an element of anticolonialism and racism (white men have built nuclear weapons, dark-skinned men can as well). There was no doubt that India considered itself a nuclear weapon state. The Indian tests also assured that Pakistan would follow India with a series of nuclear weapon tests in the near future. And that is in fact what happened as will be discussed later in this chapter.

Brazil and Argentina pursued a rivalry for some years when both had military governments. Each suspected the other of pursuing a nuclear weapons program.

In any case these programs were abandoned by both countries once they returned to civilian rule.

South Africa began mining uranium in 1944 and increased production in the 1950s. In 1965 construction began at Pelindaba on the Safari-1, a 20-megawatt research reactor sold to South Africa by the United States under the Atoms for Peace program, becoming operational in 1967. This reactor was under IAEA safeguards. At the inauguration ceremony for the commencement of construction of Safari-1, Prime Minister H. F. Verwoerd implied that South Africa should acquire nuclear weapons. In 1970, construction began on a pilot enrichment plant at Valindaba near Pelindaba where earlier enrichment experiments had secretly taken place, and in 1974 Prime Minister John Vorster authorized the construction of the first South African nuclear weapon. A test site was located in the Kalahari Desert [23].

The enrichment facility would begin producing highly enriched uranium (HEU) in 1978. South Africa prepared a test shaft at the prospective test site in advance in 1977. These preparations were detected by a Soviet reconnaissance satellite and the Soviets passed this information on to Washington urging action. After reconnaissance of its own the United States agreed with the Soviets that this looked like an impending test. Britain, France, and Germany joined the United States and the Soviet Union in protests to the South African government. After some days of denial the South African government gave the assurances that were demanded and declared that South Africa had no intention of developing nuclear explosives for any purpose. The test site had been dismantled overnight. After the 1977 clamor had died down, the Valindaba plant began producing HEU. By the end of 1978, the plant was beginning the process to provide enough HEU for the assembly of one unsophisticated gun-type nuclear weapon per year. South Africa built six with a yield of 15–20 kilotons each. Some believe that a mysterious double flash of light detected by a US satellite in 1979 was an Israeli test of a tactical nuclear weapon, with South African assistance; near remote South African islands in the South Atlantic. This incident, after years of debate, is now thought to have been a test by Israel alone on South African territory. South Africa did not have enough HEU by the time of the alleged Israel test in 1979 to fabricate a device. And in 1986 when Mordechai Vanunu, an Israeli Arab working at the Israeli nuclear weapon center at Dimona defected he brought with him many pictures of the internals of the facility. These he subsequently gave to the *London Times* and their subsequent publication on October 5, 1986, informed the world that far from being a "bomb in the basement" the Israeli nuclear program was a highly sophisticated one, consistent with 100-200 weapons and perhaps a thermonuclear capacity, similar to that of France from which it was largely derived [24].

F. W. deKlerk was elected to the presidency of South Africa on September 14, 1989, at the end of the Cold War. Shortly after assuming office de Klerk announced his intention to end Apartheid and shut down South Africa's nuclear weapon program. Nelson Mandela was released from prison in February 1990, the dismantlement of the nuclear weapons began in July, and by September 1991 the six nuclear weapons were disassembled and the components scattered into South Africa's nuclear power and medical isotopes industries. On July 10, 1990, South Africa became a party to the NPT and on March 24, 1993, President de Klerk released much of this publically in a speech to the South African Parliament.

Four other nuclear programs came upon the scene during these years, those of Pakistan, North Korea, Iraq, and Iran. In addition, Libya and Syria – while

NPT nonnuclear weapon state parties, covertly attempted to procure the bomb from outside sources.

Libya made numerous attempts to acquire nuclear weapons or nuclear weapon technology. In 1970 Muammar Qadhafi sent a senior official to China in an effort to buy a nuclear weapon; he was politely rebuffed by Zhou Enlai. Numerous efforts were made to acquire nuclear weapon-related assistance from both India and Pakistan to no avail [25]. Libya approached the Pakistani rogue proliferator A.Q. Khan in the 1990s, reaching an agreement finally approved in 2000 to deliver centrifuges and the design of an atomic bomb – the same Chinese design that had been supplied to Pakistan in the early 1980s. This arrangement was disrupted by British and American intelligence and it was terminated in 2003 [26]. And not long after this Khan's entire program was shut down by the Pakistani government under American pressure and Khan placed under house arrest for some five years.

Syria apparently entered into an agreement with North Korea to construct at Al Kibar, a remote site in North Syria, a nuclear reactor with the same design as the plutonium producing five megawatt (electric) reactor at Yongbyon, North Korea. It was destroyed by Israel in an air raid on September 6, 2007, as it was nearing completion [27].

It was Saddam Hussein himself who led Iraq's efforts to acquire weapons of mass destruction, in particular nuclear weapons. The Iraq Atomic Energy Agency had been established in 1959 at the Nuclear Research Center at Tuwaitha, near Baghdad. In 1974 French Prime Minister Jacques Chirac visited Iraq and this led to the signing in 1976 of an agreement to sell to Iraq a 70-megawatt research reactor similar to the Osiris reactor in France. The purchase was subsequently modified to be a 40-megawatt materials testing reactor (MTR). The MTR design is useful for countries with established reactor programs – which Iraq did not have – but not particularly useful for a country without such a program unless it is interested in producing plutonium to make a bomb [28]. The standard fuel for a MTR reactor was HEU on which the Iraqis insisted. Saddam Hussein himself proclaimed that this reactor was part of "the first Arab attempt at nuclear arming" [29].

The reactor was destroyed on June 7, 1981, by an Israeli air strike shortly before it was to become operational. Thereafter the Iraqi program went underground. It made considerable progress using highly outmoded technology but was completely destroyed in early 1990s in the aftermath of the first Gulf War.

The defeat by India in the 1971 War was a humiliating experience for Pakistan. Pakistani armed forces surrendered to Indian forces in the Pakistani province of West Bengal which became the independent nation of Bangladesh on December 16, 1971. On December 20, the military government resigned and

Foreign Minister Zulfikar Ali Bhutto became the national leader. He vowed to rally and restore the nation by invoking a deep sense of nationalism to "never again" suffer defeat and dismemberment. The Pakistanis vowed to build a "new Pakistan." Nuclear weapons were seen a central to this and possession of such weapons would be the ultimate guarantee of national self-reliance [30]. To quote General Feroz Khan, one of the architects of the Pakistani nuclear weapon program directly " ... nuclear weapons are the only guarantee of Pakistan's national survival in the face of both an inveterately hostile India that cannot be deterred conventionally and unreliable external allies that fail to deliver in extremis" [31] and while Bhutto had made his first "we shall eat grass" comment in 1965 while Foreign Minister to the Manchester Guardian in the context of India acquiring the bomb, General Khan has him indicating the following to a scientific gathering on January 20, 1972 that Pakistan needs to acquire nuclear weapons because "We are fighting a thousand year war against India" and like Israel and India, Pakistan never signed the NPT [32].

Munir Kahn was appointed at this meeting as the new Chairman of the Pakistan Atomic Energy Commission. Dr. A.Q. Kahn, a young Pakistani who had received his graduate education in Europe, at this time was working as a subcontractor for the European enrichment corporation URENCO where he had access to sensitive information relating to uranium enrichment and the nuclear fuel cycle. Traumatized by the 1971 defeat he volunteered as, in essence, a spy in 1974 and transferred centrifuge plans and other important information to Pakistani agents. He returned to Pakistan in 1975 and, reporting directly to Bhutto, established the Engineering Research Laboratories (ERL) which soon established what became a large, secret plant at Kahuta, near Islamabad. Khan then went on a huge shopping spree in Europe to purchase the necessary technology for the Pakistani program. He, for example, purchased from a Swiss company a large system of pipes and vacuum valves to feed uranium hexafluoride gas into centrifuges, without an export license. Three Pakistani C-130 cargo planes arrived in Switzerland a few months later to transport this equipment to Pakistan. After many such purchases Khan invited European technicians that he had known while at URENCO to come and train the "local boys" [33]. Soon, as Washington began to realize, all was in place to produce the material for a bomb. And after Bhutto was overthrown by General Muhammad Zia-al-Haq, Khan's role only increased. In 1981 ERL became the Khan Research Laboratories (KRL). The United States was fully aware of all this by the mid-1980s and by May 1990 concluded that Pakistan possessed one or more nuclear weapons. By 1994 the estimated number was six to eight and it was believed Pakistan could produce one or two more a year. The United States was also aware that China had passed to Pakistan a design for a 20-kiloton weapon [34]. Over the years the Pakistani stockpile has greatly increased and on May 28 and May 30, 1998, after the Indian tests and an intense internal debate, Pakistan carried out six nuclear weapon tests – one more than India, also claiming that it was now a nuclear weapon state [35]. CIA Director George Tenet once famously described A.Q. Khan in Congressional testimony as "at least as dangerous as Osama bin Laden" [36].

Further, Khan made an offer to provide uranium enrichment technology to North Korea which was carried out in the mid-1990s. In the early 1990s he accompanied Prime Minister Benazir Bhutto on a state visit to Pyongyang, North Korea and on the margins of the meeting arranged a deal to exchange uranium enrichment technology for designs and parts of North Korea's effective medium range missile, the Nodong, which became the Ghauri, in Pakistan [37]. And he also made the sale to Libya mentioned above as well as a sale to Iran discussed below.

The North Korean dictator Kim Il Sung sent two delegations to China, in 1964 and 1974, seeking assistance to acquire nuclear weapons without success. In the late 1970s he gave the order for North Korea to build nuclear weapons on its own. In 1986 North Korea brought on line a 5-megawatt (electric) nuclear reactor which made enough plutonium for one bomb a year. The Soviets pressured North Korea to join the NPT which they did in 1986 but only signed their NPT required IAEA Safeguards Agreement in 1992. A dispute broke out between North Korea and the IAEA about access to two waste storage sites (as well as the IAEA discovering a reprocessing facility) and the IAEA demanded an inspection of the sites in early 1993. North Korea rejected the demand and shortly after gave their 90-day notice of withdrawal from the NPT. This led to a complicated negotiation with the United States – on the 89th day the DPRK "suspended" its withdrawal – which led to the Agreed Framework Agreement which shut down, but did not eliminate, the North Korean program. In 2000 the Clinton administration signed a "no hostile intent" communiqué with North Korea and was close to an agreement terminating North Korea's missile program. Up to that time, North Korea had done nothing with the uranium technology that it had acquired from A.Q. Khan.

However, the Bush administration chose not to pick up with North Korea where the Clinton administration left off. The "no hostile intent" communiqué was not renewed, North Korea was included in the "Axis of Evil" group in President Bush's January 2002 State of the Union message and, admittedly on no new information since the Clinton administration certified North Korea to be in compliance with the Agreed Framework the previous year, the Bush Administration found North Korea to be not in compliance with the Agreed Framework [38].

In January 2003, North Korea with one day's notice "completed" its withdrawal from the NPT, conducted reprocessing campaigns at Yongbyon – after restarting the reactor there – in 2003 and 2005, built ten to twelve nuclear weapons, and conducted four nuclear weapon tests in 2006, 2009, 2013, and early 2016, with a fifth, in the thirty-kiloton range, coming in September 2016.

Iran has had a long interest in nuclear weapons dating back to the Shah. Since the 1990s it has had a significant program substantially advanced by the uranium enrichment technology acquired clandestinely from A.Q. Khan. He sold to Iran uranium enrichment technology – centrifuges – and probably a copy of the bomb design given to Pakistan by China. Iran made two attempts to negotiate with the US in 2001 and 2003 which were ignored by the Bush administration. Subsequent negotiations yielded little until the election of President Rouhani in June 2013. In July 2015, after a lengthy but intense negotiation, the Joint Comprehensive Plan of Action was signed by the five permanent members of the Security Council plus Germany known as the P-5 + 1 and Iran. The JCPOA is a complete agreement putting stringent controls on Iran's entire nuclear program for ten to fifteen years, twenty-five years for some elements.

And why would Iran want nuclear weapons? Common assumptions point to Israel, as a perceived nuclear threat, and also to the US, whose fifth fleet patrols the Persian Gulf and Indian Ocean. The motivations of the Islamic Republic today are different from those of Iran under the Shah, but both regimes share one reason for pursuing the bomb: international prestige. Since early in the Cold War with respect to major states, the possession of nuclear weapons has distinguished great powers from other states. Iran is a proud country. The Persian cultural heritage is one of the world's richest and the Persian Empire was once the world's most powerful. Many Iranians believe that as a great civilization with a long history, Iran has a right to acquire nuclear weapons [39].

With the demise of Saddam Hussein, nuclear weapons could enhance Iran's role as a regional power. The Islamic Republic was deeply scarred by the horrific casualties of the Iran-Iraq war and there is a strong "never again" sentiment in Iran as well. Nuclear weapons can be seen as insurance that something like that war will never happen again. And there are sectarian issues as well, if a radical Sunni regime were ever to come into power in Islamabad and thereby into possession of Pakistan's nuclear stockpile, Iran, as a Shia Muslim state, would have a right to be concerned [40].

The NPT: Origin, History, and Significance

The Nuclear Non-Proliferation Treaty, the NPT, arguably the most important international security agreement that exists, or which will probably ever exist until one day when nuclear weapons are permanently and verifiably eliminated worldwide, is somewhat of a hybrid. It is built on three pillars: nuclear non-proliferation, disarmament, and peaceful uses. Put another way, originally, the intent of the negotiators was to reduce the threat of nuclear weapons to the world while at the same time creating a regime for the peaceful use of nuclear technology.

But the Treaty ultimately established an international legal regime of non-proliferation which has two objectives: establishing a norm of international behavior that the further acquisition of nuclear weapons by any additional country – beyond the five nuclear weapon states endorsed by the NPT, that is the five that had carried out nuclear weapon test explosions prior to 1967 (the United States, the United Kingdom, France, Russia, and China)–is contrary to international law; and to guarantee the right to the peaceful use of nuclear technology to all NPT parties in good standing but to very heavily regulate this technology in order to prevent it from being used to breach the norm of behavior established by the Treaty. Further, the NPT declares the objective of the ultimate elimination of the nuclear arsenals possessed by the five NPT-approved nuclear weapon states.

Yet in the course of the negotiations toward the NPT, the two Superpowers, the United States and the Soviet Union, the co-managers of the NPT negotiations taking place at the Eighteen Nation Committee on Disarmament (ENCD) in Geneva, found the fifteen other negotiating partners (France, a member, refused to participate in these negotiations at the ENDC) insisting on balance in the Treaty. This was forecast in the Sweden/India sponsored United Nations General Assembly Resolution in 1965, referred to in Chapter One.

As a result of this the NPT became more than a normative treaty establishing the principle that there should be no more proliferation beyond those five states that already possessed arsenals of such weapons in 1968 (Articles I and II) – regarded as a particularly serious threat – but rather evolved into a treaty which also attempted to establish the principle that at some point in the future the possession of such weapons by anyone would be contrary to international law (Article VI), as well as a regime which guaranteed access to peaceful nuclear technology as in "inherent right" (Article IV) thereby necessitating the heavy regulation which now characterizes the NPT regime: the extensive development of related safeguard regulation established by the International Atomic Energy Agency (IAEA); the additional Model Protocol, also administered by the IAEA, which gives the IAEA much more in inspection rights; and the rules developed to govern trade in nuclear technology, first by the Zangger Committee, which established a list of sensitive nuclear technology items subject to special controls and later by the Nuclear Suppliers Group (NSG), which now requires that no sensitive nuclear technology will be exported by its large membership unless safeguards on all nuclear facilities are established by the importing country – the full scope safeguards rule. This rule was long championed by the United States and was attained only after an effort of many years. But then some years later in 2008 the US pushed through the NSG an exception to this rule for India. All this is discussed in more detail below.

It can be said that, based on the negotiating history of the NPT and the immediate aftermath of its signing, Article VI meant to the nonnuclear weapon states participating, first and foremost a comprehensive nuclear weapon test ban and, in addition, other measures such as reductions in nuclear weapons worldwide leading to their eventual elimination from the arsenal of states.

One other issue from the 1968 period that should be mentioned here is Article X.2, on NPT duration. The United States and others had pressed for a provision for indefinite duration for the NPT, as was the custom with respect to other arms control/nonproliferation treaties with many parties. But important states involved in the negotiating process were unwilling to agree to this for the NPT. These states included Germany, Sweden, and Italy. Among the concerns expressed were the commercial impact of the NPT safeguard system, the potential effectiveness of the NPT, and the prospects for widespread membership. Therefore, it was agreed that twenty-five years after entry into force of the treaty, the state parties would meet and decide by majority vote the ultimate duration of the NPT. In this regard an aide-mémoire sent to the ENCD in November 1967 by the Swiss government said, in part, referring to the issue of the duration of the non-proliferation treaty under negotiation, "The non-nuclear weapon states certainly cannot take the responsibility of tying their hands indefinitely if the nuclear weapon states fail to arrive at positive results in that direction," (the adoption of specific measures aimed at a limitation of armaments) [41].

The first NPT Review Conference in 1975 produced a strong reaffirmation of support for the Treaty by the parties. It also expressed good support for IAEA safeguards [42]. However, progress on Article VI by the nuclear weapon states was regarded as disappointing and a complete impasse was reached on the test ban. Some twenty nonnuclear weapon states proposed adding a protocol to the NPT mandating a test moratorium until France and China joined the treaty and after that a comprehensive test ban. This was rejected by the nuclear weapon states and, in order to permit agreement on a conference final document, conference president Inga Thorsson gaveled through a presidential statement as a compromise, among other things expressing the desire of the conference that a test ban treaty be concluded as soon as possible.

The second review conference in 1980 was similar to 1975 only worse. There was a continued strongly held view of a majority of the parties that the nuclear weapon states had not lived up to their Article VI obligations. The nonaligned NPT members insisted on commitment by the nuclear weapon states to a comprehensive test ban treaty and, failing to achieve that, blocked conference agreement on a final document. This was so, even though substantial agreement was reached in other areas such as peaceful uses and safeguards. At the 1985 conference, a final document was agreed upon by the pasting together of disparate views, primarily on Article VI issues using the on-the-one-hand/on-the-other-hand approach. Once again there was substantial agreement on peaceful uses and safeguards issues. Virtually all nonnuclear weapon states parties present supported immediate negotiations on, and the urgent conclusion of, a comprehensive test ban treaty. The Fourth Review Conference in 1990 ended in failure, even though once again there was substantial agreement on peaceful uses and safeguards. In the last days of the conference, many nonnuclear weapon states parties insisted on a commitment from the nuclear weapon states to a comprehensive test ban treaty, and the nuclear weapon states were unwilling to agree to this.

In the spring of 1995, the long-awaited NPT Review and Extension Conference took place. In the words of Article X.2 of the treaty, "Twenty-five years after the entry into force of the treaty, a conference shall be convened to decide whether the treaty should continue in force indefinitely, or shall be extended for an additional fixed period or periods. This decision shall be taken by a majority of the parties to the treaty." This being a one-time decision, otherwise such a measure would be treated as an amendment subject to ratification in 1995 by 178 national legislatures. Now it would be 190. Thus this was without question the decisive moment for the NPT and the outcome would turn primarily on how the Article VI issues were dealt with. The United States from the beginning of the run-up to the conference took a position for indefinite extension, strongly desiring to make the NPT permanent. Approximately 110 of the then 178 NPT states parties were nonnuclear weapon states parties (NNWS) considered to be in the nonaligned camp, and states in this group as well as a number of other nonnuclear states were of the view that the nuclear weapon states (NWS) had not fulfilled their Article VI obligations. The NPT was not a gift; it was a strategic bargain in their view; they had lived up to their side of the bargain, but the nuclear weapon states had not lived up to an important part of their side of the bargain – disarmament. As a result, most of these states were highly reluctant to agree to extend the NPT indefinitely, believing that if they did, they would lose all leverage over the nuclear weapon states and that the nuclear weapon states would never carry out their Article VI obligations.

The manager of the Review and Extension Conference was Ambassador Jayantha Dhanapala, a diplomat highly experienced in the nonproliferation field from Sri Lanka who had been elected president of the conference. The delegation that played the pivotal role was South Africa. South African Foreign Minister Nzo, in his speech on the first day of the conference, supported indefinite extension but proposed the establishment of benchmarks for disarmament progress linked to the permanent extension of the treaty. This provided the impetus for Ambassador Dhanapala to create a presidential consultations group, essentially to address the Article VI issues. The task of the consultations group was to develop an agreed document on arms control and nonproliferation objectives that all parties – including the nuclear weapon states – would agree to in the context of a strengthened and permanent NPT. There would also be a document enhancing the NPT review process to permit the almost annual monitoring of disarmament progress. The group was established in the second week of the four-week conference held in New York in April–May 1995.

Ambassador Dhanapala's goal in this procedure was to try to find a way to make an indefinite extension more attractive to those states parties that still wanted a shorter-term extension. If the main concern of many of the NNWS related to the fear of the loss of "leverage" over the NWS on disarmament, he believed that there might be some alternative ways for the NNWS to retain or perhaps even to expand that leverage. Limiting the extension was, in short, not the only means available to achieve such a goal – and the Treaty's review process offered the key to enhancing accountability [43].

The presidential consultations group continued its work after the second week of the conference. The countries included on this advisory committee were Algeria, Australia, Canada, China, Colombia, Egypt, France, Germany, Hungary, Indonesia, Iran, Japan, Malaysia, Mexico, the Netherlands, Poland, Romania, the Russian Federation, Senegal, South Africa, Sri Lanka, Sweden, Venezuela, the United Kingdom, and the United States. These countries represented all the nuclear weapon states, the leaders of the various regional groups, and other countries that conference president Ambassador Dhanapala believed had significant points of view that should be represented [44]. By the end of the second week of the conference, it was clear that a majority of the NPT states parties favored indefinite NPT extension. Early in the third week, on May 5, the Canadian representative,

Ambassador Chris Wesdahl, introduced a resolution for indefinite extension without conditions, sponsored by 105 states parties, easily a majority. Thus, Ambassador Dhanapala's efforts began to focus less on securing indefinite extension and more on achieving it by consensus, in the most positive way for the NPT regime, and therefore what would accompany indefinite extension as its political price, "indefinite extension plus," as he put it [45]. On April 21, South Africa circulated a working paper setting forth several proposals that it wished to see attached to a decision on indefinite extension. The paper identified five substantive goals to be included: a comprehensive test ban treaty, a fissile material cutoff treaty, security assurances, strengthening IAEA safeguards, and nuclear disarmament [46]. Added later were a few more issues such as more nuclear weapon free zones, particularly in the Middle East and improved NPT verification. Once again, these objectives followed the proposals of India and Sweden in 1965, part of the inspiration for NPT Article VI. The South African paper built on the general proposal of South Africa of April 19 of various "principles" of nuclear nonproliferation and disarmament in a strengthened review process to be in effect the "quid" for the "quo" of a conference decision indefinitely extending the NPT for the great benefit of all countries.

Ambassador Dhanapala assembled the "package" which would accompany a legally binding decision on indefinite extension, by consensus. This package, which would be termed "politically binding," but was intended to be the price for indefinite extension itself which would be internationally legally binding, and would consist of a resolution on "Strengthening the Review Process" and "Principles and Objectives for Nuclear Non-Proliferation and Disarmament." The package was approved by the presidential consultations group by consensus, and Ambassador Dhanapala was authorized to propose the three decisions to the conference plenary: "Strengthening the Review Process" (decision 1); "Principles and Objectives for Nuclear Non-Proliferation and Disarmament" (decision 2); "Extension of the Treaty on the Non-Proliferation of Nuclear Weapons" (decision 3). The enhanced review process provided for Preparatory Committee meetings in three of the four years prior to each five-year NPT Review Conference and these Preparatory Committee meetings were specifically authorized to monitor progress on the principles and objectives or, in other words, Article VI. The three decisions were approved by the conference by consensus on May 11, 1995. Added at the last minute was a fourth resolution calling on all Middle East states to join the NPT and to establish a zone free of weapons of mass destruction in the Middle East. It was the result of a long fruitless effort during the period leading to the 1995 Conference to persuade Israel to do something positive towards the NPT to the satisfaction of Egypt and its allies so they would support NPT indefinite extension. It also has caused much trouble later such as we shall see.

Ambassador Dhanapala made clear that his use of the terms "legally binding" and "politically binding" in no way diminished the nature of decision 1 and 2 as the basic "price" for NPT indefinite extension by consensus. Decision 2, like 1 and 3, was approved by all NPT states parties and should be considered a clear articulation of the meaning of Article VI, both as a central part of the basic NPT bargain of 1968 and the political justification for NPT indefinite extension in 1995. It binds all NPT states parties and is ignored at peril to the NPT regime.

A comprehensive test ban treaty to be negotiated in one year was the most important element of the Principles and Objectives Statement. The CTBT was signed after a vigorous negotiation completed in 1996 in Geneva dissented from only by India, approved at the United Nations General Assembly with the United States being the first country to sign. However, in subsequent years, negative developments for the NPT regime overshadowed positive ones. In 1998, both India and Pakistan carried out a series of nuclear weapon tests, declaring themselves to be nuclear weapon states and undermining the NPT regime from the outside. In April 1999, NATO issued its Strategic Concept outlining a nuclear doctrine that continued to assess nuclear weapons as essential in meeting NATO security needs, implicitly retaining the first use of nuclear weapons option; essentially contrary to the 1995 NPT Security Assurances statements as far as many NPT parties were concerned. The following year, Russia announced its new National Security Concept, which included a provision for the first use of nuclear weapons. In October 1999, came the most grievous blow, the rejection by the US Senate of the Comprehensive Test Ban Treaty, the most important element of Article VI, the long-term "litmus test" of nuclear-weapon-state compliance with Article VI.

The CTBT is the essential "glue" that holds the NPT together. It was the most important commitment by the NPT nuclear weapon states in the eyes of nonnuclear weapon NPT states parties in 1968. Giving up the testing of nuclear weapons is the "quid" for the "quo" of giving up nuclear weapons forever as nonnuclear weapon NPT states parties see it. But the Republican Party in the US has adopted an intransigent position on CTBT ratification which prevents the US from ratification and thus the CTBT cannot come into force. This situation still prevails today and as a result there is much concern about the long-term viability of the NPT. If the NPT was ever to be lost probably it could never be regained as the essential compromises could not be made again.

Against this backdrop the NPT parties came together again at the 2000 NPT Review Conference in an attempt to rescue the NPT regime. Led by the New Agenda Coalition of seven nonnuclear weapon states: Brazil, Egypt, Ireland, Mexico, New Zealand, South Africa and Sweden, and assisted by solid leadership from the United States, the NPT states parties agreed on a final document which set forth specific "practical steps for the systematic and progressive efforts to implement Article VI" of the treaty, along with the disarmament section of the 1995 Principles and Objectives document. Importantly, the nuclear weapon states agreed to an "unequivocal undertaking" for the total elimination of nuclear weapons [47]. The practical steps were intended to reinforce Article VI and afterwards became known as the "13 steps." Some of these steps included: the early entry into force of the Comprehensive Nuclear Test Ban Treaty; a moratorium on nuclear test explosions until entry into force of that treaty; a diminishing role for nuclear weapons in security policies; and engagement of all the nuclear weapon states in the process leading to the total elimination of nuclear weapons.

But in the years following the 2000 NPT Review Conference, there was little progress in implementing the 1995 statement of Principles and Objectives or the 13 steps. The 2005 NPT Review Conference was the worst ever. This time, there was no final document and no agreement on Article VI issues, which had happened before, but for the first time ever there was no agreement on peaceful uses or safeguards, either. And the US delegation took the position that, in effect, the 1995 statement of Principles and Objectives and the 2000 13 steps were no longer relevant.

Like most significant international agreements, the NPT is a political document more than a legal instrument. It is grounded in a central bargain: most of the world's states, now some 190, pledge to never acquire nuclear weapons; in return, the five nuclear weapon states recognized by the treaty pledge to assist nonnuclear-weapon states in peaceful nuclear technology and to pursue nuclear disarmament negotiations aimed at the ultimate elimination of their nuclear arsenals. However, giving up forever the most powerful weaponry ever created and joining a treaty which enshrines this principle is not a natural act for a sovereign state, and as this treaty permits a small number of states to have these weapons for many years in the future, it is a political necessity for many states, in order to create a semblance of equality among the treaty parties, not only to have a general article committing the treaty's nuclear weapon states to eventual nuclear disarmament but also to achieve specific steps in that direction in the shorter term. Since early in the Cold War and still today, the possession of nuclear weapons has to a large degree distinguished "great powers" from other states. The United Kingdom, France, and India have all made clear that this was the rationale behind their nuclear arsenals [48]. No major state wants to remain perceived as second class forever. In the words of French President Charles de Gaulle a "great state" that does not have nuclear weapons when others do "does not command its own destiny" [49]. Hence, political balance is essential to the survival of the NPT for the indefinite future and that is what the CTBT represents.

In 2009 there was a new US administration and President Obama early on, in April 2009, made a strong declaration on behalf of strengthening the NPT at Prague and advocated the entry into force of the CTBT as well as movement toward the eventual complete elimination of nuclear weapons.

Approximately one year later the 2010 NPT Review Conference took place in New York. The contrast between the 2010 Review Conference and 2005 could not have been more pronounced. The 2010 Conference was able to achieve a fully agreed final document, agreed to by all NPT parties – only the second time since the Review Conference process began in 1975, the other time being the 2000 Review Conference, a real achievement.

However, two issues should be noted, first a substantial number of NPT parties signed on to the objective of achieving a nuclear weapon convention. This would be the negotiation of a multilateral treaty prohibiting nuclear weapons, modeled on something general in scope like the Chemical Weapon Convention. It is most unlikely that a verification system for such a treaty could ever be found that was satisfactory, given the great advantage that would accrue to a state were it to secretly fabricate nuclear weapons and also there probably would be no way to enforce it. Such a concept is anathema to the NPT nuclear weapon states – this is emphatically not the process President Obama had in mind when he advocated the achievement one day of a nuclear weapon free world in Prague – and it is a highly divisive idea for the NPT community. Nevertheless, it was clear that this was going to be a problem issue for the NPT Review Conference process, as it was in 2015 and promises to be in 2020.

Second, and perhaps more immediately important, the 2010 final document contained an agreement to convene a conference in 2012 to discuss – not negotiate – a nuclear weapon free zone for the Middle East, with the participation of all relevant states, including Iran and Israel. As the principal advocate for the Middle East resolution in 1995, which was included in the final package along with indefinite extensions, Egypt at the conference made clear that they were tired of waiting and wanted action. They proposed long before the Review Conference a conference of all Middle East states to negotiate a nuclear weapon free zone for the Middle East. The US offered after some time a nonnegotiating conference on this subject, implying it seemed, at least for some, that by doing this Israel could be persuaded to attend. This was ultimately agreed between the US and Egypt and the UN Secretary-General appointed a Finnish diplomat as facilitator with Helsinki proposed as a site. Many discussions among relevant states were held, but in the end the US could not deliver Israel. All other Middle Eastern states agreed to come. But even so with the absence of Israel the conference initiative failed and this created a very serious problem for the 2015 NPT Review Conference.

The draft final document of the 2015 Review Conference contained a procedure to proceed to the negotiation of a nuclear weapon free zone for the Middle East, once more promoted by Egypt and supported by all NPT parties except the United States, the United Kingdom, and Canada. The provision would have established a March 2016 deadline for convening a conference to negotiate a nuclear weapon free zone. Last minute language added to the final proposal was supplied by Russia (cosponsor of the 1995 Middle East Resolution along with the US and the UK). The US denounced an "arbitrary deadline" and Canada demanded that Israel – a non-NPT party – be added to the negotiation on this formula. In the end, the US, the UK, and Canada blocked the final document because of this provision and the 2015 NPT Review Conference failed. All other issues of the moment had been resolved as the UK representative said it was "this issue and this issue alone [that] was the stumbling block" [50].

The Right to Peaceful Nuclear Energy

It is difficult to say where the NPT goes now. The CTBT, the essential commitment of the NPT nuclear weapon states since the signing of the NPT in 1968, has not yet entered into force, largely because of the US. However, it must be said that for whatever reason the Obama administration, very positive for arms control, has been long in rhetoric and short on action for the CTBT. A NPT Review Conference has recently failed over a different issue that must eventually be resolved for the NPT to remain viable in the long term. The US has not performed particularly well here either. And with the large nuclear weapon modernization programs underway in the US, Russia, and China, as outlined in the lead article in the *New York Times* on April 17, 2016, the NPT continues under threat [51].

Article IV is an essential part of the NPT basic bargain of nonprolifera-tion in exchange for nuclear disarmament and access to peaceful nuclear technology. It represents thus far the strongest of the three pillars sup-ported unequivocally by all parties. Many of the states negotiating the terms of the NPT were deeply concerned that the NPT would block or significantly inhibit their access to peaceful nuclear technology which they regarded as a sovereign right and essential to their economic development. Without Article IV there would have been no NPT. In an address to the Bundestag, on April 27, 1967, then Foreign Minister of the Federal Republic of Germany Willy Brandt said with respect to the negotiation of a nonproliferation treaty that Germany was not willing to accept anything which hindered the peaceful utilization of nuclear energy saying that "the future of the Federal Republic of Germany as a modern industrial state depended on this principle" [52].

In May of 1968 in the final debate on the NPT at the United Nations the Belgium Representative stated in arguing against a doubly unbalanced treaty (weapons and peaceful uses), "The needs of industrial and scientific development make this co-operation (as found in Article IV) imperative if we want to avoid introducing into the civilian area the distinction in the military area, which would be unacceptable and would inevitably lead to the calling into question of the treaty" [53]. Indeed, concern over this issue was one of the principal reasons that the Treaty was not made permanent from the beginning but rather was given a twenty-five-year term, renewable on a one-time basis at the end of that term. Article IV is appropriately interpreted to provide that a Party is not required to export nuclear technology on demand but rather that NPT Parties are free to adopt restrictive export rules to promote the objectives of the NPT. But with respect to a nuclear program in a State which is a NPT Party that is entirely indigenous, that Party has an absolute right to have such a program, "inalienable right" in the language of the Treaty, as long as that State remains a NPT Party in good standing – in other words in full compliance with Articles I and II, as specified in Article IV.

Since the beginning of the nuclear age and the military use of nuclear power in 1945, humanity nevertheless has managed to use nuclear technology for welfare and prosperity as well as weapons. But the expected widespread use of nuclear energy for peaceful purposes created potential risks as well as benefits due to the overlap between peaceful and military nuclear technologies. One of the principal objectives of the NPT is to prevent peaceful nuclear technology from being exploited for military purposes. Articles II and III (Safeguards) are the basic instruments of the Treaty in this regard. However, concerns were expressed by the nonnuclear weapon states during the NPT negotiations that by instituting such controls in the Treaty for the purpose of preventing proliferation, a further unwelcome result could be that their full access to the knowledge and the technology of the peaceful use of nuclear energy, which was needed for their future development and economic success, in their view, would be significantly restricted. International inspections might become industrial espionage and thus the NPT could place the nuclear weapon states in a position of permanent economic advantage. Freedom to exploit peaceful nuclear technology was considered an important part of the balance of obligations by the nonnuclear weapon states [54].

It is against this background that the emergence and the significance of Article IV and the corresponding preambular paragraphs must be understood [55]. In this regard perhaps the most important NPT preambular clauses are the sixth and seventh which respectively declare that the benefits of the "peaceful applications of nuclear technology ... should be available for peaceful purposes to all Parties of the Treaty, whether nuclear weapon or non-nuclear weapon states" and that "all Parties to the Treaty are entitled to participate in the fullest possible exchange of scientific information" in order to advance the "further development of the applications of atomic energy for peaceful purposes." As mentioned in Chapter One, Article IV became an important part of the NPT central bargain of nonproliferation in exchange for disarmament and access to peaceful nuclear technology. The Italian ambassador to the ENDC went so far as to describe the content of Article IV as the codification of a new human right. Article IV is essential to the long-term viability of the NPT [56].

The language of the first paragraph of Article IV containing the "inalienable right" phrase did not undergo further change after the August 1967 Co-Chairmen's draft. Later, however, it was placed in a separate paragraph so as to separate it from the right to participate "in the fullest possible exchange" of nuclear technology, pursuant to a Mexican proposal. This would suggest that these two "rights" were viewed differently by the negotiators, which is consistent with the subsequent state practice under the Treaty. The "inalienable right" paragraph is properly viewed as an implementation of the preambular clause that peaceful nuclear technology should be available to all "whether nuclear weapon or non-nuclear weapon states" [57].

During the various phases of the negotiation of the NPT, there was unanimity among the negotiating Parties that the Treaty should not interfere with access to peaceful nuclear technology. As a delegate to the 1968 Conference of Non-Nuclear Weapon States, which Conference was held two months after the signing of the NPT, put it, "the right of every State to use nuclear energy for peaceful purposes was inherent in its sovereign right to independent economic development, and was an essential attribute of national sovereignty and independence," [58] as of course qualified by the Treaty as required to be "in conformity with" Articles I (no transfer of nuclear weapons to nonnuclear states) and II (no acquisition of nuclear weapons by nonnuclear states) of the Treaty.

This "right" to develop peaceful nuclear technology domestically (as opposed to any right to import such technology) is not one that was intended to be able to be abrogated or modified in the course of subsequent state practice short of an actual amendment to the Treaty. The 1975 Review Conference of the NPT in its Final Declaration asserted that nothing in the NPT should be interpreted as affecting, and noted with satisfaction that nothing in the Treaty had been identified as affecting, the inalienable right set forth in paragraph one of Article IV [59].

Now turning to the second "right" granted by Article IV, that of the "fullest possible exchange" of nuclear technology "for the peaceful uses of nuclear energy." This provision is found in the second paragraph of Article IV and its text is set forth in Chapter 1 of this book. Nigeria during the negotiations wanted this provision to be more compelling so it proposed language that calls on all Parties to "undertake to facilitate" as well as having "the right to participate" in the "fullest possible exchange" arguing that to make the right of participation meaningful, the participation of those Parties that in fact will make it meaningful "must be guaranteed." The United States initially opposed this language but later accepted it and, when commenting on the final formulation of Article IV toward the end of the negotiation, said ". . . the right to such sharing is recognized explicitly not only as a right of non-nuclear Powers but also as a commitment to action by nuclear Powers and all others in a position to contribute thereto" [60]. Therefore, it was intended that participation in such exchanges by nuclear-capable states cannot be turned on and off without strong reason.

Some countries interpreted this language as not requiring reciprocity and were of the view that nuclear capable states were simply supposed to make the technology available; others such as Australia and Canada took the position that what was intended was not a program of unlimited grants but rather genuine cooperative efforts. Dr. Glenn Seaborg, then Chairman of the US Atomic Energy Agency, explained "fullest possible exchange" to the Senate Armed Services Committee as meaning that "the parties will be expected to cooperate only to the extent they are in a position to do so, and that reciprocity may be a factor in determining what may be done in certain circumstances" [61].

Thus, it may have been that nonnuclear weapon states expected more from this language than the nuclear weapon states and the advanced nonnuclear weapon states were prepared to deliver. This is highlighted by the passage in the United States of the Nuclear Non-Proliferation Act of 1978 – ten years after NPT signature – which required many states to renegotiate their Agreements for nuclear cooperation with the United States. However, the situation becomes more complex because some of the advanced nonnuclear states as well wanted commitments to the transfer of nuclear materials that others were not prepared to give. Italy, in early 1968, introduced a proposal which would have amended Article IV to say that it was the "inalienable right" of all parties to have access to "source and fissionable materials" and related equipment. This proposal received widespread support among nonnuclear weapon states, as many were concerned that the NPT would inhibit their access to the fuel for nuclear power. The Italian proposal ultimately was not accepted although the words "equipment" and "material" were added to Article IV as a partial response and a new preambular paragraph was added to the UN General Assembly resolution of May 28, 1968, commending the Treaty which stated that all parties have the right to engage in peaceful nuclear activities and to have access to source and fissionable material and related equipment [62]. Thus, the concerns were clear. At the 1968 Conference of Non-Nuclear Weapon States, Spain asserted that the nuclear weapon states keeping the information about uranium enrichment to themselves was contrary to the spirit of Article IV. Switzerland at the same Conference emphasized the importance of providing access to nuclear enrichment technology [63].

In testimony before the Senate Foreign Relations Committee on this issue during the ratification process of the NPT, Director William Foster of the US Arms Control and Disarmament Agency (the US government agency that had managed the NPT negotiations for the US) said: "It may be useful to point out, for illustrative purposes, several activities which the United States would not consider per se to be violations of the prohibitions in Article II. Neither uranium enrichment nor the stockpiling of fissionable material in connection with a peaceful program would violate Article II so long as these activities were safeguarded under Article III. Also clearly permitted would be the development, under safeguards of plutonium fueled power reactors, including research on the properties of metallic plutonium, nor would Article II interfere with the development or use of fast breeder reactors under safeguards" [64].

Some assert that access to uranium enrichment and plutonium reprocessing technology should be denied to additional states, including those in good standing under the NPT. The former Director General of the IAEA, Mohamed ElBaradei, as well as others, has pressed for a multilateral fuel bank in an attempt to achieve voluntary renunciations. Such a fuel bank has recently been established under control of the IAEA. The more extreme position is represented by a speech of the President of the United States at National Defense University on February 11, 2004, in which he proposed that the members of the Nuclear Suppliers Group (NSG) deny access to enrichment and reprocessing technology to any state that does not already possess such technology [65]. For the NSG to do what President Bush proposed would be a de facto amendment of the Treaty and would raise the question of double discrimination under the NPT, both weapons and fuel cycle technology reserved to the nuclear weapon states, which the Belgian delegate warned against in 1968 asserting that the Treaty could not stand with such a double level of "distinction." Adoption of a proposal such as this would not be positive for the long-term health of the NPT regime.

But early on, first the NPT Exporters Committee, which became known as the Zangger Committee and then the London Suppliers Group, which became the NSG, decided not to make available such technology as that for uranium enrichment, plutonium reprocessing and heavy water without stringent controls. The NPT in Article III provides that "source or special fissionable material" or related equipment shall not be transferred to a nonnuclear weapon state for peaceful purposes unless such export is made subject to Article III safeguards. In 1970 a group of States began informal meetings on how to implement this commitment. This Group, the Zangger Committee after Professor Zangger of Switzerland, its Chairman, defined "source or special fissionable material" to include such items as nuclear power reactors, uranium enrichment technology, plutonium reprocessing technology, heavy water, and related equipment.

This definitional list became known as the "Trigger List," as a request for export "triggers" a request from the supplier that the Committee conditions, including safeguards, be met. The Zangger Committee decided to apply the NPT Article III condition to any NPT non-Party seeking such exports as well, along with a non-explosive use assurance and retransfer approval rights. The Nuclear Suppliers Group, incorporated the work of the Zangger Committee and added one item to the trigger list and several new conditions. The NSG guidelines go significantly beyond NPT Article III and apply to NPT Parties and non-Parties alike [66]. Secure access by nonnuclear weapon states to nuclear material remained a contentious issue for many years after the signing and entry into force of the NPT with States criticizing the restrictive rules of the NSG. At the 1975 Review Conference there was an emphasis on the importance of access to nuclear materials, equipment and technology.

Thus, Article IV became a compensatory article for the benefit of the nonnuclear weapon states. It became one of the obligations intended to apply largely to the nuclear weapon states to balance the nonproliferation obligations of the nonnuclear weapon states. It makes up, therefore, an integral part of the NPT central bargain. How much was gained by the nonnuclear weapon states was not entirely clear in 1968 due to the vagueness of the language of Article IV itself. However, one can say, from the negotiating history of this provision, that the negotiators intended to guarantee the right of all NPT Parties to the use of nuclear energy for peaceful purposes as long as a program is an honest one –

that is, consistent with the nonproliferation undertakings of Articles I and II. This right, with respect to a national indigenous program of a State, is absolute. Second, in Article IV, the intent of the negotiators was to provide a more qualified right to participate in nuclear trade involving materials, equipment and information, and to place an obligation on all nuclear capable states – not just nuclear weapon states – able to do so to facilitate this trade. It was recognized that this trade, the exchange of material, equipment and information, and the commitment of nuclear capable states to cooperate, should be limited by prudence in order to support the nonproliferation goals of the Treaty.

In summary, the right to develop peaceful nuclear technology, if a program is in compliance with the Treaty, is unqualified, the right to participate in nuclear trade can be subject to restriction even if a program is in compliance with the Treaty. A significant example is the current rule of the Nuclear Suppliers Group that a member of the Group should not export technology directly applicable to a nuclear energy program to any state (except the NPT nuclear weapon states) unless that state places safeguards on all its nuclear activities, not just on the facility that is to receive a particular shipment of nuclear technology. In 2008, the NSG, under great pressure from the United States, agreed to a waiver of this restriction for India. This was required to implement the US-India nuclear agreement of 2005 in which India is granted an exception from US non-proliferation constraints – an amendment to US law was required – and ultimately an exception to the full scope safeguard rule of the NSG. The effect of this exception was to bring India into international nuclear commerce even though it is not a NPT party and possesses a sizeable nuclear weapons arsenal. Pakistan with the support of China has sought a similar exception not yet granted. This exception, given the shortage of uranium in India has permitted India to have a large domestic nuclear power program as well as a large nuclear weapon establishment. In 2016, the US was supporting Indian actual membership in the NSG.

In developing the subsequent state practice of the Parties for the NPT the Five-Year Review Conferences are important, but perhaps of greater signifi-cance for Article IV are the deliberations of the Nuclear Suppliers Group, the NSG. First was the Review Conferences, referred to earlier in the context of progress on Article VI.

Review Conferences for the NPT have been held at five-year intervals beginning in 1975. Traditionally the Conferences have divided into three main Committees for disarmament, peaceful uses (Article IV) and safeguards. There has been an agreed report at every Conference on peaceful uses except in 2005. Beginning in 1975, the Review Conferences regularly emphasized the importance of the "inalienable right" of NPT Parties to develop nuclear energy for peaceful purposes. The Final Declaration of the 1975 Conference, referred to above, set the standard in this regard. "The Conference reaffirms, in the framework of Article IV, that nothing in the Treaty shall be interpreted as affecting, and notes with satisfaction that nothing in the Treaty has been identified as affecting, the inalienable right of all the Parties to the Treaty to develop research, production and use of nuclear energy for peaceful purposes without discrimination and in conformity with Articles I and II of the Treaty" [67]. As noted during the negotiation of the NPT, there was considerable controversy as to whether the "fullest possible exchange" language in Article IV should be interpreted as requiring cooperation in all aspects of the nuclear fuel cycle, including the so-called sensitive technologies of uranium enrichment and plutonium reprocessing. However, this issue has not been significantly featured in discussions at NPT Review Conferences given the polarity of views between suppliers and recipient states but rather has been conducted elsewhere, particularly within the Nuclear Suppliers Group [68].

To sum up the history of rules regarding international trade of nuclear technology, we should begin by nothing that the NPT was signed in 1968 and entered into force in 1970. The Treaty affirmed "that all states party to the Treaty in good standing have a right to benefit from the peaceful uses of the atom."[69] The NPT Parties that were supplier states subsequent to Treaty signature sought to determine what specific materials should be shared with non-nuclear weapon states. This led to the formation of the aforementioned Zangger Committee, the objectives of which were to define source and special fissionable material which were to be controlled, to harmonize export policies and to require States outside the NPT to adopt IAEA safeguards and make other commitments before being allowed certain items of nuclear technology which could be used to pursue nuclear weapons. As said, the list of these items came to be known as the Trigger List [70]. Initially the Zangger Committee was composed of seventeen Western nations. Eastern bloc nations began joining in 1974 [71]. This list was later adopted as an IAEA official document.

As a response to India's diversion of nuclear technology imported from the United States and Canada for peaceful purposes to a program leading to the explosion of a nuclear device in 1974, the London Suppliers Group, which became the NSG, was formed in 1975. The Group adopted what later became Part I of its Guidelines. Part I, first published in 1978, lists material and technology specifically designed for nuclear use, including fissile material, nuclear reactors and equipment and reprocessing and enrichment technology. This includes largely items from the Zangger Committee Trigger List [72]. Restraint was to be exercised in the export of such technology and safeguards as well as additional conditions required. It had seemed, after the explosion by India of a nuclear device in 1974 and the announcement in early 1975 of major nuclear technology export plans by France and Germany to Pakistan and Brazil respectively, that the NPT was not good enough protection against proliferation. Thus, in April, 1975, the US, USSR, Canada, the UK, Japan, Germany, and France (which had refused to join the Zangger Committee) met in London to establish the NSG.

By 1977 the NSG had expanded to fifteen members. The Group did not meet again after 1978 until 1992 while steadily expanding its membership. Thus, there were an increasing number of states observing the Guidelines, which, although voluntary, had considerable force. In 1992, as a result of learning how close Iraq came to acquiring a nuclear weapon by illicitly importing so-called dual-use items, the NSG began meeting again on a regular basis, which practice has continued to this day. In 1992 the NSG adopted Part II of its Guidelines identifying certain dual-use items, which are nonnuclear items with legitimate civilian applications which also can be used to develop nuclear weapons, such as machine tools, certain computers and lasers. In addition, the NSG in 1992 provided that, in order to import Part I items from a NSG member, a state must have comprehensive IAEA safeguards on all its nuclear activities and facilities, as opposed to safeguards on the specific nuclear activity for which the import is destined, which are required for Part II imports. In 2004, NSG members adopted a so-called "catch-all" provision which permits members to block any export suspected to be sought for use in a nuclear weapon program even if it does not appear on either the Part I or Part II lists. By 2009 the NSG had expanded to forty-six members [73].

Thus, subsequent state practice unequivocally demonstrates that the "fullest possible exchange" language in Article IV is very much subject to the rule of prudence with respect to the basic purpose of the NPT, preventing the proliferation of nuclear weapons. At the same time, consistent with the negotiating record, subsequent practice upholds the sanctity of the "inalienable right" of all NPT Parties to participate in peaceful nuclear energy programs if they are in good standing under the Treaty.

What Have We Learned?

So what have we indeed learned in seventy years of living with nuclear energy and living with its wartime product, nuclear weapons?

We have learned that the gigantic nuclear weapon confrontation in which the United States built more than 70,000 weapons and the Soviet Union some

55,000, many, many thousands of which remained for forty-five years on hair trigger alert must remain part of history and never return. We escaped from world destruction by the narrowest of margins and we know this is a situation that must never be repeated. But while the Cold War ended twenty-five years ago, the United States and Russia have turned hostile again, over a thousand nuclear weapons in each country remain on alert available to be launched against the other; twenty years ago one of these two parties, by mistake, nearly launched an all-out nuclear war during a time of relatively peaceful relations between the two states, and both the United States and Russia have announced huge nuclear weapon modernization plans at the cost of many billions, in the case of the United States up to $1 trillion in the course of coming decades.

We also know now that the nuclear disarmament process, which began with the SALT negotiations and continued in fits and starts through the end of the Cold War and beyond, has come to an end at least for the foreseeable future. The president of Russia wants to emphasize nuclear weapons and does not want to negotiate on this subject with the United States. Likely he will be in office for at least another decade. And the most important international security treaty of them all, the NPT, remains under threat because the United States is unable to implement one of its central commitments made as part of the NPT central bargain: to bring into force a comprehensive test ban treaty and establish a permanent legal ban on further nuclear weapon tests. Now a new threat, or perhaps an old threat become more intense, has appeared on the scene – the inability of the entire NPT community to address the question of a nuclear weapon free zone treaty for the Middle East, much desired by NPT parties. This risks the serious destabilization of the NPT regime. The US has to some degree a working relationship with Russia and the Cold War is over but with all the above as background, at least in the security area we do not appear to have learned very much.

In the field of peaceful use of nuclear energy the situation is different. All countries agree on most things about nuclear power and peaceful nuclear technology. That all nations that are parties in good standing under the NPT have the right to access peaceful nuclear energy but that the more sensitive elements of nuclear technology (the technology that presents the greatest risk of diversion from civil power programs into weapon programs, although this has never happened) such as uranium enrichment and plutonium reprocessing technology can be subject to heavy international regulation. Efforts to limit the number of countries that have access to this technology – such as the establishment of an international fuel bank to ensure access by all countries to nuclear fuel for their reactors – have had limited success to date in accomplishing this. This is because all NPT parties in compliance with the NPT have a right to all peaceful nuclear technology, including such sensitive technology, there would not have been an NPT without this right, even though very few countries would ever want to pay the money necessary to acquire such technology, they do not want to surrender their sovereign rights in this domain. And there is no chance of amending the NPT on this or probably any other issue. The amendment process is too difficult.

A shining example of what countries can do is provided by the UAE "gold standard" discussed in Chapter 11. An agreement for nuclear cooperation with the US remains the sort of Good Housekeeping seal of approval, so since virtually no country, beyond the few that have built enrichment or reprocessing facilities, actually believes that acquiring such technology for its nascent nuclear program would make economic sense, why not advocate a pledge not to build enrichment or reprocessing facilities and try to make it a condition in some way for a nuclear cooperation agreement with the United States. Any state that does this could perhaps be – with government support – granted cheaper and easier access to nuclear power plant fuel. This could strengthen cooperation with the international community, enhance the prestige of national programs – the UAE has greatly benefited – and make economic sense. But national sovereignty appears to a degree to stand in the way, recent examples include Jordan and Vietnam.

So the big issues in the nuclear technology field would appear to be, in no particular order:

1. Can the world community, intellectually and emotionally, get past the origins of the nuclear age and accept nuclear power for what it is: a huge benefit for humanity if managed properly? It can bring reliable electricity to billions of people and is an indispensable tool for combatting the greatest threat that humanity has ever faced, climate change.
2. Can the world community cooperate sufficiently to derive the maximum benefit from nuclear power and also use it as it can be used: as a principal response to climate change? It is indeed as the title of Gwyneth Cravens' book proclaims – "Power to Save the World."
3. Can the United States Senate pull itself together to do what is right and in the best interests of itself and the world and permit US ratification of the CTBT? Entry into force likely would follow not long after. And the essential "glue" to hold together for the indefinite future the most important treaty protecting us all, the NPT, will be fully in place.
4. Can we, that is the international community, finally learn something from the past seventy years and get ourselves on a path to reach the worldwide, complete, verifiable elimination of nuclear weapons and banish these weapons forever?

5. And, finally, can the new administration recapture the ambition and vision of Presidents Reagan and Gorbachev and (1) promote the widespread deployment of nuclear power plants to ensure eventual victory for civilization over climate change, plus (2) aggressively pursue CTBT entry into force and a nuclear weapon free Middle East to ensure that the NPT will survive until one day the worldwide elimination of nuclear weapons becomes possible.

References

[1] M. Krepon, Reagan, Gorbachev and Reykjavik (Internet), *The Non-Proliferation Review*, 22:2 (June 2015). Available from: www.armscontrolwonk.com/archive/404308/reagan-gorbachev-and-reykjavik

[2] Ibid.

[3] R. Rhodes, *Arsenals of Folly* (New York: Vintage Books, 2007), p. 240–241.

[4] Ibid., p. 241.

[5] Ibid., pp. 252, 261–262.

[6] Ibid., pp. 265–267.

[7] Ibid., p. 306.

[8] Ibid., p. 308.

[9] Ibid., pp. 308–309.

[10] T. C. Reed and D. B. Stillman, *The Nuclear Express* (Minneapolis: Zenith Press, 2009), p. 158.

[11] J. T. Richelson, op. cit., pp. 219–221.

[12] Ibid., pp. 221–222.

[13] Ibid., p. 224.

[14] Reed and Stillman, op. cit., p. 159.

[15] Hymans, op. cit., p. 186.

[16] Hymans, op. cit., p. 184.

[17] Ibid., p. 190.

[18] Richelson, op. cit., p. 433.

[19] Hymans, op. cit., pp. 195–196, 198.

[20] Reed and Stillman, p. 243.

[21] Hymans, op. cit., pp. 201, 202.

[22] Ibid., p. 202.

[23] Richelson, op. cit., pp. 243–245.

[24] Richelson, *Spying on the Bomb, American Nuclear Intelligence from Nazi Germany to Iran and North Korea* (New York: W.W. Norton, 2006), p. 361–367.

[25] Richardson, op. cit., pp. 325–326.

[26] G. Corena, *Shopping for Bombs: Nuclear Proliferation, Global Insecurity, and the Rise and Fall of the A.Q. Khan Network* (Oxford & New York: Oxford University Press, 2006), pp. 176–194.

[27] Reed and Stillman, op. cit., pp. 290–291.

[28] World Nuclear Association. Nuclear Proliferation Case Studies: Iraq (Internet). Available from: www.world-nuclear.org/information-library/safety-and-security/ non-proliferation/appendices/nuclear-proliferation-case-studies.aspx

[29] Ibid.

[30] F. H. Khan, *Eating Grass: The Making of the Pakistani Bomb* (Stanford, CA: Stanford University Press, 2012), pp. 70–71.

[31] Ibid., p. 6.

[32] Chung Min Lee, *Fault Lines in a Rising Asia*, (Washington, D.C., Carnegie Endowment of International Peace, 2016), p. 288.

[33] D. Frantz and C. Collins, *The Nuclear Jihadist: The True Story of the Man Who Sold the World's Most Dangerous Secrets ... and How We Could Have Stopped Him.* (New York: Hachette Book Group, 2007), pp. 68–71, 76, 82.

[34] Richelson, op. cit., 342–345.

[35] Khan, op. cit., pp. 269–283.

[36] G. Correra, *Shopping for Bombs: Nuclear Proliferation, Global Diversity and the Rise and Fall of the A. Q. Khan Network* (New York: Oxford University Press, 2006), X111.

[37] Frantz and Collins, op. cit., p. 208–210.

[38] M. Chimoy, *Meltdown: The Inside Story of the North Korean Nuclear Crisis* (New York: St. Martin's Press, 2008), pp. 77–78.

[39] R. Takeyh, *Hidden Iran: Paradox and Power in the Islamic Republic* (New York: New York Times Books, 2006), p. 154.

[40] Ibid., p. 144.

[41] Documents on Disarmament, United States: Arms Control and Disarmament Agency, Vol. 6. (November 7, 2009), p. 573.

[42] History of the NPT 1975 – 1995, *Reaching Critical Will* (Internet), Available from: http://www.reachingcriticalwill.org/disarmament-fora/npt/history-of-the-npt -1975-1995#NPT1975

[43] Dhanapala with Randy Rydel, Multilateral Diplomacy and the NPT: An Insider's Account, New York: United Nations, 2005, 48. (Internet), Available from: http://www.unidir.org/files/publications/pdfs/multilateral-diplomacy-and-the-npt-an-insider-s-account-323.pdf.

[44] Ibid., pp. 47, 48.

[45] Ibid., p. 46.

[46] Ibid.

[47] Dhanapala, op. cit., p. 90.

[48] T. Graham, Jr., *Common Sense on Weapons of Mass Destruction* (Seattle: University of Washington Press, 2004), p. 66.

[49] K. Campbell, R. Einhorn, and M. Reiss, *The Nuclear Tipping Point: Why States Reconsider Their Nuclear Choices* (Washington, D.C.: Brookings Institution Press, 2004).

[50] W. Wan, Why the 2015 NPT Review Conference Fell Apart (Internet), *UNU-CPR (Centre for Policy Research)* (May 28, 2015). Available from: https://cpr.unu.edu /why-the-2015-npt-review-conference-fell-apart.html

[51] W. J. Broad and D. E. Sanger, Race for Latest Class of Nuclear Arms Threatens to Revive Cold War, *The New York Times* (April 17, 2016), p. 1.

[52] M. I. Shaker, *The Nuclear Non-Proliferation Treaty, Origin and Implementation, 1959–1979* (London: Oceana Publications, 1980), p. 294.

[53] Ibid., p. 330.

[54] Ibid., pp. 274, 295.

[55] Ibid., p. 275.

[56] Ibid., pp. 273–277.

[57] Ibid., pp. 293–294.

[58] Ibid., p. 294.

[59] Ibid., p. 299.

[60] Ibid., p. 301.

[61] Ibid., p. 302.

[62] Ibid., pp. 303–305.

[63] Ibid., pp. 313, 314.

[64] Personal Communication: Letter from Fred McGoldrick, September 1, 2009.

[65] Remarks at the National Defense University, February 11, 2004 (Internet), Administration of George W. Bush 2004, Government Publishing Office, pp. 216–220. Available from: https://www.gpo.gov/fdsys/pkg/WCPD-2004-02-16/pdf/WCPD-2004-02-16-Pg216.pdf

[66] Other Activities Relevant to Article III, Background Paper by the United Nations Secretariat, NPT/Conf. 191995/7 Part II, April 18, 1995, paragraphs 9–28 (Internet). Available from: www.un.org/Depts/ddar/nptconf/2136.htm

[67] Final Declaration of the First Review Conference of the NPT 1975 (Internet), p. 3. Available from: www.nti.org/media/pdfs/NPTRevCon75.pdf?_=1316545426

[68] C. Stoiber, The Evolution of NPT Review Conference Final Documents, 1975–2000, *The Nonproliferation Review* (Fall–Winter 2003), pp. 129–130, (Internet). Available from: www.nonproliferation.org/wp-content/uploads/npr/103stoi.pdf

[69] US Department of State, Fact Sheet: Article IV of the NPT (Internet), *US Support for Peaceful Nuclear Cooperation, Bureau of Nonproliferation*. Available from: www.fas.org/nuke/control/npt/news/article4.htm

[70] Arms Control Association, The Nuclear Suppliers Group (NSG) at a Glance (Internet) (July 2009). Available from: www.armscontrol.org/factsheets/nsg

[71] Tadeusz Strulak, The Nuclear Suppliers Group (Internet). Available from: www.nonproliferation.org/wp-content/uploads/npr/strula11.pdf.

[72] Nuclear Suppliers Group: History, NSG, (Internet). Available from: www.nuclearsuppliersgroup.org/en/history1

[73] Ibid.

13

Conclusion: Is Nuclear Power Essential?

Weighing the Future

Questions about energy are questions about the present and the future. They are also questions about life, its quality, options, and welfare. Today, and for decades ahead, noncarbon energy is not only needed; it is life-saving. And this will only increase with each coming year.

Nuclear power continues to be the largest form of noncarbon energy in the world. It is also the most concentrated and reliable, with the smallest environmental impact among all baseload sources and the lowest number of accidents, injuries, and fatalities. To say that it has saved a good many lives by replacing what would have been many hundreds of coal plants defines a clear truth. To say that its expansion will make this even more true in the future, when climate concerns are taken into account, is no less accurate.

As such, it is not only necessary but *essential*. The idea of letting it die off, a reactor at a time, like something marginal and without consequence, is a pathway to carbon and climate failure. Maintaining and expanding it defines a required goal if we are truly serious about preventing such failure and protecting millions of lives from the lethal impacts now clearly defined, whose victims we are already counting on a yearly basis. A single nuclear plant, built with today's technology, can supplant three or even four coal plants erected decades ago or planned for the future. Some nations, like China, have taken this truth as a spur for action and are building new nuclear plants along with renewable energy capability as part of a strategy to change how they power their growing cities. Other countries have plans to do the same, even though they lack a nuclear program right now. Indeed, dozens of developing

354

nations in a like position have declared an interest in nuclear for these and other reasons.

It helps to review why this make sense. In previous chapters, we have seen that nuclear power defines a mature and advancing technology, with distinct plans for the future. These plans include a carefully chosen set of new reactor designs intended to be cheaper to build, easier to operate, much more efficient, proliferation resistant, and producing less waste. We don't mention increased safety, though this, too, defines a core objective. We don't highlight this because over six decades nuclear power has had the smallest number of serious accidents and fewest fatalities, as well as the lowest deaths and injuries per terawatt-hour, of any energy source except solar PV. Another key factor is that nuclear produces by far the largest amount of electricity per acre (hectare), giving it the smallest environmental footprint (especially per unit of power). Due to a global fuel market that is well established and carefully monitored and that handles a fuel of low and stable price, nuclear power plants greatly improve energy security. As a baseload source, nuclear substitutes directly for fossil fuels and can act to stabilize the grid where variable power from renewables is significant. It produces small amounts of waste that can be stored in the subsurface like the vastly larger volumes of toxic material from other industries that have been injected and buried underground for many decades.

At the same time, nuclear power has two major limiting factors. First, its plants are expensive to build and finance and therefore take a long time to become profitable. This has always been true. Even in the 1950s, when the first power plants were built, their costs were much higher than expected. As a result, the economic competitiveness of nuclear has depended on regulated markets and on fossil fuel prices. Challenges here are significant today, in partially or wholly deregulated markets. Such markets work by short-term competition among sources, which grants strong advantage to cheap natural gas but also to subsidized wind/solar. The challenge to nuclear could be met were it given financial recognition, as solar and wind are, for its noncarbon nature – its role in keeping carbon emissions, not to say pollution, far lower than they would otherwise be. This has elevated meaning in OECD nations, because when nuclear plants have closed in recent years they have been mainly or entirely replaced by fossil fuel stations, both gas and coal. Moreover, the year 2016 saw emissions from gas consumption in the US surpass those from coal for the first time. The underprivileged status of nuclear in the OECD nations is already proving a problem, therefore. Again, if reducing carbon energy to mitigate both climate change and toxic air pollution define a goal for the future, it will not be achieved without nuclear power.

The second limiting factor has been still more significant in certain nations. It involves public fear and related myths that have come to surround nuclear power. These are myths that urge people to use nuclear power as a scapegoat for deep-seated anxieties about radiation, the threat of nuclear war, deceitful government and indifferent corporate power. Among them are fables about nuclear reactors as inherently unsafe, with dangers similar to those of weapons, having killed many thousands, even tens of thousands, in accidents like Chernobyl, poisoning huge areas for centuries, and routinely creating waste more perilous and lethal than anything civilization has ever produced. None of these dark fairy tales, which emerged from the fearful childhood of the Atomic Age, come anywhere near the truth, as shown by this book (and others). Yet they persist, because the fears they embody – about the destructive powers of society – persist. It requires little effort from a knowledgeable person to dispel any of them, individually. But together they define a worldview, unfortunate as it is, that connects nuclear energy with the sense of immeasurable damage that modern humans have wreaked upon the environment and themselves. For many, indeed, it is the presumed connection between nuclear power and nuclear weapons that matters most – images of the rising mushroom cloud and the steaming hyperboloid tower. Yet sixty years of reactors producing electricity for society have proven, that this link is untrue. No material from a single civilian power reactor has ever been diverted into a weapon. On the contrary, tens of thousands of weapons once deployed by the US and the Soviets have had their fuel consumed in nuclear plants to power cities once targeted by those same weapons. Rather than imperiling society, these plants have been key to a reduction of threats. Similarly, the terrors of Chernobyl and Fukushima do not stand up to unbiased scrutiny. Hundreds or thousands have not died in the case of one and won't in the case of the other, while a great many more could have returned home if the land were not deeply contaminated with fear and distrust.

Such fears, coveted by some, are unlikely to write the future story of nuclear. Not only is a new generation less persuaded by myths and gravely concerned about climate change, but there now seems every possibility that nuclear power has entered a period of globalization. We see this in the new nuclear programs for nations like the UAE, Ghana, Turkey, and Nigeria, and in the export interests pursued by nuclear vendors in Russia, China, South Korea, and Japan. Present indications are that the number of operating reactors may rise from 449 in late 2016, distributed among thirty nations, to over 900 reactors in fifty-five or more countries by 2040. This takes into account a number of reactors that might be retired and not replaced. The new builds will include not only large-scale reactors with capacities of 1.2 GW or more, but an array of medium- and smaller-sized models all the way down to micro-reactors

(<25 MW) and floating nuclear power plants (10–200 MW). They will also involve a number of new reactor designs with significantly higher efficiencies than those now operating.

None of this constitutes a wish or dream. All of it is planned and much of it is already in the testing and demonstration phase. We see this especially in China, where several new designs are being tested, including a high temperature gas-cooled reactor, molten salt reactor, fast reactor, and floating nuclear power plant. This, however, is only the beginning. It is a foregone conclusion that the Chinese will be very interested in SMR technology for a variety of local uses and for export to developing nations in Asia and Africa especially.

Russia, too, is working on advanced designs. These include sodium-cooled fast neutron reactors, breeder reactors, floating nuclear plants, and more. Its long-term plans are to replace nearly all its current fleet and to increase nuclear's share of total power generation from under 20 percent in 2017 to 50 percent by 2050. Russian scientists and engineers have an ultimate goal of eliminating nuclear waste and developing several closed fuel cycles. The current government of Vladimir Putin has few climate-specific policies for reducing emissions. Putin himself has shown little interest in the Paris Climate Agreement or other treaties and agreements of like kind. Yet Russia's plans for expanded nuclear power stand to reduce the country's use of coal and natural gas consumption by more than 20 percent over the next two decades. This would cause its emissions to fall a nearly equal amount. It has also decided to pioneer an idea proposed by the IAEA regarding multinational collaboration on building and testing multiple prototypes of new designs. Russia has discussed with India, for example, creating a regional nuclear "use center" in the form of a multipurpose sodium-cooled fast research reactor, supported and used by several or more nations. Therefore, even without any real climate policy – a situation we must hope will change – the Russian Federation could aid to a significant degree the global movement toward noncarbon energy.

All three of these countries, China, Russia, and India, are focusing on closed fuel cycles. A shared goal is to develop reactors able to burn and generate electricity from existing excess plutonium as well as other actinides in fuel waste. South Korea, too, plans to build advanced reactors at home and abroad, including a sodium-cooled fast reactor for burning LWR spent fuel and an air-cooled modular reactor designed for export to Saudi Arabia. But perhaps more importantly, South Korea, like Russia, has also become an international training center for nuclear scientists and engineers.

The point here is that nuclear power continues to grow and advance, particularly in Asia, but not in its original homeland, the US and Europe. Yes, there is some activity in the West. US federal laboratories are partnering with other nations' firms to provide technical assistance and advice on advanced nuclear systems, and there are several new reactors planned in southern states (where power markets remain more regulated). At this writing, new reactors are under construction in England, France, Finland, Slovakia, and Romania, with others planned for Poland, Hungary, and Bulgaria. As of 2016, however, more reactors were being shut down in the US than built, and the same could soon be true in Europe. Much of the world will be moving ahead with an energy source that brings advantages of noncarbon electricity, sustainability, energy security, and more. How quickly nuclear power will globalize using Gen III and Gen IV technology isn't yet clear. It will take decades, no doubt. But it is already happening and will help reduce carbon emissions billions of tons annually. Will the West join the new nuclear era in a full sense, or be left behind? The answer here, too, isn't yet available. Perhaps something more should be said.

Einstein Has an Opinion

"Reality is an illusion," said Albert Einstein, "albeit a very persistent one." Realism, in other words, is a needed approach in all things, unless we prefer self-deception. Such is the course of those who continue to reject nuclear power by refusing to accept the facts that now exist. Placing coal and nuclear in the same category of risk, or saying that nuclear represents only the lesser of these two "evils," reveals an inability to distinguish between a carbon energy source that causes death on a massive scale every year and a noncarbon source that kills no one.

Such fundamental errors of perception and judgment cannot be allowed to direct a significant portion of the energy future. How nations decide to power their societies impacts the biology of planet Earth. This is a relatively new realism and defines a context we are only now beginning to fathom. But it is a context that humanity will be living with permanently, without pause, for centuries. Climate change, in fact, is only part of the setting. Another part is the toxic air pollution that injures and erases literally millions of lives every year. This, too, is new to our world view. Most of the lives lost each year are poor and less visible. Yet, we should know by now that this is fast changing. Global warming and lethal pollution do not discriminate on the basis of income.

In this urgent new context, there is no such thing as a "soft" or "hard" energy path. These are distinctions whose intended implications will not help us. Talk of more decentralized energy production, more local forms of control and choice, are fine, indeed necessary, in certain cases. Such is the province of renewable energy for the next few decades. But the world continues to urbanize. Small may be beautiful, in some estimations, but cities are huge and growing. Such is particularly true in developing nations, where nearly all future rise in energy demand will be. People in these countries are moving into cities at a high rate, for better, more interesting lives, and this includes hundreds of urban areas of a million or more up to megacities of over 10 million. Cities are epicenters of energy use. They demand it in huge, reliable concentrations twenty-four hours a day, every day of every year. There is no question of powering these centers except with commensurately large amounts of electricity, supplied consistently and dependably, aided by more locally adjusted sources like rooftop solar.

But, again, climate change and global demographics are not the only reasons nuclear is essential. In the world today, many cities in major developing nations, from China and India to Nigeria and Pakistan, are also centers of the worst air on Earth. The overriding reason is the use of coal in power plants and factories without modern pollution protections. Coal use in homes defines yet another contribution to a public health peril that takes millions of lives each year and would exist even without climate change but in the event doubles or triples its impact. Yet coal remains the default choice for many developing nations for many reasons. Not only is it cheap, abundant, and widely distributed – India, Ukraine, Turkey, Vietnam, Indonesia, Zimbabwe, and Colombia all have large reserves. It needs only roads and railways to be transported, not an expensive network of pipelines, and its power plants can be built quickly, especially when they lack pollution controls. Coal is the default choice because poorer nations usually have limited resources and limited time. Their economies and their social advancement in many domains are being held up by a lack of electricity, fundament of modern life.

Nuclear and renewable energy are the noncarbon sources that will change this situation, while also lowering carbon emissions worldwide. In scientific terms, these sources of power are intimately allied. Just as fission generates the energy for one of them, nuclear reactions within the Sun create the heat and radiation for the other, driving the movements of ocean and atmosphere. Instead of "hard" and "soft" the categories of "carbon" and "noncarbon" make the most sense to employ for the sake of realism. Nuclear and renewables together provide us with the technological capability for meeting core challenges to a more sustainable energy future. As this book has emphasized, these sources are not in the least antithetical, any more than are factories and workshops. The view that they inhabit separate worlds, with nuclear in a lower circle of hell and renewables inhabiting a heavenly orbit, defines a narrow, absolutist vision whose lack of realism will not help the world move forward. Nuclear fear is not a force for either social or technological progress, nor for public health or environmental protection.

Much of the advanced world, including the US, seems content to let the new nuclear era move ahead without any active leadership from the West. While new ideas, designs, and technologies have emerged, there has been little overall government interest and even less funding, making it necessary for such ideas to be tested in other countries where support exists. This will mean, over time, that all progress in nuclear power will shift to Asian nations and Russia, who will be its developers, builders, *and* exporters. This would not necessarily be regrettable, economically speaking, though it might well bring worries in the non-proliferation domain. But it would surely be foolish and wasteful in a number of ways. Today, in fact, an innovative US company wishing to build and test a reactor design with exciting potential is unlikely to find the support and financing it needs at home. It would have to go to China, perhaps South Korea, to gain a needed partner. This situation, to put it mildly, is revealing.

Everything today suggests that the US and most of Europe are not ahead of the curve in noncarbon energy but behind it, and falling further behind every year even as more renewables are installed. How is it that the South Koreans and Chinese can build reactors on time and on budget, but the US can't? The Koreans can do this not only at home but in nations on the other side of the world, in the Middle East. This reality shows that it is not the technology itself that defines the problem. Nor can it be claimed that South Korea and China routinely sacrifice safety for economy; this is simply untrue.

Moreover, there are major security issues to consider. These operate, in fact, on more than one level. Western nations are still the world's most scientifically and technologically advanced, and for them to largely ignore or turn their backs on a realm of energy technology that they largely conceived, a realm moreover that has gained new importance as a zero-carbon source, would be profligate at the very least. It would weaken significantly the world's effort to deal with climate change. Nuclear now provides more than half of the EU's noncarbon electricity and over 60 percent in the US. Letting this seriously decay and be replaced mainly by cheap natural gas defies any rational commitment to sustainability.

In another sense, the US has been the global leader in nuclear energy for six decades. It has been involved in every nonproliferation concept, treaty, and agreement during this long period. It has acted as a chief authority in preventing the spread of weapons and illegal sharing of nuclear material and technology. No small part of this, in other nation's eyes, has been US expertise and status in the nuclear power domain. Allowing its own nuclear industry to weaken and seek better pastures abroad, failing to produce and motivate future generations of nuclear scientists and engineers, would come to seriously erode US standing and negotiating authority.

We cannot blame public anxiety and antinuclearism for what has happened, not entirely. Thirty years without a new nuclear plant on American soil is the result of other factors, too. Ideas demanding less government involvement in the economy, including energy, have helped reduce support for nuclear in many areas. Related to this has been the movement, dating mainly from the 1990s, to deregulate electricity markets. This has brought very mixed results, lowering prices in some states but raising them in many others. The US electricity system has become a ridiculously complex "experiment" of regulated, deregulated, half-deregulated, and re-regulated state power markets, most of which now also operate with renewable portfolio standards – government rules requiring certain percentage use of solar and wind. Little support for nuclear exists in this "experiment,", despite its supply of noncarbon, nonvariable power. The exceptions of New York and Illinois, which have provided support to keep their nuclear plants open, will hopefully provide a model for other states. Still, there is also the hurdle of the licensing process; in the name of public safety (for a technology that has never injured or killed one member of that same public), this process typically requires five-to-eight years and sometimes more. Since 2012, the understaffed NRC has licensed a total of eleven new reactors whose applications were submitted in the early-to-mid 2000s. But due to rising costs over the decade required for approval, the advent of cheap natural gas, new regulatory demands, and public opposition, most of these projects are now in doubt. All of which makes it simple to say that changes are sorely needed if the nation a as a whole, and the states individually, seriously want to reduce emissions and advance the effort to deal with climate change and air pollution.

In the end, it makes little sense for the US especially, to back away from an industry of noncarbon energy that it started six decades ago and largely gave to the world. And here we come to a different but no less pressing kind of obligation. The United States brought nuclear energy into existence and did so both in the form of weapons and reactors. Dropping the bomb in 1945 set in motion a monstrous construction of arms that, at one point in the 1980s, included over 70,000 nuclear weapons. During the same period, a few dozen nations built 420 civilian power reactors, the great majority of them based on American light water designs. To say that the US has a degree of historical responsibility in the nuclear realm, therefore, is to stunningly understate the truth. Once we accept the fact that America gifted humanity with the possibility of annihilation through nuclear weapons, then sought to balance this out with "the peaceful atom," we are forced to admit that this same country has a profound moral responsibility over the nuclear realm. Such is a responsibility, furthermore, that the US will always have; there is no abandoning it or pretending its truth is irrelevant. At present, America has put itself in the mutant position of strengthening, perhaps even increasing, its nuclear arsenal once again, its use of nuclear energy for death and war, while at the same time allowing the peaceful use of this energy, with all its needed potential, to decline. Such is not a choice for progress but for absurdity and squander.

And so there emerges a deeper argument for American involvement in this same realm. The US, more than any other country, has an obligation to stay in the field of nuclear power, to ensure it has a productive and valuable future, and to therefore get things right in a new century where new global risks abide.

In the new nuclear era, these risks are both new and old. If they include global changes in the climate and the need to reduce carbon-based energy, they also return to the challenge of nonproliferation. It is possible to envision two existential threats for humanity in the twenty-first century – the ever-more deadly impacts of global warming and the unrelieved danger of nuclear war. If the US has a responsibility in both these realms, so does every nation that seeks to acquire nuclear power. This does not in the least cast a shadow over the essential need for nuclear power. The chances of a country seeking a weapon are enormously less if it has a nuclear power program that has been guided, monitored, and legitimated by the IAEA and required to allow inspections thereafter. History has made this abundantly clear.

This noncarbon energy source, with benefits for emissions, breathable air, energy security, and reliable power, is now expanding to nations that have not been a home to it before. While many uncertainties exist, this expansion could easily double the number of nuclear power nations over the next twenty to thirty years. Such nations will have the advantage of more advanced reactors provided by foreign vendors jostling in a new and highly competitive export market. How this will playout in different parts of the world is not yet known. But playout it certainly will. Perhaps the greatest uncertainty about this expanding nuclear reality is whether those nations who contributed most to its evolution in the past will be an important part of its future. For if they are not, humanity's chances of an ultimate triumph over climate change will remain a wish in search of a reality.

Index

363